P9-CRL-090

D0015353

# BEST-LOVED
# STORIES OF THE LDS
# PEOPLE
# VOLUME 3

# Best-Loved Stories of the LDS People
# Volume 3

Edited by Jay A. Parry, Jack M. Lyon,
and Linda Ririe Gundry

DESERET BOOK COMPANY
SALT LAKE CITY, UTAH

*Also available from Deseret Book*
BEST-LOVED POEMS OF THE LDS PEOPLE
BEST-LOVED HUMOR OF THE LDS PEOPLE
BEST-LOVED STORIES OF THE LDS PEOPLE, VOLUME 1
BEST-LOVED STORIES OF THE LDS PEOPLE, VOLUME 2

**Library of Congress Cataloging-in-Publication Data**

Best-loved Stories of the LDS People / edited by Jay A. Parry, Jack M. Lyon, and Linda Ririe Gundry.
    p.   cm.
    Includes bibliographical references and index.
    ISBN 1-57345-802-3 (hardcover)
    1. The Church of Jesus Christ of Latter-day Saints—History—19th century—Sources. 2. Mormon Church—History—19th century—Sources. 3. Mormons—History—19th century—Sources. I. Parry, Jay A. II. Lyon, Jack M. III. Gundry, Linda Ririe.
    BX8611.B36    2000
    289.3'32—dc21                                                                    97-24195
                                                                                          CIP

Printed in the United States of America                                        72082-6690
10   9   8   7   6   5   4   3   2   1

# CONTENTS

## Faithfulness

## Healing

## Honesty

## Humor

## Joseph Smith

## Miracles

## Prayer

## Protection and Deliverance

## Repentance

## Restoration

## Revelation

# PREFACE

The gospel of Jesus Christ is founded on true stories. Almost any child can tell you the stories of Noah and the ark, Moses in the bulrushes, David and Goliath, or Daniel in the lion's den. Primary children sing "Tell me the stories of Jesus." The Book of Mormon gives us the thrilling stories of Nephi, King Benjamin, Alma the Younger, Samuel the Lamanite, and many more. We also love to hear the stories of our dispensation—of the boy Joseph, who went into a grove of trees in upstate New York with a question about truth and came out with an experience that was destined to change the world. We tell of the angel Moroni, the "latter-day Pentecost" at Kirtland, and the days of trial and triumph in Liberty Jail. The stories have continued from that day to this, building testimony and increasing faith.

Stories can strengthen as little else can. They add sparkle to a talk or lesson—or deepen the sense of the Spirit. In some important ways, our very understanding of the gospel is based on stories, true stories that change the lives of those who read them and make them part of their own experience.

This collection—following in the tradition of volumes 1 and 2 of the *Best-Loved* series—contains some of the best true, faith-promoting stories in the Mormon experience. Some will already be familiar to the reader. Others will be new discoveries. But each one is a treasure.

The stories in this volume are reproduced substantially as they were originally published. We have, however, made some changes in spelling, punctuation, capitalization, and paragraphing to enhance their readability.

We owe a debt of gratitude to those who have recorded and

collected stories in our past. Such writers and compilers as Andrew Jenson, Kate Carter, Bryant S. Hinckley, Preston Nibley, Nels B. Lundwall, and Leon Hartshorn have created a literature that continues to bless. We stand on a foundation which they established. We also thank the many writers who have graciously given us permission to use their material. Special thanks goes to Edward L. Kimball and Susan Arrington Madsen.

We thank those at Deseret Book Company who have helped to turn our collection into a finished book: Ronald A. Millett, Sheri L. Dew, Kent S. Ware, Jennifer Adams, Laurie Cook, Ronald O. Stucki, Tom Hewitson, and Sheryl Dickert.

# BOOK OF MORMON

# MARTIN HARRIS'S TESTIMONY OF
# THE BOOK OF MORMON

⌒‿

## MARTIN HARRIS

Joseph Smith, Jr., found at Palmyra, N. Y., on the 22d day of September, 1827, the plates of gold upon which was recorded in Arabic, Chaldaic, Syriac, and Egyptian, the Book of Life, or the Book of Mormon. I was not with him at the time, but I had a revelation the summer before, that God had a work for me to do. These plates were found at the north point of a hill two miles north of Manchester village. . . .

. . . On the 22d of September, 1827, before day, Joseph took the horse and wagon of old Mr. Stowel, and taking his wife, he went to the place where the plates were concealed, and while he was obtaining them, she kneeled down and prayed. He then took the plates and hid them in an old black oak tree top which was hollow. . . .

Joseph did not dig for these plates. They were placed in this way: four stones were set up and covered with a flat stone, oval on the upper side and flat on the bottom. Beneath this was a little platform upon which the plates were laid; and the two stones set in a bow of silver by means of which the plates were translated, were found underneath the plates.

These plates were seven inches wide by eight inches in length, and were of the thickness of plates of tin; and when piled one above the other, they were altogether about four inches thick; and they were put together on the back by three silver rings, so that they would open like a book.

The two stones set in a bow of silver were about two inches in diameter, perfectly round, and about five-eighths of an inch thick at the centre; but not so thick at the edges where they came into the bow. They were joined by a round bar of silver, about three-eighths of an inch in diameter, and about four inches long, which, with the two stones, would make eight inches.

The stones were white, like polished marble, with a few gray streaks. I never dared to look into them by placing them in the hat, because Moses said that "no man could see God and live," and we could see anything we wished by looking into them; and I could not keep the desire to see God out of my mind. And beside, we had a command to let no man look into them, except by the command of God, lest he should "look aught and perish."

These plates were usually kept in a cherry box made for that purpose, in the possession of Joseph and myself. The plates were kept from the sight of the world, and no one, save Oliver Cowdery, myself, Joseph Smith, Jr., and David Whitmer, ever saw them. Before the Lord showed the plates to me, Joseph wished me to see them. But I refused, unless the Lord should do it. At one time, before the Lord showed them to me, Joseph said I should see them. I asked him, why he would break the commands of the Lord. He said, you have done so much I am afraid you will not believe unless you see them. I replied, "Joseph, I know all about it. The Lord has showed to me ten times more about it than you know." . . .

. . . I hefted the plates many times, and should think they weighed forty or fifty pounds.

When Joseph had obtained the plates he communicated the fact to his father and mother. The plates remained concealed in the tree top until he got the chest made. He then went after them and brought them home. While on his way home with the plates, he was met by what appeared to be a man, who demanded the plates, and struck him with a club on his side, which was all black and blue. Joseph knocked the man down, and then ran for home, and was much out of breath. When he arrived at home, he handed the plates in at the window, and they were received from him by his mother. They were then hidden under the hearth in his father's house. But the wall being partly down, it was feared that certain ones, who were trying to get possession of the plates, would get under the house and dig them out. Joseph then took them out, and hid them under the old cooper's shop, by taking up a board and digging in the ground and burying them. When they were taken from there, they were put into an old Ontario glass-box. Old Mr. Beman sawed off the ends, making the box the right length to put them in, and when they went in he said he heard them jink, but he was not permitted to see them. He told me so.

The money-diggers claimed that they had as much right to the plates as Joseph had, as they were in company together. They claimed that Joseph had been traitor, and had appropriated to himself that which belonged to them. For this reason Joseph was afraid of them, and continued concealing the plates. After they had been concealed under the floor of the cooper's shop for a short time, Joseph was warned to remove them. He said he was warned by an angel. He took them out and hid them up in the chamber of the cooper's shop among the flags. That night some one came, took up the floor, and dug up the earth, and would have found the plates had they not been removed.

These things had all occurred before I talked with Joseph respecting the plates. But I had the account of it from Joseph, his wife, brothers, sisters, his father and mother. I talked with them separately, that I might get the truth of the matter. The first time I heard of the matter, my brother Preserved Harris, who had been in the village of Palmyra, asked me if [I] had heard about Joseph

Smith, Jr., having a golden bible. My thoughts were that the money-diggers had probably dug up an old brass kettle, or something of the kind. I thought no more of it. This was about the first of October, 1827. The next day after the talk with my brother, I went to the village, and there I was asked what I thought of the Gold Bible? I replied, The Scripture says, He that answereth a matter before he heareth it, it is foolishness unto him. I do not wish to make myself a fool. I don't know anything about it. Then said I, what is it about Joe's Gold Bible? They then went on to say, that they put whiskey into the old man's cider and got him half drunk, and he told them all about it. They then repeated his account, which I found afterwards to agree substantially with the account given by Joseph. Then said I to them, how do you know that he has not got such gold plates. They replied, "D—— him, he ought to be tarred and feathered for telling such a d——d lie!" Then I said, suppose he has told a lie, as old Tom Jefferson said, it did not matter to him whether a man believed in one god or twenty. It did not rob his pocket, nor break his shins. What is it to us if he has told a lie? He has it to answer for if he has lied. If you should tar and feather all the liars, you would soon be out of funds to purchase the material.

I then thought of the words of Christ, The kingdom divided against itself cannot stand. I knew they were of the devil's kingdom, and if that is of the devil, his kingdom is divided against itself. I said in my heart, this is something besides smoke. There is some fire at the bottom of it. I then determined to go and see Joseph as soon as I could find time.

A day or so before I was ready to visit Joseph, his mother came over to our house and wished to talk with me. I told her I had no time to spare, she might talk with my wife, and, in the evening when I had finished my work I would talk with her. When she commenced talking with me, she told me respecting his bringing home the plates, and many other things, and said that Joseph had sent her over and wished me to come and see him. I told her that I had a time appointed when I would go, and that when the time came I should then go but I did not tell her when it was. I sent my boy to harness my horse and take her home. She wished my wife and daughter to go with her; and they went and spent most of the day. When they came home, I questioned them about them. My daughter said, they were about as much as she could lift. They were now in the glass-box, and my wife said they were very heavy. They both lifted them. I waited a day or two, when I got up in the morning, took my breakfast, and told my folks I was going to the village, but went directly to old Mr. Smith's. I found that Joseph had gone away to work for Peter Ingersol to get some flour. I was glad he was absent, for that gave me an opportunity of talking with his wife and the family about the plates. I talked with them separately, to see if their stories agreed, and I found they did agree. When Joseph came home I did not wish him to know that I had been talking with them, so I took him by the arm and led him away from the rest, and requested him to tell me the story, which he did as follows. He said: "An angel had appeared to him, and told him it was God's work." . . .

Joseph said the angel told him he must quit the company of the money-diggers. That there were wicked men among them. He must have no more to do with them. He must not lie, nor swear, nor steal. He told him to go and look in the spectacles, and he would show him the man that would assist him. That he did so, and he saw myself, Martin Harris, standing before him. That struck me with surprise. I told him I wished him to be very careful about these things. "Well," said he, "I saw you standing before me as plainly as I do now." I said, if it is the devil's work I will have nothing to do with it; but if it is the Lord's, you can have all the money necessary to bring it before the world. He said the angel told him, that the plates must be translated, printed and sent before the world. I said, Joseph, you know my doctrine, that cursed is every one that putteth his trust in man, and maketh flesh his arm; and we know that the devil is to have great power in the latter days to deceive if possible the very elect; and I don't know that you are one of the elect. Now you must not blame me for not taking your word. If the Lord will show me that it is his work, you can have all the money you want.

While at Mr. Smith's I hefted the plates, and I knew from the heft that they were lead or gold, and I knew that Joseph had not credit enough to buy so much lead. I left Mr. Smith's about eleven o'clock and went home. I retired to my bedroom and prayed God to show me concerning these things, and I covenanted that if it was his work and he would show me so, I would put forth my best ability to bring it before the world. He then showed me that it was his work, and that it was designed to bring in the fullness of his gospel to the gentiles to fulfill his word, that the first shall be last and the last first. He showed this to me by the still small voice spoken in the soul. Then I was satisfied that it was the Lord's work, and I was under a covenant to bring it forth.

---

Martin Harris, in Francis W. Kirkham, *A New Witness for Christ in America*, 2:377–82.

# "What Have You Done with the Book of Mormon?"

## B E N J A M I N   B R O W N

I procured a Book of Mormon, and took it home to read, determined to investigate until I was fully satisfied. But I had scarcely begun to read, before I felt greatly to dislike the book. Ere I had perused ten pages, I rejected it altogether.

Acting in this bigoted manner, I had resigned myself to the evil influence that was gaining power over me, so that, directly after, I felt a similar dislike seize me towards the Bible. Its statements of miracles, etc., appeared to me to be compounds of the grossest absurdity possible. I could see no light or good in it, and actually resolved never to read it again!

But, oh! the darkness that seized me as soon as I had made this resolution! The light that was in me became darkness, and how great it was, no language can describe. All knowedge of religious truth seemed to forsake me, and if I attempted to quote scripture, my recollection failed, after the first word or so! So remarkable was this, that it excited reflection, and caused me to marvel, and finally I determined to repent of my resolve respecting the Bible, and I commenced to read again.

The book was hardly in my hand, when, as in a moment, my light and recollection returned as usual. This made me rejoice, and immediately the idea flashed across my mind, "What have you done with the Book of Mormon? Behave as fairly to that." I soon reprocured it. But, even this time, I felt prejudiced against the book. I resolved, however, to read it through, and I persevered in its perusal, till I came to that part where Jesus, on visiting the continent of America, after His resurrection, grants the request of three of the apostles whom He had chosen, to permit them to live until His second coming on the earth (like unto John spoken of in the Bible).

Here my mind half yielded to the belief which arose within me, that perhaps it might be true, whereupon I took the book and laid it before the Lord, and pleaded with Him in prayer for a testimony whether it was true or false, and, as I found it stated that the three Nephites had power to show themselves to any persons they might wish to, Jews or Gentiles, I asked the Lord to allow me to see them for a witness and testimony of the truth of the Book of Mormon, and I covenanted with Him, if He complied with my request, that I would preach it, even at the expense of my life, should it be necessary.

The Lord heard my prayer, and, about five days afterwards, two of the three visited me in my bedroom. I did not see them come, but I found them there.

One spoke to me for some time, and reproved me sharply on account of my behavior at the time when I first attended the meeting of the Saints, and treated so lightly the gift of tongues. He told me never, as long as I lived, to do so again, for I had grieved the Spirit of the Lord, by whose power that gift had been given.

This personage spoke in the Nephite language, but I understood, by the Spirit which accompanied him, every word as plainly as if he had spoken in English. I recognized the language to be the same as that in which I had heard Father Fisher speak at the meeting.

Such a rebuke, with such power, I never had in my life, before nor since, and never wish to have again. I was dumb before my rebuker, for I knew that what he said was right, and I felt deserving of it.

How these men went, I do not know, but directly they were gone, [and] the Spirit of the Lord said to me, "Now, you know for yourself! You have seen and heard! If you now fall away, there is no forgiveness for you."

Did I not know then, that the Book of Mormon was true, and that Joseph Smith was a prophet of the Lord? Surely I did, and I do now, as surely as I know that I live.

_Gems for the Young Folks_, 59–61.

# "DOES NOT THIS AGREE WITH YOUR FAITH?"

## BRIGHAM YOUNG

I have read [to those of other faiths] many and many a time out of the prophecies, and the sayings of the Savior and His apostles what the Bible contains, until they who listened have got up and declared they would hear no more from that wicked book, believing it to be the Book of Mormon. Priests and deacons [of these other churches] have declared they would hear no more from that vile record. I have said, "Does not this agree with your faith and feelings?" "No, it does not, and if we had it in our houses, we would take the tongs and put it in the fire." "Well," I have replied, "the book I have been reading from is the Holy Bible, the Old and New Testaments, translated by the order of King James."

*Journal of Discourses*, 12:57–58.

# "THIS IS MY BOOK, NOT YOURS"

EDWARD JAMES WOOD

We have recently had an Indian by the name of Brother Warner, from Parker, Idaho, come up and do missionary work among the Blood and Blackfoot Indians across the border in Montana from our country [Alberta, Canada]. He [accompanied] a young man named Galbraith. . . . [Galbraith's] mother was an Indian, a Blackfoot woman. His father was an honorable Scotchman living very close to our country on the Blackfoot reservation.

This Brother Galbraith had a dream. He said he came to our meeting. He saw in the meeting, in his dream, four or five old Indian chiefs sitting on the stand. He knew these Indians were dead and had been for a long time. One of them was his uncle. The highest point on the Rocky Mountains near us was called Old Chief. That was the name of his uncle, the highest chief among the Blackfoot nation. He said as he went into the audience that this uncle of his told him to come up on the stand with him, and he said he wondered how it was, because this man was dead; he knew this. He went up and he heard his uncle stand up and preach a sermon to the audience there and turn around and say, "This nephew of mine must be our representative among our people." . . .

When he got to this, Brother Galbraith said, "What have I got to do?" He said, "You see a book on the table"—and he pointed to a book on the table. "That book contains the history of our people. We are what people call all dead, and you are in the life, with the book. It will be told to you what to do." He awoke, and after two long years of investigating, he joined the Church.

When Brother Warner came up, by permission of President Ballard, he went over and visited Brother Galbraith, and they went among the Indians, and they aroused a lot of interest among the Indians. [In one meeting, after] he spoke about the Book of Mormon . . . the [investigator] stood up and said, "I know more about that book than you do, Brother Galbraith. I can see that. Let me tell you what I know. For three consecutive years I have taken my family and gone off into the woods, and when I got there (the first year was 1914), pitched my tepee and went off in the forest. I was told by a man who came there to meet me that I was to lie down under the trees, wrap my blankets around me, and go with him on a journey. So I did it. I went right off, and looked down on my body when I went with this visitor—saw an Indian there wrapped in his blankets, and I wondered how it was that I was living and yet it was I there wrapped in my own blankets. I wondered if anybody would come along and bury my body before I returned. We were gone a day, and the visitor had taught me, oh, so many things—many things you would not believe if I told you, because my own family do not believe them. The messenger said I was to come in 1915, and I did it. I went again on the journey. In 1916 the messenger said to me, . . . 'During this year you will have a little dark man come to you with a book. That is the book that will tell you of the history of your people.'"

The man stood up and said, "There is the little dark man, Brother Warner. I saw him here yesterday. He had the book in his hand. The old Indian told him to give me the book. . . . And he took it and wrapped it in what they call their sacred cloth, and said to the man, "Brother Warner, this is my book, not yours."

---

Conference Report, April 1917, 128–29.

# CALLINGS

# "My Ideal Apostle"

F . A . H A M M O N D

On the 6th day of September 1848, we arrived in Great Salt Lake City. I remember thinking the name was much larger than the city, which consisted of three mud forts called the North, South and Middle Forts, enclosing ten acres in each fort, if my memory is not at fault. The Saints . . . were all located inside these forts or enclosures, probably in round numbers not exceeding fifteen hundred souls. . . .

On the 20th of September, 1848, President Brigham Young and company arrived in the valley from Winter Quarters. I sought and obtained an introduction to him. I was profoundly impressed with his appearance. Never did a man make such an impression upon me as he did; and I was more than willing to accept him as the great leader and prophet and counselor to the people of God. This testimony has never wavered in the least from that day to the present.

I had a great desire to make the acquaintance of Apostle Parley P. Pratt, for I revered him as my father in the gospel, on account of the *Voice of Warning,* which had much to do in converting me to the faith. Brother John Van Cott used to visit frequently at Brother Riter's [where I was living,] and I was introduced to him. I soon came to esteem Brother Van Cott very highly for his many virtues and strict honesty, and unflinching fidelity to the cause of truth.

One afternoon soon after my arrival, I dressed myself up in my best bib and tucker, and Brother Van Cott took me up to introduce me to Apostle Parley P. Pratt. We found him threshing beans before his door, with a wagon box with sides turned down for a floor. He was barefooted, in shirt sleeves, and wore a home-made straw hat with brim nearly separated from the crown, and his ears protruding between crown and brim of his hat. I must confess I was a good deal surprised to find my ideal Apostle in such a plight, and forced to labor in such a manner for his support, for I had the old sectarian idea about the grave and reverend appearance of prophets and apostles, who had little if anything to do with secular or temporal affairs. With such views I could hardly receive Brother Pratt as the man who wrote so many inspired books.

In introducing me, Brother Van Cott stated that I was lately from the Sandwich Islands, and had resided there some three years. Brother Pratt flung down his flail and, seating himself on a fence, began talking about the people on those far-off isles belonging to the house of Israel. A flood of light and truth flowed in a perpetual stream from his lips, and his whole soul was inspired with his theme. I soon lost all sight of his bare feet, his dilapidated hat and general appearance, and was all imbued with the spirit of the great latter-day gathering promised by the Lord to His people, the house of Israel. Never in all my life had I heard such a discourse so full of inspiration and prophecy concerning the great work of the Lord in the latter days. I found my ideal Apostle to be all that I had imagined and far more.

---

*Juvenile Instructor* 29:518–20.

# "I HAVE ANOTHER MISSION FOR YOU"

## REINHARD MAESER

In the spring of 1876, just prior to the April conference, a terrific explosion of powder occurred on Arsenal Hill, near the present site of the State Capitol. Several lives were lost, and extensive damage was done to adjacent property, such as the breaking of window glass, crashing of roofs by the large boulders, etc. Nearly all of the plaster was shaken from the ceiling of the Twentieth Ward schoolhouse, where Professor [Karl G.] Maeser was teaching. Immediately he started in search of his bishop, John Sharp, the one person to whom, when in trouble, he always went first; it seemed that his difficulties could not be adjusted otherwise. He found the bishop at the President's office and reported to him what had just happened, adding that the school would have to be dismissed until the house could be repaired.

But at this point, President Young interrupted the conversation with the remark: "That is exactly right, Brother Maeser; I have another mission for you."

What! Another mission! What could it be? Financial daylight was just beginning to dawn upon him. And now another mission! It fairly took his breath away. What did it all mean?

"Yes," said the President, "we have been considering the establishment of a Church school, and are looking around for a man—the man to take charge of it. You are the man, Brother Maeser. We want you to go to Provo to organize and conduct an Academy to be established in the name of the Church—a Church school." . . .

In a few days, Elders George Q. Cannon, George Reynolds, and Warren N. Dusenberry waited upon Professor Maeser at his home, to discuss the matter further, and invited him to attend a board meeting at Savage's Art Gallery the next day. At this meeting all necessary arrangements were made for a preliminary session of school to be held April 24, 1876. The principal was to receive $1200 a year for his salary, in such commodities as the treasurer might take on tuition. . . .

He knew full well there would be perplexing problems to solve, difficult situations to meet, soul-trying times to endure, when he would have to go up to his Gethsemane to seek relief. This struggle continued within him for several days. At last he decided that he must accept the appointment, or, cowardlike, back out. He went to President Young, whom he found in his office, busy on important matters. Addressing the President, he said, "I am about to leave for Provo, Brother Young, to start my work in the Academy. Have you any instructions to give me?"

The President looked steadily forward for a few moments, as though in deep thought, then said: "Brother Maeser, I want you to remember that you ought not to teach even the alphabet or the multiplication tables without the Spirit of God. That is all. God bless you. Good-bye."

---

Reinhard Maeser, *Karl G. Maeser,* 77–79.

# "I Think I Will Not Call You"

## WILFORD WOODRUFF

Perhaps I may be permitted to relate a circumstance with which I am acquainted in relation to Bishop Roskelley, of Smithfield, Cache Valley. On one occasion he was suddenly taken very sick—near to death's door. While he lay in this condition, President Peter Maughan, who was dead, came to him and said: "Brother Roskelley, we held a council on the other side of the [veil]. I have had a great deal to do, and I have the privilege of coming here to appoint one man to come and help. I have had three names given to me in council, and you are one of them. I want to inquire into your circumstances." The bishop told him what he had to do, and they conversed together as one man would converse with another. President Maughan then said to him: "I think I will not call you. I think you are wanted here more than perhaps one of the others." Bishop Roskelley got well from that hour. Very soon after, the second man was taken sick, but . . . Brother Roskelley did not go to him. By and by this man recovered, and on meeting Brother Roskelley he said: "Brother Maughan came to me the other night and told me he was sent to call one man from the ward," and he named two men as had been done to Brother Roskelley. A few days afterwards the third man was taken sick and died. Now, I name this to show a principle. They have work on the other side of the [veil]; and they want men, and they call them.

---

*Journal of Discourses*, 22:333–34.

# "THE BEST BISHOP IN
# THE CHURCH"

ORSON F. WHITNEY

My installation as bishop came about in this manner. On my way to church that Sabbath evening I pursued an indirect course, lengthening my walk from the parental home on City Creek to the Deseret Bank corner, where, as I turned to go east, I was accosted by Laron Cummings, who had a room on an upper floor of the bank building.

"Come up to my room," said Laron.

"Thank you," said I, "but I must go to meeting. They are going to put me in as bishop tonight."

He laughed, and I laughed and passed on, little dreaming that I had uttered in jest a prediction that was about to be fulfilled. I had been told that a new bishopric could be installed that night, but as to the proposed personnel I knew nothing.

When the president of the stake said to the congregation:

"It has been moved and seconded that Orson F. Whitney be the bishop of the Eighteenth Ward," I was astounded. If the earth had opened and swallowed me, I could scarcely have been more surprised. An unmarried youth, just turned twenty-three, with scarcely any experience in Church work, to preside over a ward where Youngs, Kimballs, Caines, Calders and other noted families dwelt!—the thought was overpowering; it almost took my breath.

Called upon to express my feelings, I tremblingly took the stand and tremulously addressed the large congregation. I told them— what they already knew—that I was young and inexperienced; but that time would cure those defects; and I accepted my call to the bishopric as I had accepted my call to the mission field, trusting in the Lord to qualify me for my duties.

President Daniel H. Wells, for many years one of the First Presidency, but since President Young's death a counselor to the Twelve Apostles; George Q. Cannon, Joseph F. Smith and Brigham Young, Jr., all members of that quorum; with the stake presidency, . . . then laid their hands upon my head, and President Wells ordained me a high priest and set me apart to preside over the Eighteenth Ward as its bishop.

George Q. Cannon then addressed the meeting. "Bishop Whitney," he remarked, "said a good thing when he told us that time would remedy in him the defects of youth and inexperience. And I will add this: If the people of this ward will rally round him and hold up his hands, the time will come when they will think they have the best bishop in the Church."

He did not say that I would be the best bishop—and of course I never was; but he said the people would think so; and that prophecy was abundantly fulfilled. During the well-nigh twenty-eight years of my bishopric, I had the love and loyal support of the good people of the Eighteenth Ward. They thought me the best bishop, just as children in a family think their father the best of men. It does not have to be fact. It is a sentiment, and a wholesome one, an expression of loyalty akin to patriotism, the love of one's own native land.

The president of the stake followed with a jocular allusion to my unmarried status, quoting Paul the Apostle on "blameless" bishops and matrimony, and adding: "We are pleased to hear Brother Whitney say that he will endeavor to qualify himself."

Orson F. Whitney, *Through Memory's Halls*, 106–7.

# "BEHAVE YOURSELF, HEBER"

## HEBER J. GRANT

My mother always told me: "Behave yourself, Heber, and some day you will be an apostle. If you do not behave yourself, you will not be, because we have in a revelation, recorded in the Doctrine and Covenants, the following statement: 'There is a law, irrevocably decreed in heaven before the foundations of the world, upon which all blessings are predicated—and when we obtain any blessing from God, it is by obedience to that law upon which it is predicated.'" I said: "Mother, get it out of your head. I do not want to be an apostle. I do not want to be a bishop. I do not want to be anything but a business man. Just get it out of your head."

After I was called to be an apostle, she asked me about that meeting where this blessing was given, and whether I remembered it. I said, "No, I do not remember anything, only that when Aunt Zina was talking she said, 'You will become a great big man,' and since I have grown tall I have often thought of that." She said, "She did not promise you any such thing; she said that you should become a great big man in The Church of Jesus Christ of Latter-day Saints, and one of the apostles of the Lord Jesus Christ. That is the reason I have told you to behave yourself. I knew it would not come true if you did not live worthily, but it has come true." Then she said: "Do you remember Heber C. Kimball's picking you up when you were a young boy, and putting you on a table and talking to you, at a great dinner he was having with a lot of his friends?"

"Yes."

"Do you remember anything he said?"

"No. I only remember he had the blackest eyes, I thought, I ever looked into, and I was frightened. That is all I can remember."

"He prophesied in the name of the Lord Jesus Christ that you should become an apostle of the Lord Jesus Christ and become a greater man in the Church than your own father; and your own father, as you know, became one of the counselors to Brigham Young. That is why I told you to behave yourself."

—————

Heber J. Grant, *Gospel Standards*, 11–12.

# "OH, HE'S INACTIVE"

## LUCILE C. TATE

Bishop [LeGrand] Richards sat in his office going over the priesthood rolls with his counselors. Like him, Elliott C. Taylor was a newcomer to the ward. Alexander R. Curtis had lived all his life in Sugar House, so it was mainly to him that the questions were directed.

"What about Brother A——?" the bishop would ask.

"Oh, he's inactive. You can't get him to do anything," would be the answer.

Night after consecutive night they continued to review the alphabetical list, the bishop putting a check mark against all the "can't gets." When they had completed the survey, the bishop said: "Brethren, let's ask the stake president not to send us any home missionaries for a few months (only high councilors to check up on us), and let's ask each of these inactive men to speak in our sacrament meetings. By giving them twelve minutes apiece, we can have four speak every Sunday but fast day."

They visited each man on the list, became acquainted with his family, and invited him to speak, not upon a gospel subject but about what the Church meant to him, his family, and his pioneer ancestors. If the brother said he preferred not to give a talk, the bishop would smile and say, "Well, it's up to you, but on [giving a date about two weeks hence] we will announce you, and if you are not there we will tell the people that we came to your house and personally invited you, so they will know we didn't overlook you."

Almost to a man the inactive brethren responded, and with tears flooding their eyes and voices they would tell at the pulpit that in the twenty or thirty years since their mission reports, this was the first time they had been asked to speak in sacrament meeting. This experience taught Bishop Richards that "you can rehabilitate a man better spiritually by putting him at the pulpit than in any other way." His aim was to apply Granite Stake's motto, "Everybody Working," and this reactivation project was a significant start.

---

Lucile C. Tate, *LeGrand Richards: Beloved Apostle,* 111–12.

# REAL AUTHORITY

## HUGH B. BROWN

If you will pardon me, I shall refer to a personal experience that I had during World War I. . . . At the outbreak of the war I held a commission in the Canadian army, and it became my duty to go and do what little I could during the war. I had the privilege of serving for a little over three years, and during that time I had the opportunity to preach the gospel more than I had during my missionary experience in England, some seventeen years prior. Quite a number of Latter-day Saint boys went from southern Alberta, and some of them did not return.

Upon several occasions, while I was in England and France, appeals came to me from some of the boys who were sick in the hospital, asking me to intercede for them with officers higher up, asking that they might be returned home while they were convalescing; asking, perhaps, that they might have leave of absence. On several occasions it was my privilege to intercede for the boys and to get favors for them.

When in London, one morning, I received a message that some boy wanted to see me in the hospital; and immediately I thought, here is another boy who would like to return to his mother, who perhaps will ask me to intercede for him, by reason of the authority that I hold as an officer in the army. And as I went in response to that call to the hospital referred to, I believe that I felt just a little pride in my heart because I had the honor of wearing an officer's uniform; by virtue of that fact I held the right to intercede as an officer of the king. With this feeling I went into the hospital, and as I was ushered into the little ward where that boy was sick, with a feeble hand he reached out and said, "Brother Brown, I sent for you to come and administer to me; I'm afraid I'm going to die, and I want you to ask God to spare my life that I can return home to my mother."

Upon that occasion it seemed to me my uniform fell from me. All the pride that I had felt in standing in that uniform of the king vanished. And at that moment I was made to realize, that there is an authority, there is a power inestimably greater than any authority or power that can be given by man. And as I laid my hands upon the head of that boy, I interceded for him, not with the king of England, not with any man, and not by virtue of my authority as an officer in that army. But as I laid my hands upon his head, I said, "In the name of Jesus Christ, and by authority of the Melchizedek Priesthood."

Brethren and sisters, I came to realize that the most valuable thing in this world is the priesthood of God, the right to speak and to act in the name of God. And as I stood there, as it were clasping hands with that boy and his Maker, by virtue of the priesthood that had been given unto me, I forgot any honor that had come to me in the army. And as I knelt at his bedside, my prayer to God was, that never again in my life would I be found seeking the honors of men, that I would remember that the things that are really worthwhile in this life come to us through the gospel of Jesus Christ.

---

Hugh B. Brown, *Continuing the Quest*, 27–28.

# CONVERSION

# "She Could Only Find
a Small Potato"

## BENJAMIN BROWN

My wife, who had managed to be present when I was going to the water [for baptism], and even threatened that she would not live with me, was, for a long while after, (perhaps a year and a half,) bitterly opposed to the work, but I knew from the Lord that she would come into the Church, and I told her so. As the way she was at last brought in was very curious, I will mention it.

She dreamed one night that a large company of visitors had come to her house, for whom she had to prepare supper. On going into her buttery to procure the necessary food to cook, she could only find a small potato, about the size of a robin's egg, lying on a wooden trencher. However, with this small stock she commenced, and by some wonderful means converted this little affair into a splendid preparation of pies, puddings, etc.

When they were ready she stood still, wondering how it had all been done, for, as may be supposed, it puzzled her sorely to conceive how, from a small potato, and that on a wooden trencher, she had produced such an elegant entertainment.

Just at this moment while she was thus marveling, I was awakened from my sleep, with a command sounding in my ears that I was to say to my wife, "Don't you remember hearing that you should not despise the day of *small things*?" I was to speak at once, without waiting. So I awoke her, and without any preface did as I was bid.

The wonderful concurrence of these words with her dream, and the self-evident interpretation of it, referring as it did to her past conduct (for one of the principal reasons of the opposition she felt to my joining the Church was, that she considered it disgraced her to have her husband belong to a church that was so poor, and everywhere spoken against), so impressed itself upon her mind, with other confirmations, that she was baptized, and has remained firm to the Church ever since.

*Gems for the Young Folks*, 63–64.

# "YOU MAY BREAK SNOW CRUST, BUT I WILL PRAY"

SHERI L. DEW

In July 1840 Ezra's [Ezra T. Benson, grandfather of President Ezra Taft Benson] curiosity was aroused when he observed Joseph Smith, prophet and president of the Church, as the Prophet attended a religious debate. Ezra determined that Joseph seemed too pleasant a man to be the rogue his detractors made him out to be. . . .

Some time later Ezra and his wife attended a gathering in which Orson Hyde, a member of the Church's Quorum of the Twelve Apostles, delivered a moving discourse. . . .

Late one night, after learning much more about the Church,

Ezra retired to a snow-covered grove to seek spiritual guidance. Shortly after beginning to pray, he heard a sound as though someone were walking toward him on the frozen snow; instinctively he jumped up, but he could see nothing. The noise recurred three times. After the last encounter he became convinced it was an opposing power trying to discourage him from prayer. At that point he shouted out, "Mr. Devil, you may break snow crust, but I will pray!" Ezra did pray, and the sounds did not return. . . .

Things began to move quickly, and Ezra soon gained a witness of the truth.

Sheri L. Dew, *Ezra Taft Benson*, 2–4.

# "GO ON, MY SON"

## JACOB HAMBLIN

In February, 1842, a neighbor called at my house and told me that he had heard a "Mormon" Elder preach. He asserted that he preached more Bible doctrine than any other man he had ever listened to, and that he knew what he preached was true. He claimed that the gospel had been restored to the earth, and that it was the privilege of all who heard it to know and understand it for themselves.

What this neighbor told me so influenced my mind, that I could scarcely attend to my ordinary business.

The Elder had left an appointment to preach again at the same place, and I went to hear him. When I entered the house he had already commenced his discourse. I shall never forget the feeling that came over me when I saw his face and heard his voice. He preached that which I had long been seeking for; I felt that it was indeed the gospel.

The principles he taught appeared so plain and natural, that I thought it would be easy to convince anyone of their truth. In closing his remarks, the Elder bore testimony to the truth of the gospel.

The query came to my mind: How shall I know whether or not these things are so, and be satisfied? As if the Spirit prompted him to answer my inquiry, he again arose to his feet and said: "If there is anyone in the congregation who wishes to know how he can satisfy himself of the truth of these things, I can assure him that if he will be baptized, and have hands laid upon him for the gift of the Holy Ghost, he shall have an assurance of their truth."

This so fired up my mind, that I at once determined to be baptized, and that too, if necessary, at the sacrifice of the friendship of my kindred and of every earthly tie.

I immediately went home and informed my wife of my intentions.

She told me that if I was baptized into the "Mormon" Church, I need not expect her to live with me any more.

The evening after the Elder had preached I went in search of him, and found him quite late at night. I told him my purpose, and requested him to give me a "Mormon Bible." He handed me the Old and New Testament.

I said, "I thought you had a new Bible." He then explained about the coming forth of the Book of Mormon, and handed me a copy of it.

The impressions I received at the time cannot be forgotten.

The Spirit rested upon me and bore testimony of its truth, and I felt like opening my mouth and declaring it to be a revelation from God.

On the 3rd of March, 1842, as soon as it was light in the morning, I started for a pool of water where I had arranged to meet with the Elder, to attend to the ordinance of baptism. On the way, the thought of the sacrifice I was making of wife, of father, mother, brothers, sister and numerous other connections, caused my resolution to waver.

As my pace slackened, some person appeared to come from above, who, I thought, was my grandfather. He seemed to say to me, "Go on, my son; your heart cannot conceive, neither has it entered into your mind to imagine the blessings that are in store for you, if you go on and continue in this work."

I lagged no more, but hurried to the pool, where I was baptized by Elder Lyman Stoddard.

It was said in my confirmation, that the spirits in prison greatly rejoiced over what I had done. I told Elder Stoddard my experience on my way to the water.

He then explained to me the work there was for me to do for my fathers, if I was faithful, all of which I believed and greatly rejoiced in.

---

Jacob Hamblin, in James A. Little, ed., *Jacob Hamblin*, 203–5.

# "PLEASE COME BACK AND SING THAT SONG AGAIN"

HEBER J. GRANT

I have related here, upon more than one occasion, the incident of J. Golden Kimball and Charles Welch being about to baptize some people who had been converted to the gospel of Jesus Christ. A mob gathered upon the bank of the river and notified the elders that if they dared to baptize their converts they would throw them into the river. Brother Kimball was a large man, not only tall but he weighed probably a couple of hundred pounds, and was two or three inches taller than I; and he did not scare worth a cent, neither did Brother Welch. So they advised the mob that they were going to baptize their converts, but before doing so they sang the hymn, written by Eliza R. Snow, to be found on page 297 of our hymn book. I recommend that the Saints read it over again when they go home. It will not hurt them.

> Truth reflects upon our senses,
> Gospel light reveals to some.
> If there still should be offenses
> Woe to them by whom they come.

The Lord says in section 25 of the Doctrine and Covenants "For my soul delighteth in the song of the heart, yea, the song of the righteous is a prayer unto me, and it shall be answered with a blessing upon their heads."

The blessing answered upon the heads of these two elders was that this song had such a wonderful effect upon the mob that they

36

did not disturb the elders while they baptized their converts. After baptizing them, and starting to leave the river, one of the mob followed them and asked if they would not please come back and sing that song again. The elders did so. One of the men in that mob, who had come out to try and persuade the mob to leave the elders alone, followed the elders and converts to the testimony meeting and confirmation and afterwards embraced the gospel. . . . I have interviewed his widow, and she said he bore testimony that while listening to that song, written by Eliza R. Snow and paraphrasing the teachings of the Savior, there was burning into his very soul a testimony that the men singing that song had in very deed the truth of God to deliver to the people.

*Deseret News,* 24 April 1920.

# "A TALL, HANDSOME MAN, WITH BEAUTIFUL WHITE HAIR"

MILTON R. HUNTER

The following is Daniel Mich's story. He lived in Patzicia, Guatemala, a small town not far from Lake Atitlan. A few years ago an Indian rebellion against the government officials, who were primarily of Spanish blood, took place in Patzicia. The government officials decided to put to death all the

Indians who had participated in this rebellion and especially those who had instigated it.

Daniel Mich [who was not a member of the Church] had taken no part in the rebellion; however, the government officials thought he was guilty. The Spirit of God whispered to him and told him and his brother to flee to the mountains and hide in a certain place. If they did not, they would be killed. They did as the Spirit instructed. As they arrived at the hiding place suggested by the Spirit, they lay on a ledge and looked over the precipice. Below them they could see the government officials searching for them along the mountainside.

A number of Indians were captured at this time and put to death. Daniel Mich and his brother stayed in seclusion for two years, but finally they also were captured. Conditions had changed during the two years to the extent that the Mich brothers were not killed but were thrown into prison. For four long years they lay in prison, living under the most terrible conditions. Their clothing wore out. They had a scant amount of bedding. It was very cold, and the jail was unheated. The caretakers of the prison gave them very little food; in fact, they practically starved to death. And to make matters much worse, Daniel Mich received word from his wife that she and the children were practically starved to death. During the six years' time that he was in hiding and in prison, they had not been able to make a livelihood.

In desperation, and, of course, in great grief, Daniel Mich kneeled down and prayed to God, pleading that the Eternal Father would be merciful unto him and let him die. He also prayed that the Lord would extend his mercy unto his wife and children, that they all might soon die. He pleaded with the Lord to release him and his family members from the misery and suffering that they were enduring.

But God did not let them die. Instead, Daniel Mich had a

vision, or a dream, or whatever it might be called. He was going up the side of a steep mountain on a definitely defined trail. He came to a place where a side trail forked off the main trail. A man stood on the side trail and said, "Follow me."

Daniel Mich replied, "No, I cannot follow you. I must follow this trail straight ahead."

He went some distance farther, and another man stood on another trail, He also said, "Follow me."

And again Daniel Mich replied, "No, I cannot follow you. I must go straight ahead." This experience repeated itself three or four times.

Daniel Mich explained, "Finally I came to the summit, and there standing in front of me was a tall, handsome man, with beautiful white hair. He had a very kindly and beautiful smile. This man said to me, 'Daniel, follow me.' I replied, 'I will follow you,' because as I made that remark, the Spirit of God whispered to me and said, 'That man has the truth.'"

Shortly after having this dream, or vision, Daniel Mich and his brother were released from jail. They returned to their home town. Soon thereafter and possibly about a year before I visited Guatemala, missionaries came to Patzicia, Brother Mich's home town. They had not been working there long until one day the mayor sent for them to come to his office. When the missionaries arrived, they saw a large crowd of Indians, perhaps two hundred or more, collected in front of the mayor's office. As the missionaries approached, according to the description given by the missionaries, "The crowd of Indians opened as the Red Sea opened for the Israelites to go through. We walked between two columns of Indians and on into the mayor's office."

The elders said to the mayor, "You sent for us?"

"Yes, I did," was the reply.

"What do you want?" they asked.

The mayor answered, "I have here in front of me a petition signed by two hundred citizens of our community in which they demand that you young men leave town immediately and that you refrain from teaching your religion any more in our community. Will you go?"

"No, we will not go," the missionaries replied. "We will not leave this town until our mission president tells us to leave."

The elders sat silently in the mayor's office for several minutes, and then one of them asked, "What do you intend to do?"

The mayor replied, "I do not know."

Thereupon one of the missionaries suggested that he telephone the governor, and perhaps the governor could instruct him. The mayor immediately picked up the telephone, called the governor, and explained the situation.

The governor emphatically instructed, "Let those Mormon missionaries alone. They have a right to teach their religion in your town or in any other town or city in Guatemala, because we have religious freedom in our country."

After this favorable solution of the problem, the missionaries came out of the mayor's office. Once again they described the crowd, stating that it opened as the Red Sea opened for the Israelites. The elders passed between those two long lines of Indians. As they arrived at the edge of the crowd, two men approached them and said, "Will you come to our homes and talk to us?" One of the men was Daniel Mich.

The missionaries were happy to accept the invitation. They went to Daniel Mich's home and taught him the gospel. He received all they taught with much faith and sincerity. They had taught him only three or four lessons when a very important event occurred. One day while in the midst of one of the lessons, one of the missionaries opened his book, and Daniel Mich saw a photograph of a tall, handsome man, with beautiful white hair.

Brother Mich immediately and excitedly exclaimed, "This is the man! It is he whom I saw!"

Of course the missionaries wondered what he was talking about, and so they questioned him. In response he told them the wonderful story that I have just told you good people today.

Then Daniel Mich asked, "Who is this man whose photograph you have in your book?"

"His name is David O. McKay," the missionaries replied. "He is the president of The Church of Jesus Christ of Latter-day Saints. He is God's holy prophet, seer, and revelator upon the earth at the present time. He is the man who holds the keys of the kingdom of God and stands as Christ's representative in the true church and the leader in spreading the true gospel of Jesus Christ."

In deep sincerity Daniel Mich replied, "I know that all of the things you have told me are true. I know that you missionaries have the true gospel of Jesus Christ." Then he asked, "Do you know why I invited you to come to my home that day as you came out of the mayor's office?"

"Of course we do not know but would certainly like to know," they replied.

Then Daniel Mich explained, "At the time that the tall, handsome man, with beautiful white hair—whom you have told me was President David O. McKay—said to me, 'Daniel, follow me,' the Spirit of the Lord whispered to me and said, 'This man has the truth.' The Spirit also said, 'Two young men will bring you the truth,' and when you came into our town recently and began to teach your religion, I became curious. I had been watching you and attempting to find out all about you that I could. When the citizens of Patzicia signed the petition to have you thrown out of town and when you called to see the mayor, I joined the crowd in front of the mayor's office to see what would take place. And now," he said, "all the things that I believed have been verified. I know that David O. McKay is a prophet of God. I also know that you have the true religion of Jesus Christ."

---

Conference Report, October 1959, 29–32.

# "YOU HAVE GIVEN ME THE KEY"

## HAROLD B. LEE

The president of the Alberta Temple told me this incident. He said, "A group of young people came to the temple for the first time to do baptisms for the dead. After they had participated in two or three baptismal sessions and were about ready to go home, I suggested that they could come down to my office and I would attempt to answer any questions they might have. I talked to them about their own baptisms. I said, 'After your own baptism, you were told to receive the Holy Ghost, which means that the Holy Ghost will guide and bless you if you are worthy. If anyone should oppose you, or bring harm to you, you can overcome that opposition by the influence of the Holy Ghost.'

"I looked around and saw a pleasant young girl sobbing. She said, 'When I was baptized, my mother cursed me. Every time I would go out she was vile and called me wicked names. When I told her I was going to the temple, she profaned and said I was no daughter of hers. I have been fasting ever since I left home that here in the temple I would be given a guide and the power to overcome the opposition of my mother. I was going away disappointed. But now, at the last moment, you have given me the key.' A smile lit up on her face as she said, 'I am going to bring Mother within the influence of the power of the Holy Ghost which I have a right to enjoy.'"

Then the president said, "Weeks went by, and a letter came from this girl that said, 'When I returned home and entered the house, Mother greeted me similarly to the way she had when I left, by profaning. On other occasions I had fought back, but this time I walked over and put my arm around her shoulder and said, "Mother, I am not going to quarrel with you today. I want you to come over on the couch and sit down beside me. I want to tell you something." This surprised Mother. As we sat down, we touched cheeks so that in actuality the Spirit would emanate from me to her, and I bore my testimony. I told her what a wonderful experience I had had in the temple. And to my amazement, Mother burst into tears and begged my forgiveness.'

"The girl closed her letter by saying, 'We are now preparing Mother to be baptized a member of the Church.'"

Harold B. Lee, *Stand Ye in Holy Places*, 94–95.

# Courage

# "Come on with Your Tar and Feathers"

⌒

B . H . ROBERTS

Near Columbus, the capital of Ohio, [John Taylor and a company of other Latter-day Saints] stayed at a town where a number of brethren resided, and all were anxious to hear Elder Taylor preach. As they had no hall, it was arranged that he should speak in the open air.

A little before meeting time a number of the brethren came running to the house where he was stopping with the information that the whole town was gathering and that a number of men had proposed tar and feathers, and boasted they would dress him with them if he undertook to preach. The brethren advised him not to attempt it as they were not strong enough to protect him. After a moment's reflection, however, he decided to go and preach. The brethren remonstrated; they knew the tar and feathers were prepared and that he could not escape. He replied that he had made up his mind to go; they could go with him if they chose—if not, he would go alone.

A very large concourse of people had assembled to listen to him. He began his remarks by informing them that he had lately come from Canada—a land under monarchical rule; that standing as he then did on free soil, among free men, he experienced peculiar sensations.

"Gentlemen, I now stand among men whose fathers fought for and obtained one of the greatest blessings ever conferred upon the human family—the right to think, to speak, to write; the right

47

to say who shall govern them, and the right to worship God according to the dictates of their own consciences—all of them sacred human rights, and now guaranteed by the American Constitution. I see around me the sons of those noble sires, who, rather than bow to the behests of a tyrant, pledged their lives, fortunes and sacred honors to burst those fetters, enjoy freedom themselves, bequeath it to their posterity, or die in the attempt.

"They nobly fought and nobly conquered; and now the cap of liberty is elevated on the tops of your liberty poles throughout the land, and the flag of freedom waves from Wisconsin to Louisiana—from Maine to Missouri. Not only so, but your vessels— foremost in the world—sail over oceans, seas and bays; visiting every nation, and wherever those vessels go your flag flutters in the breeze, a hope is inspired among the down-trodden millions, that they, perchance, if they cannot find liberty in their own land, may find it with you. . . . Gentlemen, with you liberty is more than a name; it is incorporated in your system; it is proclaimed by your senators; thundered by your cannon; lisped by your infants; taught to your school-boys; it echoes from mountain to mountain; reverberates through your valleys, and is whispered by every breeze. Is it any wonder, gentlemen, under these circumstances—having lately emerged from a monarchical government, that I should experience peculiar sensations in rising to address you?

"But, by the by, I have been informed that you purpose to tar and feather me, for my religious opinions. Is this the boon you have inherited from your fathers? Is this the blessing they purchased with their dearest hearts' blood—this your liberty? If so, you now have a victim, and we will have an offering to the goddess of liberty." Here he tore open his vest and said: "Gentlemen, come on with your tar and feathers, your victim is ready; and ye shades of the venerable patriots, gaze upon the deeds of your degenerate sons! Come on, gentlemen! Come on, I say, I am ready!"

No one moved, no one spoke. He stood there drawn to his full height, calm but defiant—the master of the situation.

After a pause of some moments he continued his remarks and preached with great boldness and power for some three hours.

At the conclusion of his discourse, he was waited upon by some of the leading citizens of the place who expressed their pleasure at what they had heard, and disclaimed, in behalf of the people, any intention of tarring and feathering him; but the brethren still insisted that such was the intention of the crowd, and that the tar and feathers had been provided; but they had been awed into silence by the boldness of Elder Taylor.

B. H. Roberts, *Life of John Taylor*, 53–55.

# "ARMED WITH WEAPONS YOU KNOW NOT OF"

## ANDREW JENSON

Elder [David] Patten preached three times at the house of father Fry in Benton County, Tenn., May 22, 1835. Many hardened their hearts, and a Mr. Rose, who rejected his testimony, asked him to raise the dead. Bro. Patten rebuked him for his wickedness, when he and others came with arms and threatened to mob the brethren. At the close of the meeting Elder Patten walked out into the door yard and told the mob to shoot him, if they wished. He had nothing but a walking stick in his hand, but the mob fled and left him.

A few days later Warren Parrish arrived from Kirtland and joined Elders Patten and Woodruff. These three brethren then traveled together from town to town, through Kentucky and Tennessee, preaching the gospel, and healing the sick. The Spirit of God was with them and attended their administrations.

While Elders Patten and Parrish were staying at Seth Utley's house in Benton County, Tenn., on June 19, 1835, about forty men, armed with deadly weapons, led by Sheriff Robert C. Petty, a colonel, a major, and other officers, besides a Methodist priest with a gun on his shoulder, surrounded the house. The sheriff informed the brethren that he had a states' warrant for David W. Patten, Warren Parrish, and Wilford Woodruff, issued on complaint of Matthew Williams, the Methodist priest, who swore that those brethren had put forth the following false and pretended prophecy: "That Christ would come the second time, before this generation passed away, and that four individuals should receive the Holy Ghost within twenty-four hours." After examination Elders Patten and Parrish were bound over to appear on June 22nd, under $2,000 bonds.

"Early on the 22nd," writes Wilford Woodruff, Patten and Parrish had their trial. The mob gathered to the number of one hundred, all fully armed. They took from Elder Patten his walking stick and a penknife, and went through with a mock trial; but would not let the defendants produce any witnesses; and without suffering them to say a word in defense, the judge pronounced them guilty of the charge preferred.

Brother Patten, being filled with the Holy Ghost, arose to his feet, and by the power of God bound them fast to their seats while he addressed them. He rebuked them sharply for their wicked and unjust proceedings. Bro. Parrish afterwards said, "My hair stood up straight on my head, for I expected to be killed."

When Patten closed, the Judge addressed him, saying, "You must be armed with concealed weapons, or you would not treat an armed court as you have this."

Patten replied, "I am armed with weapons you know not of, and my weapons are the holy priesthood and the power of God. God is my friend, and he permits you to exercise all the power you have, and he bestows on me all the power I have."

The court finally concluded to let the brethren go, if they would pay the cost of court and leave the country in ten days. The sheriff advised the brethren to accept these propositions, as it was the only means of escaping the violence of the mob. The Saints in that vicinity paid the cost.

Elders Patten and Parrish left and went to Bro. Seth Utley's. They had not been gone long when the mob began to quarrel among themselves and were mad because they had let the prisoners go. They soon mounted their horses and started after them with all possible speed. The news of this movement reached the brethren and they immediately mounted their mules and went into the woods. By a circuitous route they reached the house of Albert Petty, put up their mules, went to bed and slept.

They had not been long asleep when some heavenly messenger came to Bro. Patten and told him to arise and leave that place, for the mob was after them and would soon be at that house. Elder Patten awoke Parrish and told him to arise and dress himself, as the mob would soon be upon them. They arose, saddled their animals and started for Henry county in the night. They had not been gone long before the house was surrounded by a mob, who demanded Patten and Parrish. Bro. Petty informed them that they were not there, but the mob searched the house and remained till daybreak, when they found the tracks of the brethren's animals, which they followed to the line of the next county, when they gave up the chase.

Andrew Jenson, *LDS Biographical Encyclopedia*, 1:78–79.

# COURAGE BEFORE A MOB

EDWARD W. TULLIDGE

Here we meet another of these Spartan women of Mormondom in the person of Louisa [Free] Wells. . . . In July, 1837, her father, Absalom Free, . . . emigrated with his family to Caldwell county, [Missouri].

In Caldwell, Brother Free purchased a farm and built a good house. . . .

The saints had been driven out of Jackson county, and mobs were ravaging in Davies county, but there was peace in Caldwell until the Fourth of July, in 1838, when the anti-Mormons, who were waiting and watching for a pretext, took occasion . . . to commence a crusade against the city of Far West.

When the father of Louisa joined the organization for defence of the city of Far West, he left a sick son at home, with the women folks of his own and five other families, who had gathered there. These were left to defend their homes.

Louisa and her sister Emeline, with their cousin, Eliza Free, stood guard, on a ridge near the house, for three weeks, night and day, to warn the families of the approach of the mob. . . .

While thus standing guard, one day, the girls saw a number of horsemen near, marching with a red flag and the beating of drums. They had with them a prisoner, on foot, whom they were thus triumphantly marching to their camp. . . . The prisoner was grandfather Andrew Free, though at the time the sisters knew it not.

It was almost night. The horsemen made directly for their camp with their "prisoner of war," whom they had taken, not in arms, for he was aged, yet was he a soldier of the cross, ready to die for his faith.

Already the veteran disciple had been doomed by his captors. He was to be shot; one escape only had they reserved for him.

Before the mob tribunal stood the old man, calm and upright in his integrity, and resolved in his faith. He stood alone, face to face with death, with those stern, cruel men. . . .

Then the captain and his band demanded of the old man that he should swear there and then to renounce Jo. Smith and his d——d religion, or they would shoot him on the spot.

Drawing himself up with a lofty mein, and the invincible courage that the Mormons have always shown in their persecutions, the veteran answered: "I have not long to live. At the most you cannot deprive me of many days. I will never betray or deny my faith which I know to be of God. Here is my breast, shoot away, I am ready to die for my religion!"

At this he bared his bosom and calmly waited for the mob to fire.

But the band was abashed at his fearless bearing and answer. For a time the captain and his men consulted, and then they told their prisoner that they had decided to give him till the morning to reconsider whether he would retract his faith or die.

Morning came. Again the old man was before the tribunal, fearless in the cause of his religion as he had been the previous night. Again came from him a similar answer, and then he looked for death, indeed, the next moment.

But he had conquered his captors, and the leader declared, with an oath: "Any man who can be so d——d true to any d——d religion, deserves to live!"

Thereupon the mob released the heroic disciple of Mormonism, and he returned to his home in safety.

Edward W. Tullidge, *Women of Mormondom,* 156–58.

# ESCAPE FROM RICHMOND JAIL

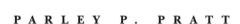

## PARLEY P. PRATT

After eight months of weary confinement [in a jail in Richmond, Missouri, in 1839] . . . the Lord had shown me in a vision of the night the manner and means of escape. And, like Pharaoh's dream, the thing had been doubled— that is, shown to me on two occasions in the same manner.

Mrs. Phelps had the same thing shown to her in a vision previous to her arrival; my brother, Orson Pratt, also came to us with a firm impression that we were about to be delivered. . . . As we sat pondering upon these things, and comparing our visions and manifestations of the spirit on this subject, my brother Orson opened the Book of Mormon, when the first sentence that caught his eye was the words of Ammon to King Lamoni: "Behold, my brother and my brethren are in prison, in the land of Middoni, and I go to deliver them!" This was indeed a similar instance to ours. Ammon, on that occasion, had [his] own brother in prison, and also brethren in the ministry, and did deliver them. Our case was exactly similar, not in Middoni, but in Missouri. And, what was still more strange, in a book of six hundred pages, this was the only sentence which would have fitted our case. . . .

It was the second of July, and our friends could only make an excuse for staying to spend the great national holiday with us (the 4th) before they must leave or excite the suspicions and ill will of the people; and, as that day had been a lucky one for our fathers and our nation, we had determined on that time as the proper one to bid farewell to bondage and gain our liberty. . . .

Our plan was this: My brother, Orson Pratt, . . . and the young Mr. Clark were to take leave with their horses, and also with the horse and saddle on which Mrs. Phelps had ridden, on pretense of taking him home with them to Illinois, while she stayed with her husband a few weeks in the prison. . . . These three horses were to be stationed in a thicket, or forest, about half a mile from the prison, and there the two friends were to await, in readiness for us to mount, should we be so fortunate as to reach the thicket alive.

Sundown, on the evening of the fourth, was the moment agreed upon, and if we did not then appear they were to give us up for lost, and make the best of their way to Illinois and inform our friends that we had gone to Paradise in attempting to come to them. The reason for appointing this hour was this: Our door would be opened at sundown to hand in our supper, and we must then make the attempt as our only chance. . . .

The prison at Columbia was situated in the same square with the court house, being on the north edge of the town. Between it and the wilderness, where our friends held the horses in waiting, there were several fields and fences, say for the distance of half a mile, consisting of meadow and pasture land, and all in full view of the town. The prison consisted of a block house, two stories high, with two rooms below and two above. The keeper and his family occupied one end, and the other was used as the prison— the only entrance being through the lower room of the dwelling part, which was occupied by the family, and then up a steep flight of stairs, at the head of which was a heavy oaken door, ironed, locked and bolted as if to secure a Bonaparte or a Samson. On the inside of this was still another door, which was but slender, with a square hole near the top, of sufficient size to hand in the food and dishes of the prisoners.

The large, heavy door had always to be opened when food, drink, or other articles were handed in; and while open, the inner door served as a temporary guard to prevent prisoners from escaping, and was not always opened on such occasions, the food being handed through the hole in the top of the door, while the door itself remained locked. However, as a fortunate circumstance for us, the coffee pot when filled would not easily slip through the hole in the door, and, rather than spill the coffee and burn his fingers, the keeper would sometimes unlock and open the inner door, in order to set in this huge and obstinate pot; and once in, the door would immediately close, and the key be turned, while the outer door would perhaps stand open till the supper was finished, and the dishes handed out. [This incident occurred before the Word of Wisdom was widely understood and practiced.]

Now, our whole chance of escape depended on the question, whether the inner door would be opened that evening, or the coffee pot squeezed in at the hole in the top. . . .

The sun was now setting, and the footsteps of the old keeper were heard on the stairs—the key turned, the outer door grated on its huge hinges, while at the same moment we sprang upon our feet, hats and coats on (rather an unusual dress for a hot day in

July—for, by the bye, my hat proved to be a fur cap, which I wore when first taken in November previous), and stood by the door to act the part of waiters in receiving the dishes and food for supper, and placing them on the table. Dish after dish was handed in through the small aperture in the door, and duly received and placed upon the table by us, with as much grace and as calm countenances as if we thought of nothing else but our suppers. And I will now venture to say that famishing men never watched the movements of a coffee pot with more anxiety than we did on this occasion. At length the other dishes all being handed in, the huge pot made its appearance in the hole in the top of the door, but one of us cried out to the keeper—"Colonel, you will only spill the coffee by attempting to put it through, besides, it burns our fingers; it will be more convenient to unlock and hand it in at the door." With this it was lowered again, and the key turned on the inner door.

In this, as in most other fields of battle, where liberty and life depend on the issue, every one understood the part assigned to him and exactly filled it. Mr. Follett was to give the door a sudden pull, and fling it wide open the moment the key was turned. Mr. Phelps being well skilled in wrestling was to press out foremost, and come in contact with the jailer; I was to follow in the centre, and Mr. Follett, who held the door, was to bring up the rear, while Sister Phelps was to pray.

No sooner was the key turned than the door was seized by Mr. Follett with both hands; and with his foot placed against the wall, he soon opened a passage, which was in the same instant filled by Mr. Phelps, and followed by myself and Mr. Follett. The old jailer strode across the way, and stretched out his arms like Bunyan's Apollion. . . . One or two leaps brought us to the bottom of the stairs, carrying the old gentleman with us headlong, helter skelter, while . . . Mrs. Phelps exclaimed, "O Lord God of Israel, thou canst help." Old Mrs. Gibbs looked on in silent amazement, while the jailer's wife . . . not only assisted in the scuffle, but cried out so loud that the town was soon alarmed. In the meantime we found ourselves in the open air, in front of the prison and in full view of the citizens, who had already commenced to rally, while Mr. Phelps and the jailer still clinched fast hold of each other like two mastiffs. However, in another instant he cleared himself, and we were all three scampering off through the fields towards the thicket.

By this time the town was all in motion. . . . The streets on both sides of the fields where we were running were soon thronged with soldiers in uniform, mounted riflemen, footmen with fence stakes, clubs, or with whatever came to hand, and with boys, dogs, etc., all running, rushing, screaming, swearing, shouting, bawling and looking, while clouds of dust rose behind them. The cattle also partook of the general panic and ran bellowing away, as if to hide from the scene. The fields behind us also presented a similar scene. Fences were leaped or broken down with a crash; men, boys and horses came tumbling over hedge and ditch, rushing with the fury of a whirlwind in the chase; but we kept our course for the thicket, our toes barely touching the ground, while we seemed to leap with the fleetness of a deer. . . .

As soon as the prisoners drew near, they were hailed by their friends, and conducted to the horses. They were breathless and nearly ready to faint; but in a moment they were assisted to mount, and a whip and the reins placed in their hands, while the only words interchanged were—"Fly quickly, they are upon you!" . . .

I had taken about the third jump with my horse when I encountered a man rushing upon me with a rifle, and, taking aim at my head, he said, "G——d d——n you, stop, or I'll shoot you." He was then only a few paces from me, and others were rushing close in his rear, but I turned my horse quickly in another direction, and rushed with all speed into the thickest of the forest, followed for some minutes by him and his dog; but I soon found myself alone, while I could only hear the sound of distant voices, the rushing of horsemen in every direction, with the barking of dogs. What had become of my companions or our friends, I knew not. I rode on at full speed. . . . [Eventually I] dismounted, tied my horse in a thicket, walked some distance from him and climbed a tree— intending to wait in this situation amid the concealment of the thick foliage till the darkness of evening would enable me to proceed with safety. Seating myself in one of its forked branches, and placing my arms in two other similar forks, I was supported from falling, although in a moment after I had ceased my exertions I fainted away. In this situation I remained for some time, without the least power to change my position or help myself; my breath was gone through over exertion, and my mouth and throat parched with a burning thirst, my stomach sickened, and as I began to breathe I was seized with vomiting, and threw up nearly all the food which my stomach contained. I then gradually recovered my strength till I could speak, when I began to call on the Lord, saying, "O Lord, strengthen me this once, deliver me from my persecutors and bring me in safety to a land of liberty, and I will praise thy name and give thee all the glory, and the remnant of my days shall be wholly devoted to thy service; for surely my life is now at stake, and if preserved, it is thy gift, therefore I shall owe it all to thee."

The darkness of evening was now fast setting in, and every moment seemed to increase my safety and security from immediate discovery. . . . I now came down from the tree and felt my way to the place where I had tied my horse, but as good or ill luck would have it, he had loosed himself and gone, leaving me to my fate. I then groped my way amid the dark shades of the forest to a small stream of warm, muddy water, and, stooping down, partly quenched my thirst. I then made my way to the highway and commenced my journey on foot, carefully watching on either hand lest I should be surprised and taken.

I was an entire stranger to the country—having no guide but the polar star. My road lay nearly northward, and upwards of a hundred miles of a wild country, peopled only by enemies, still lay between me and [Illinois. I had to] . . . make my way through this wilderness of enemies, on foot, after the weakness and debility caused by eight months' confinement, and after the fatigues of my evening's race, and neither inquire the way nor make my appearance at any house for entertainment and refreshment. . . .

At length the morning began to dawn. . . . I now sat down in safety, and took a small biscuit from my pocket which Sister Phelps had kindly provided, and which was my only store of food for the journey. With a hearty drink from the crystal stream and this biscuit I made my first breakfast, after my imprisonment, as a free son of Columbia. I recollect that while I sat enjoying this solitary meal, far from friends and home, surrounded with a scenery strange and wild, and without any guide or any knowledge where I should claim the next refreshment, I thought of the sweets of liberty I now enjoyed, and with a thankful and joyous heart I exclaimed aloud, "Thank God for this hour, it is the happiest of my life; I am free, although lost in the wilderness, and if I cannot find myself, thank God nobody else can find me." . . . My brother, O. Pratt, and the young Mr. Clark, who furnished us with the horses, must now be looked after.

When we parted in the thicket, as has been before described, they had only time to flee a few paces, when they found themselves completely surrounded on every hand, and no possibility left them of escape by running; they, therefore, dropped down into a small ravine which had been made by the water during some former freshet, and there lay as close to the earth as a young quail when its nest is disturbed. The enemy passed close by them a number of times, and so very near that they dared not to make the least motion—not even to look up to see whether they were discovered.

At length night came on; the pursuers retired, and they arose and pursued their journey on foot, and arrived safely in Illinois soon after the arrival of Mr. Phelps. My brother immediately repaired to the residence of my wife and children, who were waiting his return in anxious suspense, in hopes to hear some news from me, whom they considered still in prison—not having as yet heard any news of the escape. As he entered the door Mrs. P. raised her anxious and sorrowful eyes, and eagerly inquired:

"Have you seen my husband?"

"I have."

"Is he yet alive?"

"Yes."

"Is he well?"

"He is."

"O, thank God for that! Is there any prospect that he will ever get free and return alive?"

"Well, I hope so; for the last time I saw him he was astride a horse in the woods, and headed towards home on a gallop." . . .

She soon set about preparing for the reception of her husband, in case he should arrive, faint and exhausted with hunger and fatigue. The table was spread, and food placed upon it; the house was illuminated through the night, during which her anxious and beating heart would not suffer her for one moment to sleep. She watched during the entire night, and on several occasions opened the door and looked abroad; but still the morning dawned and he came not. Surely, thought she, he is slain or again confined in a dungeon. . . .

The suspense and anguish of her aching bosom now became intolerable. . . . Another long day passed and another night set in, and still no news—except that the ferries on the Missouri side were all strictly guarded, and the entire people on the lookout to take him dead or alive. She had now kept her table spread both day and night, and had watched for three entire nights without sleep. "He cannot be alive and free," exclaimed she, "or I know he would fly to meet the fond welcome of his wife and children, and relieve their aching hearts." . . .

[After a dangerous, exhausting journey of several days, I finally crossed the Mississippi River, leaving Missouri.] I immediately stepped a few paces into the woods, and, kneeling down, kissed the ground as a land of liberty, and then poured out my soul in thanks to God. I then arose and made my way down the river for some two miles through woods and swamps, and finally came to a house. I entered it, determined to call for something to eat; no one was in but a little boy, but he said his mother would be in in two or three minutes. I asked him for some milk, and he gave me a vessel which was full, probably containing between one and two quarts. I intended only to taste of it to keep me from fainting, and then wait till the woman came, and ask her leave to drink the remainder, as it was all she had; but once to my famishing mouth it never ceased to decrease till it was all swallowed; I now felt somewhat abashed and mortified at what I had done, but concluded money would pay all damages. Hearing the footsteps of the woman at the door, I was fixing my mouth for an awkward apology, when I heard a sudden scream; on looking up, Mrs. Sabery Granger stood before me, with both hands lifted up in an ecstasy of amazement. I said to her, "Be not afraid—handle me and see, for a spirit hath not flesh and bones as you see me have." She exclaimed, "Why, good Lord, is that you? Why, all the world is hunting you—both friends and enemies; they had almost given you up." She then flew around, scolded the children, talked to the ducks and chickens to keep out of the house and out of the garden, and not stray off. She washed my feet, gave me some clean stockings, got me some dinner, told me a thousand things about our friends, asked five hundred questions, laughed, cried and again scolded the children and chickens.

This over and dinner eaten, she on with her bonnet and accompanied me to her husband, who was clearing a small spot of land near by. (I had forgotten to say that this woman had been one of our nearest neighbors in Ohio for several years.) Her husband now dropped his work, and accompanied me as a guide for five miles across a wet, low, untimbered bottom, covered mostly with high grass and stagnant water, and entirely destitute of shade or refreshment of any kind. The air was now extremely sultry, and the sun poured in scorching beams, while we could get no water to drink, nor any rest or retreat for a moment. . . .

I had not proceeded more than a mile or two before I became so weak and faint that I could hardly speak or stand, and parched with a burning thirst. I was upon the point of lying down in the hot and stagnant water, but he took me by the arm and partly supported me, and drew me along for some distance, exhorting and begging of me to try my utmost to hold up a little longer. In this way I finally reached the upland and the shade of a fence, within about half a mile of a settlement of the Saints and other citizens, which extended along the bluff. I dropped down under the shade of this fence, and fainted entirely away; the man ran to the house of a Brother Brown and got some cool spring water and a little camphor, and was returning with it. Sister Brown, who had never seen me, came running before him to my relief; while they were yet distant I had partly come to, and feeling a dreadful faintness at my stomach, and a raging thirst which knew no bounds, I made an effort to arise and run towards them, at the same time making signs for them to hasten; I staggered a few paces like a drunken man, and again fell to the earth. This singular appearance, and my dirty clothes and long beard so frightened the woman that, instead of hurrying, she halted till the man came up with her, and then she exclaimed, "It cannot be Elder Pratt, of whom I have heard so much—it must be some old drunkard." But the man assured her it was me, and they then came on together. They bathed my temples and wrists in cold water and camphor, and finally gave me a spoonful or two at a time to drink. In about half an hour I was so far revived as to be able to arise and be led to the house. I then shaved and washed myself, and borrowed a change of linen, and got into a comfortable bed.

Next morning I felt quite refreshed, and, after resting through the day, I was so far recruited as to be able to mount a horse at evening and ride towards Quincy, which was still twenty-five miles distant. . . . We rode on at a brisk rate, and arrived in Quincy at about two o'clock the next morning. Riding up to the dwelling which . . . we judged was my wife's residence, we dismounted and gave a gentle knock at the door. She had watched for four successive nights and most of the fifth, and had now just lain down and given up all for lost. On hearing the knock she sprang from bed and opened the door, and in another instant I had clasped her in my arms.

Parley P. Pratt, *Autobiography of Parley P. Pratt,* 208–10, 212–15, 217–18, 220–24, 240–42.

# "WE WERE HORROR-STRICKEN"

JOHN R. TALMAGE

James Edward [Talmage's] . . . baptism, performed by his father . . . actually was delayed until he was nearing his eleventh birthday. . . .

In the spring of 1873, when James was in his eleventh year, he suffered an illness that became so critical that his life appeared imminently threatened. His father, in deep parental despair, associated the illness with the fact that the boy's baptism had been so long delayed. Father Talmage made a solemn covenant with the Lord that, if his boy's life should be spared, he would be baptized as soon as possible after his recovery. The boy did recover, and arrangements for the baptism were promptly made.

Due to opposition which at times "threatened persecution" of the Latter-day Saints in the community, baptisms were performed at night. James's baptism was set for the night of June 15, 1873, in a millrace paralleling the Kennet river, only a short distance from the cottage the Talmage family was occupying in Eddington, a suburb of Hungerford. A young girl of the Hungerford Branch, Ellen Gilbert . . . , was to be baptized on the same occasion.

When the hour appointed for the ordinances approached, Father Talmage and Ellen's brother Elijah, a deacon in the branch, left the Talmage cottage where the little baptismal party had assembled, and carefully reconnoitered the neighborhood. No one appeared to be abroad, and the Latter-day Saint group quickly proceeded to the waterside.

Father Talmage stepped into the stream and held out his hand for young James. At that moment, James later related, "we were horror-stricken by such a combined scream, howl, shriek, yell—I know not how to describe the noise—as none of us had ever heard before." It seemed to be "a combination of every fiendish [utterance] that we could conceive of," and to his dying day James never forgot "how I trembled at the awful manifestation, which had about it the sharpness of a thunderclap followed by an angry roll.

"Father asked me if I was too frightened to be baptized, and I answered by directly stepping into the water," James recalled. "The unearthly noise ceased the instant I stepped into the water."

Both his baptism and Ellen Gilbert's immediately afterward were performed without further unusual incident.

James rarely spoke of this peculiar experience, and even in his private journal he refrained from drawing any specific conclusion. Certain facts, however, speak for themselves:

The diabolical noise was heard by every member of the baptismal party, but by no one else. A cautious round of inquiry the next day failed to turn up any hint that anyone in the area had heard an unusual disturbance during the night. The horrifying screaming began as the candidates for baptism approached the water, and ceased abruptly when young James stepped into the millrace so that the ordinance could be performed.

---

John R. Talmage, *The Talmage Story*, 1–6.

# "THE LADY PUT ON A VERY FINE WHITE DRESS"

⌒

### EDWARD JAMES WOOD

I was traveling among the natives on one of the largest islands of the group. I was living in a large village with a good man and his wife, who had joined the Church on another island. The native ministers—"teachers" they were called, by the natives— were very bitter toward me and did all they could to get me to leave the island. However, the couple I was staying with were very kind. While the people of the village were getting ready to visit another island, this couple asked me to go along with them in their large native-made boat, as the village they were to visit was the home of her parents. All the villages of any size are near the coast, and the natives always travel from one village to another by boat or native canoe. I was glad to accept the invitation, although I learned on the boat that I was a very unwelcome member of the company of seventy-five people.

We had scarcely left the little bay and were getting out to sea when a terrible storm came up. It was a real typhoon; it soon blew so hard we could not return and expected to be swamped with every white-capped wave. The natives decided that it was all brought about by having a "Mamona"—Mormon missionary— aboard. They called me Jonah and decided to throw me over- board. The whole boatload seemed conspired against me, except our brother and his good wife. They made advances to take hold of me, and when our sister stood up in the swaying boat with waves threatening to engulf us and dared any of them to lay hold of me, and prophesied that anyone that tried to throw me out of the boat would cause the boat to capsize.

. . . Then as several of the hostile ones attempted to take hold of me, a wave almost mountain high lifted the boat high in the air and the cyclonic wind sent us whirling toward the coast, and as we neared a coral reef, the boat struck the reef and broke into pieces. We all had to swim for our lives. Our brother took his knapsack with books and a change of clothing in it and swam for shore, and some of the natives, crazed with fear at their attitude toward me, helped me to make a safe landing.

This village turned out to be the place where the parents of our sister lived, much to our surprise, as we didn't think we had sailed the boat fast enough to have made the village. I could now see the hand of the Lord in our being shipwrecked. The parents were pleased to see our sister and her husband, but the father, being a teacher in one of the churches, was not at all pleased to entertain me. Soon the word circulated through the village that a "Mamona" was in the village. Some sent word that they wanted me to hold a meeting. Our brother and sister were very loyal to me; they went ahead, against the wishes of the parents, and sent out that a meeting of the "Mamona" Church would be held that evening, and mostly out of pure curiosity, the whole village attended . . . [a congregation of] several hundred, and a very exceptional spirit for good was felt.

After the meeting they all filed out of the fine native building except one couple and the parents. The lady of the one couple who remained said she was deeply impressed with the glad news of the "Old Church" being revealed anew to the earth in our day, and she wanted another meeting called for the next afternoon. I answered that if our hosts—the parents—were willing, I would be pleased to hold another meeting; the parents reluctantly consented. Our brother and sister had several of their friends come in the next day but not much interest was shown, mostly I could see because of the unfriendly attitude of our hosts, the parents. Meeting time came and a larger crowd than before attended, but this time full of animosity toward me; we had good attention, however, to my further explanation of the restoration of the true gospel.

At the close of the meeting, the council of chiefs remained a few minutes and notified me to leave the village at once. While they were deliberating, the lady of the couple who had requested that I hold this second meeting also remained; she now stood up and with a fine humble spirit told them she was ready to be baptized and become a "Mamona." The chiefs left without further comment; the lady asked me if I had authority to baptize her, as she was converted the first time she heard me speak. I told her I had that authority, but that she must get the consent of her husband, who was all the time sitting by her; she asked if I had the authority to refuse to baptize her—I had never heard such a question before; finally her husband spoke up by her request and said that while he thought it unwise, she could suit herself.

While we were talking, the council of chiefs sent word that if this woman joined our church, her house and all the belongings would be burned to the ground. This edict only made the good woman all the more anxious to be baptized, and she said she would be ready to be baptized that night when the tide came in, in a very fine freshwater stream about a half mile down the coast. The word soon went out and the whole village came out to see the baptism. The lady put on a very fine white dress—a dress not many had seen before; then she told me to follow her and her family to the stream. She walked with the dignity and bearing of a chieftess; the entire village lined the walk through the beautiful palms to the water's edge. It was a glorious moonlit night, and it appeared that through the trees the light of heaven was present.

As we stood around the water, the hundreds of natives were very respectful; they sang as only natives can sing. . . . I baptized her and led her to the water's edge, and as she knelt I confirmed her; the glory of the light seemed brighter than ever, and then when she started for home, the crowd . . . became a howling mob of wild natives.

As we neared the village we saw many men running around with torches waving above their heads, calling on villagers to burn the house of the Mormon woman. The chiefs and others of the village authority were gathered around the home of the new convert, and as we drew near, they called the woman to renounce her new religion or they would set fire to the house.

She stood erect before all of them and, in the light of the moon, bore one of the most sincere testimonies of the divinity of the "new" church and of my mission among them. . . . The house was soon in flames, including all the families' belongings; the husband and children were grief-stricken. The good woman too was sorry, but she kept all the time telling me not to feel it was my fault. . . . I felt very keenly the loss to the family, and for a moment I wished that I had never seen the village.

The family was taken to a neighbor's house, and I remained in the home of the parents of our sister with whom I was traveling. Early in the morning, our new sister convert asked me to accompany her to a nearby village where her father lived, saying that her father was one of the head chiefs of the whole island. We found him sitting alone in his hut. He seemed greatly worried, but said nothing. He listened intently to the story of his daughter—our new convert—and of the burning of her home and its contents; he then left and called his chiefs together in an adjoining house. In about thirty minutes he returned and asked me to go back with him to the village where the house of his daughter had been burned. I noted as we went through the village that all the chiefs came out and did homage to my new friend; the spirit of persecution had left them when they saw this chief of chiefs stand before them. He called upon the chiefs to go through the village with him and me, and, to my great surprise, he asked me to select a site where I would like to have a church house and a dwelling house.

I told him I was not prepared to erect any house; he then turned to the chiefs who had burned his daughter's house and told them that he and his council had decided that they who had anything to do with burning the house should set at once and build me a house and a house for church on any site I chose. He returned to the village and I was at once taken into the council of the chiefs who last night had been like a lot of savages, and was given the authority to say the kind of house I would like. In six weeks I had a fine house and meeting house combined, made out of split bamboo. I held meetings and made many converts, and when the house was completed, we held one of the biggest celebrations and dedicated the house and grounds, the site having duly and legally been transferred to our church. We at this time had a very fine branch organized and the whole village became our friends, as we did also villages far and near; and all this and many cases of healing of the sick through administrations and faith—all out of the most severe persecutions and trials an elder could pass through.

Edward James Wood, in Melvin S. Tagg, *The Life of Edward James Wood, Church Patriot*, 38–41.

# FAITH

# "THERE IS A BLESSING FOR YOU"

BENJAMIN F. JOHNSON

I was born July 28, 1818, in the town of Pomfret, Chatauqua County, New York. . . . To my parents were born sixteen children, namely: Joel Hills, Nancy Maria, Seth Gurnsey, Delcina Diadamia, Julia Ann, David, Almera Woodard, Susan Ellen, Joseph Ellis, Benjamin Franklin, Mary Maria, Elmer Wood, George Washington, William Derby, Esther Meleta and Amos Partridge. Excepting Elmer W., who died in infancy, all arrived at maturity, and all were among the first to embrace the fullness of the gospel. . . .

Previous to the dedication of the [Kirtland] Temple on the 27th of March, 1836, all who had labored upon it were called together, and in the public congregation received their blessings under the hands of the First Presidency. I [was seventeen years old and] had attended all the meetings, listened to the blessings given, and felt a great joy in these prophetic words that filled and thrilled me. Yet all the time I was thinking that these blessings would only be for those who had labored with their hands upon the temple, and as I had not myself worked upon it, not being strong enough for such labor, I would not receive any blessing, and it grieved me exceedingly to think that perhaps . . . I was to be deprived of that which to me appeared of more worth than all earthly things. When on the last day of blessings, I was standing by the door in the crowded congregation, and oh! how I did yearn for a blessing! And as the last blessing, apparently, was given, the Prophet earnestly looked towards the door where I was standing, and said to his brother Hyrum, "Go and see if there is not one more yet to be blessed." Brother Hyrum came to the door, and seeing me, put his hand upon my shoulder and asked me if I had not worked upon the temple. I said, "No sir," but it seemed like passing a sentence upon my fondest hopes. He then asked if I had done nothing towards it. I then thought of a new gun I had earned and given as a donation, and of the brick I had helped to make. I said, "I did give often."

"I thought," he said, "there was a blessing for you," and he almost carried me to the stand. The Prophet blessed me, with a confirmation of all his father had sealed upon me [in a patriarchal blessing given some time earlier], and many more also. I felt then that the Lord had respect for my great desire. Even to be the youngest and last to be blessed seemed to me a high privilege. When the Prophet had looked towards the door, I felt as though he would call for me, though I could not see how I had merited so high a privilege. But so it was, and my joy was full.

Benjamin F. Johnson, *My Life's Review,* 7, 23.

# "TELL HIM NOT TO WORRY"

LORENZO SNOW

Early in the spring of 1840, I was appointed to a mission in England, and I started on or about the twentieth of May. . . .

Brigham Young, Heber C. Kimball, Parley P. Pratt, Orson Pratt, and others of the Quorum of the Twelve, nine in all, were at this time laboring in England, and before leaving Nauvoo, the home of the Saints, I visited several of their families. I found Sister Young occupying an unfinished log hut, with a loose floor, and no chinking between the logs; consequently the sides and ends of the hut were open, leaving the inmates exposed to wind and storms. When I called, she had just returned from a long, fatiguing and fruitless search for her milk cow, which had strayed the day before, and on which she much depended for sustenance for her little ones. On my asking her what she wished me to say to her husband, she replied, "You see my situation, but tell him not to trouble, or worry in the least about me—I wish him to remain in his field of labor until honorably released." Her apparent poverty-stricken, destitute condition deeply stirred my sympathy. I had but little money—not sufficient to take me one-tenth the distance to my field of labor, with no prospect for obtaining the balance, and was then on the eve of starting. I drew from my pocket a portion of my small pittance, and presented her, but she refused to accept it; while I strenuously insisted on her taking, and she persisting to refuse—partly purposely, and partly accidentally, the money was dropped on the floor, and rattled through the openings between

the loose boards, which settled the dispute, and bidding her good-
bye, I left her to pick it up at her leisure.

---

Lorenzo Snow, in Eliza R. Snow, *Biography and Family Record of Lorenzo Snow,* 46–47.

# "I LIKE THAT KIND OF FAITH"

## BRYANT S. HINCKLEY

A man had gone on a mission and left his wife and children
poorly provided for. One night when all of the flour had
been used one of the children before going to bed prayed
that the Lord would open the way so that they could have more
flour. The mother listened to it and thought about it and got the
inspiration. No sooner had the children gone to bed than this
woman discovered among her scanty belongings a little yarn and
she went busily to work knitting. Finally she had a small pair of
stockings knitted. In the morning she said to the boy: "Take these
stockings and this bread pan over to our neighbor and see if he
won't give you some flour in return for the stockings." The boy did
so and came back with the pan filled with flour. I like that kind of
faith. That is faith backed by works. They had to couple their faith
with works in those days. Roads were not built just by saying prayers.

I remember one time while traveling in the southern part of
the state I saw a man with a thin, frail team of horses attached to a
loaded wagon. He was sitting down at the base of a hill and was

figuring on something. I said to him: "Lee, what are you doing?" He replied: "I am trying to figure myself over that hill." Besides figuring it took muscle and energy to get over the hill.

A man in Idaho told me this story. I like this also. He said: "You know we used to ford the Snake River here, and when it was high it was dangerous. Your uncle and another man had to cross the river. They had a light wagon and a small team and when they got in the middle of the stream it looked as if the thing would capsize, and one of them said, 'I want to pray.' The other man said, 'I prayed before I got into this stream. You get into the back of this wagon and hold the bedding in and keep this box balanced, and when you get on the other side then you can offer your gratitude.'" I like that quality of faith also.

Conference Report, October 1932, 34–35.

# "ED IS ALL RIGHT"

HEBER  Q.  HALE

When Captain Lot Smith had his company of volunteers with their teams lined up in front of the Lion House, in Salt Lake City, to be reviewed by President Brigham Young, before embarking on the perilous expedition of the spring of 1862, it was discovered that his organization was not complete—he lacked a wagon-master.

When questioned by the President as to whom he would like for the position, the captain replied, "I want Sol Hale." A man from the line spoke up, stating that he had just seen Mr. Hale drive into town. J. Q. Knowlton was immediately dispatched to bring him before the President, in his office.

When Mr. Hale entered, President Young informed him that he was organizing a company to go east and set in order the stage lines and stations which had been much interfered with and, in many instances, burned by the Indians, and to protect incoming immigrant trains, and that he was wanted to go with the company as its wagon-master. "Now can you go?" interrogated the President.

The young man replied, "President Young, I have given my promise to old Father and Mother Austin that I would go in search of their son, Ed, who is reported by parties who arrived yesterday as having been killed by the Indians, near Beaver, on his return from San Bernardino with a band of horses, and his brother and I have our wagon and horses in readiness to leave in search for the body and to recover the horses, if possible. We were just in buying a few supplies when Quince came for me."

"Well," said the President, "if you are ready to go south, you are certainly ready to go east."

"Yes, but what can I tell Father and Mother Austin?" inquired Sol, upon whom rested a responsibility which he dared not shirk.

President Young's mind was in deep thought, and before the last words of the closing question were spoken, he bowed his head and rested it upon his hand, with his elbow upon the railing enclosing the desk in the general office. Nearly a minute elapsed before he raised his head to speak. Fixing his eyes squarely upon those of the anxious face before him, President Young made this extraordinary statement:

"Sol, you can tell Brother and Sister Austin that I say their son is still living, and is safe, and will return to them in a few days."

"Then I will go with the company," responded the ever-ready young man.

Sol mounted his horse and rode back to the store where he had left "Nute" with the team and wagon. He related the incident that he was called to go east with Lot Smith's company, and told him the words of President Young to his parents. Whereupon young Austin began crying, and begged Sol to yet go with him in search of his brother.

Sol answered in about these words: "No; I have now promised to go out with the volunteers, and my faith in President Young's word tells me that Ed is all right and will soon be home." He then bade his friend good-bye and joined the ranks, and the company began its march.

The third day out the company reached a station in Echo Canyon, and Captain Smith sent back to President Young a statement of their progress. The last words of the President's return message were: "Tell Sol, Ed Austin just arrived with horses O. K."

Heber Q. Hale, in Preston Nibley, comp., *Pioneer Stories,* 106–8.

# A PROMISE TO KEEP

## AUTHOR UNKNOWN

Brother Wm. J. Parkin, of South Bountiful, tells this story of how the Lord can and will open up the way for those who have faith to fulfill their promises and accomplish their righteous desires.

He arrived in Utah in the year 1863, fresh from England, and very poor. He had not succeeded in accumulating much when, in the following year, he ventured to get married. While attending conference in Salt Lake City the following spring he heard President Brigham Young announce to the assembly that he wanted a collection taken up in the several wards for the immigration of the poor, and wished every man to subscribe to the extent of his ability. The following Sunday he attended meeting in Bountiful and heard Bishop Stoker repeat the call.

Brother Parkin is a man of generous impulses, and felt like doing his full duty in so worthy a cause, but was absolutely without funds, and didn't know where or how he would be able to obtain any, but he was the first man to arise and say what he would do. He said, "Bishop, you may put me down for $2.50." The money was to be paid within two weeks.

When he returned home from meeting, his wife, who had not been at the meeting, met him at the gate with tears in her eyes. She had already heard from a neighbor of what her husband had promised to do, and knew too that he had no money. Her heart was in the work of the Lord, and she would have been more than willing to help migrate the poor if she had been able so to do, but her high sense of honor would not brook the making of a promise she could not fulfill. She greeted him reproachfully with the exclamation: "What have you done?" He had no guilty feeling, and asked her what she meant. "You have promised to give two-and-a-half dollars, and haven't a cent, nor any way of getting any. Do you know that I had to sit up and wash and iron a shirt for you after you went to bed last night, so that you might have a decent shirt to wear today?"

"Well, I know that we are very poor," he replied, "but I believe the Lord will provide a way for me to fulfill the promise. Perhaps he will make the chickens lay more eggs, or the cow give more milk, so you will have butter to sell."

"How can you expect that," said she, "when we only have three hens and a rooster, and the cow is almost dry?"

Peace was patched up between the couple by his assurance that what he had done in the matter of making that promise was done from a strict sense of duty, and because he had faith that the Lord would somehow enable him to fulfill it. She knew him too well to doubt his good intentions, and was too good a woman to further reproach him therefor, though she did not share his faith about his being able to keep his promise.

Time passed without his securing any money until the day before he was to pay it. On the morning of that day when he was out in the yard attending to his chores he noticed a fairly well-defined path, that he had not observed before, leading from his chicken coop into a patch of brush that grew near. Following the path out into the brush, he there found a big nest full of eggs. Carrying them into the house, he met his wife at the door, who was just coming out to exhibit to him a good-sized chunk of butter which she had just taken out of the churn—ever so much more than she had been in the habit of getting. Their surprise was mutual when he counted out before her eyes thirty clean, fresh-looking eggs—all the more surprising because they had both previously thought they were getting all the eggs their hens produced.

While they were still beaming with satisfaction over their good fortune, a knock was heard at the door, and upon opening it a stranger, an overland immigrant, was met, who inquired if they had any butter and eggs to sell. The eggs just brought in were pointed out with the remark that he might have them, and the good wife also produced the lump of freshly-made butter. The stranger said he would be glad to buy both, and if they could spare him some buttermilk also he would regard that as a favor. He was assured that they would be glad to do so, and that he could have them at his own price.

He produced from his wallet a diminutive coin, such as they had never seen before, and offered it to them, and Brother Parkin inquired, "What is that?" "That is a two-and-a-half dollar gold piece," the stranger replied.

"Well," said Brother Parkin, "I have no change and that is entirely too much. Have you no small change?"

The stranger told him to keep it. He was welcome to it. That he was glad to get the butter, eggs and buttermilk at any price, as he had applied in vain at so many houses for them that he had begun to despair about being able to get any.

The stranger carried away his small purchase, rejoicing, and Brother and Sister Parkin were profuse in their thanks to him, and very grateful to the Lord, for having inspired him to supply them with the means of fulfilling the promise made to the bishop.

Sister Parkin was so impressed with the fact that the money had come as a special providence from the Lord, and so thankful that her husband's honor could now be saved, that she actually shed tears of joy, and assured him that she would never more reproach him for being too rash in trying to do his duty as a

Latter-day Saint, and hoped never again to be lacking in faith that the Lord will provide.

The day following, being Sunday, he attended meeting as usual, and presented the gold piece to the bishop with the remark that it was his donation to help immigrate the poor. The bishop accepted it with a "God bless you, Brother Parkin; yours is the first money paid of all that was promised."

George C. Lambert, comp., *Gems of Reminiscence*, 33–36.

# "THIS IS THE MAN THAT SHALL TAKE CHARGE"

## DANIEL WEBSTER JONES

One little incident I will relate, to show how I came to be called to explore Arizona in connection with this mission to Mexico, which could have been made in an easier way than traveling so far with pack mules. I was in President Young's office one day when several others were present. Brother W. C. Staines came in and was telling about having heard a Brother McMaster, of the 11th Ward, [who] related a remarkable occurrence whilst on this first Arizona trip. Brother McMaster's statement, as told by Brother Staines, was that there were several hundred persons, with teams, in a perishing condition. They had passed some forty-five miles beyond the Colorado and no water could be found. Someone had gone on up the Little Colorado and found that entirely dry. Brother McMaster being chaplain went out and pled with the Lord for water. Soon there was a fall of rain and snow depositing plenty of water for the cattle, and to fill up all their barrels. They were camped in a rocky place where there were many small holes that soon filled up. In the morning all were refreshed, barrels filled up, and all turned back rejoicing in the goodness of the Lord in saving them from perishing. They all returned to Salt Lake and reported Arizona uninhabitable.

After Brother Staines had finished, some remarks were made by different ones. I was sitting near by and just in front of Brother Brigham. I had just been telling him something about my labors among the Indians. He said nothing for a few moments, but sat looking me straight in the eye. Finally, he asked, "What do you think of that, Brother Jones?"

I answered, "I would have filled up, went on, and prayed again." Brother Brigham replied putting his hand upon me, "This is the man that shall take charge of the next trip to Arizona."

---

Daniel W. Jones, *Forty Years among the Indians*, 234–35.

# "HALF OF ONE PERCENT A DAY"

BRYANT S. HINCKLEY

The story of how Heber J. Grant saved two Church banks during the prolonged and disastrous panic of 1891–93 is so characteristic of his faith that we give this account of it. He made a trip to New York City in 1891 to sell one hundred thousand dollars worth of Z.C.M.I. notes owned by one of the banks. Money was then lending on the New York Stock Exchange at one-half percent a day, one hundred eighty-two and one-half percent per year. These notes bore six percent interest. Think of it! He states:

"Before starting, I was talking with President Woodruff, who knew why I was going. He smiled and said, 'You are going east on a very difficult mission. Sit down and let me give you a blessing.' I sat down and he gave me a wonderful blessing, stating that I would get all the money I needed and more would be offered to me if I needed it. I went out with a feeling of perfect assurance that I would be successful. I heard that the directors of the Deseret National Bank were laughing at the idea of my being foolish enough to think I could cash Z.C.M.I. notes in the East at six percent per annum when money was one-half of one percent a day."

He stopped, on the way, at Omaha and asked the president of the Omaha National Bank, a correspondent of one of his banks, to cash a note of twelve thousand dollars. The president smiled and said: "The idea of your coming down here, trying to get money when it is one-half of one percent a day. Your banks are as well fixed financially, if not better, than ours. Young man, let me give you some advice. Go home and call your bank friends together and decide to lend a little more than would be considered strictly safe and the money will circulate around and come back into your bank again to take care of your own bank."

Brother Grant told this gentleman he was not asking for advice, that he had to go east for one hundred thousand dollars, that he intended to get it and on his return he would call on him and tell him where he got it. The bank president said: "Well, Mr. Grant, it will be a long time before I will see you."

When Brother Grant got to Chicago, he asked the vice-president of a bank there to cash two notes for twelve thousand dollars each. This bank was also one of their correspondents. He did not even ask Brother Grant to come into the bank. He stood on the outside of the counter, smiled, and declined to cash the notes. He said: "Young man, have you read the morning papers?" "Certainly," Brother Grant replied. "Have you read the financial sheet?" "Yes." "What is money loaning for in New York?" Brother Grant answered: "One-half of one percent a day." "Well, do you expect to get any money at six percent per annum?" "Yes, I do," responded Brother Grant, "because that is a rate you charge your customers if their balances are good enough to justify your making loans." Again, he replied: "I did not come to Chicago to get advice. I had the same advice from the president of the Omaha Bank. I told him I would go on my way, then on my way home I would call and tell him how I got the money, and I'll do the same with you." The vice-president smiled and said that he did not expect to see him for a long time.

When he reached New York, he had not sold one of his notes, but from then on he was divinely guided. It is a long and interesting story, but this is what he said in conclusion: "I borrowed $336 thousand all told. Before going to the train to go home, I received a telegram saying that we needed forty-eight thousand dollars more. I felt sure it was a mistake, that they did not need it, and I started for Chicago and wired one of my insurance friends at Hartford, and he made arrangements to get forty-eight thousand dollars if I needed it after I got home. After I got home, it was not needed; therefore, it was never borrowed."

From the day President Woodruff blessed him and promised him that he would get all the money he wanted and more if he needed it, he proceeded with the most perfect assurance that this promise made by a prophet of God would be fulfilled; and it was fulfilled to the very letter. This is the same faith that heals the sick and works miracles, but its application is in a different way. On his return, he called on the banker in Chicago who didn't expect to see him for a long time. He had only been gone a short time, and had much more money than he expected. When he got to Omaha, he did the same thing. The banker was utterly astonished. He felt he was a marvel; he wondered how Brother Grant did it.

---

Bryant S. Hinckley, *Faith of Our Pioneer Fathers*, 76–78.

# "LITTLE CHANCE THE BABY WOULD SURVIVE"

⌒

LEONARD J. ARRINGTON AND
SUSAN ARRINGTON MADSEN

After George [Benson] and Sarah [Dunkley] were married October 19, 1898, in the Logan Temple, they returned to Whitney to live in the two-room house George had built for his bride—with a shanty in back for washing. This was their home for thirty years, and in it their eleven children were born.

The arrival of their first child a year later was an event of considerable concern and anxiety, for the life of both mother and child seemed to hang in the balance as the childbirth progressed. The attending doctor told George and the two grandmothers who were present that there was almost no chance Sarah would live and very little chance that the baby would survive. The three of them almost instantaneously fell to their knees and prayed to God for the preservation of these two precious lives. As the doctor worked quickly to try to save Sarah, Margaret Dunkley and Louisa Benson worked to save their grandchild. The black and blue, nearly eleven-pound baby boy was put first in a pan of cool water and then a pan of warm water until finally he began to breathe and let out a boisterous cry. Tears of joy were shed as it soon became clear that both mother and child would survive. The child was blessed and given the name of his great-grandfather: Ezra Taft Benson. Thus was ushered into the world the man who would be sustained as prophet and president of the Church in 1985.

---

Leonard J. Arrington and Susan Arrington Madsen, *Mothers of the Prophets,* 202–3.

# A Child's Faith

HENRY D. MOYLE

My labors this winter [1953–54] in the great countries of Europe have brought me close to the people. I have had the opportunity of visiting them in their towns and in their villages, seeing them in their homes, feeling of their faith and of their devotion, and understanding to some slight extent the difficulties that confront them in their daily lives, the manner in which they are still ostracized by their neighbors the moment that they join the Church and begin to proclaim the gospel of Jesus Christ to their neighbors and friends and their families. My heart goes out to them. . . .

I might take you . . . down into Switzerland. . . . A little black-haired boy, not more than eight or nine years of age, came up to me after our meeting in Basel, and with fear and trembling he said he wanted to shake hands with me, and when he got hold of my hand, he looked up into my eyes with his big black eyes and he said, "Brother Moyle, would you come and administer to my father?"

When I went to that boy's home, I met a faithful mother, and an older brother. That mother threw her arms around me, and she said, "Brother Moyle, we have fasted and prayed, and especially this youngest son of mine, that he might have the courage that we older ones lacked to ask you to come to our home and bless our father who is so critically ill."

I tell you when I saw the faith of that boy, and the faith of that mother and of that son, and of the appreciation that they had for the priesthood of God, it touched my heart to the very core. It gave me a sense of humility I would like to keep all the days of my life. The Spirit of the Lord and his power were there present, and we blessed that good father and gave to that family the desires of their heart through the gift and power of our heavenly Father.

Conference Report, April 1954, 120.

# "DO YOU BELIEVE THE LORD CAN HEAL YOU?"

### DAVID O. MCKAY

A number of years ago President Francis M. Lyman and President B. H. Roberts had attended a quarterly conference at Loa, Wayne County, Utah. In those days traveling was by team and whitetop. The brethren had started early that morning to catch the train at Sigurd—fifty or sixty miles distant. They stopped for breakfast at Koosharem. While they were eating, a very singular incident occurred. A young man, seeing the whitetop, knowing the elders were in the house, dismounted from his horse, entered, and eagerly asked: "How long are you brethren going to stay here?"

"Just long enough to finish our breakfast. Why?" queried Elder Lyman.

"Because I should like to bring my uncle here and have you administer to him."

Before the brethren had finished their breakfast, there entered the living room of the house a man who was led in his physical blindness by his wife and this young, outstanding rancher. As the elders entered the living room, Brother Lyman, in his big-hearted way, putting his hand on the man's knee, said: "Well, so you want to be administered to, do you?"

"No, I do not," was the surprising reply.

"Well, then," said President Lyman, "why are you here?"

"Because my wife and my nephew put me in the wagon and brought me here," was his frank statement.

"How long has it been since you lost your sight?" asked President Lyman. The man told him. And Brother Lyman said: "Well, you believe the Lord can heal you, do you not?"

The man answered, "Well, I think he can. I don't know if he will."

There seemed to be an absolute absence of faith so far as the man was concerned.

"Do you belong to the Church?" asked President Lyman.

"No, I do not," was the reply.

"Well, if the Lord heals you, you would be glad to acknowledge his power, should you not?"

"Yes, if he did, I think I should."

Let me tell you at this point now what seemed to me in that instance to be most significant, and then I will finish the story. That young man had seen in a dream or vision the night before two men who had administered to his uncle, and the latter had received his sight through that administration. That is what prompted him to dismount from his horse, and make the request.

President Lyman and President Roberts performed the administration. The man, his wife, and nephew returned to their home. Presidents Lyman and Roberts resumed their journey to Salt Lake City.

Two or three months later, President Lyman was attending a conference in Blackfoot, Idaho. Among those who greeted him, walking unaided, was this man to whom they had administered. "Do you remember me?" the man asked.

President Lyman said, "Yes, and I see you have received your sight."

"Yes, I have," said the man; "I can read a newspaper as well as you can."

During the brief interview that followed, President Lyman remarked: "I remember our conversation—how do you account for your having received your sight?"

"Well," said the skeptic, "I believe that the medicine I was taking had just begun to work."

There was a miracle, but its effect in converting the man to the power of God was nil.

To me a most important phase of the story is the pre-vision of that young rancher, for I know that pre-vision is an actual fact in life, and it was through his faith that the man had been blessed.

You young men who pass through periods of doubt about the reality of the spirit in man, and of the possibility of its being in contact with divine influence, should ponder earnestly on the fact that there is something within you which can become cognizant of happenings or incidents that are entirely beyond the limit of any one or all of your five physical senses.

David O. McKay, *Gospel Ideals*, 515–17.

# "I Prayed Your Voice Would Hold Out"

DAVID O. McKAY

Sunday morning, April 24, 1921, dawned in a cloudless east and promised a clear day [in Huntly, New Zealand]. We held the usual prayers and scripture repeating exercises, and at 10 A.M. met in the Sunday School session of conference.

Having wet my feet yesterday, I have aggravated my cold. As a result, I'm so hoarse I can scarcely speak above a whisper. A condition that forebodes difficulty and disappointment for me and for the people on this the heaviest day of our tour!

Ten A.M. I managed to tell the children a story, but my voice was weak and husky. However, Brother [Hugh J.] Cannon was at his best, so we had an excellent meeting.

A thousand people—Maoris and Pakehas, sitting, reclining, and standing—assembled for the afternoon service. They came with curiosity and high expectations. It was my duty to give them a message, but I was not only too hoarse to speak and be heard by that crowd, but I was also ill!

However, with a most appealing prayer in my heart for divine help and guidance, I arose to perform my duty. My voice was tight and husky. Five minutes after I began, someone shouted from the group standing on my right, "Joseph Smith didn't receive the revelation on polygamy!"

Evidently the emissaries of the devil had chosen an opportune moment to obtain some free advertising. I hesitated a moment, turned my head in his direction, saw some men scuffling, and the crowd beginning to sway towards them. Motioning to the audience to remain quiet, I said with as much good nature as I could muster, "When the sons of God met, the devil came also." Many grasped the application and broke into laughter. Some began to clap, but I motioned for order, and continued with my discourse.

Then happened what had never before happened to me. I entered into my theme with all the earnestness and vehemence I could command and spoke as loud as possible. Feeling my voice getting clearer and more resonant, I soon forgot I had a voice and thought only of the truth I wanted my hearers to understand and accept. For forty minutes I continued with my address, and when I concluded, my voice was as resonant and clear as it ever was!

Brother Cannon concluded with a fervent testimony; and thus our fifth meeting closed with thanksgiving and rejoicing in every heart!

When I told Brother Cannon and some other brethren how earnestly I had prayed for the very blessing I had received, he said, "I, too, was praying—never prayed more fervently for a speaker in my life."

---

David O. McKay, *Cherished Experiences,* 85–87.

# "THEY ALL STARTED TALKING
# TO ME IN MAORI"

ROBERT L. SIMPSON

I want to tell you . . . that the Lord moves in mysterious ways, his wonders to perform. He protects his people and he watches out for them. He is mindful of his own.

As I was being set apart for my mission . . . , Brother Rulon S. Wells, then of the First Council of the Seventy, laid his hands upon my head and said, "I bless you, Brother Simpson, with a knowledge of the language of the people amongst whom you will labor," and I was grateful for this blessing. So I went to New Zealand elated that I was going to learn a foreign language and that this blessing had been given to me, and no one could take it away from me.

But as I got to New Zealand I did not do very much about learning that language. I was with a companion that was on the verge of going home, and he had other things to think about, so we did not do much about studying the Maori language. After about three or four weeks had gone by with not much activity on the Maori language, I had a dream. I would like to tell you about this dream. To me it is very real. To me it is one of the significant events of my life. In this dream I had returned home from my mission. I was getting off the boat down in Los Angeles harbor from whence I had left, and there was my bishop, my stake president, my mother and dad, all of my friends. As I came down the gangplank of the boat they all started talking to me in Maori, every one of them—my mother, my father, my bishop—all talking in Maori,

97

and I could not understand a word they were saying. I was so embarrassed. I was humiliated. I thought to myself, "This is terrible. How am I going to get out of it?" And I started making excuses.

Right then I woke up and I sat straight up in bed and the thought came to my mind so forcefully, "You will *have* to do something about learning this language. The Lord has given you a blessing, but you are going to have to do something about it yourself. You are going to need this language when you get through with your mission. You are going to need it." This thought kept ringing through my ears all through that day, so arrangements were made and we had study time allotted each day to learn the Maori language. The Lord blessed me and we were able to bear testimony in the language after a short time.

Then, to make a long story short, the mission was finished; I came home and came into Los Angeles harbor. They were all there to meet me, but they all spoke English. Not one of them spoke Maori to me.

World War II had broken out. All of the missionaries had been called home. I thought, "Now if I am called into the Army, I am just sure that I will be sent right back down to New Zealand where I can also help President [Matthew] Cowley. Maybe the Lord will send me down there to help him with the mission activity between military assignments."

I went into the Air Force, and sure enough, when it came time for overseas processing after a few months, I was sent to San Francisco. All the Pacific processing was done here. I thought to myself, "Here I go right back to New Zealand." About two days before the ship was to sail with all of our groups of several hundred men, they took out about five of us. That is all—just five— and sent us all the way back to the Atlantic seacoast for shipment over to Europe. I thought to myself, "Well, I guess I can always preach to the Maori spirits in prison when I get on the other side!"

We joined a convoy and went across the Atlantic Ocean. I saw the Rock of Gibraltar go by, and finally the ship stopped in Egypt. We got off the ship in Egypt and we were taken to our American air base. There was a very small Air Force group in Cairo, Egypt. Of all the Air Force units throughout the world, this was one of the very smallest groups. Well, if you know anything about [geography, you know you] cannot get further away from New Zealand than Cairo, Egypt. I thought, "Well, I don't know what the Lord has in mind, but I'll just do the best I can, and I am sure that everything will work out all right."

I want to tell you . . . that not more than forty-eight hours had gone by when I found that right there within the very shadows of this American air base was the entire Maori battalion—the entire Maori battalion were stationed there! This was *their* overseas base for processing, for all of their fighting in North Africa and Italy. For nearly two years I had the privilege of being there and meeting each Sunday with these Maori boys, bearing testimony with them in their own tongue, organizing them into small groups as they went up into the front lines in order that they might have their sacrament meetings and do the things that they needed to do. They needed me. I needed them. I want to tell you that the Lord had a hand in writing military orders, because of all of the places in this world that Air Force men were being sent very few were sent to Cairo, Egypt. Why one of them should be selected who knew a few words of Maori and who had an abiding love for the Maori people only the Lord can answer.

---

*BYU Speeches of the Year,* 4 April 1962, 9–10.

# "TELL SISTER KIMBALL
# WE'RE GOING"

~

## CAROLINE EYRING MINER AND
## EDWARD L. KIMBALL

In 1976 nine area conferences were scheduled in the Pacific. Spencer and Camilla [Kimball] . . . flew to American Samoa for conference first, then Western Samoa. Suddenly she and Spencer both fell ill, with temperatures of 104, nausea, coughing, and total misery. They needed help to board the airplane for New Zealand, but they insisted on going. Spencer had a television interview and a meeting with the Prime Minister scheduled immediately upon arrival, and the conference sessions had to go forward.

During the long hours of flight they slept, and then woke as they were about to land, fever broken. Spencer buttoned the collar of his damp shirt, pulled up his tie, and asked Camilla to brush his hair. She had enough sense of humor left to ask, "Which one?"

When they left the plane, they greeted the enthusiastic crowd there to welcome them, showing nothing of their illness. After the television interview and just as the luncheon with Prime Minister Muldoon was ending, Spencer's fever returned after a two-hour remission and he went immediately to bed.

In Hamilton, New Zealand, Spencer asked President N. Eldon Tanner to represent him at the cultural program planned for Saturday evening, hoping to conserve his strength for the Sunday conference sessions. But in the evening, he awakened with a start and asked Dr. Russell Nelson, who sat watching over him, "Brother Nelson, what time was that program to begin this evening?"

"At seven o'clock, President Kimball."

"What time is it now?"

"It is almost seven."

Spencer was soaked with perspiration. His fever had broken again. He said, "Tell Sister Kimball we're going."

Camilla got out of bed, and they both hurriedly dressed and then drove the short distance to the stadium where the program had just convened. President Tanner had explained at the beginning of the meeting that they were too sick to attend. In the opening prayer a young New Zealander petitioned fervently, "We three thousand New Zealand youth have gathered here prepared to sing and to dance for thy prophet. Wilt thou heal him and deliver him here." As the prayer ended, the car carrying Spencer and Camilla entered and the stadium erupted in a spontaneous, deafening shout at the answer to their prayer.

---

Caroline Eyring Miner and Edward L. Kimball, *Camilla,* 182–84; see also Russell M. Nelson, *From Heart to Heart* (Salt Lake City: Russell M. Nelson, 1979), 177–79.

# FAITHFULNESS

# "HE HAD SAVED $600"

ANDREW KARL LARSON

The story [of Peter Neilson Sr.] is concerned with the glass in the windows of the stately old Tabernacle in St. George. . . . The window panes for the Tabernacle had been ordered from New York City, and since the railroad had not yet reached Utah, the glass had to be shipped to the Pacific coast by boat. The word came that the glass was at Wilmington, California, and preparations under David H. Cannon's direction were made to send teams via the Old Spanish Trail to bring it to St. George. [Cannon was later called as president of the St. George Temple.] There was one hitch in his plans: there was a freight bill of $800 due on the panes, and Brother Cannon had been unable to raise more than $200 of the required amount. . . . At any rate David Cannon proceeded to speed preparations for the freighters' departure at the time planned—early morning. Whether they actually would get away [with sufficient money] rested with Providence, he reasoned. . . .

Peter must have known about Brother Cannon's predicament. . . . Peter was uneasy on this particular evening and passed a sleepless night wrestling with his problem. . . . He was careful in handling his property, both in Sanpete and in Dixie, and he had succeeded, by a frugality born of his Scandinavian upbringing and the stern necessity imposed by the frontier, in saving a considerable sum of money in gold. He had plans to enlarge his two-room adobe house and make it more commodious and comfortable for his family. He had saved $600. . . .

He thought of these things and what they meant to his family and to himself. He thought, too, of the reasons why he had left Denmark to come to America. At that time he felt that he could sacrifice anything for the sake of the kingdom. . . . This night, as he lay there weighing his $600 against the need of the kingdom, he again arrived at the same decision.

Before daylight he arose from his bed, put on his clothes, and lighted a candle. From its hiding place he brought the $600 in gold coin—half-eagles, eagles, and double-eagles—and tied it up in a clean red bandana. His wife, Karen, aroused by this activity at such an hour, asked why he was up so early. He replied that he had to take the $600 to David Cannon, who would know what to do with it. . . .

. . . As the first shafts of the rising sun touched with gold the somber dark red of the Sugar Loaf, there was a knock at David Cannon's door. Opening it, he was greeted by Peter Neilson, who handed him the heavy bandana. . . ."Good morning, David," said Peter; "I hope I am not too late. You will know what to do with this money."*

*Peter was never again able to save sufficient money to add to his house. He continued to "make do" with a small and humble two-room adobe dwelling for the rest of his life.

Andrew Karl Larson, *Red Hills of November*, 311–13; see also Jeffrey R. Holland, "As Doves to Our Windows," *Ensign*, May 2000, 75–77.

# "HOLD FAST TO THE IRON ROD NO MATTER WHAT"

WARREN M. JOHNSON

*On 29 July 1891 Warren Johnson wrote to Wilford Woodruff:*

In May 1891 a family residing in Tuba City, came here from Richfield Utah, where they . . . spent the winter visiting friends. At Panguitch they buried a child, . . . without disinfecting the wagon or themselves, [and] not even stopping to wash the dead child's clothes, they came to our house, and remained overnight, mingling with my little children. . . .

We knew nothing of the nature of the disease [diphtheria], but had faith in God, as we were here on a very hard mission, and had tried as hard as we knew how to obey the Word of Wisdom, [to] attend to the other duties of our religion, such as paying [our] tithing, family prayers, etc. etc. that our children would be spared. But alas, in four and a half days [the oldest boy] choked to death in my arms. Two more were taken down with the disease and we fasted and prayed as much as we thought it wisdom as we had many duties to perform here. We fasted [for] twenty-four hours and once I fasted [for] forty hours, but to no avail, for both my little girls died also. About a week after their death my fifteen year old daughter Melinda was [also] stricken down and we did all we could for her but she [soon] followed the others. . . . Three of my dear girls and one boy [have] been taken from us, and the end is not yet. My oldest girl nineteen years old is now prostrate [from] the disease, and we are fasting and praying in her behalf today. . . .

107

I would ask for your faith and prayers in our behalf however. What have we done that the Lord has left us, and what can we do to gain his favor again[?]

*On 16 August 1891 Brother Johnson wrote to a friend, Warren Foote:*

It is the hardest trial of my life, but I set out for salvation and am determined that . . . through the help of Heavenly Father that I [would] hold fast to the iron rod no matter what troubles [came] upon me. I have not slackened in the performance of my duties, and hope and trust that I shall have the faith and prayers of my brethren, that I can live so as to receive the blessings you having authority . . . placed on my head.

Warren M. Johnson, in P. T. Riely, "Warren Marshall Johnson, Forgotten Saint," *Utah Historical Quarterly,* Winter 1971, 19; spelling modernized; "Autobiography of Warren Foote of Glendale, Kane County, Utah," LDS Church Archives.

# THE FAITH OF THE GERMAN SAINTS

ELDRED G. SMITH

When I talk about unity in the gospel, I am often reminded of an experience that I had while on a mission in Germany. When this German choir sang for us yesterday in the conference meetings, I was reminded again of those experiences, especially when I was assigned to work in Celle in the Hanover District in Germany. Once a month we went to the little town of Uelzen, which was a self-sustaining branch. We went there to get their reports and to help them as we could. Since my companion was assigned to the branch at the same time I was, this first visit to Uelzen was a new experience for both of us.

We took our seats in the first meeting we attended in the front of the hall. The branch president announced that the meeting would be started by the choir singing such and such a song. I looked about and found no choir up in front, but before I could ask any questions or discover an answer to the problem in my mind as to where the choir was coming from, my companion and I found ourselves the only ones sitting in the audience. The entire congregation, except for my companion and me, had gone up to the front and sang as a choir. It is no wonder we have Saints who can come here and produce a chorus such as we had yesterday.

I found from the reports that they not only all sang together, but they also worked together. I found that there was 100 percent membership of the branch paying 100 percent tithing, and that was not just the month that I went there on that one visit, but that was the report I got all the time I was there. Attendance in their meetings was the same. They worked together in everything they did. I discovered, also, that there were two women in the branch at that time whose husbands had gone to America, and that the branch had agreed together, before these two men left, that they would all work together; they would keep the commandments of the Lord to the best of their ability; they would do all that was required of them without excuse; nothing would stop them from fulfilling the responsibilities given to them. Those who remained in the branch would see to it that the wives of these two men were taken care of, that they would not be in need.

The two men who left for America agreed that they would do likewise in living the commandments of the Lord and that they would find jobs and work hard and save their money and send for their wives as soon as possible. It was not long until I was transferred from that section of Germany, and then soon after, I was released to come home.

Some twenty years later, after I became Patriarch to the Church, I had an appointment to give a blessing to a young girl. When she arrived, her mother was with her. I found that the mother was one of those two sisters whose husbands had left Uelzen when I was over there. I had a long talk with this sister and her daughter. The daughter, of course, had grown up from a small child, and her mother told me this story: . . . One by one, or two at a time, as occasion came, different members of the branch would have the opportunity of leaving and coming to America, until before World War II broke out, there was not one member of the Church left in that branch in Uelzen. They had all come to America safely before the war broke out.

Then she told me also that in the end of the war, when the American soldiers invaded that section of Germany, for some reason unknown to her, the German soldiers set up a resistance in Uelzen which resulted in a four-day battle. The bombings and general destruction were such that there was not a house left in the section where most of the Saints had lived, yet there was not a member of the Church left in Uelzen—a result and reward of unity, working together to keep the commandments of the Lord.

---

Conference Report, October 1955, 62–64.

# "TIME IS ON THE SIDE OF TRUTH"

E Z R A   T A F T   B E N S O N

On the way to the airport our last night in Moscow [during an official visit to Europe and the Soviet Union in 1959], I mentioned again to one of our guides my disappointment that we had had no opportunity to visit a church in Russia. He said a few words to the chauffeur, the car swung around in the middle of the avenue and we eventually pulled up before an old stucco building on a dark, narrow, cobblestone side street not far from Red Square. This was the Central Baptist Church.

It was a rainy, disagreeable October night with a distinct chill in the air. But when we entered the church, we found it filled; people were standing in the hall, in the entry, even in the street. Every Sunday, Tuesday, and Thursday, we learned, similar crowds turn out.

I looked at the faces of the people. Many were middle-aged and older but a surprising number were young. About four out of every five were women, most of them with scarves about their heads. We were ushered into a place beside the pulpit.

A newsman who was present described what happened: "Every face in the old sanctuary gaped incredulously as our obviously American group was led down the aisle. They grabbed for our hands as we proceeded to our pews which were gladly vacated for our unexpected visit. Their wrinkled, old faces looked at us pleadingly. They reached out to touch us almost as one would reach out for the last final caress of one's most-beloved just before the casket is lowered. They were in misery and yet a light shone through the misery. They gripped our hands like frightened children."

The minister spoke a few words, and then the organ struck a chord or two and began a hymn in which the entire congregation joined as one. Hearing a thousand to 1,500 voices raised there became one of the most affecting experiences of my entire life. In our common faith as Christians, they reached out to us with a message of welcome that bridged all differences of language, of government, of history. And as I was trying to recover balance under this emotional impact, the minister asked me, through an interpreter who stood there, to address the congregation.

It took me a moment of hard struggle to master my feelings sufficiently to agree. Then I said, in part, "It was very kind of you to ask me to greet you.

"I bring you greetings from the millions and millions of church people in America and around the world." And suddenly it was the most natural thing in the world to be talking to these fellow Christians about the most sacred truths known to man.

"Our Heavenly Father is not far away. He can be very close to us. God lives, I know that He lives. He is our Father. Jesus Christ, the Redeemer of the world, watches over this earth. He will direct all things. Be unafraid, keep His commandments, love one another, pray for peace and all will be well."

As each sentence was translated for the congregation, I saw the women take their handkerchiefs and, as one observer put it, begin to "wave them like a mother bidding permanent goodby to her only son." Their heads nodded vigorously as they moaned, *ja, ja, ja!* (yes, yes, yes!). Then I noticed for the first time that even the gallery was filled and many persons were standing against the walls. I looked down on one old woman before me, head covered by a plain old scarf, a shawl about her shoulders, her aged, wrinkled face serene with faith. I spoke directly to her.

"This life is only a part of eternity. We lived before we came here as spiritual children of God. We will live again after we leave this life. Christ broke the bonds of death and was resurrected. We will all be resurrected.

"I believe very firmly in prayer. I know it is possible to reach out and tap that Unseen Power which gives us strength and such an anchor in time of need." With each sentence I uttered, the old head nodded assent. And old, feeble, wrinkled as she was, that woman was beautiful in her devotion.

I don't remember all that I said, but I recall feeling lifted up, inspired by the rapt faces of these men and women who were so steadfastly proving their faith in the God they served and loved.

In closing I said, "I leave you my witness as a Church servant for many years that the truth will endure. Time is on the side of truth. God bless you and keep you all the days of your life, I pray in the name of Jesus Christ, amen."

With that I brought this broken little talk to an end, because I could say no more, and sat down. The whole congregation then broke into a favorite hymn of my childhood, "God Be with You Till We Meet Again." We left the church as they sang and as we walked down the aisle, they waved handkerchiefs in farewell—it seemed all 1,500 were waving at us as we left.

It has been my privilege to speak before many church bodies in all parts of the world, but the impact of that experience is almost indescribable. I shall never forget that evening as long as I live.

Seldom, if ever, have I felt the oneness of mankind and the unquenchable yearning of the human heart for freedom so keenly as at that moment.

Ten members of the American press who were present felt it, too. Without exception they told me later what a moving experience it had been. One of them wrote in the next issue of his magazine: "The Communist plan is that when these 'last believers' die off, religion will die with them. What the atheists don't know is that God can't be stamped out either by legislated atheism or firing squad. This Methodist backslider who occasionally grumbles about having to go to church, stood crying unashamedly, throat lumped, and chills running from spine to toes. It was the most heart-rending and most inspiring scene I've ever witnessed."

On the drive to the airport one of the interpreters, a young Russian girl who had never known any life save that under communism, said, "I felt like crying."

So did I.

Ezra Taft Benson, *Crossfire*, 485–88.

# "A MOST REMARKABLE PRIESTHOOD MEETING"

## DAVID O. McKAY

I was on my first mission, president, at the time, of the Scottish conference in the year 1899. Presiding over the European Mission were Elders Platt D. Lyman, Henry W. Naisbitt, and James L. McMurrin. President McMurrin represented the European Mission presidency at a conference held in Glasgow, Scotland. Following a series of meetings, we held a most remarkable priesthood meeting—one that will never be forgotten by any who was present.

I remember as if it were but yesterday, the intensity of the inspiration of that occasion. Everybody felt the rich outpouring of the Spirit of the Lord. All present were truly of one heart and one mind. Never before had I experienced such an emotion. It was a manifestation for which as a doubting youth I had secretly prayed most earnestly on hillside and in meadow. It was an assurance to me that sincere prayer is answered "sometime, somewhere."

During the progress of the meeting, an elder on his own initiative arose and said, "Brethren, there are angels in this room." Strange as it may seem, the announcement was not startling; indeed, it seemed wholly proper, though it had not occurred to me there were divine beings present. I only knew that I was overflowing with gratitude for the presence of the Holy Spirit. I was profoundly impressed, however, when President James L. McMurrin arose and confirmed that statement by pointing to one brother sitting just in front of me and saying, "Yes, brethren, there are angels in this room, and one of them is the guardian angel of that young man sitting there," and he designated one who today is a patriarch of the Church.

Pointing to another elder, he said, "And one is the guardian angel of that young man there," and he singled out one whom I had known from childhood. Tears were rolling down the cheeks of both of these missionaries, not in sorrow or grief, but as an expression of the overflowing Spirit; indeed, we were all weeping.

Such was the setting in which James L. McMurrin gave what has since proved to be a prophecy. I had learned by intimate association with him that James McMurrin was pure gold; his faith in the gospel implicit; that no truer man, no more loyal man to what he thought was right ever lived; so when he turned to me and gave what I thought then was more of a caution than a promise, his words made an indelible impression upon me. Paraphrasing the words of the Savior to Peter, he said: "Let me say to you, Brother David, Satan hath desired you that he may sift you as wheat, but God is mindful of you." Then he added, "If you will keep the faith, you will yet sit in the leading councils of the Church." At that moment there flashed in my mind temptations that had beset my path, and I realized even better than President McMurrin, or any other man, how truly he had spoken when he said, "Satan hath desired thee." With the resolve then and there to keep the faith, there was born a desire to be of service to my fellow men, and with it a realization, a glimpse at least, of what I owed to the elder who first carried the message of the restored gospel to my grandfather and grandmother who had accepted the message years before in the north of Scotland, and in South Wales.

David O. McKay, *Cherished Experiences,* 13–14.

# THIEVES HAD SLIT HIS THROAT AND STOLEN HIS VOICE

EDWARD L. KIMBALL AND
ANDREW E. KIMBALL JR.

In November, [months after a throat operation,] Dr. Cowan pronounced Spencer [W. Kimball]'s throat fully healed and freed him to use his voice as he could, so long as he did not strain it or subject it to fatigue.

But he had still not spoken at a conference with his gruff, unfamiliar voice, and he feared the experience.

In December Elder Kimball attended stake conference in the Gila Valley. Elder Delbert L. Stapley, the appointed conference visitor, offered him a chance to speak. Elder Kimball was tempted to pass the opportunity by, but he decided that if ever he were to speak in public again he would have to brave a first time and there would be no more sympathetic group in the whole Church for him than this one. He started by telling the congregation that he had gone to New York and fallen among cutthroats and thieves who had slit his throat and stolen his voice. The audience laughed heartily and both he and they relaxed. He was home, he was back at his work again.

He spoke briefly three times that day, with no apparent harm, and he found that with good electronic equipment he could be heard reasonably well. The doctors had told him that to keep his voice he must now use it, with restraint but regularly. He appealed almost plaintively to the First Presidency to allow him to take regular assignments again. "My service, my time, my energies and my life are in your hands. Please command me." They agreed. He felt "like a resurrected person."

In January he was assigned, with Elder Harold B. Lee, to divide the Dallas Stake and organize a Shreveport Stake. It was a hard week. He had a cold, diarrhea, two boils starting in his nostrils, some nosebleeds, and an excruciating back pain. Elder Lee, who shared his bedroom, asked him several times if there was anything he could do for him.

After denying any difficulty until three in the morning, he decided that Elder Lee must know perfectly well from his twisting and turning that something was wrong. He then admitted he had been in constant pain for two days. Elder Lee gave him a sleeping pill and a blessing. Then Spencer slept a few hours and the pain was gone and did not return. "The Lord is so good to me and so far beyond my deserts."

At the Houston conference Elder Lee, the senior of the two apostles, announced Elder Kimball as the next speaker. He stood, opened his mouth, but only an ugly grating noise came out. He swallowed and gulped and tried again, with the same sickening feeling. The thought came: "Better quit—you can't do it—you can't impose on the people like this." But he tried again, this time found his voice, and delivered his short sermon. Then he turned to Elder Lee, shrugged helplessly and sat down. Elder Lee put his hand on him and said, "Thank you, Brother Kimball."

The next day there was another meeting in Houston. Elder Lee, in charge, announced Elder Kimball as the next speaker. He stood and "made the most terrible sound you can imagine" until finally he found his voice and gave his sermon. Then he sat down, buried his head in his hands and mourned. "I was crying gallons of tears inside. I don't think they showed. But I really thought I was through, that I'd never preach again, that I wouldn't even try."

Three days later, driving by car to Texarkana, he passed Elder Lee a note: "I hope you won't embarrass me again." Elder Lee jovially responded, "Oh, I'm sure we'll call on you again. I think it's important for the people to hear your witness." Elder Kimball answered nothing. He knew he would do anything Elder Lee, his senior, asked. But inside he rebelled at the thought.

The conference at Texarkana was held in a long, narrow Methodist chapel. True to his word, Elder Lee called on his companion apostle to speak. It seemed impossible. The public address system was out. The chapel was huge. Outside the window was the highway, with trucks climbing a hill, grinding and shifting gears. Elder Kimball stood and began, "Brothers and Sisters. . . ."

He prayed silently, he strained, the words came. For ten minutes he bore his testimony. Every person in the chapel heard him. He sat down and Elder Lee put his arm around him and said, "That's right, Spencer."

Spencer wrote home to Camilla: "I realize I cannot quit for

anything, though the temptation is terrific when I stumble and stammer and halt."

In the 1958 April Conference he spoke in the Tabernacle, on missionary work, and reactions from listeners reassured him he need not worry too much about his raw voice. Indeed, Elder Lee had earlier observed that when he spoke people leaned forward and listened with special intentness. President Clark asked about a boil on his neck and Elder Kimball said he was so glad to be able to speak that he could not be bothered by anything so minor as a boil.

That summer a nephew, talking about frustrating dreams, asked him, "Have you ever been in a dream and tried to scream, but just couldn't get it out?" "Yes," answered Spencer immediately, "for a whole year now." They both laughed.

---

Edward L. Kimball and Andrew E. Kimball Jr., *Spencer W. Kimball*, 311–13.

# HEALING

# "I Had Been Healed Instantly"

## BENJAMIN BROWN

The doctrine of the gathering had been taught the Saints, at Pomphret, and, in common with the others, I felt a great desire to gather up and live with the body of the Church. With this idea I endeavored to dispose of my farm, but failure in my efforts to do this was the only thing that saved me from a share in the Missouri persecutions. . . .

For several months I was preparing to remove, getting teams, wagons, etc. When the time arrived, with my wife and children, and part of the branch, . . . I started to find the Church, thinking it was still in Missouri, though we had heard that it had been mobbed and broken up.

We journeyed until we came to Springfield, about a hundred miles from Nauvoo, where we met with some brethren who had been driven out of Missouri, and who told us that the Church was collecting in Nauvoo, then called Commerce. We turned our course in that direction, and arrived there in June, the weather being very warm at the time.

We found brothers Joseph Smith and Sidney Rigdon there, with a few others. The rest were coming in daily, in a most distressed condition. Many of them were sick, and they had no house to enter when they arrived. The nature of the climate, combined with the hardships they had endured, soon made those ill who were not so previously.

Numbers of the sick and dying had to lie on the ground, with only a blanket over them. No springs or wells were handy, and the

123

Mississippi water was unfit to drink, so that many had to go miles for water to give to the afflicted. Sometimes one would go on horseback with a jug, and fetch a little for the sick, and take it round to them. It was frequently declared that the persecutions in Missouri were small matters compared to the miseries endured at this period in Nauvoo.

My family, with myself, were also taken sick, and I laid so for two or three weeks. I was so far gone that I was quite senseless, and all thought I was dying. Doubtless I should have died, but one day Joseph Smith was passing by my door (for I had managed to procure a house) and was called in, and, as I was afterwards informed, laid his hands upon me, and commanded me to arise and walk, in the name of the Lord. The first thing I knew was that I found myself walking on the floor, perfectly well, and within ten minutes afterwards I was out of the house visiting my daughter, whom I had not seen for nearly a month. I felt so full of joy and happiness, that I was greatly surprised that every one else was not as full of praise as myself.

This was the second time that I had been healed instantly by the power of God, through His servants.

---

*Gems for the Young Folks,* 73–75.

# "HERE COMES THE MORMON"

## BENJAMIN BROWN

A young man named Jesse W. Crosby . . . had been engaged with his brother and brother-in-law, in felling trees in a wood. The trees grew very close together, and one which they cut down had, in falling, struck another, and broken off one of its limbs, which hung suspended by the other branches.

It is a very common thing in forest country, to see dry, detached limbs hanging in this way for months, and sometimes years, without falling. This one was about ten or eleven feet long, and as thick as a man's thigh, and very high up the tree.

Not apprehending danger, Jesse was working without his hat, just under this branch. Suddenly, a movement, caused by the wind, shook the tree, and the loose branch fell from a height of at least sixty feet, striking him on the crown of his head, crushing him to the earth. The violence of the blow broke in a portion of his skull, forming a hollow about as large as the palm of a man's hand. His neck and shoulders were also much injured. Altogether, a more deplorable object I never saw in my life.

He was carried home by his friends, most of whom were members of the Church, and his father, who was not a member, procured a doctor, who pronounced Jesse's case desperate, unless, on removing the broken part of the skull, it should be found that the skin of the brain was still entire, when, by using a silver plate over the exposed portion, a chance might still exist of his life.

The doctor proceeded to cut Jesse's head for that purpose,

but was stopped by his mother, who strongly objected to this experiment, and sent for me to administer to him.

I was then eight miles off, and at the time of my arrival he had not spoken, nor scarcely indicated any signs of life. Going into the room where he lay, I found it filled with the neighbors, who were mostly enemies of the Church. Sneers and jeers of "Here comes the Mormon, we'll soon see whether he can heal now," saluted my ears on all sides.

From a sign which I had received while on my way, I knew Jesse would recover, and being reminded . . . that such people should not be privileged to behold a manifestation of the power of God, I, like Peter of old, cleared the house of all but Jesse's relatives, and administered to him in the name of the Lord. Jesse then recovered sufficiently to speak, after which he fell into a peaceful sleep, and, before morning, was altogether better.

In less than four days from the time of receiving this terrible accident, from which there seemed no human probability that he could recover, or, if he did, only to survive the loss of reason, he was again at work in the woods hauling timber, the wound being entirely healed up.

Since then, he, as an elder of this Church, has been on missions to various parts of the world, including England, and has also fulfilled a mission to Nova Scotia.

---

*Gems for the Young Folks*, 68–70.

# "THE MOBOCRATIC SURGEON
# WENT TO WORK"

⌒

## O.  B.  HUNTINGTON

I will relate what Zera Cole (spoken of in the Doctrine and Covenants) told me about five years ago at the Logan Temple. He said he was in Zion's Camp and marched with Joseph Smith from Kirtland to Missouri. A few days after they had ended their journey and the company was still in camp, he was cutting wood at a house of some brother and there was present, talking with him, one of the mob that drove the brethren from their homes.

Brother Cole made a miss lick with the axe and cut a big toe off, all but a bit of skin on the bottom side. The mobocrat said that *he* could sew it on, when Brother Cole said something about saving the toe if he had someone to sew it.

A needle and thread were obtained and the mobocratic surgeon went to work, took seven stitches and tore out the most of them, if not all. Brother Cole then told him to stop.

The toe was placed in proper shape and position, tied fast and bandaged. With some help he got to the camp of the brethren, where he was administered to by the elders for the first time in his life.

It was evening and he soon went to bed with the bandages all on his foot, and slept soundly all night.

After breakfast next morning he would dress his toe and see what should be done to it. To his great astonishment, when the bandages were removed, his toe was well and grown fast as any of them, but showed the scars of the cut and every stitch that was torn out. He immediately went on foot to the man that witnessed the accident and made the stitches, pulled off the shoe and showed him the scars; there was the toe, all sound, which the day before he had tried to sew on, or tried not to, as Brother Cole thought.

Brother Cole said that God did that, through the elders laying on their hands and praying.

The man gazed deliberately and intently at it a few moments, then turning away, remarked in a very awkward way, "D——! the devil did that."

Every right-minded person knows that the devil doesn't do such things—but his business and mission is to destroy.

*Young Woman's Journal,* 2:411–13.

# HEALED BY THE
# WATERS OF BAPTISM

## REUBEN BRINKWORTH

On the 2nd July, 1839, I entered on board the *Terror,* Commodore Sir John Franklin being then about to set out on a voyage of discovery for a northwest passage to India. Upon returning to England, we landed at Bermuda on the 16th of July, 1843, and in the afternoon of the same day a terrible thunder storm occurred, in which I was suddenly deprived of my hearing and speech. At the same time five of my comrades, viz., John Ennis, William Collins, John Rogers, Richard King, and William Simms were summoned into eternity. I remained insensible fifteen days—perfectly unconscious of all that was passing around me; but upon the return of reason, came the dreadful conviction that I was deprived of two of my faculties. I well remember the period, and shall for ever continue to do so—language cannot describe the awful sensations that pervaded my mind when I became fully sensible of the reality of my condition.

I will here remark, that the subject of religion had never troubled my mind; nor did the calamity I was called to suffer awaken any feeling akin to it; nevertheless I felt a certain feeling of gratitude that I had not met with the same fate as my more unfortunate companions; yet I must, to my shame, confess that it was not directed to the Great Disposer of all events, who could have taken my life as those of my companions, had he willed it. But it was not his design. I was spared, and am now a living witness of his loving kindness to the most abandoned sinners, if they will turn and seek his face. At that time I was about nineteen years old.

After remaining at Bermuda for about three weeks, we again set sail for England, and reached Chatham on the 14th December. I remained there only fourteen days, after which I went to London, and by the kind assistance of some gentlemen, entered the deaf and dumb school in Old Kent Road, where I remained for two weeks, but not liking the confinement, and being from home, I became dissatisfied and unhappy, and resolved to leave it, and accordingly did so. I then went to George Lock's, Oxford Arms, Silver Street, Reading, with whom I lived eighteen months, supporting myself the whole of that period upon the wages I earned on board the *Terror*. . . .

. . . I then went to Newport, Monmouthshire, and occupied

my time in teaching the deaf and dumb alphabet for about three years, at the end of which I became acquainted with the Latter-day Saints. At that time I was lodging at a public house, kept by James Durbin, sign of the Golden Lion, Pentonville. One of the customers of this house became acquainted with me and prevailed upon me to go . . . with him and his brother, who was a member of the Latter-day Saint's church. There I first became acquainted with the doctrines taught by this people, by reading and by means of the finger alphabet. I continued to investigate them for about three months, when I felt convinced of the truth of those doctrines which have since become so beneficial to my temporal and eternal welfare.

On the 22nd September, I had been, by means of the deaf and dumb alphabet, conversing freely with some of the Saints, and had fully determined to be baptized that evening, therefore I expressed my desire to receive the ordinance of baptism, and was taken to the canal early on the morning of the 23rd, and baptized in the name of the Father, Son, and Holy Ghost; and upon my head emerging from the water, I heard the voices of persons upon the towing path, and this was the first sound I had heard since my deprivation upon the island of Bermuda, in 1843. With my hearing came also my speech, and the first words that I uttered were—"Thank the Lord, I can speak and hear again as well as any of you." I scarcely need state my own surprise at the moment, but such it was, and it appears marvelous in my own eyes, not that God is possessed of such power, but that he should manifest it in my behalf.

I have much cause to praise him and glorify his holy name, for in obedience to his divine commands, I not only received the remission of my sins, which I esteem above all earthly blessings, but also the removal of my deafness and dumbness; and now I can hear as distinctly and speak as fluently as I ever did, although I had been deprived of both these faculties for upwards of five years not being able to hear the loudest notice, or to use my tongue in speech.

---

*Millennial Star*, 2:301–2.

# "HOW DID THE MAN HEAL YOUR EYES?"

## PARLEY P. PRATT

Mrs. Walton requested me to call on a friend of hers, who was also a widow in deep affliction, being totally blind with inflammation in the eyes; she had suffered extreme pain for several months, and had also been reduced to want, having four little children to support. She had lost her husband, of cholera, two years before, and had sustained herself and family by teaching school until deprived of sight, since which she had been dependent on the Methodist society; herself and children being then a public charge. Mrs. Walton sent her little daughter of twelve years old to show me the way. I called on the poor blind widow and helpless orphans, and found them in a dark and gloomy apartment, rendered more so by having every ray of light obscured to prevent its painful effects on her eyes. I related to her the circumstances of my mission, and she believed the same. I laid my hands upon her in the name of Jesus Christ, and said unto her, "Your eyes shall be well from this very hour." She

131

threw off her bandages; opened her house to the light; dressed herself, and walking with open eyes, came to the meeting that same evening at sister Walton's, with eyes as well and as bright as any other person's.

The Methodist society were now relieved of their burden in the person of this widow and four orphans. This remarkable miracle was soon noised abroad, and the poor woman's house was thronged from all parts of the city and country with visitors; all curious to witness for themselves, and to inquire of her how her eyes were healed.

"How did the man heal your eyes?" "What did he do?—tell us," were questions so oft repeated that the woman, wearied of replying, came to me for advice to know what she should do. I advised her to tell them that the Lord had healed her, and to give Him the glory, and let that suffice. But still they teased her for particulars. "What did this man do?" "How were your eyes opened and made well?"

"He laid his hands upon my head in the name of Jesus Christ, and rebuked the inflammation, and commanded them to be made whole and restored to sight; and it was instantly done."

"Well, give God the glory; for, as to this man, it is well known that he is an impostor, a follower of Joseph Smith, the false prophet."

"Whether he be an impostor or not, I know not; but this much I know, whereas I was blind, now I see! Can an impostor open the eyes of the blind?"

"Perhaps, then, you intend to be his disciple, to join the 'Mormons'?"

"He said nothing to me about joining the 'Mormons,' but taught me the gospel, and bore testimony that God had restored its power to the earth. Would you like to be partakers thereof? Or why do you inquire so earnestly about my eyes being healed?"

"Oh, we are John Wesley's disciples. We are the Christian

Church. We know John Wesley, but as to this man, we know not whence he is."

"How is this that you know not whence he is, and yet he hath opened my eyes? Did John Wesley open the eyes of the blind? Can an impostor do it?"

"Ah, we see how it is. You are determined to forsake the Christian Church, the good old way, for the sake of these fools, these weak impostors—the Mormons. Well, farewell. But remember, you will have no more support from our society, no more encouragement of any kind; you shall not even teach a school for us. How then will you live?"

Such contentions and discouragement as these, poured into the ears of a poor mother from day to day, together with railings, lyings, and various sophistry and slander, soon caused her to waver, and like thousands of other poor, weak mortals, she shrank back into the net of sectarian delusion, and was seen by the Saints no more. In the meantime our meetings commenced at Mrs. Walton's. At first very few attended, but they gradually increased till her rooms, and sometimes her yard, were well filled with attentive hearers.

---

Parley P. Pratt, *Autobiography of Parley P. Pratt*, 117–18.

# "HERE I AM A LIVE MAN"

LEVI CURTIS

About the month of August, 1856, William D. Huntington and I went into Hobble Creek Canyon to get a log suitable for making drums. After we started for home, our conversation turned upon the experiences of the past, when the life and labors of the Prophet Joseph were touched upon. This subject aroused into more than usual earnestness the mind and conversation of my associate.

He said that in Nauvoo he lived in the family of and worked for Joseph Smith at the time the Prophet had such a wonderful time with the sick. He said he had been sick some weeks and kept getting weaker, until he became so helpless that he could not move. Finally he got so low he could not speak, but had perfect consciousness of all that was passing in the room. He saw friends come to the bedside, look at him a moment, commence weeping, then turn away.

He further stated that he presently felt easy, and found that he was in the upper part of the room near the ceiling, and could see the body he had occupied lying on the bed, with weeping friends standing around.

About this time he saw Joseph Smith and two other brethren come into the room. Joseph turned to his wife Emma and asked her to get him a dish of clean water. This she did; and the Prophet with the two brethren washed their hands and carefully wiped them. Then they stepped to the bed and laid their hands upon the head of his body, which at that time looked loathsome to him, and as the three stretched out their hands to place them upon the head, he by some means became aware that he must go back into that body, and started to do so. The process of getting in he could not remember; but when Joseph said "Amen," he heard and could see and feel with his body. The feeling for a moment was most excruciating, as though his body was pierced in every part with some sharp instruments.

As soon as the brethren had taken their hands from his head he raised up in bed, sitting erect, and in another moment turned his legs off the bed.

At this juncture Joseph asked him if he had not better be careful, for he was very weak. He replied, "I never felt better in my life," almost immediately adding, "I want my pants."

His pants were found and given to him, which he drew on, Joseph assisting him, although he thought he needed no help. Then he signified his intention to sit in a chair at or near the fireplace. Joseph took hold of his arm to help him along safely, but William declared his ability to walk alone, notwithstanding the continued help.

Throughout the room, astonishment had taken the place of weeping. Every looker-on was ready to weep for joy; but none were able or felt inclined to talk.

Presently William said he wanted something to eat. Joseph asked him what he would like, and he replied that he wanted a dish of bread and milk.

Emma immediately brought what he called for. Every hand was anxious to supply the wants of a man who, a few moments before, was dead, really and truly dead! Brother Huntington ate the bowl of bread and milk with as good a relish as any he ever ate.

In a short time all felt more familiar, and conversation upon the scene that transpired followed. William related his experience, and the friends theirs.

Joseph listened to the conversation and in his turn remarked that they had just witnessed as great a miracle as Jesus did while on the earth. They had seen the dead brought to life.

At the close of his narrative to me, William Huntington remarked, "Now I have told you the truth, and here I am a live man, sitting by the side of you on this log, and I testify that Joseph Smith was a prophet of God."

*Juvenile Instructor,* 27:385–86.

## "THE EFFECT WAS INSTANT"

### ORSON F. WHITNEY

It was April 8, 1877, when I left Columbia for Elyria, Ohio. Arriving at my destination, I walked three miles into the country, to the farm where dwelt the Frinks. They were not aware of my coming, but had been praying that an Elder of the Church might be led that way, several of their neighbors, with whom Sister Frink had conversed, having expressed a desire to hear more of the gospel, and hear it from the lips of a "Mormon" missionary. I was the only one in that part of the country.

On the other side of the country road passing the farm house where I was staying, stood the residence of Truman Frink's brother, a bitter anti-Mormon, who had been heard to say that if one of our elders crossed his threshold he would kick him into the street. . . . His wife, Margaret Frink, was an excellent woman, childless by him but by a former husband the mother of several daughters, all married. The eldest, a widow with one child, shared her mother's home.

Mrs. Frink had been confined to her room with an attack of neuralgia, which for many weeks had caused her intense pain. Her daughter had learned . . . that . . . healing was practiced by the Latter-day Saints. . . . She therefore invited me to come and bless her mother, that she might be healed. Sister "Angie" seconded the suggestion—if, indeed, she did not originate it—and again I was all but paralyzed at the prospect.

Never did I feel so helpless—or so humble. I besought the Lord with all my soul to stand by me in this critical hour, to perfect my faith, and use me, if He could consistently, as an instrument for showing forth His merciful power upon the afflicted one. I then consecrated, as best I could, some olive oil provided by Sister Frink, and went with her and her husband to Mrs. Frink's abode.

It was evening and the family were all at home. The daughter met us at the door, and ushered us into her mother's apartment, on the right of a hallway leading through the house, with rooms on either side. We had heard, as we entered, men's gruff voices and loud laughter in a room to the left; and presently Eli Frink thrust his head through a rear doorway, glanced around suspiciously, and then retired without uttering a word.

Mrs. Frink, with her head bandaged, was sitting up, but still suffering much pain. Laying my hands upon her head, which I previously had anointed, I proceeded to bless her. Scarcely had I begun, when a power fell upon me that I had never felt before. . . . It was a warm glow in my throat and breast—not painful, but powerful, almost preventing utterance, and it ran like liquid flame to the very tips of my fingers. The effect was instant. "Thank God!" said the sufferer, "the pain has gone." . . . I was so overcome by a sense of gratitude for this signal manifestation of divine favor, that I sank into a chair and burst into tears.

———————

Orson F. Whitney, *Through Memory's Halls*, 85–87.

# "THEY HAD GATHERED THE SICK FROM ALL PARTS OF THE VILLAGE"

### LLEWELLYN HARRIS

I arrived at the Zuni village on the 20th of January, 1878, on my way to the Mexican settlements, to preach the gospel. Circumstances caused me to stay at Zuni eight days, thus giving me an opportunity to become acquainted with their traditions, customs and history. . . . At present they are nearly all Catholics. A few of them have been baptized into our Church by Brothers Ammon M. Tenney and R. H. Smith, and nearly all the tribe say they are going to be baptized.

I put up with a Zuni Indian known as Captain Lochee, who had three children sick with the smallpox. After I had been asleep two or three hours, I was awakened by the cries of the family and some of the neighbors who had come in. I arose and inquired the cause of the crying, and was informed by Captain Lochee that his daughter, a child of about twelve years of age, was dying. I saw she was gasping for breath. I felt like administering to her then, but the Spirit of the Lord prompted me to wait a little longer. I waited until she had done gasping and did not appear to breathe. The Spirit of the Lord moved upon me very strongly to administer to her, which I did; she revived and slept well the remainder of the night. I also administered to the other two who were sick in the same house that night. All was quiet the remainder of the night, and all seemed much better in the morning.

The news of this spread through the town, and the next day I was called to visit about twenty-five families, all of whom had one or more sick with the smallpox. They also wished me to administer to the sick, which I did. I was called upon to visit from ten to twenty families a day for four days after my arrival, and administered to their sick. The power of the Lord was made manifest to such a degree that nearly all I administered to recovered. The disease was spreading so rapidly that I was unable to visit all the houses.

One morning about eight o'clock one of the Zuni women came for me to go and visit the sick; she took me to a house which had a large room in it, about twenty by forty feet. When I entered the room I found they had gathered the sick from all parts of the village, till they had completely filled the house. The stench that arose and the horrible sight that met my eyes is beyond description. They had a Spaniard there, who understood the Zuni language, for an interpreter, who told me they wanted me to administer to so many, and I called on the Lord to strengthen me.

I commenced, and as fast as I administered to them they were removed, but other sick ones were continually being brought in. It was late in the afternoon before I could perceive that they began to diminish in numbers. When I had administered to the last one and went out, the sun had set and it was getting dark. The Spaniard who had stayed there all day asked me if I knew how many I had prayed for. I told him that I did not keep count; he

139

said he had, and that it was 406. The next morning my arms were so sore that I could hardly move them.

There was a Presbyterian minister in the village, who became jealous of the influence I was gaining with the Indians. He persuaded two Spaniards, one Navajo Indian, one albino Zuni, and one of the Zuni medicine men to circulate lies and frighten the Zunis, telling them that those who were healed were healed by the power of the devil.

I felt weak from the effects of administering so much, and, on the second day after administering to the 406, I started for the settlement in Savoia valley. The next day after arriving in Savoia I was taken down with a severe fever, which lasted about a week. I stopped with the family of Brother John Hunt, who treated me very kindly. It was about three weeks before I was able to resume my journey to the Mexican settlements on the Rio Grande. I spent about four months preaching to the Mexican people in New Mexico.

When I arrived at Savoia on my return, I was informed by the brethren that the minister who had opposed me at Zuni had passed there and was nearly dead with the consumption. When I arrived at Zuni I was told by some of the most reliable Zunis that all to whom I had administered recovered, excepting five or six that the minister gave medicine to, and four or five that the medicine man had tried to cure by magic. The medicine man that opposed me had died during my absence, and the Navajo who opposed me, on returning home, was killed by his people to keep the smallpox from spreading among them.

This is a true statement of the manner in which the power of God was made manifest among the Zunis, and also the judgments of God which followed some of those who opposed it. It seemed that I was, by the providence of God, cast among them; and I felt that I was one of the weakest of my brethren, and to ask the Lord to strengthen me if it was his will to make his power manifest through me. If the Lord had not strengthened me I could not have borne up under what I passed through at Zuni.

---

*Juvenile Instructor*, 14:160.

# "HE LOOKED LIKE HE WAS DEAD"

MARGARET MᶜNEIL BALLARD

During the summer of 1874, there was an epidemic of scarlet fever in Logan. Many families were severely afflicted with it. My brother, Joseph McNeil, contracted the disease and died on Saturday June 13, 1874, at the age of fourteen and one-half years old. My children all came down with it and were very sick. Our little son George Albert died of it on Tuesday, July 7, 1874. Our daughter Margaret Hannah was sick with the same disease when her little brother died. The day after his death his little body was taken to her bedside for a last farewell on earth. This parting was not for long for she too died six days later. He [George Albert] was buried Wednesday, 8th of July, and Margaret [Hannah] died Monday, July 13, 1874 at the age of nearly twelve years. She was buried the next day, Tuesday, July 14th by her brother.

Thus I had been the mother of seven children with but three remaining—three boys; Henry, Thomas and my baby Melvin.

Within ten days we had buried our twins, [then,] less than five years later, within six days we buried our other two dear children. How lonely and empty our home was and sad were our hearts.

Not long after we had buried our children, my son, Henry, was helping his father haul peas from the field. In some way he fell on the pitchfork which ran through his bowels. His father prayed over him at the time and asked the Lord to spare his life until he could get him home. When they brought him in he looked like he was dead. I hurried and made an herb plaster and put his whole body in it. We also offered up a mighty prayer for him. He was again restored to health and we know that it was the power of the Lord that saved him, for at that time we had no doctors to help us.

---

Margaret McNeil Ballard, in Douglas O. Crookston, ed., *Henry Ballard*, 231–32.

# "THE BULLETS HAD GONE CLEAR THROUGH HIM"

### HEBER J. GRANT

In the days of the "underground" when more than a thousand of our men went to the penitentiary for living with their wives whom they had married in good faith, a man by the name of Joseph W. McMurrin was guarding the servants of the Lord.

The brethren were holding a meeting in the Social Hall. A deputy U.S. marshal came to the back door where Joseph W.

McMurrin was standing, and Joseph put his arms around him to keep him from going through that door. The deputy finally got his hand loose and took his pistol and, pressing it against Brother McMurrin's body, fired two bullets clear through his vitals. Those bullets lodged just under the skin in his back. He was attended by Dr. Joseph Benedict who told Joseph W. McMurrin that no man could live after two bullets had passed through his vitals, and then added: "If you wish to make a dying statement you should do so immediately."

I went with John Henry Smith to Brother McMurrin's home and saw where the flesh was burned away around those terrible gaping wounds. I saw where the bullets had gone clear through him. I heard John Henry Smith say, "By the authority of the priesthood of the living God which we hold, and in the name of the Lord, Jesus Christ, we say that you shall be made absolutely whole, and that there shall be no physical weakness left upon your body because of these terrible wounds that you have received while guarding the servants of the living God."

Joseph W. McMurrin is alive and well, and has never had any physical weakness because of those terrible wounds. Tell me that sickness is not cured by spiritual power, by the power of God, in the Church of Jesus Christ! I know that it is as well as I know that I live.

---

Heber J. Grant, *Gospel Standards*, 310–11.

# "HAVE YOU FAITH
# TO BE HEALED?"

GEORGE ALBERT SMITH

My great-grandparents lived in New England. When the message of the restored gospel was first taken to that section by Orson Pratt and others, the houses of worship were not open to them. They had difficulty in finding a place in which to preach. They came to a small village and they thought surely they would readily find someone who would offer to open a place for the preaching of the gospel, but they found none. At length they inquired of a man on the street as to where they could secure a place. He said, "Go find Winslow Farr. I think he can help you."

So they went to see Winslow Farr: he was easily found; everyone knew him. They told him what they wanted—to find a place in which to preach the gospel.

He asked, "What are you going to preach about?"

They answered, "Jesus Christ and his gospel."

He said, "I will help you."

They found a place and invited the people to come. Orson Pratt told them God had spoken again from the heavens, and that a young man named Joseph Smith had received heavenly manifestations. The Lord had directed him to an ancient record which the Prophet translated—the Book of Mormon. It was a divine record, the story of the ancestry of the American Indians.

Orson Pratt's testimony was so effective that Winslow Farr came up to him, took his hand, and said, "I have enjoyed your meeting tonight. Where are you going to stay?" On learning that they had no place to stay, he said, "You come home with me."

The missionaries didn't know that Winslow Farr's wife was dying of a dread disease—tubercular consumption. But this servant of the Lord, Orson Pratt, seeing her condition and realizing how kind her husband had been, looked at her and asked, "Have you faith to be healed?" The doctor had said she could not be healed, could live but a few days. When asked that question she said, "I don't know if I have that faith or not, but I know God could heal me if he wanted to."

And then this servant of the Lord said, calling her by her given name, "Olive, in the name of Israel's God, I command you to be healed." She was healed and in a few days was going about performing her household duties.

It was not long after that the Farrs came down where our people were situated in Nauvoo. And when our people came farther west, the Farrs were among the first to come. Winslow Farr, my great-grandfather, and Olive Farr, his wife, had three sons and a daughter born to them. They were among the first people to live in Ogden. The last time the Farr family assembled to celebrate Olive Farr's birthday, they found she was grandmother, great-grandmother, or great-great-grandmother to more than three hundred and twenty people, and I was one of the great-grandchildren.

I record these facts as one more witness of the power of God, and of the validity of his promises to all who will hearken and obey. . . . I am grateful for my great-grandmother who was healed by the power of the Lord, and passed her last days in the valleys of the mountains, where she lived to be ninety-three years old.

George Albert Smith, *Sharing the Gospel with Others*, 91–95.

# "I'VE BEEN FASTING AND PRAYING"

## MATTHEW COWLEY

We have a . . . friend down in Honolulu, . . . a man who is a young bishop down there, very wealthy, and yet a young man with a lot of humility. He was called one day from the Queen's Hospital to come and bless a boy who had polio. A native sister had called him. He was her bishop, and she said, "Bishop, come up here, my boy is stricken with polio, and I want you to come up here and administer to him and bless him." All day she waited for him, and the bishop never showed up. All night he never showed up, the next morning he never showed up, but early in the afternoon here he came. She turned loose on him. She called him everything she could think of. "You, my bishop, I call you and tell you my boy is here stricken with polio. And you your own boss, you have your cars; you have a beautiful yacht; you have everything you want; and your time is your own; and you don't show up. You just come now after a whole day." After she had finished and couldn't think of anything more to call him, he smiled and said, "Well, after I hung up the receiver yesterday, I started to fast, and I've been fasting and praying for twenty-four hours. I'm ready now to bless your boy." At five o'clock that evening the boy was released from the hospital entirely cured of his polio. " . . . this kind goeth not out but by prayer and fasting."

---

Matthew Cowley, *Matthew Cowley Speaks*, 149–50.

# "YOU ARE NOW FREE TO GO"

MATTHEW COWLEY

I am grateful that I learned to pray in my infancy because I had only passed from infancy when I was called as a missionary to the uttermost bounds of the earth; I had just turned seventeen. I was called to faraway New Zealand, and in that mission I was assigned, without a companion, to one of the most humble places I have ever seen in all my life, one of the most poverty-stricken places, and in that little village, I had to pray. I was there but a few days when a woman came rushing to my room, and I have a picture of that room—no floor, just the ground with a woven mat and a blanket or two. She came rushing to that room and asked me to arise from my bed and hurry to her little hut, and when I arrived there, I found her companion lying on the ground, being consumed by the fire of typhoid fever. All I could do was pray; and I knelt beside that suffering native and I prayed to God, and opened up my heart to him; and I believe the channel was open; and then I placed my hands upon that good brother; and with the authority of the priesthood which I as a young boy held, I blessed him to be restored to health. The next morning the wife came again to my room and said, "If you have anywhere you desire to go, you are now free to go; my husband is up."

---

Conference Report, October 1953, 107.

# "WHO IS GOING TO GET THE CREDIT?"

J . GOLDEN KIMBALL

I got a telephone message some time ago, I think a year ago, maybe, that I had some relatives in the hospital. They wanted me to hurry up there and administer to them. They were two sisters. They were married, and they were not city people, and, by the way, their father and mother were good Latter-day Saints, and these young girls had been taught and they had been active, but they were not healed, so they came to the hospital. When I arrived I found one of them in one room, and she had been operated upon, and getting along very nicely. The other sister wanted me to bless her before she was operated upon. I asked her how much she was paying for her room. She told me, "And how much are you paying the doctor?"

"Three hundred dollars."

"Well, haven't you got confidence in him? He is charging you enough. Why don't you trust him?"

"Well," she said, "Uncle Golden, I have been administered to, but I was not healed, and I felt forced to come to the doctor."

I said, "I am a little jealous for God, and if I bless you, and you arc hcalcd, who is going to get the credit? If the doctor gets all the money and all the credit, and God heals you, I don't think that fair."

So I blessed her as best I knew how, and I blessed the doctor. I made a full anointing and blessed the nurse, and asked God that his spirit might be there and the patient's life be spared. I realize that hospitals, physicians, and surgeons, do wonderful things, and that faith without works is dead. I want to bear testimony to you, and I know it, I don't think it, I don't imagine it: I have seen God heal the sick. I know it isn't in me, but I know that where there is faith there is nothing impossible, and these young elders who are sent out now, it may not be wisdom to send them out as we went, but when we were in the South, God had to take care of us, whether it was stormy or sunshine, as we had no choice. I know the Lord can take care of us and will take care of us if we have faith.

---

Conference Report, October 1927, 54.

# HONESTY

# "I Know Jacob Send You Back"

<br>

## JACOB HAMBLIN JR.

When I was about twelve years old our family lived in Kanab, Utah. A band of Piute Indians were camped a few miles away, across the wash. My father, Jacob Hamblin, the Indian missionary, said to me, "Son, I want you to go to the Indian camp this afternoon and trade the little bay pony for some blankets, which we will need this winter."

When the midday meal was over I climbed astride old Billy the horse and, leading the little bay pony, rode across the flat toward the Indian camp.

When I rode in, the chief helped me off the horse and asked, "You Jacob's boy. What you want?"

When I told him my errand, he looked at the trade pony and grunted his assent. He led me to his wigwam, where there was a pile of hand-woven Indian blankets. He pulled out a number of them. Determined to show my father that I was a good trader, I asked for another blanket. The chief looked at me out of the corner of his eye and added another blanket to my pile. Then I asked for another and another and still another. By now the chief was grinning broadly, but he continued to add as many blankets as I demanded.

Satisfied that I had made a really good trade, I closed the deal. The chief piled the blankets on the back of old Billy and lifted me up.

Father met me in the yard and looked at the blankets. Then he made two piles of about equal size. One pile he placed on the horse and put me back on, saying, "Go back and give these to the chief. You got enough blankets for two ponies."

As I approached the camp, I could see the old chief. When I rode up, he laughed and said, "I know Jacob send you back. He honest man. He my father as well as your father."

*Several years later when Jacob was alone with a band of angry hostile Indians, the fact that he had always been honest with them saved his life.*

---

*A Story to Tell*, 359–60.

# THE POWER OF GOSSIP

~

## GEORGE F. RICHARDS

Once upon a time I was a high council member in a stake and somebody made a serious accusation against a man. We debated whether to have him in and try him. Finally, the stake president decided he would talk to the man privately, and apparently he did, and the man proved to the satisfaction of all of us that not only was he *not* guilty of the accusation, but he hadn't even been in the country when it was supposed to have taken place. He was away somewhere, and he couldn't possibly have done it.

Forty years went by, and that man's name came up for a very high appointment in the Church. In spite of myself, I caught myself wondering if the story about the man was true, even though it had been proven false. I had to get hold of myself to keep from voting negatively against that man on a false story, told forty years before, which was proved false.

―――――――

*BYU Speeches of the Year*, 7 May 1968, 6–7.

# "WHAT IF I'D LIED TO HIM?"

❧

## S . D I L W O R T H Y O U N G

I had another experience one time. My wife was very ill. I was here in Provo to some Scout affair—I don't recall what it was now—and I had promised her that I would come home by six o'clock that night. I had left food at the side of her bed so that she could have something to eat because she couldn't get off the bed—she wasn't able—and I had to leave her alone.

Things took place here so that I didn't get away from Provo until eleven o'clock that night, and I was worried as I headed for home. . . . I passed through Salt Lake at midnight. Going north on the highway—the moon was full, the light was bright, I could see as easily as in daylight and I was the only person on the road— I went quite rapidly until I got to Farmington Junction, where I was to turn off to go up over the mountain road toward home. I turned off on that road and I really hit it up. I had that car going 70 miles an hour, which was good for those days over that road, and I whipped past the road going over to Hill Field, and down into Weber Canyon. I got about half way down the hill when through the rear view mirror I saw the flashing red light. The patrolman had been hiding up Hill Field road. So I pulled to a stop and got out. (One always wants to get out of his car when a policeman comes, and hold out his hands so he can see that one is not armed—at midnight, anyhow!) It was now nearly one o'clock.

So I walked back a few yards and stood there and his headlights picked me up and he came to a stop about thirty yards away. He got out of his car and came up to me. He said, "May I see your driver's license and your car registration." So I got the car registration and he took a look at it—he didn't bother to look at my license.

I said, "Well, give me the ticket. I've got to get home; my wife is ill and helpless. That's why I was speeding."

He said, "Yes, you were going faster than sixty miles an hour."

And I said, "I was going faster than seventy miles an hour."

He said, "Well, I'm not going to give you a ticket. I'm going to give you a *warning* ticket so you won't do it again, but I'll just warn you. This will make it so you will not have to go to court; but if you do it again, of course, then they'll collect on both counts."

I couldn't imagine why he had given me just a warning ticket. He got the ticket written out and he handed it to me—then he smiled, and he put his hand out, which a cop seldom does, and he said to me, "My name is Bybee. I used to be one of your scouts at Camp Kiesel."

All the rest of the way home, every time the wheels turned, I said to myself, "What if I'd lied to him—what if I'd lied to him—what if I'd lied to him."

I've learned by what little experience I've had with lies that anyone who tells a lie—I can guarantee that that lie will last him all his life and he'll have it burned into his soul over and over again until he dies.

---

*BYU Speeches of the Year,* 7 May 1968, 4–6.

# HUMOR

# CHRISTMAS IN ORDERVILLE

⌒

A U T H O R   U N K N O W N

oward Orson Spencer was chosen to be bishop and
leader in the little community of Orderville, in southern
Utah. One December evening some of the sisters of
Orderville met to plan a Christmas treat for the children. The
Order had no luxuries and the necessities were strictly rationed.
About the only sweets the people had was molasses, so, the sisters
decided to make molasses candy and cookies for the youngsters.
But on Christmas Eve, they came to grandmother Spencer with
news that the brother in charge of the molasses "won't let us have
any. He says our allowance for the month is already used."
Grandmother's lips tightened. "The children are going to have
something for Christmas, I'll speak to my husband after dinner—
he'll give us permission."

When grandfather came in tired and hungry, grandmother
hovered over him and after dinner urged him to rest by the fire.
As he sat looking drowsily into the flames, she said in a low voice,
"You do think the children should have some candy and cookies
for Christmas, don't you Howard?" "Ummhmm," was the sleepy
response and grandmother went away smiling. She reported to
the ladies that everything was all right, "My husband has given us
permission." "Did he say we could have the molasses?" asked one
doubting Thomas. "He didn't say 'No,'" replied grandmother
truthfully. "Now we won't wake up the brother in charge of the
molasses. We'll just slip out and take what we need."

The man in charge of the molasses barrel was very conscious

of his responsibility. On the lid of the barrel he had placed a section of heavy logging chain and a large boulder. Only a thin wooden partition at the head of the bed separated him from the barrel outside, and he was a light sleeper. Shivering from the cold the women crunched through the snow toward the barrel. It was beginning to snow again and the night was very dark. With infinite caution they removed the heavy chain without so much as one betraying clank. It took the combined efforts of all the women to lower the boulder noiselessly to the ground. There was a breathless pause as grandmother raised the lid and dipped into the barrel with a saucepan. She emptied its contents into a bucket and dipped again, and again. "We have enough now," whispered one of the women. "Let's go back."

With the same caution the chain and boulder were replaced and the women filed back to the warm kitchen to make the Christmas goodies. But, there was a dismayed gasp when they looked into the pail: "Oh dear, we haven't enough molasses. We'll have to get some more." "Oh no, Sister Spencer. It's so cold and dark. It's too risky." "Well just the same, we must unless we want the children to be disappointed."

There could only be one answer to such a statement and the little band of mothers went again to the molasses barrel. They returned safely and set to work. When morning came, every child in Orderville had two molasses cookies and one big slightly sticky lump of candy in his stocking. Santa Claus had not forgotten them.

Grandfather insisted all his life that he could not remember ever having given the women permission to get the molasses.

---

In Kate B. Carter, comp., *Our Pioneer Heritage*, 18:160–61.

# A JUMPING TOOTHACHE

## AUTHOR UNKNOWN

*Emeline Grover Rich, wife of Charles C. Rich, was a nurse and mid-wife who was "set apart to administer to the sick and to act as nurse and midwife by President Brigham Young."*

A young man who had been suffering with a "jumping toothache" hurried to Emeline's home and said, "Sister Rich, I have a terrible toothache; will you please pull it?" When Emeline appeared with the forceps, he became frightened and said, "My tooth has stopped aching now, Sister Rich. I will be going." After he had repeated this act twice, Emeline instructed her sons Sam and Heber to nab this young man if he returned the third time. In a few minutes he knocked at the door again. This time Sam exclaimed, "Young man, this time you are going to lose your tooth." Emeline, being of a sanitary nature, always sterilized the forceps by holding them over a flickering candle—then she would wipe them off on her apron. Having no dental chair and no anesthetics, she used ingenuity and whatever aid was handy. She put the patient flat on his back on the floor, and in this case, with Heber holding the boy's two arms, Sam on the two legs and Emeline on the boy's chest—she pried out the offending tooth. The boy's opinion on her technique is not recorded, but we do know that upon being released and raised to his feet, he exclaimed, "Sister Rich, father is out of town and I don't have fifty cents. If you can't trust me, please put the tooth back in." He apparently had a lot of faith in her ability.

---

In Kate B. Carter, comp., *Our Pioneer Heritage*, 6:420.

# "SHELL OUT HANDSOME"

## WALLACE STEGNER

J Golden Kimball's . . . shrewd dramatic sense told him when to soft-pedal, when to harangue, when to stop. He practiced tricks on his audiences and they loved him for it. In St. George, when he was stumping with an apostle to raise money, the two high dignitaries showed up in town on the monthly fast day. There hadn't been an apostle in town for a long time. His coming put a burden on the good farmers of Dixie. They were gaunt and sad-eyed as they came to meeting. Not a chew of tobacco or nip of Cisie wine had been snitched all day. The Word of Wisdom and the midsummer heat rode heavily on them. They sat glumly while the apostle inched his way like a measuring worm through a tedious sermon. By the time J. Golden arose they were restless and a little resentful. It was a hundred and ten in the hall; they steamed slowly, waiting for the inevitable and dreaded time when the contribution box would come out, wondering how small a donation they could get away with.

"Brethren and Sisters," J. Golden said, "you have heard good counsel. I don't aim to add much to it, even if I thought I could." He paused, his skinny six-feet-three leaning forward over the pulpit. "I know times are hard," he said. "I know it's a fast day. I know it's hot. . . . But I want to prophesy, Brothers and Sisters . . . ," his hand went up in a gesture of benediction, "I want to prophesy that if you shell out, and shell out handsome, Apostle Lyman and I will get out of town in half an hour." They paved the platform with silver dollars.

---

Wallace Stegner, *Mormon Country,* 193–94.

# ROAST CAPON IN BURGUNDY

## HEIDI S. SWINTON

President [George Albert] Smith had a fine wit and a great sense of humor. In August 1950 he sailed to Hawaii for the celebration of the centennial of the Hawaiian mission. In the party were his daughters Emily and Edith, Elder and Sister Henry D. Moyle, and Arthur and Maurine [Haycock].

They sat at the captain's table. While the others dined on steak and eggs for breakfast, pork chops for lunch, and prime rib for dinner, President Smith ate his regular fare of steamed wheat, boiled eggs, bread, and milk. Looking over the dinner menu one evening, he saw "Roast Capon in Burgundy" and thought he'd try it, since he'd grown fond of chicken dishes while serving on his mission in the Southern States. Emily nudged him, saying, "Papa, you don't want that; it's been cooked in burgundy." President Smith replied, "I don't care if it's been cooked in Australia. I still want it."

---

Heidi S. Swinton, *In the Company of Prophets,* 33.

# "THE RESULT WAS SPECTACULAR"

⌒

## JOHN R. TALMAGE

*While serving as president of the University of Utah, James E. Talmage learned to ride a bicycle for transportation.*

Some time after James had achieved reasonable proficiency in handling his machine on standard roads, he showed up at the front door one evening a full hour late for dinner and scarcely recognizable.

[His wife, May,] nearly went into shock, for her husband was a frightening sight. Battered, bruised, and bleeding profusely, clothes torn in a dozen places and covered with dust and mud, James looked as though he had been caught in a riot, or at least a fight of unusual violence. Neither, it developed, had been the case.

Half a block from the Talmage home a single-plank footbridge crossed the ditch of running water that separated the street from the footpath. Until now, James had dismounted when he reached this point in a homeward journey, and crossed the narrow bridge on foot. Today, he had decided that he had reached the point in his development as a cyclist where he should no longer resort to this prudent maneuver, but rather ride over the bridge in the manner of an accomplished veteran of the two-wheeler.

Having so decided, James approached the bridge resolutely, confident that he would negotiate the tricky passage in a manner to be proud of and to impress neighbors, if any should chance to be watching, with his skill and casual daring. He turned sharply from the road toward the bridge with scarcely any diminution of speed. The result was spectacular and observers, if any there were, must indeed have been impressed, but in a very different way from that intended. The professor's bicycle went onto the plank at an oblique angle and quickly slid off the side, throwing its rider heavily into the ditchbank.

Dazed, bruised, bleeding, and humiliated, Dr. Talmage was not convinced that the difficult maneuver was beyond his skill. Rather, he was stubbornly determined to prove that he could and would master the difficulty.

For the next hour, the president of the University of Utah might have been observed trundling his bicycle fifty yards or so down the road from the bridge, mounting and riding furiously toward the plank crossing, turning onto it with grim-lipped determination—and plunging off it in a spectacular and bone-shaking crash into the rough ditchbank. Uncounted times this startling performance was repeated, but in the end mind triumphed over matter, will power over faltering reflexes, and the crossing was successfully made. Not just once, but enough times in succession to convince James that he was capable of performing the feat without mishap at any time he might desire to do so. From then on, he never again dismounted to cross the bridge, albeit he never made the crossing without experiencing deep-seated qualms which he kept carefully concealed from any who might be watching.

---

John R. Talmage, *The Talmage Story*, 138–40.

# "I'M THAT BOY"

EDWARD L. KIMBALL AND
ANDREW E. KIMBALL JR.

W hen Spencer W. Kimball was a new Apostle], many Church members did not know him yet. In New Mexico the counselor conducting stake conference introduced him in the morning session as Elder Ezra Taft Benson. "That's all right with me," Elder Kimball began his sermon. "Just don't tell Brother Benson." In another conference session the flustered stake president announced him as Richard R. Lyman. Some in the audience tittered in embarrassment; Richard Lyman had just been excommunicated.

While he was waiting in the Salt Lake Temple, an aged man from Sanpete struck up a conversation. Learning he sat next to a Kimball, the man asked, "You related to Heber C. Kimball?"

"He's my grandfather."

"Did you know Golden Kimball?"

"That's my uncle."

"I read some on that Kimball just made an apostle. You related?"

"I'm that boy."

"What's that?"

"I'm that boy."

"You're *his* boy?"

"No. I am the man you are talking about."

The old man pumped Elder Kimball's hand ecstatically and declared those two new apostles, Kimball and Benson, were *real*

LDS. "But," he added in surprise, "you don't look more than twenty-eight years old." Spencer, forty-eight, penned in the margin of his diary, "Ha."

---

Edward L. Kimball and Andrew E. Kimball Jr., *Spencer W. Kimball*, 207.

# JOSEPH SMITH

# "Tell Your General to Withdraw His Troops"

⌒

## JOHN TAYLOR

Some . . . years ago, in Far West, a mob—one of those semi-occasional occurrences—had come against us with evil intent, placing themselves in position to give us battle; and there were not more than about 200 of us in the place. We had one fellow who was taken with a fit of trembling in the knees, and he ordered our people to retreat.

As soon as Joseph heard this sound, he exclaimed, "Retreat! where in the name of God shall we retreat to?" He then led us out to the prairie facing the mob and placed us in position; and the first thing we knew a flag of truce was seen coming towards us. The person bearing it said that some of their friends were among our people for whose safety they felt anxious. I rather think it was a case in which the wife was in the Church but not the husband, and the mob wished these parties to come out as they, he said, were going to destroy every man, woman and child in the place. But these folks had a little "sand" in them, as the boys say; they sent word back, that if that was the case they would die with their friends.

Joseph Smith, our leader, then sent word back by this messenger, said he, "Tell your General to withdraw his troops or I will send them to hell." I thought that was a pretty bold stand to take, as we only numbered about 200 to their 3,500; but they thought we were more numerous than we really were, it may be that our numbers were magnified in their eyes; but they took the hint and left; and we were not sorry.

*Journal of Discourses,* 23:37.

# "Don't You Worry about This Little Man"

## JOHN R. YOUNG

In the early years of my life I remember meeting the Prophet Joseph Smith. I was a sickly child: had suffered for two weeks, perhaps, with the chills and fever. I was a little skeleton, and peevish, everything would annoy me.

I remember that one morning my father had led me out to give me a little sunshine, and in that walk we met the Prophet Joseph Smith, his brother Hyrum, and Sidney Rigdon. When they met my father, they shook hands with him, and the Prophet asked father if I was the little boy that father had requested the elders to pray for.

Now, the Latter-day Saints were a praying people: they had faith in the Lord Jesus Christ, and that faith was strengthened in their bosoms by the testimonies of the Prophet Joseph Smith; and on that occasion, when we met them. I knew the Prophet. I had seen him in the congregations of the Saints, and I knew that he was a man that our people honored and loved: and hence I felt a thrill of pleasure pass over my little frame when he paid some little attention to me.

When my father had told him that I was the child he had requested the elders to pray for, the Prophet stepped toward me, and took my little straw hat from my head. He ran his fingers through my curly hair, and for the moment it seemed to me that he was looking far away, and then he said to father, "Brother Young, don't you worry about this little man, he will live to grow up to manhood, and will help carry this gospel to the nations of the earth."

That is one of my strongest and earliest recollections of things that came to me in this life, and hence I have answered to those who have met me out in the world, and asked me why I was a Latter-day Saint, that from my childhood, lessons came to me that gave me faith in the prophet of the last days, the Prophet Joseph Smith.

---

Conference Report, April 1916, 113.

# "YOU WOULD DO WELL TO TIE YOUR HORSE"

JOHN LYMAN SMITH

When playing in the yard of the old white mansion, in Nauvoo, with Joseph and Frederick, two of his sons, a gentleman drove to the gate and asked if the Prophet Joseph Smith was at home; when he (the Prophet) sprang up from the grass plat, and, shaking the dust from his clothing, replied that he was. The gentleman then drove his one horse up to a tie post and left the lines lying loose, and got out and came into the house. When about half way to the house Joseph said, "Mr., I think you would do well to tie your horse; he might get a scare and run away and break your carriage."

The gentleman replied, "I have driven that horse for some years and never tie him. I am a doctor and cannot afford to tie up at every place I call."

Joseph repeated, "You had better tie, all the same. Your horse might get a scare and run away."

The doctor replied, "No fear."

Joseph seemed quite uneasy, and got up several times from his chair on the porch or stoop. Suddenly the horse started up the street and struck a wheel against a post and scattered the pieces for a block or more. The doctor sprang to his feet, and looking after the horse, cried out to Joseph, "I'll be d——d if you ain't a Prophet!"

*Juvenile Instructor*, 27:172–73.

# "I SEE YOU ARE HAVING TROUBLE"

⌒

T .   E D G A R   L Y O N

*A boy who was nine years old shortly before Joseph Smith was killed related this account years later.*

It was Temple Tithing Day (they had two tithings in Nauvoo, the regular tithing on one's increase or earnings, and the other on time, so that each person was expected to work every tenth day on the temple without pay). This boy's father had hitched his team to his wagon and with his son had gone to the quarry to load a large stone into the wagon; then, they started for the temple. Pulling out of the quarry with its stone floor was no problem, but when they started across the "Flat" their wagon became stuck in a mud hole. The father whipped the horses and they lurched forward against their collars, but this sudden pull merely jiggled the wagon and made it sink a bit deeper in the mire. The father handed the reins to his son telling him to stay with the team while he went up to the temple and secured someone to come down with a team or two of oxen and pull his wagon out of the mud.

His father had just stepped off the wagon when a man walking along the side of the street (where they had planned sidewalks, but had not yet constructed them) called to him and said, "I see you are having trouble, Brother Bybee."

"Yes," replied the latter, "I'm going to the temple to get someone to pull me out."

The man waded into the mud and said to the father, "Brother Bybee, you get by that left rear wheel and put your right shoulder under a spoke. I'll get my left shoulder under a spoke of the right wheel." Then to the nine year old boy he said: "Get your whip ready and when I say 'Lift,' we'll lift with our shoulders, and don't you spare the horseflesh."

So saying, each in position, the man said "Lift." Each did his part. The horses jumped at the sting of the whip, the wagon moved a bit, and the horses were able to keep it going. After going about a hundred feet onto dry ground the boy let the team rest. The two men caught up with the wagon and as Brother Bybee climbed up to the driver's seat and took the reins from his son, the father called out, "Thank you, Brother Joseph."

The boy had been greatly impressed that a prophet of the Lord, probably on his way to pay his temple tithing in labor, was not above wading in mud halfway to his knees and getting his shoulder covered with mud to help another man in distress.

*BYU Studies*, Winter 1978, 18:148.

# "RELEASE THEM TO MY CUSTODY"

## T. EDGAR LYON

A man with a long, white beard testified to a great lesson the Prophet had taught him. As a teenager, he and another boy had gotten into some sort of devilment, unthinking of the seriousness of what they were doing. He failed to state exactly what they did, but they had destroyed some property. They might have done what was common sport in those days, setting fire to a rail fence, or tearing out a few panels of such a fence so that cattle, sheep, horses, and hogs could get out of the enclosure and wander for miles; perhaps some of the cows bloated and died from eating too much of the wrong kind of forage. The owner of the farm where they had committed their destructive act was furious. He found out who they were, swore out a warrant for their arrest, and the sheriff took them to Carthage before the county judge. They were found guilty and sentenced to six months in the Hancock County jail, and fined $50.00. (This may not seem a heavy fine to an affluent society, but when one considers that skilled craftsmen and mechanics at that time earned a dollar a day, it was a heavy fine for youths in the 1840s.)

The father of the boys complained to Joseph Smith about the severity of the sentence, the need of the parents for the help of the young men with the harvest and fall planting, and the fear of boys spending six months in an unheated stone jail. Wouldn't the Prophet intercede with the judge for a reduction of the sentence?

Joseph Smith went to Carthage and talked to the judge, whose answer was, "They did wrong and I'm going to teach them a lesson never to do such a thing again."

Joseph Smith's reply was, "I'm afraid you won't teach them that lesson by an imprisonment. After six months they'll come out of that jail hating you and the sheriff and the man whose property they destroyed, and perhaps antagonistic against the ordered society we stand for. With nothing worthwhile to do they'll spend their time planning how they could do the same thing again and not get caught. They might even be persuaded to join one of the gangs of outlaws who infest this country and become professional criminals."

The judge asked Joseph Smith what he could propose as a better punishment to which he replied, "Release them to my custody for six months. Our Nauvoo streets are difficult to travel because of mud holes. We'll employ them to haul stone chips from the temple quarry and gravel from the river banks to improve our streets. We'll pay them fifty cents a day to reimburse the man whose property was destroyed. This will save the county money as they won't have to be fed for six months at county expense. Let them pay the costs of the court procedures and all will be better off than a jail sentence would achieve."

Contemporary Nauvoo notes show that from time to time Joseph Smith, the mayor, or Brother Sherwood, the city surveyor and supervisor of streets, checked on the boys. Once they found them loafing, another time not on the job, and docked them a day's pay for their indolence.

Then the [bearded storyteller] said something to this effect: "That was the greatest training I ever had not to wantonly or willfully destroy property of another. It was the best training to work consistently and earn an honest day's pay I ever had. Here I am advanced in years and I've never done anything since that episode that brought me into a court for misconduct." To this man Joseph Smith was a man of warm feeling, great compassion, and wonderful insight into the minds of youths in training them to avoid delinquency.

---

*BYU Studies*, Winter 1978, 18:146–47.

# "WHY DON'T YOU HOLD YOUR HEAD UP?"

~

## HENRIETTA COX

In the spring of 1841 my parents were both baptized into the Church of Jesus Christ of Latter-day Saints, and soon after started for Nauvoo in company with some other Saints. After reaching their destination the company camped for a few days on the bank of the Mississippi until they had opportunity to find homes, a Brother Sherwood kindly giving them the use of one small log house which he owned.

While the Saints camped here the Prophet visited them. A meeting was held in the aforementioned log house. I remember that when the Prophet came into the room he shook hands with all, old and young, who had assembled. I cannot remember much that was said that day in meeting, as I was so very young, but one incident of the day's proceedings fastened itself so firmly upon my mind that I have never forgotten it.

Brother Joseph was sitting with his head bent low, as if in deep thought, and had not spoken for a few minutes, when one of the elders present began to chide him for being bowed in spirit, and said, "Brother Joseph, why don't you hold your head up and talk to us like a man?"

Brother Joseph presently answered the elder by calling his attention to a field of ripening grain, saying that many heads of grain in that field bent low with their weight of valuable store, while others there were which, containing no grain to be gar-nered, stood very straight.

Proof of the correctness of his words was given shortly after, as the elder to whom they were addressed soon after apostatized and went back east.

I know of a surety that Joseph Smith was a Prophet of God, and have had abundant testimony that the work which he established is the work of our Father in Heaven.

*Juvenile Instructor,* 27:203.

# A GENTILE'S TESTIMONY OF JOSEPH SMITH

## OLIVER B. HUNTINGTON

I will relate a testimony that Joseph Smith was a prophet, which was borne by a gentile as witnessed by Brother Packard and told to us that evening, or night. He said that he was in a saloon in the Sweet Water, when gold was first found there, and a very tall lank westerner came in finely dressed in the best of broadcloth and everything on him corresponding. He looked rather out of place among a lot of rough miners, and one of his old comrades meeting him asked where he got such fine clothes, or how he could afford to wear such.

The tall man replied that it was because they cost him nothing. His comrade asked how that happened.

The reply was "because Joseph Smith was a true prophet."

"What has that to do with your getting that suit of clothes?"

The tall man said, "I will tell you. I went into a store in Carson, an old friend of mine kept it. I was dead broke and had on next to nothing, and the storekeeper asked me why I didn't wear better clothes? I told him, 'I'd like to.'

"He said for me to 'pick out the best suit I could find in the store and pay him when Stephen A. Douglas was elected President.' Now that occurred when Douglas was running for President of the U.S.

"A little before the election I told the storekeeper I'd take two suits on them terms, but he said one was all he proposed to let me have."

The interlocutor asked how he dare take them on that condition. "Well, you see, Joe Smith told Douglas before he thought of trying to be President, that he would try it some day, and that if he used his influence against the Mormons, he should never sit in the President's chair; and I kept watch and kept thinking of that prophecy, just to see if Joe was a true Prophet. When I see Douglas trying to be President, I knew Joe Smith was a true prophet and that Douglas would not be elected because he had turned against the Mormons. I have watched Joe's prophecies and never have seen one of them fail."

---

Oliver B. Huntington Journal, typescript, 10 February 1883.

# EXPERIENCES IN LIBERTY JAIL

#### ALEXANDER MCRAE

Sometime during our stay in Liberty Jail an attempt was made to destroy us by poison. I supposed it was administered in either tea or coffee, but as I did not use either, I escaped unhurt, while all who did were sorely afflicted, some being blind two or three days, and it was only by much faith and prayer that the effect was overcome.

We never suffered ourselves to go into any important measure without asking Brother Joseph to inquire of the Lord in relation to it. Such was our confidence in him as a Prophet, that when he said "Thus saith the Lord," we were confident it would be as he said; and the more we tried it, the more confidence we had, for we never found his word fail in a single instance.

A short time before we were to go to Daviess county for trial, word came to us that either General Atchison or Doniphan, would raise a military force, and go with us to protect us from the wrath of that people. The matter was discussed by the brethren (except Brother Joseph), and they naturally enough concluded it would be best; and although I had nothing to say, I concurred with them in my feelings. Brother Hyrum asked Brother Joseph what he thought of it. Brother Joseph hung his head a few moments, and seemed in a deep study, and then raised up and said, "Brother Hyrum, it will not do; we must trust in the Lord; if we take a guard with us we shall be destroyed."

This was very unexpected to us, but Brother Hyrum remarked, "If you say it in the name of the Lord, we will rely on it." Said

Brother Joseph, "In the name of the Lord, if we take a guard with us, we will be destroyed; but if we put our trust in the Lord, we shall be safe, and no harm shall befall us, and we shall be better treated than we have ever been since we have been prisoners."

This settled the question, and all seemed satisfied, and it was decided that we should have no extra guard, and they had only such a guard as they chose for our safe keeping. When we arrived at the place where the court was held, I began to think he was mistaken for once, for the people rushed upon us en masse, crying, "Kill them, . . . them, kill them." I could see no chance for escape, unless we could fight our way through, and we had nothing to do it with. At this, Brother Joseph, at whom all seemed to rush, rose up and said, "We are in your hands; if we are guilty, we refuse not to be punished by the law." Hearing these words, two of the most bitter mobocrats in the country—one by the name of William Peniston and the other Kinney, or McKinney, I do not remember which—got up on benches and began to speak to the people, saying, "Yes, gentlemen, these men are in our hands; let us not use violence, but let the law have its course; the law will condemn them, and they will be punished by it. We do not want the disgrace of taking the law into our own hands."

In a very few minutes they were quieted, and they seemed now as friendly as they had a few minutes before been enraged. . . . This took place in the court-room (a small log cabin about twelve feet square), during the adjournment of the court; and from that time until we got away, they could not put a guard over us who would not become so friendly that they dare not trust them, and the guard was very frequently changed. We were seated at the first table with the judge, lawyers, etc., and had the best the country afforded, with feather beds to sleep on—a privilege we had not before enjoyed in all our imprisonment.

On one occasion, while we were there, the above-named

William Peniston, partly in joke and partly in earnest, threw out a rather hard insinuation against some of the brethren. This touched Joseph's feelings, and he retorted a good deal in the same way, only with such power that the earth seemed to tremble under his feet, and said, "Your heart is as black as your whiskers," which were as black as any crow. He seemed to quake under it and left the room.

The guards, who had become friendly, were alarmed for our safety, and exclaimed, "O, Mr. Smith, do not talk so; you will bring trouble upon yourself and companions." Brother Joseph replied, "Do not be alarmed; I know what I am about." He always took up for the brethren, when their characters were assailed, sooner than for himself, no matter how unpopular it was to speak in their favor.

Alexander McRae, in Joseph Smith, *History of the Church,* 3:258–59.

# "NOT ONE HAIR OF HIS HEAD SHALL BE HARMED"

LUCY MACK SMITH

About the first of August [1829], Samuel returned home [from Pennsylvania, where Joseph was staying], bringing us news of Joseph's success [in beginning the translation of the Book of Mormon]. This intelligence produced in Martin Harris a great desire to go down to Pennsylvania to see how they were prospering. This being made known to his wife, she resolved to prevent him from going, also to bring Joseph into difficulty, which would perhaps hinder him from ever accomplishing the work in which he was engaged.

To this end, she undertook to prove that Joseph never had the Record which he professed to have, and that he pretended to have in his possession certain gold plates, for the express purpose of obtaining money. Accordingly, she mounted her horse, rode from house to house through the neighborhood, like a dark spirit, making diligent inquiry wherever she had the least hopes of gleaning anything, and stirring up every malicious feeling which would tend to subserve her wicked purpose. Having ascertained the number and strength of her adherents, she entered a complaint against Joseph before a certain magistrate of Lyons. She then sent word to Lyman Cowdery, requesting him to come thither, prepared to go post haste to Pennsylvania (provided the decision should be given against Joseph), to assist the officers in securing and confining him in prison. This call Lyman Cowdery answered immediately, and all things seemed going on prosperously with Mrs. Harris. She made affidavit to many things herself and directed the officers whom to subpoena. Among the number was her husband, who was a principal witness in the case.

When the day of trial came on, the neighbors came and informed us, that the witnesses had gone to Lyons with the declared intention to obtain a verdict against Joseph, if it could be done by swearing. Immediately after our friends left, Hyrum came in, and I asked him what could be done.

"Why, mother," said he, "we can do nothing, except to look to the Lord: in him is all help and strength; he can deliver from every trouble."

I had never neglected this important duty, yet, seeing such confidence in my son, strengthened me in this hour of trial. Not being accustomed to lawsuits of this character, I trembled for the issue, for this was the first time a suit had ever been preferred before a court against any of my family. I retired to a secluded place, and poured out my whole soul in entreaties to God, for the safety of my son, and continued my supplication for some time; at length the spirit fell upon me so powerfully, that every foreboding of ill was entirely removed from my mind, and a voice spoke to me, saying, "not one hair of his head shall be harmed." I was satisfied. I arose, and repaired to the house. I had never before in my life experienced such happy moments. I sat down and began to read, but my feelings were too intense to allow me to do so. My daughter-in-law, Jerusha, came into the room soon after this, and when she turned her eyes upon me, she stopped short, and exclaimed, "Why! mother! what is the matter? I never saw you look so strangely in my life."

I told her, that I had never felt so happy before in my life, that my heart was so light, and my mind so completely at rest, that it did not appear possible to me that I should ever have any more trouble while I should exist. I then informed her in relation to the witness which I had received from the Lord.

In the evening the proceedings of the court were rehearsed to us, which were as follows:

The witnesses, being duly sworn, the first arose and testified, that Joseph Smith told him that the box which he had, contained nothing but sand; and he, Joseph Smith, said it was gold, to deceive the people.

Second witness swore, that Joseph Smith had told him that it was nothing but a box of lead, and he was determined to use it as he saw fit.

Third witness declared, that he once inquired of Joseph Smith what he had in that box, and Joseph Smith told him that there was nothing at all in the box, saying, that he had made fools of the whole of them, and all he wanted was to get Martin Harris' money away from him, and that he (witness) was knowing to the fact that Joseph Smith had, by his persuasion, already got two or three hundred dollars.

Next came Mrs. Harris' affidavit, in which she stated, that she believed the chief object which Joseph Smith had in view, was to defraud her husband out of all his property, and that she did not believe that Joseph Smith had ever been in possession of the gold plates which he talked so much about.

The magistrate then forbade the introduction of any more witnesses, until Martin Harris should be sworn. Martin being called upon, testified with boldness, decision and energy, to a few simple facts. When he arose he raised his hand to heaven, and said, "I can swear, that Joseph Smith never has got one dollar from me by persuasion, since God made me. I did once, of my own free will and accord, put fifty dollars into his hands, in the presence of many witnesses, for the purpose of doing the work of the Lord. This, I can pointedly prove; and I can tell you, furthermore, that I have never seen in Joseph Smith, a disposition to take any man's money, without giving him a reasonable compensation for the same in return. And as to the plates which he professes to have, gentlemen, if you do not believe it, but continue to resist the truth, it will one day be the means of damning your souls."

After hearing this testimony, the magistrate told them they need not call any more witnesses, but ordered them to bring him what had been written of the testimony already given. This he tore in pieces before their eyes, and told them to go home about their business, and trouble him no more with such ridiculous folly. And they did go home perfectly discomfited.

Lucy Mack Smith, *History of the Prophet Joseph Smith,* 143–46.

# "THE STARS SHALL FALL FROM HEAVEN"

PHILO DIBBLE

On one occasion Joseph was preaching in Kirtland sometime in the fall of 1833. Quite a number of persons were present who did not belong to the Church, and one man, more bitter and skeptical than others, made note with pencil and paper of a prophecy uttered on that occasion, wherein Joseph said that "Forty days shall not pass, and the stars shall fall from heaven."

Such an event would certainly be very unusual and improbable to the natural man, and the skeptic wrote the words as a sure evidence to prove Joseph to be a false Prophet.

On the thirty-ninth day after the utterance of that prophecy a man and brother in the Church, by the name of Joseph Hancock . . . and another brother were out hunting game and got lost. They wandered about until night, when they found themselves at the house of this unbeliever, who exultingly produced this note of Joseph Smith's prophecy, and asked Brother Hancock what he thought of his Prophet now, that thirty-nine days had passed and the prophecy was not fulfilled.

Brother Hancock was unmoved and quietly remarked, "There is one night left of the time, and if Joseph said so, the stars will certainly fall tonight. This prophecy will all be fulfilled."

The matter weighed upon the mind of Brother Hancock, who watched that night, and it proved to be the historical one, known in all the world as "the night of the falling of the stars."

He stayed that night at the house of the skeptical unbeliever, as it was too far from home to return by night, and in the midst of the falling of the stars he went to the door of his host and called him out to witness what he had thought impossible and the most improbable thing that could happen, especially as that was the last night in which Joseph Smith could be saved from the condemnation of "a false prophet."

The whole heavens were lit up with the falling meteors, and the countenance of the new spectator was plainly seen and closely watched by Brother Hancock, who said that he turned pale as death, and spoke not a word.

After that event the unbeliever sought the company of any Latter-day Saint. He even enticed Mormon children to keep him company at his house. Not long afterwards, too, he sent for Joseph and Hyrum to come to his house, which they did, but with no noticeable results, for I believe he never received the gospel.

*Juvenile Instructor,* 27:23.

# "I OFTEN FEEL TO LONG
# FOR MY DAY OF REST"

BENJAMIN F. JOHNSON

On one occasion, at Macedonia, after [the Prophet Joseph Smith] had preached to a large congregation through the day, and at evening meeting had blessed nineteen children, he said to me [Brother Johnson was serving as the Prophet's secretary], "Let us go home." We went home, and I found my wife sitting with our first born still unblessed and said, "See now what we have lost by our babe not being at meeting." Brother Joseph replied, "You shall lose nothing, for I will bless him too," which he did, and then sitting back heavily in a big chair before the fire, and with a deep-drawn breath said, "Oh! I am so tired—so tired that I often feel to long for my day of rest. For what has there been in this life but tribulation for me? From a boy I have been persecuted by my enemies, and now even my friends are beginning to join with them, to hate and persecute me! Why should I not wish for my time of rest?"

His words to me were ominous, and they brought a shadow as of death over my spirit, and I said, "Oh, Joseph! how could you think of leaving us? How as a people could we do without you?" He saw my feelings were sorrowful and said kindly, "Bennie, if I was on the other side of the veil I could do many times more for my friends than I can do while I am with them here."

Benjamin F. Johnson, *My Life's Review,* 97–98.

# "RIDE FOR YOUR LIFE"

## JOSEPH S. BARLOW

My grandfather, Israel Barlow, was a very trusted body-guard to the Prophet Joseph Smith. Shortly before the martyrdom (the exact date not being available), the Prophet called upon him and requested that he make a journey of many miles, on horseback, and deliver a message from the Prophet to a certain man who lived in a neighborhood of enemies to the Prophet and to the Latter-day Saints. He was asked to make special observations of what he might see and hear while on this mission.

It was a hazardous time in the history of the Church and the Prophet's life was constantly in jeopardy, not only from enemies without but within the Church. The Prophet told him to leave on this errand on a certain day, early in the morning, and ride to a certain man's home and there deliver the message. He was instructed to accept of their hospitality, which the Prophet Joseph assured him they would extend to him. "But," said the Prophet, "let them put your horse up for you and eat supper with them, but when it becomes sundown saddle your horse and leave. They will be insistent and try to persuade you to remain overnight, but if you value your life do not stay, but leave, and listen to the direction of the Spirit."

[Grandfather completed his errand and] left [the man's home] promptly at sundown and rode along the country road until it became dark. Just before he came to the river bridge, a voice said to grandfather, "Ride faster." He sped up his horse and the voice repeated again, with more emphasis, "Ride faster." Again he increased the speed of the animal when the voice said to him: "Ride for your life." He then sped for all the animal's strength. As the horse's feet clattered across the bridge he could hear the mob, which had gathered in the brush to intercept him, cursing at the top of their voices. He had crossed the bridge but a short distance when the voice said to him: "Turn to the right," and he turned his horse off the road into the brush toward the river. There he stood in silence as the mob, who had mounted their horses, came racing over the bridge at break-neck speed, and down the road they went, supposedly after him. After they had gone by he wound his way from the river's edge to the bed of the stream, and on through the willows. In the darkness he made his way along the river in the opposite direction from which the mob had expected him to go. Finally when he thought it was safe, several miles away, he emerged from the river and made his way over the country back into Nauvoo, just as the day was breaking.

There he saw the Prophet Joseph, walking up and down the street in front of his home. As grandfather approached and alighted from his horse, he began to tell the Prophet of his experience. The Prophet stopped him and told him he need not tell him for he already knew. The Prophet told him that he had been up all night, waiting for his return, and stated, "I saw it all, you have no need to tell me." Thereupon the Prophet laid his hand upon grandfather's shoulder and gave him a blessing and said: "Thee and thine shall never want."

---

Joseph S. Barlow, in N. B. Lundwall, comp., *Faith Like the Ancients*, 1:196–97.

# MIRACLES

# "I Want to See a
Notable Miracle"

### GEORGE A. SMITH

W hen The Church of Jesus Christ of Latter-day Saints
was first founded, you could see persons rise up and
ask, "What sign will you show us that we may be made
to believe?" I recollect a Campbellite preacher who came to
Joseph Smith, I think his name was Hayden. He came in and
made himself known to Joseph, and said that he had come a considerable distance to be convinced of the truth. "Why," said he,
"Mr. Smith, I want to know the truth, and when I am convinced, I
will spend all my talents and time in defending and spreading the
doctrines of your religion, and I will give you to understand that
to convince me is equivalent to convincing all my society, amount-
ing to several hundreds."

Well, Joseph commenced laying before him the coming forth
of the work, and the first principles of the Gospel, when Mr.
Hayden exclaimed, "O this is not the evidence I want, the evidence that I wish to have is a notable miracle; I want to see some
powerful manifestation of the power of God, I want to see a
notable miracle performed; and if you perform such a one, then I
will believe with all my heart and soul, and will exert all my power
and all my extensive influence to convince others; and if you will
not perform a miracle of this kind, then I am your worst and
bitterest enemy."

"Well," said Joseph, "what will you have done? Will you be
struck blind, or dumb? Will you be paralyzed, or will you have one

hand withered? Take your choice, choose which you please, and in the name of the Lord Jesus Christ it shall be done." "That is not the kind of miracle I want," said the preacher. "Then, sir," replied Joseph, "I can perform none, I am not going to bring any trouble upon any body else, sir, to convince you."

*Journal of Discourses,* 2:326–27.

# GOD WILL PROVIDE

ROBERT I. BURTON AND
RACHEL BURTON BALLANTYNE

At the time of the occurrence of the following incident, my parents lived in what now would be regarded as the direst poverty, for they rarely had sufficient food at any one meal to satisfy their hunger. A stew of "pig weed roots, nettles and dandelions" often supplemented the meager fare. My father was teaching school and a large number of the people, whose children attended the school, were in arrears in the payment of tuition. In the family there were several small children, which fact greatly increased the anxiety of my parents, as they saw the scant supply of flour rapidly decreasing.

Finally there came a day when the flour was all gone and they had no money with which to buy more. The children were hungry and cried for food. I have often tried to imagine what pangs my parents suffered under these circumstances. . . . Their suffering . . . must have been intense to see their children crying for food and to feel their inability to supply their wants.

Father took a flour sack and started out to visit those people who were owing him money, hoping that among the number he might be fortunate enough to find someone who could spare some flour to apply on his debt. Wherever he called, he found the people had generous hearts, but little flour. Almost without exception they would tell him to help himself to what they had, but at no home did he find more than a few pounds. Unwilling to take their small store, he would go on to the next house, hoping they would be better supplied, but always with the same result.

Toward evening, as he approached his home, weary and disheartened, the children came running to meet him, and to his amazement they were eating hot biscuits! To his question, "Where did you get the biscuits?" they replied, "Mama made them." Unable to get a satisfactory explanation from the children, he hastened to the house and asked my mother where she got the flour with which to make the biscuits. Pointing to a large, white, seamless sack, standing in the corner of the room, she replied, "Why, it's the flour you sent." "But," he replied, "I haven't sent any flour. I haven't seen that much flour all day."

They both realized, then, that something unusual had occurred. In answer to a question, she explained that two men, one much older than the other, had driven up to the front of the house and stopped. One of them came in and asked, "Is this where William Burton lives?" Upon her answering in the affirmative, he said, "We have some flour for him." He then returned to the wagon and the two men carried in the sack of flour. Mother was so amazed at seeing such a large quantity of flour that she was rather paralyzed into inactivity for a moment. Upon recovering herself, she hurried outside to thank the men and to ask them their names, but they were gone. "But," said Father, "you are acquainted with everyone who lives in this vicinity. You surely must know who they are." She insisted, however, that she had never seen them before.

Nor were my parents ever able to discover who these men were, whence they came, nor whither they went. . . .

At the time this incident occurred, and ever afterward in their memories, it was to my parents as much a divine manifestation of Providence in their behalf as was the manna from heaven to the children of Israel in the wilderness, or the Savior's feeding of the multitude with the five loaves and the two fishes.

Robert I. Burton and Rachel Burton Ballantyne, in N. B. Lundwall, comp., *Faith Like the Ancients,* 1:126–28.

# "THE RECORDS WERE SAVED"

## LUCILE C. READING

F ire! Fire!"

The warning cry brought fear to the hearts of all those who heard it in the little community of Farmington, Utah, for it usually meant complete destruction of whatever was burning. They had no equipment to fight fires, although everyone who could [do so] would form a line and pass buckets of water from the creek to the burning building.

At the first cry of "Fire," Aurelia [Spencer Rogers], who had just arrived in Farmington [for a visit], ran toward the house from which smoke was billowing up into the hot August air. It belonged to special friends of hers with whom she often stayed. . . .

Aurelia [joined] the water line. She thought of her friends' loss before she thought of her own. In the upstairs bedroom where she usually slept, she had left some clothes hanging in the closet. Then with a sick feeling she remembered she had also left on a table close to the window the Primary record books. These books contained the history of the very first Primary ever organized. "I mourned exceedingly," said Aurelia later. "I would not have minded losing my clothes . . . if the records could only have been saved."

Aurelia was heartsick as she returned to Salt Lake after helping her friends move into a nearby vacant house. But the loss of the record books haunted her, and in a few days she went back to Farmington to try to gather information to write another history of the organization of the Primary.

What thrilling news awaited her there! . . ."Brother Moroni Secrist, who was bishop of our ward at the time, felt prompted to climb onto the porch and go through the window to my room, thinking he might save some of the property; but when he went inside, the smoke was so dense he was nearly suffocated and had to be helped out by others who had followed. As he neared the window, he reached out his hand and felt the cover on the table and drew it toward him, gathering up the corners with the books and a box of notions that I had, and passed them to those on the outside. Thus the records were saved through the providence of God."

*Children's Friend,* August 1968, 15.

# "I Saw the Spirit Operate
# on That Man"

EZRA TAFT BENSON

I thought of our first interview with General McNarney, the top general in the American forces [after World War II]. It was in the I. G. Farbin building in Frankfurt, which had been spared by "pin bombing," because the Americans expected it would be their headquarters when the war was over, as it was.

We had driven our little jeep up to the building, parked it, and gone in to see if we could get an appointment with the general. We had been in Europe just a few days. We wanted to get permission from him to make our own distribution of our welfare supplies to our own people through our own channels. In those days, of course, everything was being distributed through the military. We were told by the colonel at the desk that we couldn't get an appointment for three days. The general was very busy, with important delegations coming to see him. We returned to our car and had a prayer together, then went back in. In the meantime, the secretary at the desk had been changed, and, in less than fifteen minutes, we were in the presence of General McNarney.

Then I saw the Spirit operate on that man. I heard him say, "Under no conditions can you have permission to distribute your own supplies to your own people. They must come through the military." And, of course, we recognized immediately that if we had to go through the military, our Saints wouldn't get much of the supplies. And so we started telling him about the program of the Church, and when he saw we were somewhat determined, he said, "Well, you go ahead and collect your supplies, and probably by the time you get them collected the policy will be changed." I said, "General, they are already collected; they are always collected. We have ninety warehouses full of supplies. Within twenty-four hours from the time I wire our First Presidency in Salt Lake City, carloads of food, bedding, clothing, and medical supplies will be moving toward Germany." When I said this, he said, "I never heard of people with such vision." And before we left him we had written authorization to make our own distribution to our own people through our own channels, and from that moment on we had wonderful cooperation.

So I know that the Spirit can operate on nonmembers of the Church in high positions when it is in the interests of the work of the Lord. I have seen it with my own eyes.

Ezra Taft Benson, *God, Family, Country*, 73–74.

# "WE SAW THE YOUNG MAN IN ABOUT TWELVE FEET OF WATER"

## EDWARD JAMES WOOD

I [would like to share] my experience on the islands of the Navigator Group, in 1889.

A young [missionary] from Provo . . . was told by his mother not to go in bathing. We had been accustomed to bathing every day in the ocean, and had become good swimmers before this young man arrived. I coaxed him to go in swimming with us in the ocean. Those of you who have come from the old country know what it looks like on the beach when the tide is out. Those islands are surrounded by a coral reef, and in the reef there are large holes, ten to eighteen feet deep, and when the tide is out, we wind our way, guarding ourselves from the holes, until we come to the edge of the reef. Then we dive out into deep water, where we used to anchor our boat.

I coaxed this young man to go. We got our bathing suits, and he followed me out. I wound my way through the coral reef, and swam out to where three others of our elders were. When I got there, one of the other brethren said, "Did not that brother follow you out?" I said, "Yes." But I looked around and could not see him anywhere. He had told me he could not swim, and I thought he was bathing in the shallow water.

We swam to the reef and hunted around and saw the young man in about twelve feet of water, in the attitude of prayer. We dove down, lifted his body up, and brought it up to the beach. Blood was coming from his ears and mouth and we could see that he was dead.

You can hardly imagine my feelings, feeling myself almost responsible for the death of that young man. The natives gathered around and said, "It is sacrilegious to work with a body after it is dead." But I suggested to the mission president that we take him into a house, dress him in his garments, and administer to him. Then I should feel more satisfied. We worked for over forty minutes with that young man's body, carried him onto the beach with his head down, his feet on my shoulders. No sign of life at all.

We laid his body on a table, with over five hundred natives witnessing the ceremony of the anointing with oil. We anointed him and we blessed him. I felt his eyes move under my hands, and he awoke and came to, and asked us to place him up on the table and he would tell us what he saw, "before I forget it," he said, "for I can feel it is going from me just like I might be leaving a room."

He said, "I called, when I got into deep water. You paid no attention to me, and the last thing that I thought of was of my mother's admonishing me to always pray in time of danger. When you took my body out of the water I was with you. When you walked up and down the beach I walked up and down with you. I saw my body. I prayed to God with all my soul that you would not bury me nor consider me dead until you exercised the power of your priesthood. I was told by something that it was the priesthood that had the power to return my spirit to my body. I watched you all the time. I wondered why you did not do it, having this glorious ordinance in the Church. You elders apparently were going to forget all about it. And oh, how glorious, when you exercised your priesthood and anointed me with oil in the name of the Son of God and through the priesthood which you had! As soon as you said that, my spirit body entered my physical body."

I am here to testify unto you what I know to be a positive fact.

---

Conference Report, April 1917, 130–31.

# MISSIONARY WORK

# "LET MY SERVANT HEBER GO TO ENGLAND"

EDWARD W. TULLIDGE

Mormon apostles and elders have deemed it as nothing to take missions to foreign lands, but in 1837, before the age of railroads and steamships had fairly come, going to Great Britain on a mission was very like embarking for another world; and the apostolic proposition to gather a people from foreign lands and many nations to form a latter-day Israel, and with these disciples to build up a Zion on this continent, was in seeming the maddest undertaking possible in human events. . . . [Such was the] apostolic picture of Heber C. Kimball "opening the door of salvation to the nations that sat in darkness"; and for the gathering of an Israel from every people and from every tongue.

*Vilate Kimball, Heber's wife wrote:*

"One day while Heber was seated in the front stand in the Kirtland temple, the prophet Joseph opened the door and came and whispered in his ear, 'Brother Heber, the spirit of the Lord has whispered to me, let my servant Heber go to England and proclaim the gospel, and open the door of salvation.'"

*Relative to this, Heber wrote in his journal:*

"The idea of being appointed to such an important mission was almost more than I could bear up under. I felt my weakness and was nearly ready to sink under it, but the moment I understood the will of my heavenly Father, I felt a determination to go at all hazards, believing that he would support me by his almighty power, and although my family were dear to me, and I should have to leave them almost destitute, I felt that the cause of truth, the gospel of Christ, outweighed every other consideration. At this time many faltered in their faith, some of the twelve were in rebellion against the prophet of God. John Boynton said to me, if you are such a d——d fool as to go at the call of the fallen prophet, I will not help you a dime, and if you are cast on Van Dieman's Land I will not make an effort to help you.

"Lyman E. Johnson said he did not want me to go on my mission, but if I was determined to go, he would help me all he could; he took his cloak from off his back and put it on mine. Brother Sidney Rigdon, Joseph Smith, Sr., Brigham Young, Newel K. Whitney and others said go and do as the prophet has told you and you shall prosper and be blessed with power to do a glorious work. Hyrum, seeing the condition of the church, when he talked about my mission wept like a little child; he was continually blessing and encouraging me, and pouring out his soul in prophecies upon my head; he said go and you shall prosper as not many have prospered."

*Sister Kimball continued:*

"A short time previous to my husband's starting, he was prostrated on his bed from a stitch in his back, which suddenly seized him while chopping and drawing wood for his family, so that he could not stir a limb without exclaiming, from the severeness of the pain. Joseph Smith hearing of it came to see him, bringing Oliver Cowdery and Bishop Partridge with him. They prayed for and blessed him, Joseph being mouth, beseeching God to raise him up, &c. He then took him by the right hand and said, 'Brother Heber, I take you by your right hand, in the name of Jesus Christ of Nazareth, and by virtue of the holy priesthood vested in me, I command you, in the name of Jesus Christ, to rise, and be thou made whole.' He arose from his bed, put on his clothes, and started with them, and went up to the temple, and felt no more of the pain afterwards.

"At length the day for the departure of my husband arrived. It was June 13th, 1837. He was in the midst of his family, blessing them, when Brother R. B. Thompson, who was to accompany him two or three hundred miles, came in to ascertain when Heber would start."

*In later years Brother Thompson wrote an account of the scene:*

"The door being partly open I entered and felt struck with the sight which presented itself to my view. I would have retired, thinking I was intruding, but I felt riveted to the spot. The father was pouring out his soul to

> That God who rules on high,
> Who all the earth surveys;
> That rides upon the stormy sky,
> And calms the roaring seas,

"that he would grant unto him a prosperous voyage across the mighty ocean, and make him useful wherever his lot should be cast, and that he who cared for the sparrows, and feted the young ravens when they cry, would supply the wants of his wife and little ones in his absence. He then, like the patriarchs, and by virtue of his office, laid his hands upon their heads individually, leaving a father's blessing upon them, and commending them to the care and protection of God, while he should be engaged preaching the gospel in foreign lands. While thus engaged his voice was almost lost in the sobs of those around, who tried in vain to suppress them. The idea of being separated from their protector and father for so long a time, was indeed painful.

"He proceeded, but his heart was too much affected to do so

regularly; his emotions were great, and he was obliged to stop at intervals, while the big tears rolled down his cheeks, an index to the feelings which reigned in his bosom. My heart was not stout enough to refrain; in spite of myself I wept and mingled my tears with theirs at the same time. I felt thankful that I had the privilege of contemplating such a scene. I realized that nothing could induce that man to tear himself from so affectionate a family group—from his partner and children who were so dear to him—but a sense of duty and love to God and attachment to his cause."

*Sister Vilate Kimball concluded:*

"At nine o'clock in the morning of this never-to-be-forgotten-day, Heber bade adieu to his brethren and friends and started without purse or scrip to preach the gospel in a foreign land. He was accompanied by myself and children, and some of the brethren and sisters, to Fairport. Sister Mary Fielding, who became afterwards the wife of Hyrum Smith, gave him five dollars, with which Heber paid the passage of himself and Brother Hyde to Buffalo. They were also accompanied by her and Brother Thompson and his wife (Mary Fielding's sister), who were going on a mission to Canada. Heber himself was accompanied to Great Britain by Elders Orson Hyde, Willard Richards, J. Goodson and J. Russell, and Priest Joseph Fielding."

Edward W. Tullidge, *Women of Mormondom,* 111–15.

# PARLEY PRATT'S MISSION TO CANADA

⌒

### EDWARD W. TULLIDGE

Here is the opening of the story of Parley P. Pratt's mission to Canada, in which a woman immediately comes to the foreground in a famous prophecy:

"It was now April [1836]. I had retired to rest," says he, "one evening, at an early hour, and was pondering my future course, when there came a knock at the door. I arose and opened it, when Heber C. Kimball and others entered my house, and being filled with the spirit of prophecy, they blessed me and my wife, and prophesied as follows: 'Brother Parley, thy wife shall be healed from this hour, and shall bear a son, and his name shall be Parley; and he shall be a chosen instrument in the hands of the Lord to inherit the priesthood and to walk in the steps of his father. He shall do a great work in the earth in ministering the word and teaching the children of men. Arise, therefore, and go forth in the ministry, nothing doubting. Take no thought for your debts, nor the necessaries of life, for the Lord will supply you with abundant means for all things.

"'Thou shalt go to Upper Canada, even to the city of Toronto, the capital, and there thou shalt find a people prepared for the fullness of the gospel, and they shall receive thee, and thou shalt organize the Church among them, and it shall spread thence into the regions round about, and many shall be brought to the knowledge of the truth, and shall be filled with joy; and from the things growing out of this mission, shall the fullness of the gospel spread into England, and cause a great work to be done in that land.'

"This prophecy was the more marvelous, because being married near ten years we had never had any children; and for near six years my wife had been consumptive, and had been considered incurable. However, we called to mind the faith of Abraham of old, and judging Him faithful who had promised, we took courage.

"I now began in earnest to prepare for the mission, and in a few days all was ready. Taking an affectionate leave of my wife, mother and friends, I started for Canada, in company with a Brother Nickerson, who kindly offered to bear expenses."

Away to Canada with Parley. We halt with him in the neighborhood of Hamilton. He is an entire stranger in the British Province, and without money. He knows not what to do. His narrative thus continues:

"The spirit seemed to whisper to me to try the Lord, and see if anything was too hard for him, that I might know and trust him under all circumstances. I retired to a secret place in a forest, and prayed to the Lord for money to enable me to cross the lake. I then entered Hamilton, and commenced to chat with some of the people. I had not tarried many minutes before I was accosted by a stranger, who inquired my name and where I was going. He also asked me if I did not want some money. I said yes. He then gave me ten dollars, and a letter of introduction to John Taylor, of Toronto, where I arrived the same evening.

"Mrs. Taylor received me kindly, and went for her husband, who was busy in his mechanic shop. To them I made known my errand to the city, but received little direct encouragement. I took tea with them, and then sought lodgings at a public house."

Already had he met in Canada a woman destined to bear a representative name in the history of her people, for she is none other than the wife of the afterwards famous apostle John Taylor. She is the first to receive him into her house; and the apostolic story still continues with the woman in the foreground:

"In the morning," he says, "I commenced a regular visit to each of the clergy of the place, introducing myself and my errand. I was absolutely refused hospitality, and denied the opportunity of preaching in any of their houses or congregations. Rather an unpromising beginning, thought I, considering the prophecies on my head concerning Toronto. However, nothing daunted, I applied to the sheriff for the use of the court-house, and then to the authorities for a public room in the market-place; but with no better success. What could I do more? I had exhausted my influence and power without effect. I now repaired to a pine grove just out of the town, and, kneeling down, called on the Lord, bearing testimony of my unsuccessful exertions; my inability to open the way; at the same time asking him in the name of Jesus to open an effectual door for his servant to fulfill his mission in that place.

"I then arose and again entered the town, and going to the house of John Taylor, had placed my hand on my baggage to depart from a place where I could do no good, when a few inquiries on the part of Mr. Taylor, inspired by a degree of curiosity or of anxiety, caused a few moments' delay, during which a lady by the name of Walton entered the house, and, being an acquaintance of Mrs. Taylor, was soon engaged in conversation with her in an adjoining room. I overheard the following:

"'Mrs. Walton, I am glad to see you; there is a gentleman here from the United States who says the Lord sent him to this city to preach the gospel. He has applied in vain to the clergy and to the various authorities for opportunity to fulfill his mission, and is now about to leave the place. He may be a man of God; I am sorry to have him depart.'

"'Indeed!' said the lady; 'well, I now understand the feelings and spirit which brought me to your house at this time. I have been busy over the wash-tub and too weary to take a walk; but I felt impressed to walk out. I then thought I would make a call on my sister, the other side of town; but passing your door, the spirit bade me go in; but I said to myself, I will go in when I return; but the spirit said, go in now. I accordingly came in, and I am thankful that I did so. Tell the stranger he is welcome to my house. I am a widow; but I have a spare room and bed, and food in plenty. He shall have a home at my house, and two large rooms to preach in just when he pleases. Tell him I will send my son John over to pilot him to my house, while I go and gather my relatives and friends to come in this very evening and hear him talk; for I feel by the spirit that he is a man sent by the Lord with a message which will do us good.'

"The evening found me quietly seated at her house," says Parley, "in the midst of a number of listeners, who were seated around a large work table in her parlor, and deeply interested in conversation like the following:

"'Mr. Pratt, we have for some years been anxiously looking for some providential event which would gather the sheep into one fold; build up the true Church as in days of old, and prepare the humble followers of the Lamb, now scattered and divided, to receive their coming Lord when he shall descend to reign on the earth. As soon as Mrs. Taylor spoke of you I felt assured, as by a strange and unaccountable presentiment, that you were a messenger, with important tidings on these subjects; and I was constrained to invite you here; and now we are all here anxiously waiting to hear your words.'

"'Well, Mrs. Walton, I will frankly relate to you and your friends the particulars of my message and the nature of my commission. A young man in the State of New York, whose name is Joseph Smith, was visited by an angel of God, and, after several visions and much instruction, was enabled to obtain an ancient record, written by men of old on the American continent, and containing the history, prophecies and gospel in plainness, as revealed to them by Jesus and his messengers. This same Joseph Smith and others, were also commissioned by the angels in these visions, and ordained to the apostleship, with authority to organize a church, to administer the ordinances, and to ordain others, and thus cause the full, plain gospel in its purity, to be preached in all the world.

"'By these apostles thus commissioned, I have been ordained as an apostle, and sent forth by the word of prophecy to minister the baptism of repentance for remission of sins, in the name of Jesus Christ; and to administer the gift of the Holy Ghost, to heal the sick, to comfort the mourner, bind up the broken in heart, and proclaim the acceptable year of the Lord.

"'I was also directed to this city by the spirit of the Lord, with a promise that I should find a people here prepared to receive the gospel, and should organize them in the same. But when I came and was rejected by all parties, I was about to leave the city; but the Lord sent you, a widow, to receive me, as I was about to depart; and thus I was provided for like Elijah of old. And now I bless your house, and all your family and kindred, in his name. Your sins shall be forgiven you; you shall understand and obey the gospel, and be filled with the Holy Ghost; for so great faith have I never seen in any of my country.'

"'Well, Mr. Pratt, this is precisely the message we were waiting for; we believe your words and are desirous to be baptized.'

"'It is your duty and privilege,' said I; 'but wait yet a little while till I have an opportunity to teach others, with whom you are religiously connected, and invite them to partake with you of the same blessings.'"

Edward W. Tullidge, *Women of Mormondom*, 216–22.

# "LET NO MAN DESPISE
# THY YOUTH"

BENJAMIN F. JOHNSON

When I came to Erie County, Pennsylvania, I put up at a tavern, and as I had traveled all day in the snow, and was very tired, I was just going to bed when it occurred to me that before I left home Colonel Harmon had asked me to call upon his friends in Erie County, Pennsylvania, if I ever went there. I had my slippers on, my candlestick in hand to go to my room, when the door opened and a man covered with snow came in and stood by the fire. Almost before I thought, I asked him if he knew any people named Barnes in that region. He said, "Yes, and you can go there right now if you wish to see any of them." I told him no, but their friends in the west wished me to inquire after them, and when I told him the names of their friends he was still more solicitous, insisting that I should go with him, and something said, "Go." I put on my boots, got my valise and rode eleven miles through the storm to the house of my companion, who was himself one of the Barnes. One of his sisters then living with him was a member of the Church (Huldah Barnes) and afterwards was sealed to President H. C. Kimball. When we arrived about 11 p.m., he told her he had a Mormon elder, cold and hungry, and although a large corpulent woman, her steps were nimble until all my wants were supplied.

The word at once went out that a Mormon elder had come, and all appeared anxious that I should preach. I did so the next day, and the day after I was taken by others of the kindred to

Union district, where I commenced to preach to a large congregation, and from there to a larger still. Here now a wide door for preaching was opening to me, but the enemy was not asleep. Soon the priests were out, came and filled the stand without invitation, with full expectation to overawe and squelch the Mormon boy.

I opened the meeting, and arose with very bashful and boylike feelings, and commenced to apologize for my youth, want of learning, etc. Just then at a point farthest from me in the congregation, an old man arose and said, "Young man, he that is good for excuses is good for but little else." Instantly the words of Paul to Timothy came to me, "Let no man despise thy youth." And those admonitions to me were never needed again. I spoke upon the Book of Mormon and the second coming of Christ with good liberty, after which Rev. Jesse E. Church, a great and noted preacher, arose and gave out an appointment to preach the next evening; said he would down all this Mormonism; that he had once challenged Sidney Rigdon, who would not meet him in debate. The next evening I attended his meeting, and made appointment for the next night, which was again crowded. He then appointed his meeting in his own neighborhood and I heard him again, gave an appointment for the next Sabbath at the same place, at which I invited any present who wished baptism to arise. Seven of his own members arose, and repairing to the creek and cutting through fifteen inches of ice, were baptized by the boy for whom he had shown such contempt.

---

Benjamin F. Johnson, *My Life's Review*, 78–80.

# "HOW DARE I SHRINK FROM
# MY CALLING?"

BENJAMIN F. JOHNSON

Here [in Erie Country, Pennsylvania,] lived Washington Walker, a Universalist, who took me to his house and made it my home while I remained in that country [as a missionary], often taking me in his sleigh or carriage to my appointments. He was a gentleman of culture, but of few words. At this time his sister, an eminent Presbyterian, came from Erie City to visit them. They took her to my appointments to hear Mormonism, in which she seemed to take a lively interest, and on one occasion said there was one subject that greatly interested her, on which she wanted light, and wished I would make it the subject of my next discourse. This was "Foreordination" or "Election and Reprobation."

If she had struck me with a club I could not have felt more stunned, dazed, and foolish. I felt that I must comply with her request, but how? In preaching the first principles of the gospel, the second coming of Christ, the gathering of Israel, Book of Mormon, etc., I was perfect, both in the letter and in the Spirit, but what did I know about predestination? I did not know its definition, or meaning, nor of election and reprobation. And I was expected to preach upon that subject. How could I without one gleam of light or some key of knowledge to inspire me?

I searched the scriptures and prayed, but no light came to me. The subject occupied my thoughts, and "foreordination" rang in my ear like a funeral knell. I wished to make excuse to the lady,

218

but how dare I shrink from my calling? Had I not professed that my capability to teach was from the Lord, and could I say I was not prepared? But oh, how dark it all was to me!

The day of meeting came, the hour was fast approaching, and the thought almost took my breath. I had not eaten, I had not slept, for predestination had occupied my thoughts night and day. I did not fear for myself, but for the great cause to be dishonored, perhaps by me. But the hours would not wait, the congregation had assembled, the house was full, and my feelings almost as dark as suicide.

I opened the meeting, arose, and mechanically, without a thought as to what I would read, opened the Bible and saw the first chapter to the Ephesians and read, "We were chosen from before the foundation of the world, to the adoption of children by Jesus Christ to the praise and glory of God." Here now was the key of knowledge, and with it came the light of the Lord to fill my whole being. . . .

[With new understanding] I presented and elucidated . . . a discourse delivered in a vehement and powerful manner, of over three hours' length, while the congregation sat as if riveted to their seats, and not a move did I notice from the time I arose, until I took my seat, and even yet all sat still as if in [amazement].

But though all seemed to wonder, the marvel of no one could equal my own. To me it was as though from Egyptian darkness I had been suddenly brought into the light of the sun. The heavens had seemed opened to me, and of all I was the one most instructed. I knew it was all of the Lord because I had not desired the light for my own praise and glory.

An old Methodist preacher came to me at the close and said, "My young friend, you have taken us beyond all of my comprehension but I cannot gainsay one word." The lady left the next day, seemed very thoughtful, and treated me with the greatest respect, but she was of wealth and position, and I thought was sorrowful that all the great things she had learned were through so low and poor a people as the Mormons.

Benjamin F. Johnson, *My Life's Review,* 80–82.

# "THE LORD WILL LOOSEN YOUR TONGUE"

### AMASA POTTER

I was introduced to the congregation as Elder Potter, with the remark that I would continue the subject of the gospel. I arose with fear and trembling; for it was the first time in my life that I had stood in a pulpit. Before me was a large Bible and prayer book. I must say that my mind was confused; but I took a text from the Bible that lay open before me. It was from the Prophet Amos:

"Surely the Lord God will do nothing, but he revealeth His secret unto His servants the prophets."

After reading it I spoke a few more words and became dumb that I could not speak. I stood there without speaking about two minutes, when the words of President Heber C. Kimball came to me: He said that the time would come when I should be at a loss to know what to say to the people "and, at that time," he said, "if you will commence to declare the divine mission of Joseph Smith in this our day, and the divine authenticity of the Book of Mormon, the Lord will loosen your tongue and you shall say the very things that are needful to be said to the people." When this came to my mind I commenced declaring these things to the congregation. I had spoken but a few minutes when I thought I saw several lines of large letters printed on the walls of the house, and I commenced to read them and spoke about one hour. When the letters faded from my sight I then stopped speaking. I could not tell all that I had said; but my companion told me it was an excellent discourse.

*Labors in the Vineyard,* 79.

# "I TOLD THEM OF
# THEIR WICKED DEEDS"

## WILFORD WOODRUFF

There were present [at a meeting in Memphis, Tennessee, during his mission] some five hundred persons who had come together, not to hear a gospel sermon but to have some fun.

Now, boys, how would you like this position? On your first mission, without a companion or friend, and to be called upon to preach to such a congregation! With me it was one of the most pleasing hours of my life, although I felt as though I should like company.

I read a hymn and asked them to sing. Not a soul would sing a word.

I told them I had not the gift of singing; but with the help of the Lord, I would both pray and preach. I knelt down to pray, and the men around me dropped on their knees. I prayed to the Lord to give me His Spirit and to show me the hearts of the people. I promised the Lord in my prayer I would deliver to that congregation whatever He would give to me. I arose and spoke one hour and a half and it was one of the best sermons of my life.

The lives of the congregation were opened to the vision of my mind, and I told them of their wicked deeds and the reward they would obtain. The men who surrounded me dropped their heads. Three minutes after I closed I was the only person in the room.

Wilford Woodruff, *Leaves from My Journal,* 17–18.

# "WE DID NOT HAVE ANY MONEY"

## AMASA POTTER

We had a large river to cross on the way, and we were informed that the bridge had been carried off and there was a ferry established across the river which charged five shillings each passenger. We did not have any money with which to pay this charge, and my companion was anxious to know what we should do for money to pay the ferriage with. We were then about three miles from the ferry, and were passing through timber. I told him that we would go into the woods and pray to God to open the heart of some one to give it to us. We did so, and we had traveled but a short distance through a lane between two fields, when we looked ahead of us a little way and saw an old man coming across the field. He came into the road ahead of us, and as he came to meet us he had a smile on his countenance. He reached out his hand to me, as if to shake hands, and left a crown, or five shilling piece, in my hand and went to my companion and did the same; but spoke not a word. I cannot describe the feeling that we had when the man took hold of our hands; we felt our hearts burn within us, and it did not seem that we had power to ask him his name or where he was from, as we usually did when a person gave us any article of clothing or money. He was a man about six feet high, well proportioned, and wore a suit of light gray clothes and a broad brimmed hat, and his hair and beard were about eighteen inches long and as white as snow. We passed on and came to the ferry, and the money that we had was just enough to pay our ferriage.

---

*Labors in the Vineyard,* 81.

# "GIVE US A SIGN"

BRYANT S. HINCKLEY

A large well-dressed and apparently influential man arose in the audience and addressing his remarks to Brother Morgan said, "Mr. Preacher, I have been much interested in your remarks and especially those that infer that signs will follow the believers. Now sir, I live in an adjoining county; have lived there for many years and am what you would call a really influential man among the people, but I want to say to you now that after what you have just said, unless you can give us a sign right here and now I am warning you that it would really be unpleasant for you to ever visit our community. I will see to it that you are handled pretty roughly and driven out." Thereupon Brother Morgan, in answer to the man's request, quoted the saying of the Savior to the effect that a wicked and adulterous generation seeketh after a sign, and he further said that what applies to a generation applies to a community, what applies to a community applies to an individual and "Sir, I am amazed that a man of your standing and influence would stand up before this large audience of several hundred people and proclaim yourself an adulterer."

The man, terribly enraged at Brother Morgan's rebuttal, started with an oath toward the pulpit with the intention of doing bodily injury to the elder. He hadn't gone far when an officer of the law arose. He was dressed in his official uniform and in a stern voice commanded the enraged man to return to his seat. Then turning to Brother Morgan, he said, "Mr. Preacher, I happen to be the Chief of Police in the city in which this man lives, and it is very apparent that when you stated that he was a self-confessed adulterer, you hit him in a vulnerable spot. The fact is," continued the Chief of Police, "that it was only last month that I arrested this man for that offense in our town and when taken before the court, he pleaded guilty to the charge." The man seeking for a sign, according to Brother Morgan, sneaked out a side door and he continued with his sermon.

Bryant S. Hinckley, *Faith of Our Pioneer Fathers*, 251–52.

# "I WAS PREPARED . . . IN THE HAWAIIAN LANGUAGE"

## JOSEPH F. SMITH

I was set apart [for my mission to Hawaii] under the hands of Parley P. Pratt and Orson Hyde, Parley being mouth. He declared that I should obtain a knowledge of the Hawaiian language "by the gift of God, as well as by study." Up to this time my schooling had been extremely limited. My mother taught me to read and write, by the camp fires, and subsequently by the greater luxury of the primeval tallow-candle in the covered wagon and the old log cabin, 10x12 feet in size, when first the soles of our feet found rest, after the weary months of travel across the plains. When I say, therefore, that within four months after my arrival on the Sandwich Islands—two weeks of which time were consumed by the most severe sickness I had ever known—I was prepared to enter upon the duties of my ministry, and did so with a native companion, with whom I made a tour of the Island of Maui, visiting, holding meetings, blessing children, administering the sacrament, etc., all in the Hawaiian language, it may be inferred that Parley's promise upon my head was literally fulfilled.

Joseph F. Smith, in B. H. Roberts, *New Witnesses for God*, 3:245.

# "PREACH SHORT SERMONS"

## GEORGE A. SMITH

When I was first called upon by the Prophet to go and preach the gospel, I received a little good advice, which I have endeavored to profit by ever since, and that too, to the best of my ability.

In the morning, as I was about to start on my first mission to preach the gospel, I waited upon brother Joseph, and asked if he had any advice to give me. "Yes," said he, "George A., preach short sermons, make short prayers, deliver your sermons with a prayerful heart, and you will be blessed, and the truth will prosper in your hands." I was a boy of seventeen at the time, and I called this my college education. . . .

But I ought to make some acknowledgment and confessions probably. I well remember the first time I ever broke those instructions; I was preaching in Virginia, in the County of Tyler. There was a . . . preacher by the name of West, that would follow me wherever I went, and when I got through preaching he would get up to burlesque me, and he would talk for an hour or two, and then he would get his congregation to sing, but with all he could do he could not get more than thirty or forty to come and hear him preach, whereas I had from three to four hundred attentive hearers.

So on one certain occasion he came with his . . . friends to the meeting, and I invited him to preach first, but no—he said he was "going to preach just as soon as I got through;" so I said to myself, "You will have to wait a pretty considerable spell, old gentleman;" and I then selected and read one of the longest chapters I could find in the Bible, and read it slowly; then read a long hymn and lined it off, and got the preacher to sing it for me, after which I preached about two hours and a half. I saw the preacher was in a terrible great hurry to get a chance to speak; the reason was, there were many at the meeting who had come from 10 to 30 miles on purpose to hear me, the country being very thinly settled, and some of them would have turned their pigs out of the pen if they had known West was going to preach in it, and the very moment I had done speaking, he jumped up and said he wanted to preach before I dismissed the congregation. When he commenced about 300 of the congregation left.

---

*Journal of Discourses*, 3:24–26.

# "THE PLACE HE HAD SEEN IN HIS DREAM"

⌒

BRYANT S. HINCKLEY

John Morgan's first home in Salt Lake City was with the family of Joseph L. Heywood, bishop of the Seventeenth Ward. He was not, at this time, a member of the LDS Church nor had he given it much consideration. One morning, on coming down to breakfast, he related to Mrs. Heywood an impressive dream he had had during the night in which he dreamed that he was back in North Georgia near the battlefield of Chickamauga, where he had fought in the Civil War, and he was traveling southward on a road running from Chattanooga, Tennessee, to Rome, Georgia. He was perfectly familiar with the road, as it was one the soldiers had used many times.

In this dream he suddenly came to a fork in the road and for a moment was undecided as to which fork led to Rome. Then he was amazed to see President Brigham Young standing in front of a large tree in the fork. President Young told him the right-hand road led to Rome, but that if he would take the left-hand road, he would have an experience that would give him a strong and abiding testimony of the divinity of the Book of Mormon. Laughingly, he asked Mrs. Heywood what she thought of it. "I am not interested in the Book of Mormon or its divinity, but I am interested in knowing what you think of my dream."

Mrs. Heywood answered: "Mr. Morgan, I think I can give you some light concerning your dream. It is my conviction that the time is not far distant when you will become a member of our

Church and that in due time you will be called to do missionary work in the Southern States. It is my thought that in your missionary work you will one day be following the road and will arrive at the fork you saw in your dream—but President Young will not be there. However, I counsel you to remember his instructions and take the road that will lead to the left."

Mr. Morgan thanked Mrs. Heywood for her interpretation of his dream and soon forgot about it.

A year later John Morgan became a convert to Mormonism and was baptized.

Ten years later while traveling as a missionary from Chattanooga, Tennessee, to Rome, Georgia, he came to a fork in the road that confused him and caused him to stop. He was undecided as to which of the two roads might lead to Rome. As he was pondering, he suddenly realized that the fork in the road that lay before him was the identical place he had seen in his dream when he resided in the Heywood home in Salt Lake City ten years before. The large tree in the fork was there, but as Sister Heywood had predicted, President Young was not there; however, he vividly recalled the counsel given in the dream not to take the right-hand road, which he said led to Rome, but to follow the left-hand road, which would lead him to a remarkable experience from which he would gain a testimony of the divinity of the work in which he was engaged and a knowledge of the divine teachings of the Book of Mormon. Thrilled with his experience, he took the left-hand road and continued his journey. After an hour's walk, the road led him to the rim of a beautiful valley in North Georgia. From a passerby, he learned that the name of the place was Heywood Valley, having the same spelling as the Heywood family, and that it was settled and farmed by some twenty-three prosperous families.

In high spirits he traveled on and called at the first house he came to, where he was received with true southern hospitality.

Filled with the spirit of his mission, he spent the entire evening in gospel conversation. Three hours were engaged in his effort to explain the first principles of the gospel to his newly made friends. As the interview closed, the head of the house brought out the family Bible, and, to Elder Morgan's amazement, he found that many of the passages of scripture that he had used in explaining the principles of the gospel were underscored; and in asking who had marked the passages, he was advised that ten days before, a kindly looking man in very tidy apparel, and seemingly possessed of great intelligence, had come to their home and had, with their permission, marked their Bible, explaining to them that another would come in a few days who would teach them the meaning of the marked passages and explain to them in its completeness the great plan of salvation. They knew not who the stranger was—his name, or whence he came, or where he went.

During the following six weeks, Elder Morgan called successively on each of the families in Heywood Valley; and in every home where the stranger had called and had marked the family Bible and had indicated that another would soon visit them and explain to them the scriptures in their fullness, he was successful in converting and baptizing the inhabitants thereof until all but three families were led into the water of baptism. Among those converted was a Methodist pastor, who was made the presiding elder of the Heywood Branch, and the building he had previously used as a Methodist church now became a Mormon meetinghouse.

---

Bryant S. Hinckley, *Faith of Our Pioneer Fathers,* 242–44.

# A CONVERSION IN CORNWALL

## AUTHOR UNKNOWN

The various gifts of the gospel were perhaps enjoyed to as great an extent by the Elders who labored in England in an early day as they have been by any people and in any place, at least in this dispensation. Nor were the manifestations of these gifts confined to the Elders who were engaged in the ministry, for their converts also enjoyed them to a very great extent. . . .

Brother Halliday . . . relates [an] instance in which the power of God was displayed in a rather remarkable manner . . . :

He and Elder John Chislett were sent to Penzance, Cornwall, to introduce the gospel to the inhabitants. They met with no encouragement, yet they did not feel justified in leaving the place until they had given the people a thorough warning. Their funds were so low that the two of them were forced to live on a penny's worth of bread and a penny's worth of soup per day; yet their faith was strong, and they spent much of their time in prayer. Finally, as a last resort, in the effort to awaken an interest in the message they had to bear to the people, they decided to give a course of public lectures. Elder Halliday pawned his watch to raise the necessary money to rent a hall and publish some placards announcing their meetings, and on the first evening appointed they were gratified at seeing a few come to hear them. Among the audience they noticed particularly a well-dressed gentleman and lady, the latter of whom commenced weeping almost as soon as she entered the hall and continued to do so as long as the meeting lasted.

The Elders, of course, could assign no reason for this peculiar conduct while the meeting was in progress, nor were they any more enlightened when, at the close of the services, the lady came forward with her husband and invited them to visit her at her home at St. Just, about six miles distant. This was the first invitation they had received from anyone in the place, and they accepted it joyfully, and would willingly have gone home with her that night, but, to their disappointment, she named the following Wednesday as the time when she would be pleased to receive them. Nothing further passed between them, but it was evident that a favorable impression had been made upon her, and that she was a woman of intelligence and refinement. While anticipating the pleasure of visiting her and waiting for the day to arrive, the Elders continued to subsist upon their scanty fare, and spent their time in vainly endeavoring to proselyte among the citizens of Penzance.

Wednesday morning came and with it a drenching rain storm, through which the Elders tramped the whole six miles, hungry and penniless. Shortly before arriving at St. Just, and while they were crossing a plowed field, with the mud clinging to their boots so they could scarcely walk, the Lord deigned to comfort them by giving Elder Halliday the gift of tongues and the interpretation of the same, in which it was made known to him that the lady whom they were going to visit had been favored with a vision in which she had seen himself and Elder Chislett; also that she was the owner of several houses, one of which she was going to allow them to use to hold meetings in, and that he was going to baptize her that very night.

As soon as this had passed through his mind, for he had not spoken aloud, but to himself, he joyfully slapped his companion on the shoulder and exclaimed, "Cheer up, John! I have had a revelation!" He then proceeded to relate all that had been revealed to him.

When they arrived at the house they were drenched as badly as if they had been in a river. Even their boots were full of water, so that when they pulled them off and turned the tops downward it ran out of them in a stream. Their friend, however, had been anxiously looking for them, and had prepared a blazing fire to warm them and spread the table with tempting food. She also proposed for them to change their clothes as far as she could supply them with dry ones to put on from her husband's wardrobe. "But," said she, "I can hardly wait for you to change your clothes, I am so anxious to talk to you."

"Oh, you need not be in such a hurry," remarked Elder Halliday, "for I know what you are going to say!"

She looked at him in surprise and inquired how he knew.

"Why," he said, "I have had it revealed to me on the way here." He then related to her every particular as it had been made known to him, until he got to that part relating to her baptism, when she interrupted him by exclaiming in surprise to her husband:

"There, now, is that not just as it occurred? How could he have learned that? for you know I have not talked with anyone but you about it!" She then admitted that the week previous, while lying awake in bed, she saw a bright light in the room and awoke her husband and pointed it out to him. He also saw it, and it passed around the room in the direction of Penzance, to which place it led her in her mind, and there she saw two men trying to raise a standard, in which labor the people who looked on seemed unwilling to lend a helping hand. She reproached them for their lack of interest, and took hold herself to assist. This vision was so plain that she afterwards related the whole of it to her husband and even described the appearance of the men. Then she could not rest until she had, in company with her husband, visited Penzance and attended the lecture she there saw announced. As soon as she entered the hall and saw the two elders she recognized them and could not refrain from crying. As to the other part of what had been revealed to him, she said it was true that she was the owner of a row of houses, which she pointed out to the elders, and that the last one was a school-house in which her husband taught school, and which they were welcome to use as a meeting house as long as they wanted to free of charge.

"But," said Elder Halliday, "that is not all that the Lord revealed to me. He told me that I was going to baptize you before I went to bed to-night, and now I want your husband to go and find some water for that purpose."

Brother Halliday, in telling what had been revealed to him, felt a good deal as he imagined the prophet Jonah must have felt when the Lord commanded him to go to Nineveh and declare the destruction of that city. He had before him the fear of being declared a false prophet, and it required a great deal of faith in him to tell it, especially that part relating to her baptism. However, he was soon relieved on that score, for the good lady expressed her readiness and anxiety to go immediately and be baptized. But her husband declared there was not a stream or pond in that region deep enough to baptize a person in, and it would be no use for them to think of doing such a thing that day. "Is there not a ditch or hollow anywhere around here that is deep enough?" said Elder Halliday. "Please go and see."

The husband complied with a dubious look on his face, while the elders proceeded to change and dry their clothes, and soon he returned and reported that the heavy shower which had fallen had so filled all the ditches and low places that they would have no difficulty in finding water deep enough.

Within two hours from the arrival of the elders the lady was baptized and confirmed, she being the first one to embrace the gospel in the region known as "Land's End."

The elders ever found a home at her house and enjoyed the

privilege of holding meetings in her school-house for years, and she remained faithful, but her husband, although he was kind to the elders and willing to entertain them, never joined the Church.

―――――

*Early Scenes in Church History,* 32–35.

# A BURNING DESIRE TO SPEAK

ANDREW JENSON

E lder Gearsen Bastian] had much difficulty in acquiring the language [during his mission to Denmark], and after a few weeks he became discouraged, and thought it impossible for him to learn the language. But the Lord gave him a marvelous manifestation of His power. His missionary companion was released to return home, and Elder Bastian was left in charge of the Randers branch. Only once had he attempted to speak before the public and he was not able to say but a very few words. Sunday came, and at the appointed time for worship the meeting hall was well filled. After the opening exercises he called upon one of the native Elders to speak, but he had only occupied a few minutes, when a burning desire to speak filled the soul of Elder Bastian. He arose, and under the influence and power of God he preached the gospel with much plainness in the Danish language for an hour and twenty minutes. At the close of the meeting the native brethren and sisters all flocked around him to congratulate him;

and they claimed that he had spoken the language with as much plainness as they could have spoken; and they rejoiced greatly. But as yet he could not converse with them; nevertheless the Lord had given to him a testimony that he should henceforth have freedom and power in preaching the gospel.

Andrew Jenson, *LDS Biographical Encyclopedia*, 3:667.

# "THE LANGUAGE HAS STAYED WITH ME"

O. ORLANDO BARRUS

I always had a desire to fulfill a mission and at the age of twenty-three I accepted a call for a mission to the Samoan Islands. Prior to my leaving for this mission Brother Samuel Woolley (a patriarch in Grantsville) gave me a blessing, wherein he said: "You shall be given the gift of the language and shall speak it fluently." Upon arriving in Salt Lake City, Apostle Heber J. Grant set me apart for this mission and in doing so he said, among other things, "You shall go in peace and return in safety, and you shall be given the gift of the language and you shall speak it fluently, even as a ready writer."

On August the 18th, 1893, I, with other elders, boarded the *Monowai* at San Francisco, and after one week's sailing we landed at Honolulu where we remained nine hours, at the end of which time we continued our journey to Samoa, where we landed at the end of another week. The Samoans came out to meet the boat in the Apia Harbor. They had coral and sea shells, etc., to sell and I wondered if I could ever learn to talk the language they were using. Pres. George Browning and two other elders also came out with a rowboat and took me to Fagalii, where I stayed for about three months, painting the mission house for Pres. Browning, at the end of which time I was sent to Tutuila and was then sent out among the natives. Elder Frank Vancott was my companion. He had been there nearly three years and spoke the language fluently. The first meeting Elder Vancott held after my arrival was on Thursday, this being a testimony meeting. After singing and prayer, Elder Vancott arose and said something to the congregation, which numbered about thirty Samoans. They began arising and bearing their testimonies.

I did not understand what Elder Vancott said, neither did I understand what the natives said as they arose and spoke in their Samoan tongue, but after about thirty minutes had expired I felt impressed to arise and could not resist the prompting. As I have said, I did not know the language, even enough of it to ask for something to eat, but I was just put on my feet and given the gift of the Samoan language just as Patriarch Woolley and Pres. Grant had said it would be. I started out by quoting the words of John 14th Chapter and 6th verse of Revelations, in which he says: "And I saw another angel flying in the midst of heaven having the everlasting gospel to proclaim unto them that dwell on the earth," and in Samoan it was as follows:

"Na au iloa le tasi angelu us lele i le tau loto aiga a le lagi, ia te ia le tala lellei, a faavavau a folafola atu ie, nonofo i le lalolagi."

Then I said, this angel has come and brought the gospel to the earth just as John the Revelator said he would. He brought it to a young man by the name of Joseph Smith in America and I have come down here 5,000 miles to tell you about it. I continued to talk in their language for about fifteen minutes, telling them about the Angel Moroni bringing the Book of Mormon to Joseph Smith, etc., which contained the everlasting gospel. When I sat down Elder Vancott arose and said that Elder Barrus had spoken in tongues. He said this was the same gift that was enjoyed on the day of Pentecost when Peter arose and spoke and they all understood in their own language.

The peculiar thing about it was that I could understand then everything he said to them in Samoan but I could not understand what he said at the beginning of the meeting. The natives came around me and congratulated me and I could understand them, and thanked them. I occupied all of the time in the afternoon meeting the following Sunday, speaking their language with the greatest of ease. . . .

I continued to speak, read and write the Samoan language from that hour when I arose in meeting until now, and that has been more than fifty years ago. Just recently I borrowed Elder Quinney's Samoan Book of Mormon, and I read it and enjoyed it immensely as it was not printed in the Samoan language when I was in Samoa; but the language has stayed with me for these fifty years.

---

O. Orlando Barrus, in N. B. Lundwall, comp., *Faith Like the Ancients*, 1:21–23.

# "Father Went on His Mission"

## EZRA TAFT BENSON

A rich blessing for the entire family came as a complete surprise to all. It was during the time, many years ago, when sacrament meeting was held at 2:00 p.m. in the rural wards. We usually went to meeting in the white-top buggy, which would hold the entire family. But at this particular time there was an epidemic—chicken pox, I believe—in the ward. Parents were to attend sacrament meeting, but the children were to stay home. So Father and Mother went to meeting in the one-horse buggy.

As Father and Mother returned from sacrament meeting and we all gathered around the buggy, we saw something we had never seen before in our home. Both Father and Mother were crying at the same time—and they had just returned from sacrament meeting. Being the oldest, I asked what was wrong. Mother assured us everything was all right. "Then why are you crying?" we asked. "Come into the house and we'll tell you all about it."

As we gathered around the old sofa in the living room, they explained why they were in tears. When sacrament meeting was over, the storekeeper opened the store just long enough for the farmers to get their mail, as the post office was in the store. There was no R.F.D. in those days, and opening the store briefly saved a special trip to the post office.

As our parents proceeded homeward, Father driving and Mother opening the mail, there was a letter from Box B in Salt Lake City. This was a call to go on a mission. No one asked if you were able, ready, or willing to go. The bishop was expected to know and the call came without warning.

Then Mother explained that they were happy and grateful that Father was considered worthy to fill a mission. Then Father explained, "We're crying a bit because we know it means two years of separation, and your mother and I have never been separated more than two nights at a time in all of our married life, and that has been when I've been in the canyon for poles, fence posts, or derrick timbers."

Father went on his mission, leaving Mother at home with seven children. The eighth was born four months after he left. In preparation, the small dry farm was sold to finance the mission. A family moved into part of our expanded farm home to rent the row cropland. We children, under Mother's day-to-day encouragement and Father's letters of blessings, took care of the dairy herd and the hay and pastureland.

You can well imagine who had the hardest end of that mission. But not once did we ever hear a murmur from Mother's lips as she would sing at her work the ballads of youth and the songs of Zion she and Father had enjoyed so much in the ward choir. In fact, my first baby tending—we call it sitting now—I remember was as a boy of seven years tending my younger brothers and sisters while Father and Mother went to choir practice on Wednesday evenings.

It was hard work, but a rich two years. Letters from Father from what seemed to us far away—Davenport, Iowa; Springfield, Illinois; Chicago; Cedar Rapids; etc.—coupled with family prayer and unity brought into that home a spirit of missionary work that never left it. Later, seven sons went on missions from that home, some of them on two or three missions.

Many years later at the bedside of that noble mother, who, as Father confided to me as the oldest child, had only a few weeks unless the Lord intervened, I heard her farewell words to her fifth son as he left for his mission. "Remember, George, no matter what happens at home, I want you to stay and finish your mission." A few weeks later a telegram from the First Presidency to President LeGrand Richards of the Southern States Mission told of her passing. And a year later a second telegram told of the passing of Father. But true to the wish of his mother and the missionary spirit of that true Latter-day Saint home, George stayed and finished his mission, and a summer later he returned to his old field of labor on a short-time mission. In the brief will, first call on the modest assets was provision for missions for the two younger sons.

My father, who as a young man had helped to support several of his twelve brothers and sisters on missions also, was spoken of by a prominent citizen, state senator, and nonmember of the Church in these words: "Gentlemen, today we buried the greatest influence for good in Cache Valley." How grateful we eleven children are for parents who always, by word and example, were faithful to the great missionary call of the Master.

---

Ezra Taft Benson, *God, Family, Country,* 52–55.

# "THE GREATEST EDUCATION
# IN THE WORLD"

HEBER J. GRANT

I was talking once with Captain John Codman, who owned a sailing vessel before the time of steam. He had sailed over many seas. He had had all kinds of adventures and experiences and was acquainted with all kinds of people. He also had become quite a noted magazine writer, furnishing articles to many of the leading magazines of the country. Finally he suffered from asthma, and he discovered he was better at Soda Springs, Idaho, than at any other place. And having abundance of money, he bought four or five horses, bought a little cottage there, and used to come to Soda Springs just as early as he could in the spring, and stay just as late as he could on account of the cold and snows.

He averaged spending about seven months a year at Soda Springs, and I became acquainted with him here in Salt Lake City; had some business dealings with him, and it so happened that the money that he placed in my hands as a young man of twenty-two or three, to invest for him, turned out very well. In one investment of about two thousand dollars, he made some twenty thousand out of it, and we became very familiar.

During the three years I was at Soda Springs every summer with a sick wife, I became quite intimate with him, and he said to me once, "Grant, the greatest education in the world comes from your missionary system." "Why," he said, "there is nothing like it; I am convinced that the average Mormon boy who goes out for three years to proclaim your gospel comes home improved better than he would have been if he had gone through the best university in all the world; there is nothing like it. I never was more astonished in my life than to discover the growth in your young men who go out as missionaries."

He gave me an example. He said, "There was my stable boy, currying my horses. Why, when I heard he was called on a mission to Germany, I laughed and said, 'That boy will never even learn the German language; he is not bright enough to learn a difficult language, I am sure.' He had been away about a year and a half when I got a letter from him. He had run across some of my relatives over there who had gone to Germany to live for a few years to put their children in school to get a certain education and to acquire the German language practically, by coming in contact with the actual Germans. When he heard they were relatives of mine, he thought he would get a letter of introduction from me to them, and I thought of what my cultured relatives would think of him, and I said, 'I am not going to give the ignoramus a letter.' But afterwards I thought if he was fool enough to ask for it, I would give it to him. So I sent it.

"Pretty soon I got a letter in answer from my folk, thanking me for introducing the young Mormon; that he was a very bright, intelligent young fellow, and they had thoroughly enjoyed his visit.

"I decided when he returned home I would go and hear him preach. I thought it would be a joke. He came home in another year and a half, and I went to hear him speak. He gave as logical a sermon and made his points from the standpoint of your faith as well as any one could. Why, he was away ahead of fellows who go to theological seminaries for years, and I was astounded. Now I always go to hear the boys from Soda Springs when they come back from missions. I have never been disappointed. It is wonderful."

I said, "It is not so wonderful when you stop to think that they are taught by the inspiration of the Lord."

He said, "Rubbish, rubbish."

"Well," I said, "you say they progress more rapidly than in the finest universities in the world; where do they get the progress, if it is not from the spirit of the living God that attends them in their labors?"

*Young Women's Journal,* 30:357–58.

# "I WANT YOU TO GO TO WOLF POINT"

### BRIGHAM S. YOUNG

We sometimes think that the missionaries are subjected to great sacrifice. I have an instance in mind. There is in the mission a young woman. She comes from Sevier county. Her name is Velma Nebeker. She is educated, beautiful, and possesses all of the requisites not only for a successful missionary but for a woman fitted to occupy the highest social position, a woman who some day will make her mark and write her name large in the history of this community. She is a paragon of excellence as respects appearance and dress.

The mission needed a teacher on the Indian reservation at Wolf Point [Montana], a most forbidding place. Our Church sits on a little hill, wind-swept. It is desolate. It is on the great arid bottoms of the Missouri river, mostly of mud, stunted cottonwoods, and poor growth of grass. Inhabiting that particular part of the country is a tribe of Indians, and there has been established among them, or was established during the days of Elder Ballard, of the Council of the Twelve, an Indian school. We have an enrollment of nearly thirty pupils, and we teach from the primary up to the sixth grade.

This young woman, among her other accomplishments is a school teacher. The mission needed just her stamp of woman for the performing of the duties necessary to the instructing of those little Indian children.

I called her into the office. I had been praying for a month as to the selection that should be made, because I recognized its importance. And when I called her into the office—Wolf Point is the most abhorrent to all the missionaries, because it is the most difficult and sacrificial place in which to labor—and said to her, "Miss Nebeker, I want you to go to Wolf Point," her face blanched. The tears shot from her eyes, but she set her teeth and said, "I'll go."

She went, and I said to her before she departed, "I want to say to you that when you return from your mission you will say—and I know it now as well as I shall know it in the future—that your labors in Wolf Point have been the very crown of your missionary labor." She is a heroine, and you men and women, parents in Israel, have hundreds of young people out in the mission who are just like that. They do not hesitate at any duty. There is no sacrifice they are called upon to perform that they do not go willingly, depending upon the Almighty not only for the knowledge that they disseminate but for their food and their shelter.

—————

Conference Report, October 1923, 124.

# "I Spoke in the Dutch Language"

## ALONZO A. HINCKLEY

One day, when I was alone, visiting among the people at Rotterdam, it was my duty to go back to the homes in which I had left tracts and repossess the literature. As I went I gathered the booklets, [and] some power that I cannot understand, possessed me until I quaked and trembled. I stood and looked at the house at which I was to call and felt as if I could not go to the door. But I knew my duty and so, with fortitude and determination, I went to the house, raised the knocker and dropped it. Almost instantly, the door opened and an irate woman stepped out and closed it behind her. She talked in a very loud shrill voice, berating me most severely.

I did not realize for a moment, that I was understanding Dutch as clearly as though she had spoken English. I felt no supernatural power, or influence, or feeling. I just knew every word she was saying. She spoke so loud that a carpenter, who was working across the street, building a porch on a little store, heard her and, I supposed, thought I was abusing the woman, for he came over to where we stood and brought his son with him and, greatly to my alarm, he carried a broadax. The man took his position near me and listened to the woman, who continued her tirade against me in a shouting voice.

I did not grow angry at the woman's abuse, but my soul was filled with a burning desire to speak her language and testify of the divinity of the gospel of the Lord Jesus Christ. I thought if I could only explain to her the importance of my message and the good it would do her, she would not berate me as she does now.

In a few moments she ceased her abuse, and I began speaking. I spoke in the Dutch language. I defended the truth and bore testimony of the restoration of the Gospel.

I had forgotten the big man who stood near me with his ax, and I looked at the woman and delivered my message of truth; he put his arm across my shoulders and, looking the woman in the face, said, "The Mormon Church may have its black sheep, but this is a man of God."

The woman answered, "I know it."

After our conversation, I went back home, hardly touching the ground. It dawned upon me that the prayers I had offered, and perhaps as a result in part, of the hard study I had made, and the prayers of those at home, had been answered in a moment, for I had spoken the Dutch language intelligently for the first time in my life.

In ecstasy, I rushed home to tell Brother Thatcher in the office, and to tell the president of the mission; but when I attempted to speak, to my great dismay I was the same as before, I could not understand nor speak the language.

President Farrell asked me if I would go to meeting that night. "Yes, President Farrell," I answered, "after a man has been blessed of the Lord as I have been, I will gladly go, but I beg of you not to call upon me to speak even if someone translates what I say."

"Very well," he said, "I promise you, Brother Hinckley, that if you go you will not be asked to speak." I went to meeting, and everything progressed nicely, as I thought, until Brother DeBry, the branch president, arose and, contrary to Brother Farrell's promise, said, "We will now hear from Elder Hinckley."

President Farrell stepped forward, greatly embarrassed, and asked, "Brother Hinckley, shall I interpret for you?"

I felt a power I cannot describe. "Wait, President Farrell," I said as I stood upon my feet; and then I began to speak, not in my native tongue, but in the Dutch language. And then and there, I delivered the first discourse in my life in the tongue of the mission. The following morning I was sent to preside over the Amsterdam District.

Alonzo A. Hinckley, in Joseph Fielding Smith, *Answers to Gospel Questions,* 2:32–33.

# ELDER BALLARD AT CHICKEN HILL

## JOHN O. SIMONSEN

The older Indians told us, on several occasions, the story of their first meeting with Elder [Melvin J.] Ballard. They said that one day Elder Ballard was traveling east across Montana by train. As the train approached a very small town which was just being settled, Elder Ballard noticed, from the train window, a huge encampment of several hundred Indians. Their teepees were pitched in a large circle on the prairie. Elder Ballard was instantly interested and felt a keen urge to visit with them. He obtained stopover privileges and left the train to spend the day at the encampment, with the intention of proceeding on his journey the next day. He hired a horse and buggy, secured an interpreter, and drove out to the Indian encampment at a place called "Chicken Hill," on the banks of the Missouri River. . . .

Elder Ballard left the horse and buggy and with the interpreter walked out among the people. As he approached them, they showed signs of great emotion and began talking excitedly to him. They seemed to be asking him for something. The interpreter explained that many of the Indians had seen, in dreams, a white man come among them. Always he had his arms laden with books which were of great value to the Indians from their contents. As soon as they saw Elder Ballard, they recognized him as the man they had seen in their dreams and they wanted the books he was supposed to bring to them.

Of course, Elder Ballard was exceedingly impressed and told them briefly the story of the Book of Mormon and of its significance to them. He told them he must go on his way now, but that he would return soon to bring them the books and teach them more.

When Elder Ballard returned to the town he felt impressed to buy two lots in the newly laid-out town, which he obtained for a very low price. When he returned a short time later the lots had skyrocketed in price to such a figure that he was able to sell them at a tremendous profit. The money thus obtained was used to buy building materials and some acreage further out of the town, in fact, at "Chicken Hill." There a boarding school and a chapel were built, and the Lamanites were given their Book of Mormon and were taught the Gospel, as well as general school work. Many of the Indians joined the Church there, and today their descendants and many others are firm in the faith. Great spiritual manifestations occurred in this particular place, as the writings of Elder Ballard relate. Many were the healings, and many the spiritual gifts that were made manifest among the Indians. . . .

One such instance was told to us by an Indian called "Looking." He was a young boy when Brother Ballard came among his people, and he had been blind since birth. When he heard that there was a "Mormon Prayer Man" (as the Indians called the missionaries) on the reservation, he begged to be taken to Elder Ballard that he might be blessed to receive his sight. Elder Ballard administered to him, and through the power of the priesthood and the child's simple, sincere faith, his sight was restored and he was appropriately given the name of "Looking." In gratitude, Looking insisted on giving the hay from his small field each year to help feed the Church livestock at Chicken Hill.

John O. Simonsen, in Melvin R. Ballard, *Melvin J. Ballard—Crusader for Righteousness*, 55–57.

# "NONE SHALL STAY THEM"

### EDWARD JAMES WOOD

I wish to tell you a short experience of my own. . . . I was called to take a special mission to Samoa and the South Seas. I am a British subject by naturalization. I could not leave Canada without a passport, but the President of the Church had called me to be in Salt Lake City by an appointed time, and asked if I could come. I should have obtained my passport before answering the letter, but I said, yes, I will be there. Then I set to work to make good my promise by applying through all the means available for my passport.

The time approached for my departure, and I could not get across the line without the passport, but it did not come in time for me to leave. I presented the matter to the Lord in prayer. I told him my difficulties, and I felt that I must make good my word, and at least make the attempt to come. So I boarded the train bound for Salt Lake City without any passport. When I arrived at the boundary line, the emigration officers asked for my passport. I thought all the time, "They shall go forth and none shall stay them." . . . I wished that the emigration officer believed as much as I did of its truth; but he did not. However, I was somewhat acquainted with him. He said, "I will let you go provided you furnish the passport [when you return]." "All right," I said, "I shall be pleased to do it."

When President [Joseph F.] Smith set me apart, he told me that I should go. Now he did not know anything about my not having a passport. I knew it would be more difficult to get out of the United States than to get in—leaving the port of San Francisco and getting to an American possession in Samoa. I knew, or thought I did, that I must have my passport. President Smith, laying his hands upon my head, said: "Brother Wood, you shall go upon your mission to perform the business to be attended to, and return in safety." He never mentioned any appointed time. All the time he was blessing me I was wondering about my passport. . . .

I was promised by our attorney that it should be registered to me in Salt Lake City to be here the day after my arrival. I waited, and the next day it did not come. The time came for us to leave. At the Oregon Short Line office I wired home, to learn if any news had been received from Ottawa, the Washington of Canada. I did not get any reply. But President Smith said I should go; here was the prophecy and revelation that none should stay the disciples from preaching the gospel. . . . The Lord had commanded me, not the emigration officers at all. So, I set out on the train without my passport. But I received a wire at the station that my passport would be in San Francisco before the steamer left. I felt all right again.

Well, we arrived in San Francisco, and went down to the emigration office the day before the steamer sailed. I was there without my passport. I expected it would be there that evening, but it did not come. And the steamer was to sail, and I was there without my passport. When the time came to answer at the emigration office, I got in line, and felt fine, knowing it would be all right, but I did not know how. When I saw the official ask the passengers for their passports, and some were refused, some were asked a lot of questions, and I did not have my passport, I stood there just as if I had it, and he did not know anything different. When my time came, he said, "Sit down a little while, Mr. Wood; I will talk to you later." Well, I knew it would be all right. . . . felt these promises running through my mind, but how should they be fulfilled? When it came to my turn, the emigration officer said, "Well, the time is up, you must come to the office tomorrow at 9. The steamer sails at 1, and you come up, Mr. Wood."

The time arrived for me to meet again, in the morning, and I was in line. I felt all right, though I did not have any passport. The emigration officer finally said, "Let's see, Mr. Wood, you have got your passport, go right on board the steamer." I said, "Thanks," and I did not have any passport at all, though I had the commission from President Smith, which was worth more than all the passports from all the governments in the world.

But I had yet a great many difficulties. I thought, "Now, I am on the steamer, how am I to get off?" The most important part of all is to present your documents or passports before you leave [the ship]. I had three long weeks to wear away before I should land. The purser takes a kind of genealogy of each of the people. When he came to me, he asked me to sit down; and said, "Of course, you understand you must present your passport, Mr. Wood." I said,

"All right, I understand it." "Where did you come from?" I said, "From Canada." He said, "Sit down, Mr. Wood. I am delighted to see you people from Canada so willing to go down and preach the gospel to those natives." And I spoke of the gospel with him; and he asked for no passport at all. Well, I had other difficulties, too, but I felt all right.

When I arrived at Honolulu, I escaped another very difficult situation by making a pleasant gospel conversation with the emigration officer at that port. Then we made two thousand more miles to the south. I knew the most difficult time was yet to come, that is, when we arrived at Tutuila. How in the world to work it there I did not know. But I prayed to the Lord, not only twice every day for those several weeks, but several times every day, that other avenues would be opened up so that no one could stay my passing.

I remember when that steamer entered that most beautiful harbor which Mr. Robert Louis Stevenson named Pago Pago, I went up on land, and many of the natives that I had seen before met me, and made their characteristic salutation. They were glad that I had come. I saw one of our boys from Canada leading a splendid band, and they had come to welcome me. Then again I began to wonder when I would get off again, and yet whenever I would remember these promises, I would take courage again. The steamer only stayed there six hours, and we were lined up again. Now this was the final getting through without a passport, and I had to buoy up my spirit to meet the emergency. They came within one of me, when the emigration officer said, "Sit down, I want to ask you a question." And he said to me, "Mr. Wood, get your passport ready." "All right." I had the missionary appointment from President Smith, I had the promise, and the prophecy in this revelation, that "none shall stay them." When he had called me, and it was my turn to present my passport, he turned to the man next to me and said, "Why, you are a New Yorker." And this officer went over and had a conversation with this man he called the New Yorker. When he came back, he said, "Let me see, Mr. Wood, I have had your passport all right, you may go on."

Conference Report, October 1920, 122–24.

# DEDICATION OF THE CHINESE REALM

DAVID O. McKAY

*On January 9, 1921, President David O. McKay dedicated China for the preaching of the gospel.*

Elder Hugh J. Cannon and I have traveled continuously since last Tuesday with the sole purpose in mind to be here in Peking on this Sabbath day.

Before we left home, President Grant suggested that when we were in China, if we felt so impressed, to set the land apart for the preaching of the gospel. As Peking is really the heart of China, we had concluded that this would be an appropriate place to perform this sacred and far-reaching duty.

The sky was cloudless. The sun's bright rays tempered the winter air to pleasantness. Every impression following our earnest prayers together and in secret, seemed to confirm our conclusions arrived at last evening; viz., that it seems that the time is near at hand when these teeming millions should at least be given a glimpse of the glorious Light now shining among the children of men in other and more advanced nations.

Accordingly, we strolled almost aimlessly, wondering where it would be possible to find a secluded spot for worship and prayer. We entered that part of the imperial city known as the "Forbidden City," and walked by the famous old buildings formerly used as temples. On we walked, until we came to a small grove of cypress trees on the edge of what appeared to have been an old moat running parallel with one of the walls. As we proceeded from east to west, we passed a tree with a large branch shooting out on the north side, and I distinctly received the prompting to choose that as the spot. However, we passed it and walked to the west end but returned again to the designated tree, realizing it to be the most suitable place in the grove.

Under the century-old limbs and green leaves of this, one of God's own temples, with uncovered heads, we supplicated our Father in heaven and by the authority of the Holy Melchizedek Priesthood, and in the name of the Only Begotten of the Father, turned the key that unlocked the door for the entrance into this benighted and famine-stricken land of the authorized servants of God to preach the true and restored gospel of Jesus Christ.

Brother Cannon, with well-chosen words, and with a spirit of deep earnestness and humility, blessed the chosen spot as one of prayer and supplication to the Almighty. It was plainly evident that he was sincerely affected by the solemnity of the occasion.

Acting under appointment of the Prophet, Seer, and Revelator, and by virtue of the holy apostleship, I then dedicated and set apart the Chinese realm for the preaching of the glad tidings of great joy as revealed in this dispensation through the Prophet Joseph Smith, and prayed particularly that the present government may become stabilized, if not by the Chinese themselves, then by the intervention of the civilized powers of the world.

David O. McKay, *Cherished Experiences*, 87–88.

# "WHERE ARE YE FROM?"

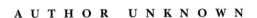

AUTHOR UNKNOWN

Two young elders were one day distributing tracts in a small village [in Ireland]. One visited on one side of the only street in the place and his companion took the opposite side. While going along in the performance of this duty one of the missionaries called at a place where he found a man and his wife digging potatoes.

A tract was offered to the man, but he was not in a humor to receive "Mormon" literature, so he gruffly ordered the elder off his premises, adding the threat that if he did not go he would brain him with his spade. His wife was not so unkind, and she remarked that she would accept the tract, saying that it would not do her any harm.

"And where are ye from?" she inquired, recognizing the elder was a stranger to the country. The young man replied that he was from Utah, in America.

"From Utah!" she exclaimed, "and do ye know our Micky?" The elder replied that he could not say as to that, for he did not know what the full name of her son might be.

256

"He works in the mine, in Utah, do you know Him!" said the woman in her anxiety to hear what he knew about her far-off son. The young man said he also had worked in that same mine, and if she would state his name he could answer the question. She at once gave her son's name, and sure enough he was known to the missionary.

"O, yes," said he, "I am acquainted with him. We used to sleep in the same bunk!"

With this the old lady clasped the young man in her arms exclaiming, "The Lord bless ye; and ye're acquainted with our Mickey! and his father was goin' to brain ye wid the spade!"

She held to the young man and wept for joy. The missionary's companion, seeing from a distance the woman's actions, thought his friend was in trouble and hastened to the premises. The situation was soon made clear to him, and both were invited into the house and treated with the greatest of kindness.

*Sketches of Missionary Life,* 78–80.

# "DID YOU LEAVE THIS
# TRACT AT MY DOOR?"

HUGH B. BROWN

In 1904 I went to England on a mission. . . . We went to Cambridge. . . . I thought the Lord had made a mistake in sending me to Cambridge. . . .

I was feeling sorry for myself, and I heard a knock at the front door. The lady of the house answered the door. I heard a voice say, "Is there an Elder Brown lives here?" . . .

She said, "Why, yes, he's in the front room. Come in, please."

He came in and said, "Are you Elder Brown?"

. . . I said, "Yes, sir."

He said, "Did you leave this tract at my door?"

Well, my name and address were on it. Though, I was attempting at that time to get ready to practice law, I didn't know how to answer [his question without incriminating myself]. So I said, "Yes, sir, I did."

He said, "Last Sunday there were seventeen of us heads of families left the Church of England. We went to my home, where I have a rather large room. Each of us has a large family, and we filled the large room with men, women and children. We decided that we would pray all through the week that the Lord would send us a new pastor. When I came home tonight I was discouraged, I thought our prayer had not been answered. But when I found this tract under my door, I knew the Lord had answered our prayer. Will you come tomorrow night and be our new pastor?"

Now, I hadn't been in the mission field three days. I didn't know anything about missionary work, and he wanted me to be their pastor. But I was reckless enough to say, "Yes, I'll come." And I repented from then till the time of the meeting.

He left, and took my appetite with him! I called in the lady of the house and told her I didn't want any tea [the evening meal in England]. I went up to my room and prepared for bed. I knelt at my bed. . . . For the first time in my life I talked with God. . . . I told Him of my predicament. I pleaded for His help. I asked Him to guide me. I pleaded that He would take [this] burden off my hands. I got up and went to bed and couldn't sleep and got out and prayed again, and kept that up all night—but I really talked with God.

The next morning I told the landlady I didn't want any breakfast, and I went up on the campus in Cambridge and walked all morning. I came in at noon and told her I didn't want any lunch. Then I walked all afternoon. I had a short-circuited mind—all that I could think of was "I have got to go down there tonight and be a pastor."

I came back to my room at 6:00 and I sat there meditating, worrying, wondering. (Let me in parenthesis tell you that since that time I have had the experience of sitting beside a man who was condemned to die the next morning. As I sat and watched his emotions I was reminded of how I felt that night. I think I felt nearly as bad as he did.) The execution time was drawing near. Finally it came to the point where the clock said 6:45. I got up and put on my long Prince Albert coat, my stiff hat which I had acquired in Norwich, took my walking cane (which we always carried in those days), my kid gloves, put a Bible under my arm, and dragged myself down to that building, literally. I think I just made one track all the way.

Just as I got to the gate the man came out, the man I had seen the night before. He bowed very politely and said, "Come in,

Reverend, sir," I had never been called that before. I went in and saw the room filled with people, and they all stood up to honor their new pastor, and that scared me to death.

Then I had come to the point where I began to think what I had to do, and I realized I had to say something about singing. I suggested that we sing "O My Father." I was met with a blank stare, We sang it—it was a terrible cowboy solo. Then I thought, if I could get these people to turn around and kneel by their chairs, they wouldn't be looking at me while I prayed. I asked them if they would and they responded readily. They all knelt down and I knelt down, and for the second time in my life I talked with God. All fear left me. I didn't worry any more. I was turning it over to Him.

I said to Him, among other things, "Father in Heaven, these folks have left the Church of England. They have come here tonight to hear the truth. You know that I am not prepared to give them what they want, but Thou art, O God, the one that can; and if I can be an instrument through whom You speak, very well, but please take over."

When we arose most of them were weeping, as was I. Wisely I dispensed with the second hymn, and I started to talk. I talked for forty-five minutes. I don't know what I said. I didn't talk— God spoke through me, as subsequent events proved. And He spoke so powerfully to that group that at the close of that meeting they came and put their arms around me, held my hands. They said, "This is what we have been waiting for. Thank God you came."

I told you I dragged myself down to that meeting. On my way back to my lodgings that night I only touched ground once, so elated was I that God had taken off my hands an insuperable task for man.

Within three months every man, woman and child in that audience was baptized a member of the Church. I didn't baptize them because I was transferred. But they all joined the Church and most of them came to Utah and Idaho. I have seen some of them in recent years. They are elderly people now, but they say they never have attended such a meeting, a meeting where God spoke to them.

---

Hugh B. Brown, "Father, Are You There?" Brigham Young University Stakes fireside address, 8 October 1967, 12–15.

# "THANK YOU FOR COMING TO MY BACK DOOR"

## HUGH B. BROWN

Fifty-six years ago I was in Norwich, England, on a mission. I had been tracting, and in those days we went three times to every door, regardless the reception. On this occasion I came to a door where I remembered the woman had been particularly antagonistic. I knocked on the door with the big brass knocker. I knocked as a mature missionary knocks, for I had been there nearly two years. New missionaries . . . sometimes knock rather carefully, hoping they won't be heard. But I knocked vigorously and had no response.

I looked through the window and saw a woman sitting in the front room knitting. I recognized her, for she had given me a tongue lashing before, and I knew she was neither deaf nor dumb. She wouldn't respond so I went around to the back door. In those days we carried a walking stick. . . . I took my walking stick and knocked on the door so hard that she came out like a setting hen comes off the nest in response to a troublesome boy.

I think for several minutes she gave me the worst Scotch blessing I have ever had. But she had an impediment of speech; she had to stop every fifteen minutes to draw her breath and when she did stop, I said, "My dear lady, I apologize for having annoyed you, but our Heavenly Father sent me 6,000 miles to bring you a message and inasmuch as he sent me I can't go home until I give you that message."

She said, "Do you mean the Lord sent a message to me?"

I said, "I mean just that. He sent it because he loves you."

She said, "Tell me the message."

And I told her as best I could the Joseph Smith story. She listened intently, apparently impressed. And then I again apologized for having been rude enough to insist on her coming out and added, "Sister, when you and I meet again, and we will meet again, you are going to say, 'Thank you, and thank God that you came to my back door and insisted on speaking to me.'"

. . . Ten years later, in 1916, I was in England again, this time in uniform. President George F. Richards was the president of the mission. He had the flu, and he called me at the military camp and asked if it was possible to get a leave and go down to Norwich to hold a conference for him. I, of course, was very glad to visit my old mission field. At the close of the morning session a woman and four grown daughters came down the aisle.

I was shaking hands with old friends, and as I took her by the hand she bowed her head and kissed my hand and wet it with her tears. She said, "I do thank God that you came to my door ten years ago. When you left that day I thought about what you had said. I couldn't get it out of my mind. I was fighting it, but I couldn't sleep that night. I kept thinking, 'God has sent a message to me.'

But," she said, "I fought it for three days. I tried to find the missionaries from the address on the tract you left, and when I found them, you had returned to Canada. We continued to investigate until my daughters and I joined the Church, and next month we are leaving for Utah."

. . . The joy that comes into the heart of a man or a woman who has been instrumental in the hands of God in carrying the message of life and salvation to some soul, be it only one, is a joy beyond anything that men in the world can know.

Hugh B. Brown, *Continuing the Quest*, 61–63.

# "THE HAPPINESS YOU . . . RADIATE"

## DAVID O. McKAY

A number of years ago, President Edward J. Wood, his counselors, and I were about to enter the temple at Cardston when an automobile stopped at the west gate. None of us recognized the travelers—a man, his wife, and two children, if I remember rightly. They came toward us, and then the gentleman introduced himself as a minister from Iowa.

He said, "We have just driven through Utah, and the first building that impressed us was the temple at St. George. We came north, and we saw the Manti Temple, a beautiful structure. We continued farther north, and visited the temple grounds and the tabernacle in Salt Lake City. Everybody around there seemed to radiate joy, and we heard the congregation sing 'Come, Come, Ye Saints.' Now in Canada we see this temple. There is something about the people whom we have met from St. George to Canada which has impressed us greatly. It is the happiness you seem to radiate. I am going to teach my congregation to sing that song, 'Come, Come, Ye Saints.'"

He was impressed with something which to him was indefinable. We are a happy people.

*Church News*, 8 August 1951, 2.

# "WHY ARE YOU SO FRIENDLY TO THE MORMON CHURCH?"

### ALVIN R. DYER

If there is any one thing that has impressed me greatly in my experiences in the Church, it is that we carry on our work under the power and influence of the spirit of God and that we receive this assistance wherever we are projecting ourselves in the work. If we can learn to abide by this magical situation, to learn to be in the right place at the right time, then the Lord will work through us, because this is God's work.

I recall a fulfillment . . . in the early part of 1961 with

President McKay. He . . . said to me, "President Dyer, I want you to go to Iceland to investigate the possibilities of sending missionaries there."

Through obedience to his request, within a few weeks we had taken an Icelandic Airways plane from Oslo, Norway, in company with the president of the Norwegian Mission, and a legal representative of our Church who was then in Europe, and my son, who was serving then in the European Mission office. . . .

But what do you do when you go to a country like this, to establish an image for the Church? . . .

We finally ended up in the office of the mayor of Reykjavik. His name is Halgrimmson.

I have been greeted and welcomed in many places throughout the world in a very cordial manner, but never so much as here this day in the office of Mayor Halgrimmson. When I suggested that we might send missionaries there, if it was the will of the Presidency and the presiding brethren of the Church, he said, "For me, I would like to see the Mormon missionaries here right now." He said, "What will you do with them when they come? Where will they live?"

I said, "They will find a place with the people."

He said, "Now I want this to be my responsibility. When they come, I will see to it that they have a place to live. Where will you hold your meetings?"

"Well, this is a little premature. We only have two members of the Church in Iceland—a Danish woman and her son."

He said, "You will need some place to meet. Let it be the responsibility of the city of Reykjavik to provide you with a meeting place at no cost."

I said, "Mayor Halgrimmson, you have been very friendly, and kind, and I would like to know the reason. Why are you so friendly to the Mormon Church?"

"Well," he said, "the answer is simple. Some years ago two Mormon missionaries came to the island of Iceland and they learned that many of the Icelanders left the island to go to Westmanna Island, some 150 kilometers off the coast of Iceland, toward the Arctic Circle. There, employed by others in one of the great fishing areas of the world, they would fish. So these missionaries, I suppose being fishermen at heart, got on a boat and away they went to Westmanna Island. While the men fished in the day, they fished at night and baptized 150 of these fishermen. They came back to the island and later, with their wives and families who were also converted, many of them immigrated to America." A good number of them . . . settled in Springville and Spanish Fork.

As he continued this story he said, "My uncle was among them. Last year (which would have been in the fall of 1960) my wife and I decided to come to America. We did not come in any official capacity, as the mayor of Reykjavik and his wife, but just as ordinary Icelanders. We told no one of our coming. We bought an automobile in Detroit, and toured America. We went of course to Utah, where we spent three weeks—three of the most wonderful weeks of my life. You ask me why I would like to see missionaries in Iceland. I lived among your people for those three weeks. I came to know them. I have never been so impressed with people, their educational inclinations, their industry, and above all, their desire to abide by what they believe and what they were taught.

"We went to Salt Lake City for the last few days of our visit in Utah. We stayed in a motel near the temple. The manager of that motel was the kindest, perhaps the finest man I have ever met. He said he belonged to some kind of quorum, but this was a man who lived completely, in my estimation, the life of a Christian."

I thought then and there of the tremendous influence that we as a people, both individually and as a community, can wield upon the lives of other people if only we live the gospel. I think that when the time comes to open Iceland for the preaching of the gospel—and this is bound to come—probably this one man with the influence he wielded on Mayor Halgrimmson and his wife will be largely responsible for the opening of the doors of preaching the gospel in Iceland. I have not been able to find this brother as yet, and I have been looking for him, but when I do I will want to convey this glad news to him.

These are happenings that indicate how the spirit of God works in the minds of people to open the way for the spreading of the gospel.

---

*BYU Speeches of the Year,* 20 March 1963, 4–6.

# OBEDIENCE

# "We Had Driven Hard
## All the Week"

⌒

BENJAMIN F. JOHNSON

We were just over the Illinois line in the prairie country and it was the Sabbath. We had driven hard all the week and needed rest, yet our anxiety was so great to get to our friends that although we knew the Lord had said, "Thou shalt rest on the Sabbath," yet in our haste we did not do so, and driving until noon we crossed a deep creek, on the opposite bank of which was an open space of beautiful grass, surrounded by timber and high brush. Our teams were tired, and heretofore on the road had given no evidence that they were easily frightened or disposed to run away. So driving into the tall grass I slipped off their bridles, as I had often done before. But no sooner had I done so than they began to show signs of fright, and commenced to plunge and start to run. My father was just doing the same with his buggy horse, and my sisters stood holding the span attached to the family carriage. I did all possible to quiet my team but they broke away. My father's did the same; the others broke from the women, and all went tearing through the timber and brush until every vehicle was smashed and with goods and harness strung piece-meal for three-fourths of a mile around. A greater smash up it was never my bad luck to see. At first I looked upon the wreck as impossible to reconstruct, but we gathered up and put the parts together and got all mechanical help possible, labored hard, and by the next Sabbath day we had so far reconstructed our vehicles that by noon we hitched up, and feeling again tempted through anxiety we drove fifteen miles to early camp, but when unhitching our horses they again—all but one— took fright, took the back track, and as though spurred by the Evil One ran the whole distance to our former camp. Upon the horse left I followed with utmost speed and found them with legs terribly lacerated by the tug chains, and streaming with blood and sweat. I made no stop, but hurried them back as fast as I could ride, arriving in camp just before sunset, and was up much of the night bathing the bruised legs of the animals, and telling the Lord if He would now forgive me and give us His blessing for the rest of our journey I would promise never to forget the experience of those two Sabbath days.

We started early the next morning, and with all the fatigue and bruises, our animals seemed all right, and made us no trouble afterwards. I knew then and I know now that this experience was given to me of the Lord for my profit, and to record as a testimony to my children, that the Lord will not hold in favor those who do not rest upon and hallow the Sabbath day.

Benjamin F. Johnson, *My Life's Review*, 89–90.

# "I COULD HAVE ENDURED
# A HUNDRED LASHES"

⌒

### J O S E P H   F .   S M I T H

W hen I was a child, somewhat a wayward, disobedient little boy—not that I was wilfully disobedient, but I would forget what I ought to do—I would go off with playful boys and be absent when I should have been at home, and I would forget to do things I was asked to do. Then I would go home, feel guilty, know that I was guilty, that I had neglected my duty, and that I deserved punishment.

On one occasion I had done something that was not just right, and my mother said to me, "Now, Joseph, if you do that again I shall have to whip you." Well, time went on, and by and by, I forgot it, and I did something similar again. The one thing that I admired more, perhaps, than any secondary thing in her was that when she made a promise she kept it. She never made a promise, that I know of, that she did not keep.

Well, I was called to account. She said, "Now, I told you. You knew that if you did this I would have to whip you, for I said I would. I must do it. I do not want to do it. It hurts me worse than it does you, but I must whip you."

Well, she had a little rawhide, already there, and while she was talking, or reasoning with me, showing me how much I deserved it and how painful it was to her to inflict the punishment I deserved, I had only one thought and that was: "For goodness sake, whip me; do not reason with me," for I felt the lash of her just criticism and admonition a thousandfold worse than I did the switch. I felt as if, when she laid the lash on me, I had at least partly paid my debt and had answered for my wrong doing. Her reasoning cut me down into the quick; it made me feel sorry to the very core.

I could have endured a hundred lashes with the rawhide better than I could endure a ten-minutes' talk in which I felt and was made to feel that the punishment inflicted upon me was painful to her that I loved—punishment upon my mother!

---

Joseph F. Smith, *Gospel Doctrine*, 317–18.

# "I WANT YOU TO GIVE HIM FIVE ACRES"

## BRYANT S. HINCKLEY

In the settlement of Spanish Fork the original settlers were given a small piece of land, perhaps five acres each. Two young men from Scotland came there, brothers. One remained in Spanish Fork, the other moved away. The man who remained was given his allotment of land and, inspired by this possession, he worked with a zeal that made him forget all his troubles. He never knew when the sun went down, he knew that every stroke of his arm would bring something to him and to his household. As a result of his thrift he was able to get five acres more. One day the bishop said to him: "Here is William, he hasn't any land and you have ten acres." William was a shiftless sort of man. The bishop said to this Scotch brother: "I want you to give him five acres of your land." . . . He said to the bishop: "Well, I will think it over." He did. On a fine fall day like this he was plowing in the field. He had thought it over carefully. He said: "Whoa!" and the horses stopped. Standing there he said: "Joseph Smith was a prophet: Mormonism is true: let them have the land."

Conference Report, October 1932, 34.

# "GO AND MARRY A WIFE"

## J. GOLDEN KIMBALL

A brother, sorely in need of bread, came to President [Heber C.] Kimball for counsel as to how to procure it. "Go and marry a wife," was Heber's terse reply, after feeding the brother. The man thought Brother Kimball must be out of his mind, but when he thought of his prophetic character, he resolved to obey counsel. He wondered where such a woman was and, thinking of a widow with several children, he got busy and proposed. As widows generally do, she accepted him. In that widow's house was laid up a six months' store of provisions. She surely grub-staked him. Meeting Brother Kimball soon after, the prosperous man of a family said: "Well, Brother Heber, I followed your advice." "Yes," said the man of God, "and you found bread."

Conference Report, April 1928, 77.

# "I DID NOT LIKE GIVING UP MY OWN ARRANGEMENTS"

## B . H . ROBERTS

Having labored some time [as a missionary] in Franklin county, Iowa, without apparently doing any good, and opportunities for preaching growing less, I concluded to go elsewhere, and find a people who were more willing to hear and obey the gospel.

I made inquiries about the surrounding neighborhoods and counties, and finally decided to go to Mason City, in Cerro Gordo county, and try to make an opening there.

The day before starting I met a number of people who had befriended me, and learning that I had decided to leave their vicinity, some gave me a dollar, others half a dollar, until I had enough to bear my expenses to Mason City on the cars, and then have some left.

All this I regarded as a good omen, thinking the Lord was opening my way to accomplish my journey to Mason City.

The morning I was to start on my journey, I awoke very early, just as the day was dawning, but feeling rather drowsy, stretched out for another nap before rising. In order to rest better I changed my posture—and in doing so, I saw a personage standing by my bedside. He was of medium size, of a light complexion, and of a very pleasing countenance. Slowly and gracefully raising his hand he pointed to the eastward and said: "You go to Rockford." He disappeared [immediately after] making this remark.

I quickly arose and walked out into the fields, all the while pondering over what I had seen and heard. I knew of no such place as Rockford, never had heard of it before, and my mind was perplexed. Had I not made up my mind to go to Mason City? Had I not told the whole neighborhood I was going there? To change my mind now would they not regard me as fickle-minded? Besides I did not like giving up my own arrangements.

Returning from my walk, I found the family [with whom I was staying] ready to sit down to breakfast. I inquired of them if they knew of such a town as Rockford; but they had never heard of such a place. Just then a young man, whom Mr. Stade had employed a few days before, came in. He was a stranger in the neighborhood, having lately come from the eastern part of the state. I asked him if he knew of such a place as Rockford; he said he did, and that it was a flourishing little town northeast of us.

I said no more about it to them, and decided at last to carry out my own plans at all hazards.

Arriving at Mason City a little before sunset, I put up at the St. Charles hotel, and at once began making inquiries about a hall in which to speak; past experiences had taught me that it was useless to ask for churches.

The only suitable place for delivering lectures was the Masonic Hall. Finding the gentleman who had it in charge, I inquired as to the terms upon which it could be obtained, and was informed they usually charged ten dollars per night, but as I was delivering free lectures, they would let me have it for half that.

I explained to him that I was traveling without purse or scrip, and received no remuneration for my services in the way of salary, but was traveling as the servants of God did anciently. This being the case, he said I could have the hall free for one night, if I could obtain the sanction of another gentleman he named, and who was associated with him in the management of the hall. Unfortunately this other gentleman had left town for a few days, and Mr. ———

did not wish to take the responsibility upon himself of letting me have the hall free.

The next day I made application for nearly every schoolhouse in town, but it was of no use, and at night I found I had only money enough to pay for a bed, and therefore missed my supper.

The next morning I paid for my lodging, and without breakfast, started out into the country. I walked on till about noon; then finding myself in a fine section of country, and a schoolhouse in sight, I inquired who had it in charge, and was told that Mr. B ——— was the director. Calling at Mr. B ———'s residence I found himself and a great number of his workmen at dinner.

After [they had] finished their repast, I introduced myself and business to Mr. B ——— by handing my Elder's certificate which I had received from the First Presidency. He read it in silence and as he handed it back to me said: "So you are a Mormon preacher, are you?"

"Yes, sir," I replied.

"Well, then, the sooner you leave my house the better you will suit me."

By this time he was pale with excitement and in a furious rage. I quietly asked him why he treated me in this manner. Said he, "It makes no difference to you why I do it, I tell you to leave—if you had been a minister of any other doctrine under heaven, I would have asked you to have dinner, but I want you to go, and I have no explanation to give you."

"Very well, sir, I will leave as you request. I came here to you with the gospel of Jesus Christ, but you drive me from your house without a cause; good day, sir." It is needless to add that I was cast down in my feelings.

I walked on all afternoon, weary and faint, without making any attempt to get a place in which to hold meetings, or to call on anyone by the wayside to tell them of the important message I had to deliver.

An hour before sunset I stopped at a house, telling the good people living in it that I was a servant of God in want of refreshments, and they kindly provided a lunch for me. Being restless in my spirit, I journeyed on. At dusk I arrived at the little village of Rockfalls [and] made some inquiries about the schoolhouse in which I desired to speak, but was informed that Mr. ——— was the director, and that he lived some three miles out of the village. Several attempts to get lodgings for the night resulted in failures; and at last I resolved to go to see the school director, thinking perhaps I could get lodgings with him, and also arrange to hold some meetings in the schoolhouse.

When I arrived at his place it was nine o'clock at night. He denied me the use of the schoolhouse, and also refused to give me lodgings; saying that perhaps his brother, who lived about half a mile further on, would accommodate me. I called at his brother's place, telling him who I was and explaining my business to him. He coolly informed me that a few miles distant, I would find a village and a hotel, where, for the money, I could find both supper and bed. He didn't wish to keep me. As I wandered out over the prairie, I concluded that I would be obliged to make the grass my couch for the night. Selecting a place, and making a pillow of my valise, I sought comfort. . . .

But all in vain. . . . The festive mosquito with his unwelcome singing, and shortly afterwards by his more painful pumping at my life's current, would arouse me from my slumber; and these things, together with the heavy dew that was falling and my aching limbs, made me realize that I was still in this "breathing world" of woe.

All night long I kept up my unequal warfare with the mosquitoes and other insects—rolling and tossing about the whole night through. At last the morning came. The mosquitoes became less ravenous, or I became less sensitive of their attacks, and dropped off into a feverish sleep. When I awoke the sun was at least an hour high, but still the fog-mists hung about the stream near which I had spent the night. I was wet through and as I arose to a sitting posture, exclaimed: "Well, this is a pretty hard way to serve the Lord!" The words had scarcely died on my lips, when a voice softly said, "You were told to go to Rockford." I leaped to my feet, looked around me—I was alone for aught I could see, but that sentence, uttered so calmly, was ringing in my ears and seemed to burn in my mind. Raising my voice almost to a shout, I said, "So I was; and to Rockford I'll go!" Those few words revealed to me the whole reason of my treatment for the last two days—the Lord was not preparing the way before me as he had hitherto done, and the difference was very perceptible—I was in the wrong way.

After bathing my face in the river, I started to retrace my steps. My limbs were stiff at first, but walk became easier as I warmed up to the work. About ten o'clock I reached the home of my friend who had so kindly given me food the day before, and again he administered to me. In the evening I reached Mason City.

My mail had been forwarded to this place, and fortunately I received a letter from a friend who had sent me two dollars to assist me in my labors. This enabled me to take the cars within a few miles of West Fork—the point from which I started to Mason City. From whence I turned my face in the direction of Rockford; where, in a few days, I arrived.

This experience to me was very severe, as the darkness of my mind and the despondency of spirit were more fruitful fountains of grief than whatever of physical inconvenience I had to endure; but if the Son of God . . . had to "learn obedience by the things which He suffered," it is not surprising that we, who are so much weaker than He, have to learn in the same manner.

---

*Juvenile Instructor* 19:178–79.

# "He Did Not Give Any Reasons"

## Heber J. Grant

As a young man Richard W. Young graduated as a cadet at West Point, and before going to the school he was set apart by his grandfather, President Brigham Young, to serve as a missionary while in the school, and then, after graduation, to continue as a missionary in the army.

After his graduation there was a surplus, so he assured me, of graduates from West Point, and more second lieutenants than the army needed, and it was considered no disgrace whatever for the graduates to resign. On the contrary, the government was pleased to receive their resignations with the understanding that they would volunteer should our country ever be engaged in war.

Richard consulted his uncle, Colonel Willard Young, and other friends including myself, stating that he would like to resign, as he was the only living child of his widowed mother. He hated to be separated from her, and an army career would not permit him to be near her.

Some of us agreed to lend him money to secure a legal education, which would cost, he thought, from four to six thousand dollars. We had no doubt he would make a success as a lawyer and would repay the loan.

After he had partially arranged for the money to pay his expenses for his education as a lawyer, he said to me:

"Heber, inasmuch as grandfather blessed me and set me apart as an army missionary, do you think it is proper for me to resign that missionary labor without consulting his successor, President John Taylor?"

I told him it would not be right. He consulted President Taylor, and was told to remain in the army. It was a great disappointment to Richard.

When he secured his appointment in the army after his graduation, he was assigned to Governor's Island, a few minutes' ride from New York City. He entered Columbia Law School in New York, was graduated with honors, and during the time of securing his education he received a salary as second lieutenant and had quarters for himself and his family on Governor's Island, then counted by many as the finest army post in the entire United States. He not only escaped being in debt several thousand dollars for his legal education, but in addition received a salary while securing his education.

After he had been graduated from Columbia Law School, General Winfield Scott Hancock, who was in command at Governor's Island, commended him on the industry he had exhibited in preparing himself for the battle of life. . . .

General Hancock also said he wished he could promote Richard W. Young. But as that was out of the question, he was pleased that he could do one thing for him, and that was to choose him as one of his own staff officers. He remarked: "Lieutenant Young, you are chosen on my staff with the rank of major."

I was in New York City at the funeral of ex-President U. S. Grant. As I recall it, the procession was over five miles long. I was watching the procession from one of the insurance offices on Broadway, and it filled my heart with pride and gratitude to see a grandson of Brigham Young riding with the commanding general on the first line of that great five mile funeral procession.

After graduation as a lawyer, Richard still kept in mind his wish to return to Salt Lake City, to be at home with his mother and to help take care of her, but feared that with the limited salary he was getting after graduation from West Point he could do little or nothing for her.

Subsequently, when the permanent judge advocate-general had been given a special assignment at Washington, General Hancock appointed Richard temporary judge advocate-general of the eastern department of the army, and . . . was working to have him permanently appointed judge advocate-general of the Missouri department at the time General Hancock died.

Richard then fell back to the rank of lieutenant, as another "Pharaoh," figuratively speaking, had arisen who did not know "Joseph." Richard came home on a vacation, and in the meantime I had become one of the apostles. He then asked me, also his uncle, Brigham Young, Jr., to plead with President Taylor to permit him to resign, as he had secured his education as a lawyer and wanted to come home and get behind him the starvation period of a young legal graduate.

Brother Brigham Young, Jr., and I argued to the best of our ability at a meeting in the old Endowment House for Richard to be released from the army. Some others spoke in favor of his resignation, and when we had finished our talks, President Taylor said: "The time has not yet arrived for that young man to resign from the army."

This was a very great disappointment to Richard. He wanted to know what the reasons were. I told him there were no reasons given, only that President Taylor said he ought not to resign.

He said: "I would like to have some reasons."

I smiled and said: "Richard, he did not give any reasons when he told you to stay in the army, and you secured your education free of debt and were paid a salary by the government while you were doing so, and upon graduation you were honored by being chosen on the staff of General Hancock. I think you can now well afford to take the advice of President Taylor." He said: "Oh, I wouldn't think of doing anything else, but I wish there were some reasons."

I assured him that when Brother Taylor said, "Your young friend ought to stay in the army," I had an impression that that was exactly the right thing.

Richard was on his way to his new assignment—I have forgotten to what place he was assigned—when he met one of his fellow students who had graduated in the same class, and he was bewailing his fate because he had to come way out to Utah. He thought Richard—as I remember the expression—was a lucky dog, in having the appointment which had been assigned to him, having previously had the best place in the army, namely, Governor's Island, and then getting another fine appointment.

Richard suggested to his fellow graduate that they apply to the secretary of war for an exchange of assignments. They did so. The exchange was made, and Richard was stationed at Fort Douglas for four years and was able to be in the law office of his relative, the late LeGrand Young, and get through what is known as the starvation period of four years as a young lawyer, drawing a good salary from the government and having a fine residence at Fort Douglas without expense.

The day that the announcement was made that Richard's assignment at Fort Douglas had expired I called at President John Taylor's office—I have forgotten for what purpose—and he said, "I see by the morning paper that your dear friend Richard W. Young's term has expired at Fort Douglas and he is about to go East. You may tell him that the time has now arrived for his missionary labors in the army to end, and he is at liberty to resign."

Faith, we are told, is a gift of God, and Richard had the faith to accept the counsel and advice of President Taylor. And it is little less than wonderful that he should have secured the finest post, so considered, in the army, secured his education without running into debt, and received a salary from the government while securing it.

Certainly God moves in a mysterious way his wonders to perform.

My experience is that men who have sufficient faith to trust in God come out of difficulties, financial and otherwise, in a most miraculous and wonderful way.

*Improvement Era*, 39:131–32.

# "DARN YOU, HEBER!"

## HEBER J. GRANT

Richard W. Young, like me and many others, invested quite heavily in Utah-Idaho Sugar stock which, at the time, paid a very generous dividend. . . .

When the trouble broke out between the United States and Spain I was visiting Richard in his office. He remarked that as a graduate of West Point it was his duty to volunteer again to enter the army. He thought that he would probably have the rank and pay of a major, and stated that his compensation as a major would not pay one-half of the interest on his debts, but honor and duty demanded his return to the army.

I replied that it would take ten times as much courage to

remain home and not enter the army, and I advised him to consult President Wilford Woodruff and take his advice, stating that if President Woodruff advised him to remain at home, I felt he ought to accept that advice notwithstanding the ridicule that might come to him by doing so. I said: "There may be some special labor that the Lord has for you to perform that is of more importance than for you to volunteer and go to the Philippines where perhaps you might lose your life."

He said that he would not think of such a thing as to speak to President Woodruff about returning to the army, and further remarked: "He is one of the most tender-hearted men in the world. He is as tender-hearted as a woman. I feel sure he would not advise me to volunteer."

I replied: "Do you accept me, Richard, as an apostle of the Lord Jesus Christ, with authority to call people on missions?"

He answered: "I certainly do."

I said: "All right, as an apostle, I call you on a mission to go to President Wilford Woodruff, and ask for his advice as to your returning to the army, and your mission is to follow that advice and counsel, no matter how much you dislike to do so. I will stay right here in your office until you return and report."

He said: "Darn you, Heber Grant." He picked up his hat and went to see President Woodruff, looking anything but happy.

He returned smiling and said: "President Woodruff is as full of fight as an egg is full of meat. He remarked, 'If you don't go back to the army, Brother Young, after graduating from West Point, you will disgrace the name you bear, and it will be a reflection upon your dear, dead grandfather, President Brigham Young.'"

Richard was very happy. He took President Woodruff's advice, joined the army, and went to the Philippines, notwithstanding the fact that he was heavily in debt and was very much concerned about leaving his unsettled obligations. But while he was still in the Philippines one of the corporations in which Richard had twelve thousand dollars' worth of stock at par value, and which was worth only nine thousand when he joined the army, paid a special cash dividend of one hundred percent and during Richard's absence paid dividends of from ten to twenty percent regularly. Soon after his return home it paid a special dividend of forty percent. These two special dividends, to say nothing of the large regular dividends that were paid, netted him enough to cancel all of his debts and leave him a home and some other valuable property in addition.

The increase in the value of Richard's securities while he was in the Philippine Islands was very remarkable. The war with Spain lasted but a short time. After the war he was appointed by the governor-general of the Philippine Islands, William H. Taft (afterwards president of the United States), one of the Supreme Court Judges of the Islands, and he was also appointed to write the code for the islands. He made an excellent record while in the Philippines, and gained the love and confidence of that splendid man, William H. Taft, who ever afterwards was a friend not only of Richard W. Young, but of the Mormon people.

When Richard returned to Utah, he resumed his law practice and was one of the prosperous, successful lawyers of our state. Subsequently, as we all know, he was blessed of the Lord by being chosen to preside over the Ensign Stake of Zion, one of the important stakes of the Church, and he made a splendid stake president.

. . . Certainly God did move in a very wonderful and mysterious way in blessing my near and dear friend when he followed the advice of . . . President Woodruff.

Faith is a gift of God, and when people have faith to live the gospel, and to listen to the counsel of those who preside in the wards and stakes and of the General Authorities of the Church, it has been my experience that they have been abundantly blessed of the Lord, and that many of them have come out of great financial and other difficulties in a most miraculous and wonderful way.

———————

Heber J. Grant, *Gospel Standards*, 271–74.

# A WIDOW'S MITE

CARL W. BUEHNER

I heard another little experience that happened somewhere up in the Uintah Basin a while ago, where for twenty-five years they talked about building a new chapel. Finally, the bishopric then in the ward decided they had talked about this thing long enough, and they would like to organize a finance committee, a building committee and go ahead, so they sent out letters assessing the membership of the ward for this purpose.

Among those who received a letter and an assessment of one hundred dollars was a little widow who had not been very active in the Church, and one that the bishopric did not know very well; but they thought they would visit this woman. When they went to her home and opened the door, they realized they had made a great mistake. They should never have assessed this poor, little old soul one hundred dollars, they said, and so in the middle of their talk of trying to justify what they had done in talking themselves out of the assessment that they had made to this woman, she said, "Just a minute, brethren, you have assessed me one hundred dollars. I would like to do my part." They said she walked over to the mantel shelf, reached her hand into a little piece of crockery, and counted out to the bishop five hundred dollars in greenbacks.

Then he said that time went on, and the building got started. They were putting the rafters on it, and one day the bishop got another call from this woman, and he thought, "Oh, dear, she wants her money back, and we have spent it on the chapel."

When they went to see her, she said, "You don't know how thrilled I am to see our building come into fruition. We have talked about it all these years, but you brethren have actually gone to work, and now I can see it grow, and the rafters are going on. I would just like to give you another five hundred dollars to be sure it is completed because I don't think I'll live until we finish the building, and I would like to have a little credit on the other side."

---

Conference Report, October 1953, 62.

# PERSECUTION

# "Sheep in the Hands
# of Wolves"

## Parley P. Pratt

October 31, 1838.—In the afternoon we were informed that the Governor had ordered this force against us, with orders to exterminate or drive every *"Mormon"* from the State. As soon as these facts were ascertained we determined not to resist anything in the shape of authority, however abused. We had now nothing to do but to submit to be massacred, driven, robbed or plundered, at the option of our persecutors.

Colonel George M. Hinkle, who was at that time the highest officer of the militia assembled for the defence of Far West, waited on Messrs. J. Smith, S. Rigdon, Hyrum Smith, L. Wight, George Robinson and myself, with a request from General Lucas that we would repair to his camp, with the assurance that as soon as peaceable arrangements could be entered into we should be released. We had no confidence in the word of a murderer and robber, but there was no alternative but to put ourselves into the hands of such monsters, or to have the city attacked, and men, women and children massacred. We, therefore, commended ourselves to the Lord, and voluntarily surrendered as sheep into the hands of wolves. As we approached the camp of the enemy General Lucas rode out to meet us with a guard of several hundred men.

The haughty general rode up, and, without speaking to us, instantly ordered his guard to surround us. They did so very abruptly, and we were marched into camp surrounded by thousands of savage looking beings, many of whom were dressed and painted like Indian warriors. These all set up a constant yell, like so many bloodhounds let loose upon their prey, as if they had achieved one of the most miraculous victories that ever graced the annals of the world. If the vision of the infernal regions could suddenly open to the mind, with thousands of malicious fiends, all clamoring, exulting, deriding, blaspheming, mocking, railing, raging and foaming like a troubled sea, then could some idea be formed of the hell which we had entered.

In camp we were placed under a strong guard, and were without shelter during the night, lying on the ground in the open air, in the midst of a great rain. The guards during the whole night kept up a constant tirade of mockery, and the most obscene blackguardism and abuse. They blasphemed God; mocked Jesus Christ; swore the most dreadful oaths; taunted brother Joseph and others; demanded miracles; wanted signs, such as: "Come, Mr. Smith, show us an angel." "Give us one of your revelations." "Show us a miracle." "Come, there is one of your brethren here in camp whom we took prisoner yesterday in his own house, and knocked his brains out with his own rifle, which we found hanging over his fireplace; he lays speechless and dying; speak the word and heal him, and then we will all believe." "Or, if you are Apostles or men of God, deliver yourselves, and then we will be Mormons." Next would be a volley of oaths and blasphemies; then a tumultuous tirade of lewd boastings of having defiled virgins and wives by force, etc., much of which I dare not write; and, indeed, language would fail me to attempt more than a faint description. Thus passed this dreadful night, and before morning several other captives were added to our number, among whom was brother Amasa Lyman.

We were informed that the general officers held a secret council during most of the night, which was dignified by the name of court martial; in which, without a hearing, or, without even being brought before it, we were all sentenced to be shot. The day and hour was also appointed for the execution of this sentence, viz: next morning at 8 o'clock, in the public square at Far West. Of this we were informed by Brigadier-General Doniphan, who was one of the council, but who was so violently opposed to this cool blooded murder that he assured the council that he would revolt and withdraw his whole brigade, and march them back to Clay County as soon as it was light, if they persisted in so dreadful an undertaking. Said he, "It is cold blooded murder, and I wash my hands of it." His firm remonstrance, and that of a few others, so alarmed the haughty murderer and his accomplices that they dare not put the decree in execution.

Thus, through a merciful providence of God our lives were spared through that dreadful night. It was the common talk, and even the boast in the camp, that individuals lay here and there unburied, where they had shot them down for sport. The females they had ravished; the plunder they had taken; the houses they had burned; the horses they had stolen; the fields of grain they had laid waste, were common topics; and were dwelt on for mere amusement, or, as if these deeds were a stepstone to office; and it is a fact that such deeds were so considered.

No pen need undertake to describe our feelings during that terrible night, while there confined—not knowing the fate of our wives and children, or of our fellow Saints, and seeing no way for our lives to be saved except by the miraculous power of God. But, notwithstanding all earthly hopes were gone, still we felt a calmness indescribable. A secret whispering to our inmost soul seemed to say: "Peace, my sons, be of good cheer, your work is not yet done; therefore I will restrain your enemies, that they shall not have power to take your lives." . . .

Next morning General Lucas demanded the Caldwell militia to give up their arms, which was done. As soon as the troops who had defended the city were disarmed, it was surrounded by the enemy and all the men detained as prisoners. None were permitted to pass out of the city—although their families were starving for want of sustenance; the mills and provisions being some distance from the city.

The brutal mob were now turned loose to ravage, steal, plunder and murder without restraint. Houses were rifled, women ravished, and goods taken as they pleased. The whole troop, together with their horses, lived on the grain and provisions. While cattle were shot down for mere sport, and sometimes men, women and children fared no better. On the third morning after our imprisonment we were placed in a wagon, in order for removal. Many of the more desperate then crowded around, cocked their rifles, and singling us out presented them to our breasts, and swore they would blow us through. Some guns were snapped, but missed fire, and the rest were in a small degree restrained by the officers, and we still lived.

We were now marched to Far West, under the conduct of the whole army; and while they halted in the public square, we were permitted to go with a guard for a change of linen and to take final leave of our families, in order to depart as prisoners to Jackson County, a distance of sixty miles.

This was the most trying scene of all. I went to my house, being guarded by two or three soldiers; the cold rain was pouring down without, and on entering my little cottage, there lay my wife sick of a fever, with which she had been for some time confined. At her breast was our son Nathan, an infant of three months, and by her side a little girl of five years. On the foot of the same bed lay a woman in travail, who had been driven from her house in the night, and had taken momentary shelter in my hut of ten feet square—my larger house having been torn down. I stepped to the bed; my wife burst into tears; I spoke a few words of comfort, telling her to try to live for my sake and the children's; and expressing a hope that we should meet again though years might separate us. She promised to try to live. I then embraced and kissed the little babes and departed.

Till now I had refrained from weeping; but, to be forced from so helpless a family, who were destitute of provisions and fuel, and deprived almost of shelter in a bleak prairie, with none to assist them, exposed to a lawless banditti who were utter strangers to humanity, and this at the approach of winter, was more than nature could well endure.

I went to General Moses Wilson in tears, and stated the circumstances of my sick, heart-broken and destitute family in terms which would have moved any heart that had a latent spark of humanity yet remaining. But I was only answered with an exultant laugh, and a taunt of reproach by this hardened murderer.

As I returned from my house towards the troops in the square, I halted with the guard at the door of Hyrum Smith, and heard the sobs and groans of his wife, at his parting words. She was then near confinement; and needed more than ever the comfort and consolation of a husband's presence. As we returned to the wagon we saw S. Rigdon taking leave of his wife and daughters, who stood at a little distance, in tears of anguish indescribable. In the wagon sat Joseph Smith, while his aged father and venerable mother came up overwhelmed with tears, and took each of the prisoners by the hand with a silence of grief too great for utterance.

In the meantime, hundreds of the brethren crowded around us, anxious to take a parting look, or a silent shake of the hand; for feelings were too intense to allow of speech. In the midst of these scenes orders were given, and we moved slowly away, under the conduct of General Wilson and his whole brigade.

---

Parley P. Pratt, *Autobiography of Parley P. Pratt*, 159–63.

# "SOME WERE FOR HANGING ME AT ONCE"

## ORRIN PORTER ROCKWELL

I ... was on my way from New Jersey to Nauvoo; and while at St. Louis, on the 4th March, 1843, was arrested by a Mr. Fox, on oath of Elias Parker, who swore I was the O. P. Rockwell advertised in the papers as having attempted to assassinate Lilburn W. Boggs. . . . Was about four days going to Independence: arrived there just at night. A large crowd gathered around, making many remarks. Some were for hanging me at once. I was then placed in the jail. In two or three days, underwent a sham trial before a justice of the peace. The courthouse was crowded, and the men were armed with hickory clubs. They set on boys from ten to twelve years of age to kick and punch me, which they did repeatedly. While in court, Fox was the main witness introduced, and he swore falsely. . . . The magistrate committed me to prison for my safe preservation, as he was afraid the people would kill me; but he could find no crime against me. This I was told by the officer who conveyed me to prison.

I was recommitted to jail, still wearing the iron hobbles, and was kept in the upper part in the daytime, and in the dungeon at night, with a little dirty straw for a bed, without any bedding, no fire, and very cold weather. For eighteen days I was not free from shaking with cold. I then got permission to buy 1.5 bushels of charcoal, which I put into an old kettle, and kept a little fire. When that was gone, I could not obtain any more. . . .

[After attempting escape] I was then put into the dungeon,

my feet ironed together, my right hand to my left foot, so close that I could not half straighten myself. The irons, when put on my wrists, were so small that they would hardly go on, and swelled them; but in eighteen days I could slip them up and turn them around my arm at the elbow. I was fed on cold corndodger and meat of the poorest description; and if I did not eat it all up, it was returned the next time.

About a month after the court sat, my irons were taken off, and I was so weak that I had to be led to the court room by the officer. I was notified that a bill was found against me for breaking jail, and that the grand jury had failed to find a bill against me on the charge of shooting Boggs, as charged in the advertisement offering a reward for my apprehension. . . .

When I was put in Independence jail, I was again ironed hand and foot, and put in the dungeon, in which condition I remained about two months. During this time, Joseph H. Reynolds, the sheriff, told me he was going to arrest Joseph Smith, and they had received letters from Nauvoo which satisfied them that Joseph Smith had unlimited confidence in me, that I was capable of toting him in a carriage or on horseback anywhere that I pleased; and if I would only tote him out by riding or any other way, so that they could apprehend him, I might please myself whether I stayed in Illinois or came back to Missouri; they would protect me, and any pile that I would name the citizens of Jackson county would donate, club together, and raise, and that I should never suffer for want afterwards: "You only deliver Joe Smith into our hands, and name your pile." I replied—"I will see you all damned first, and then I won't." . . .

The trial came on according to my last notification. I was tried for breaking Independence jail; and . . . the jury brought in a verdict of "five minutes' imprisonment in the county jail;" but I was kept there four or five hours, during which time several attempts were made to get up some other charge against me.

About 8 p.m. on December 13th, General Doniphan took me out and told me I must take across the country on foot, and not walk on any traveled road, unless it was during the night, as they would be apt to follow and again take me, as they did not care on what grounds, so they could make me trouble.

I accordingly started, accompanied by my mother, and went to the house of a widow, where I obtained my first supper in freedom for more than nine months. We then traveled two miles and obtained $4.

I then took through the woods to the road, where I heard two men riding on horseback. I hid behind a shady tree, and overheard one of them say, "He has not been gone many minutes: we shall soon overtake him."

I went round the houses and traveled in the fields by the side of the road. The moon was in its first quarter, and I traveled during the night about twenty-five miles. I carried a little food with me, and next day traveled on the road, and walked past Crooked River to a Mr. Taylor's, with all the skin off my feet. . . .

I then continued my journey about thirty miles, where I rested three days to recruit my feet. I was then carried twenty-five miles on horseback, and walked the same day twenty-five miles. The day following I walked forty miles, and then waited another day and engaged a man to carry me to Montrose, to which place I was three days in going. I immediately crossed the river to Nauvoo in a small boat, and came straight to the Mansion.

*Joseph Smith noted Rockwell's appearance in Nauvoo in his history:*

"A large party supped at my house, and spent the evening in music, dancing, &c., in a most cheerful and friendly manner. During the festivities, a man with his hair long and falling over his shoulders, and apparently drunk, came in and acted like a

Missourian. I requested the captain of the police to put him out of doors. A scuffle ensued, and I had an opportunity to look him full in the face, when, to my great surprise and joy untold, I discovered it was my long-tried, warm, but cruelly persecuted friend, Orrin Porter Rockwell, just arrived from nearly a year's imprisonment, without conviction, in Missouri."

Orrin Porter Rockwell, in Joseph Smith, *History of the Church,* 6:134–42.

# YIELDING TO PERSECUTION'S PRESSURE

## AUTHOR UNKNOWN

Elder John T. Evans . . . spent about eight years when a young man in preaching the gospel in his native country—Wales. During about five years of this time he labored as a traveling Elder in North Wales, one of the very hardest of missionary fields, where he traveled and preached without purse or scrip. Much of the time he labored alone, for, although many different Elders were sent at various times by the president of the mission to assist him, they generally became discouraged on account of the persecution and hardships they were forced to endure and soon abandoned their labors. . . .

Upon one occasion he and four other Elders were sent to an iron manufacturing district about seven miles from Neath to introduce the gospel. Among their first converts were a man by the name of William Howells and his family. This man on embracing the gospel received a strong testimony of its divinity and was fearless in declaring it unto others. He had a sister who had been so sick and helpless as to be bed-ridden for three-and-a-half years. She was a member of the Baptist church, but on hearing the doctrines of the Latter-day Saints explained she soon became dissatisfied with her religion; and when her brother testified to her that the gospel had been restored to the earth through the Prophet Joseph Smith, with all its former gifts and blessings, she declared her intention to be baptized. Her husband was bitterly opposed to the gospel, but all the reason, ridicule and persuasion that he could use failed to turn her from her purpose. She was resolute, and so zealous withal that she made a special request to be baptized on Sunday, between eleven and twelve o'clock, that the people of the whole neighborhood might see the ceremony, and had word circulated to that effect. It was a novel thing in that region to see Latter-day Saints baptizing, and the result was, that about three thousand persons assembled on the bank of the stream to witness it. She was carried from the house to the stream, the distance of about half a mile in a chair, and there Elder Evans, assisted by a man named David Matthews, carried her into the water and baptized her.

She was rewarded for her faith by being entirely restored to health, and that too, instantaneously, for she walked out of the water and to her home.

This public manifestation of the power of God seemed to be the signal for commencing a perfect storm of opposition against the Saints. Through the influence of sectarian ministers with the proprietors of the iron works a great pressure was brought to bear against the Saints. It was claimed that they were Chartists, that is, members of a political organization which had caused a great deal of trouble throughout the kingdom a short time previously, and other lies equally unreasonable were circulated about them to make them odious and unpopular.

The five Elders who had been doing the preaching and baptizing, and who were dependent upon their labor in the iron works for their living, were informed by their employers that they must renounce the "heresy" which they taught as religion, or lose their positions. They chose the latter.

About two hundred of their converts were also employed in the iron works. They were given one month's time to renounce their religion or likewise lose their situations. All efforts to obtain employment elsewhere without a recommendation from their last employers proved unavailing, on account of the rumors against their characters, and finally, when they were brought to the test, about half of them chose to renounce their religion rather than lose their work. The others were discharged and scattered to different parts in search of employment. Many of them suffered severely for want of the necessaries of life, and were only kept from starving by the collections taken up for their benefit among the more fortunate Saints in other parts of the mission.

Among others who yielded to the pressure which the enemies of the Saints brought to bear against them, was the sister who had been healed on being baptized. Notwithstanding her former zeal and resolution, and the miraculous power of God which she had experienced, she abandoned the faith. She perhaps thought she had no further need of God's mercy, but if so, the sequel proved how sadly she was mistaken, for she was soon prostrated as before and lingered in that condition until she died.

---

*Early Scenes in Church History,* 49–51.

# THE MARTYRDOM OF
# RAFAEL MONROY

⌒

REY L. PRATT *

For three years civil war had raged in Mexico. . . . All Americans were advised to leave the country. Anti-American feeling ran high and there was every indication that there would be war between the two countries.

The little band of missionaries still left were all called into the Mission office in Mexico City and it was decided to leave the country until conditions should become more settled. Letters were written to the native branch presidents throughout the mission advising them of the resolution to abandon the field for a time, and giving them instructions in the management of affairs in their respective branches. Mission effects were packed and stored and everything was in readiness for the departure of President Pratt, his family, and all of the missionaries, on the evening train, for Vera Cruz.

About 3 p.m. a young man, a convert of but three months, stepped into the almost dismantled Mission office and said:

"President Pratt, words cannot convey to you my sorrow and that of my family at the thought of yourself and the elders having to leave us. We know you have brought us the truth and we thank God that we have accepted it, but we are as children in our knowledge of the gospel. What can we do when we are left to ourselves? The older branches of the mission have their branch presidents, men holding the priesthood and who can teach the people and

---

*Rey L. Pratt was president of the Mexican mission.

keep them in the line of their duties, but we are new in the faith, and where we live there is no branch organization; what are we to do?"

"Take this seat," replied President Pratt, placing him a chair, "and we will confer upon you the Melchizedek priesthood, and ordain you an elder, and set you apart as branch president over the few Saints who live where you do. You will then go back and preside over them, teach them the gospel, and if you are faithful and humble before the Lord, he will bless you with power and great wisdom in the performance of your duties."

In all humility, the young man received the ordination and calling as branch president.

A few hours later the missionaries all left Mexico City, and up to the present, owing to unsettled conditions in the country, have not been permitted to return and resume their missionary labors. Brother Rafael Monroy, for such was the young man's name, bade them farewell at the station, and the next day returned to his home in the little town of San Marcos.

Seven were all that had been baptized members of the Church in this place, and besides them, there were as many more earnest investigators. Trusting in the promise of the Lord to him, Brother Rafael gathered them together and told them of what had been done, and that he had been called to preside over them. After this, regular meetings and Sunday Schools were held every Sunday, also once during the week. The blessings of the Lord rested upon the little branch and the noble young man called to preside over it. Through his humble and efficient labors, the number who attended the meetings regularly had increased, within a year, from about fifteen to more than seventy-five. Investigators became converts and during the two years following the organization of the branch more than fifty souls were added to it by baptism.

The little town of San Marcos was situated in a part of the country where, during the first few years of the struggle in Mexico, the horrors of war did not enter. But the revolution, like a devastating fire, afterward burned its way into and over even the most secret recesses of the land, leaving in its wake little but its blackened trail and the charred and ruined walls of what once were homes.

So it was that in May, 1915, this little town found itself on the firing line between the hordes of Zapata, the Attila of the South, on the south, and the advancing army of Carranza, under the leadership of Obregon, on the north. For three months the battle raged between the contending forces, with the town now in the hands of the Zapatistas, and now in the hands of the Carranzistas.

Our little band of Saints nobly struggled on in the midst of all this, without taking part on either side, and held their meetings and Sunday Schools many times, even while battles were being fought and bullets were flying over the house in which their services were held. Devotion to their faith had won them many friends, but, as is always the case where truth is established, Satan put hatred into the hearts of some of the people against them. Among these was a neighbor of Brother Rafael who had it in his heart not only to hate those who professed another faith to his, but also, if possible, to destroy both it and those who professed it.

On July 17, after a battle of several hours, the town, which for several weeks had been held by the Carranzistas, was taken by the Zapatistas. The neighbor spoken of saw now his opportunity to strike what he thought would be a fatal blow at the little branch, by denouncing its leader, to the conquering hordes of Zapata, as a colonel who had fought against them on the side of the Carranzistas; and further that he was a "Mormon," the leader of those who professed that strange religion in the little village, and was perverting the people and leading them off after other gods.

Zapata and his followers [were] intensely fanatic and fight their battles in the name of the Virgin of Guadalupe, avowing the destruction of all who oppose her. So Brother Rafael, soon after their entrance into the town, found his home surrounded by an armed troop of men. He and Brother Vicente Morales, who was there with him, were placed under arrest. The Zapatistas demanded that they give up their arms, but Brother Rafael, confident in the fact that he was innocent, as far as having arms, and fighting with them, simply drew from his pocket his Bible and his Book of Mormon and said:

"Gentlemen, these are the only arms I ever carry; they are the arms of truth against error."

. . . His answer only infuriated the mob. He and his companion were now held securely while his house and belongings were searched for the arms that were supposed to be hidden there. But no arms were found, so the brethren were submitted to all kinds of torture in an endeavor to make them divulge the place where arms were hidden. At last ropes were placed round their necks and thrown over the limbs of a tree; but before the knots were tightened they were told that if they would forsake their strange religion and join with the Zapatistas, they would be placed at liberty. But Brother Rafael replied:

"My religion is dearer to me than my life and I cannot forsake it."

At this they were raised from the ground by the ropes around their necks and suspended in the air till unconscious. But their tormentors were not ready to see them die, so let them down and revived them. At this stage the three sisters of Brother Rafael, even at their own peril, went to the commander of the Zapatistas to intercede for their brother and Vicente. But their tears and prayers were vain, and they, too, were made prisoners and thrown into a room under heavy guard.

This was about 10 a.m., and some time later, after all attempts, made with cruel tortures, had failed to make Brothers Rafael and Vicente divulge the hiding place of arms they did not have, and make them forsake the gospel they held dearer than life, they, too, were taken to the same room where the sisters were held. As best he could, Brother Rafael comforted his sisters, and told them to trust in the Lord and all would be well. He asked for water and bathed his hands and face and the chafed neck where the hangman's cruel rope had nearly strangled his life out. He then drew from his pocket his Bible and Book of Mormon, and occupied the remainder of the afternoon in reading the scriptures and explaining the gospel to his guards and fellow prisoners.

All day long the poor distracted mother had gone from one office to another, protesting that her children were innocent of any crime and begging for their release, but it was without avail. It was not until about 7 p.m. that she was even permitted to take them any food, and was not even then permitted to take it into them nor see them, but had to send it in by a guard. The grief and fear of the sisters were greater than their desire for food, but under the consoling and encouraging words of Brother Rafael, they were persuaded to spread out their little repast and prepare to partake of it. When all was arranged, Brother Rafael asked for the attention from the rest of the prisoners, and permission from the guards, to ask a blessing on the food. In a voice that all could hear, he thanked God for it, and for all of his blessings. Then, in a quiet way to his sisters, he said: "Partake of the food, but I will not partake, for I am fasting today."

A few moments later an orderly came in and called for Rafael Monroy and Vicente Morales, and commanded them to follow him. By this time it was getting dark, and they were conducted under guard to the outskirts of the little town. There they were stood up by a large ash tree and in front of a firing squad. The officer in charge again offered to them their freedom if they would forsake their strange religion and join the Zapatistas, but the brethren, as firmly as before, replied that their religion was dearer than life, and that they would not forsake it.

They were then told that they were to be shot, and asked if they had any request to make. Brother Rafael requested that he be permitted to pray before he was executed; and there, in the presence of his executioners, he kneeled and, in a voice that all could hear, prayed God to bless and protect his loved ones, and to care for the little struggling branch that would be left without a leader. As he finished his prayer he used the words of the Savior when he, himself, hung upon the cross, and prayed for his executioners, "Father, forgive them, for they know not what they do."

Not once did he pray that his own life might be spared; but when his prayer was finished, he stood up and folded his arms and said, "Gentlemen, I am at your service." The report of six rifles rang out on the night air, and was echoed to the sisters waiting in the little prison room, and to the mother and wife waiting in despair in their little home, conveying to them the knowledge that Rafael and Vicente had given up their lives, martyrs to the cause that they loved more than their lives!

The circumstances attending the execution were told to the family afterwards by a soldier who witnessed them, and he said that in all his experience he never saw men die with greater courage, nor had he ever heard such a prayer as that offered by Brother Rafael.

As if in grief over the great tragedy, and an effort to wash the earth clean of the stains of innocent blood, a tropical storm broke over the little village, and the rain came down in torrents. But out into the darkness, and in the face of the storm, went the heart-broken old mother of Brother Rafael, to find, if possible, the body of her dear, dead son. For, though she had pleaded with the soldiers, they would not tell her where he lay; and it was not until four in the morning that she found him. In recounting it afterwards, she said, "Surely the Lord was with me and strengthened me that night, for I, who had many times fainted at the sight of blood, was able, alone, and without fear, to keep watch over my boy and his companion from the time I found them till daylight came."

The three sisters were held all night as prisoners, and the following morning the soldiers were making preparations to take them with them, but the mother went again before the general and implored him, now that her son was dead, to spare to her her daughters. This request he granted and about 8 a.m. the girls were liberated.

Orders were given to arrest and execute any man who should attempt to move the bodies of the two murdered brethren; so, there was nothing left for the grief-stricken mother, wife and sisters to do but themselves to remove the bodies and bury them as best they could. They improvised a stretcher and carried them half a mile home, and with their own hands prepared them for burial, and buried them.

No doubt the perpetrators of this crime thought that with the death of the leader, the strange religion in their midst would come to an end. But just so thought those who put the prophets of old to death, and those who crucified the Savior of the world; and later those who murdered the Prophet Joseph Smith. But such was not the case, for the little branch has not only survived, but has grown since, and the faith of its members is stronger than ever.

Mother never loved a son with more devotion and tenderness than did the widowed mother of Brother Rafael. He was her only son, her mainstay and only support; and his love for her was only equaled by that of hers for him. Their devotion to each other in life was an inspiration to all who saw it. And only the Lord and those who have had similar experience to hers, know the depth of her grief at the death of her son!

But it has been one of the greatest inspirations that has ever come to the author of this article, to have witnessed the resignation, devotion to the Lord, and faithfulness with which she has borne her sorrow. There seems to be no bitterness in her soul, not even for those who committed the awful crime, and she says she is willing to leave their case with the Lord and let him deal with them as seemeth him good.

Her spirit is better manifest than by any description of mine, in her own words with which she closed a letter to me in describing the whole sad affair. She said: "Brother Pratt, great, great, indeed, have been our afflictions, but greater still is our faith, and we will not falter!"

_____

*Improvement Era,* 21:720–26.

# PIONEERS

# A CROWDED NIGHT IN EXILE

## ELIZA R. SNOW

We were two days on our way to Far West, and stopped over night at what was called the Half-way House, a log building perhaps twenty feet square, with the chinkings between the logs, minus—they probably having been burned for firewood—the owner of the house, Brother Littlefield, having left with his family to escape being robbed; and the north wind had free ingress through the openings, wide enough for cats to crawl through. This had been the lodging place of the hundreds who had preceded us, and on the present occasion proved the almost shelterless shelter of seventy-five or eighty souls. To say lodging, would be a hoax, although places were allotted to a few aged and feeble, to lie down, while the rest of us either sat or stood, or both, all night. My sister and I managed so that mother lay down, and we sat by (on the floor, of course), to prevent her being trampled on, for the crowd was such that people were hardly responsible for their movements.

It was past the middle of December, and the cold was so intense that, in spite of well packing, our food was frozen hard, bread and all, and although a blazing fire was burning on one side of the room, we could not get to it to thaw our suppers, and had to resort to the next expediency, which was this:

The boys milked, and while one strained the milk, another held the pan (for there was no chance for putting anything down); then, while one held a bowl of the warm milk, another would, as expeditiously as possible, thinly slice the frozen bread

315

into it, and thus we managed for supper. In the morning, we were less crowded, as some started very early, and we toasted our bread and thawed our meat before the fire. But, withal, that was a very merry night. None but saints can be happy under every circumstance. About twenty feet from the house was a shed, in the centre of which the brethren built a roaring fire, around which some of them stood and sang songs and hymns all night, while others parched corn and roasted frosted potatoes, etc. Not a complaint was heard—all were cheerful, and judging from appearances, strangers would have taken us to be pleasure excursionists rather than a band of gubernatorial exiles.

---

Eliza R. Snow, in Edward W. Tullidge, *Women of Mormondom,* 145–46.

# A DIFFICULT JOURNEY WESTWARD

## ELIZA R. SNOW

At this point [Colonel Stephen L.] Markham exchanged our buggy for a lumber wagon, in order to assist others in carrying freight; and in performing this act of generosity, so filled the wagon, as to give us barely room to sit in front. This wagon, with bags piled on bags, was my sleeping room—the [Markham] family lodged in other wagons and in a tent. Instead of comfort, necessity was the order of the move, and the best faculty for adaptation to circumstances, the best inheritance. We were thankful to be so well off—fleeing from persecution, we were in pursuit of a land of peace. The mob in the vicinity of Nauvoo, knowing that I wielded the pen, had threatened my life, lest, as they said, I should write about the tragic scene at Carthage.

When we started again, Mrs. Markham and I were seated on a chest with brass-kettle and soap-box for our foot-stools, and were happy, and well might be, in comparison with some of our sisters who walked all day, rain or shine, and at night prepared supper for their families, with no sheltering tents; and then made their beds in, and under wagons that contained their earthly all. Frequently with intense sympathy and admiration I watched the mother when, forgetful of her own fatigue and destitution, she took unwearied pains to fix up in the most palatable form, the allotted portion of food, and as she dealt it out, was cheering the hearts of her children. . . .

From exposure and hardship I was taken sick soon after with a slow fever, and as I lay sick in the wagon, where my bed was exposed to heavy rains, and, at times, unavoidably wet from head to foot, I realized that I was near the gate of death; but in this suffering and exposed condition, I did not feel that God had forsaken me—my trust was in Him, and His power preserved me. While passing through this trying scene, I not only realized the goodness of God, but experienced many kindnesses from my sisters, whose names are not only written in my Journal, but also are engraven on my heart; and I shall never forget the unceasing kindness of brother and sister Markham, with whom I journeyed from Nauvoo to this winter stopping-point.

---

Eliza R. Snow, in Kate B. Carter, comp., *Our Pioneer Heritage,* 17:332–34.

# SOPHIA GOODRIDGE'S PIONEER DIARY

◦⁓⁓

## SOPHIA GOODRIDGE

June 20th 1850.] Still in camp. Did our ironing. Picked some wild gooseberries on the banks of the creek. . . .

[June] 25th. Crossed the creek this morning. Passed five graves; they died the 15th of June. They all had grave tablets made of wood rudely hewn with the name engraved with a knife. A verse was written on the grave of Mr. Done, which was very touching. . . .

[June] 26th. We traveled ten miles today. Passed three graves, no names on them. . . . One man was sick with cholera, died, was buried in the forenoon. In the afternoon we passed three more graves, no names, died June 22. One of our company taken sick with cholera. Camped at Salt Creek. . . .

[June] 27th. Sister Green died of cholera this morning. . . .

[June] 28th. We started about noon and traveled six miles and camped on the open prairie without wood or water. Found water about one-half mile from camp. Passed the grave of a child.

[June] 29th. Our company all in good spirits this morning, and I feel grateful to my Heavenly Father for his kindness in preserving our lives and health thus far, and that He has preserved us from accident and danger of every kind. . . .

July 1st. Joseph Green died this morning of cholera, age 19 months, making three of one family that have died within five days. Came up with our first fifty, found Bro. Hall dead with cholera. Our camp felt afflicted and distressed. We felt like humbling ourselves before the Lord, and pray that He might turn from us the sickness and distress among us. We therefore met together, the speakers exhorting us to be diligent in our devotions and united. A vote was taken to that effect. They called upon the Lord in prayer that he would bless and preserve us on our journey to the Valley. We then started on our journey rejoicing. . . .

[July] 4th. Stopped to wash. Lucy Johnson was taken sick this afternoon and died at 12 o'clock.

[July] 7th. Camped for the day. Sister Snow died this morning, making five that have died in our division. . . .

[July] 11th. Heavy showers, very warm and sultry. Sister Huntington of the first division died of a fever. The road very wet and hard to travel. . . .

[July] 14th. Sunday. Camped for the day, both divisions camped in one corral. We held a meeting in the afternoon. Bros. Whipple, Hardy and Woodruff were the speakers. We felt very much encouraged by what they said.

[July] 15th. We traveled seven miles. . . . A thundershower came up and Wm. Ridges was struck by lightning and instantly killed. Three of his cattle were killed at the same time, and one of his children injured but not seriously. A number of people felt the shock. We went two miles farther and camped. . . .

[October 14, 1850] . . . Bro. Woodruff came up with us this morning and we all drove into the Valley of Salt Lake and camped in the Fort. It was a rather dreary homecoming. It was very dry and dusty, and the wind was blowing the dust in clouds. Only a few little log and adobe houses to be seen, fenced in with rail and willow fences. A few shade trees and fruit trees were to be seen here and there. I thought at first; "Have I got to spend the rest of my days here in this dreary looking place?" But I soon felt all right about it and loved my mountain home.

---

Sophia Goodridge, in Kate B. Carter, comp., *Our Pioneer Heritage*, 15:254–56, 264.

# BRIGHAM YOUNG REPROVES THE
# PIONEER COMPANY

*B . H . R O B E R T S*

T he camp in its march usually observed "The Lord's Day" by resting from their journey and holding religious services. Only the emergencies of securing food for their animals, the necessity of making some point for encampment or fording streams to that end, seem to have occasioned the breaches of the custom. There was at times much merriment in camp. There were musical instruments brought along and those who could play them. There was dancing, too, occasionally, notwithstanding the absence of ladies; the games of quoits, of checkers, some card-playing for amusement, scuffling, wrestling, the telling of humorous stories of doubtful propriety, loud laughter, the playing of practical jokes and the like were indulged.

. . . All this . . . did not appeal to the leader, Brigham Young, whom, it should always be remembered, was of Puritan extraction. . . . He had engaged if the camp would attend strictly to its duties, "abide his counsels and observe his directions, they should go safely, and they and their teams be preserved from the Indians and from every enemy." . . .

Finally, respecting these matters, things reached a climax on Saturday the 29th of May. The morning of that day was cold and rainy. The horn for gathering up the horses and cattle was sounded, but instead of proceeding on the journey, President Young required each captain to call out his men and each group to stand by itself. It was found that when this was done the whole camp, excepting two, were present, and these two were out hunting. President Young then addressed himself to the camp in the following terms—the account is from Woodruff's Journal:

"I think I will take for my text to preach my sermon from— [these words]:

"'I am about to revolt from traveling with this camp any further with the spirit they now possess.'"

He then proceeded to say:

"I had rather risk myself among the savages with ten men that are men of faith, men of mighty prayer, men of God, than to be with this whole camp when they forget God and turn their hearts to folly and wickedness. Yes, I had rather be alone; and I am now resolved not to go any further with the camp unless you will covenant to humble yourselves before the Lord and serve him and quit your folly and wickedness. For a week past nearly the whole camp has been cardplaying, and checkers and dominoes have occupied the attention of the brethren, and dancing and 'hoeing down'—all this has been the act continually. Now, it is quite time to quit it. And there has been trials of law suits upon every nonsensical thing; and if those things are suffered to go on, it will be but a short time before you will be fighting, knocking each other down and taking life. It is high time it was stopped."

So he continued in this spirit to admonish and reprove the camp, showing the brethren how inconsistent the course of the camp had been for a week past or more, for men who were going "to seek out a location in the mountains for a resting place for the saints, even the whole church of God, who have been driven out from the Gentiles and rejected of them; . . . a resting place for the saints where the standard of the kingdom of God would be reared, and a banner unfurled for the nations to gather unto."

Finally he called first upon his fellow apostles of the twelve to know if they were willing to humble themselves before the Lord and covenant to do right; if so they must manifest it by the uplifted hand. Every hand in that council was raised. The same question was put to the high priests, to the seventies, to the elders, and to the members, and all unanimously covenanted to repent of their sins and keep the commandments of the Lord. President Young then addressed himself to the few members of the camp who were not members of the church—"as there were some present." He informed them "that they would be protected in their rights, but they must not introduce wickedness in the camp, for it would not be suffered."

The day following—which was Sunday—was set apart as a day of fasting, humiliation and prayer. Prayer meeting was held by the whole camp; and a second meeting at which the sacrament of the Lord's Supper was administered. "The Lord seemed to accept the offerings of our hearts," wrote Erastus Snow that day, "and poured out his spirit upon us." The twelve and a few others, in addition to attending these public services, "went into the valley of the hills; and, according to the order of the priesthood, prayed in a circle." Two of the brethren were stationed on guard to protect these brethren from interruption by the Indians.

The repentance of the camp seems to have been most effectual as we hear no more complaint of their conduct en route for their destination.

---

B. H. Roberts, *A Comprehensive History of the Church*, 3:182–86.

# FAITH IN HIS FATHER

## SUSA YOUNG GATES

In April the first company in the spring of 1848 left Winter
Quarters, led by Pres. Brigham Young, who had returned to
bring the rest of his own family back to the retreat in the
Valley. Brigham [Junior], who was then a boy of twelve, was made
driver of two yoke of oxen. He was quite equal to the oxen and to
the occasion. He was faithful to his trust. One of his father's wives
[Eliza B. Young] sat on the seat, while the boy trudged by his
oxen, cracking his whip and piping a song to beguile the weari-
ness of the way.

When the company halted at Sweetwater, women were tired,
men were discouraged. Day after day passed, and the discontent
of the party grew with every passing hour. Among any other
people, there would have been mutiny and sharp turn backward
to the shelter of civilization.

Always alert to the pressure of influences about him, President
Young felt the resistance that manifested itself in silence rather
than in words. One afternoon at three o'clock he hitched up his
coach and with the terse statement that he was "going to the
Valley; if anybody wants to follow, the road is open," the President
put the whip to his horses and gave not a glance behind. Like a
flash, the boy flung the yoke upon his oxen, hitched them to his
wagon, picked up his whip and drove as rapidly as he could after
the coach rolling away to the west.

This instance illustrates, as perhaps no other could, the
keynote of this boy's after life. The determination which filled his

whole soul and which stiffened the youthful lips into the iron line across his face so much like his father's, was expressed in the words which he uttered to his father's wife who hastily took her seat in the wagon: "Father's started; I'm not going to lose sight of his wagon wheels while daylight lasts."

Susa Young Gates, in Preston Nibley, comp., *Faith Promoting Stories*, 143–45.

# "We Obtained a Little Musty Corn-Meal"

## RELIEF CRAM ATWOOD

Among the pioneers who came to this country in 1847, and returned to Winter Quarters at Council Bluffs the same year was [Millen Atwood,] the man who subsequently became my husband. We first met early in the Spring of 1848, and in a short time we were married. In one month we were on our way to the valley in President Brigham Young's company. In just four months to a day we arrived here, it being on the 19th day of September. We had a small store of provisions, a little clothing, our team and our hands with which to help ourselves. We found our new home a barren desert. With the exception of a few patches of ground which the pioneers had broken up and planted, scarcely a tree or shrub was to be seen and not more than one or two houses were outside the fort.

My husband made enough adobes to rear a house of two small rooms, and with much difficulty he obtained the lumber to cover the roof, lay the floor and make the doors. In the erection of this adobe, wooden pins were used exclusively instead of nails, as the latter were so very hard to obtain. The house was lighted with six broken panes of glass which he procured by plastering for a neighbor by candle light. Our furniture consisted of one chair with a rawhide seat, a bed-stead hewn out with an ax, a cupboard of three rough shelves in a corner of the room, and a table.

On the 23rd of December we moved into our humble dwelling with joy and gratitude to our Heavenly Father that we had so good a habitation to shield us from the piercing cold and storms of Winter. Until then we had lived in our wagon. The snow had already fallen and covered the earth to a depth of a foot or more, and the hungry wolves could be heard prowling about at night in search of food. One night they came near enough to take a chicken from the back of the wagon where we had retired to rest. The wild Indians, also, were roaming about by day and begging for food. Our store of provisions being very scant we had to put ourselves on very small rations. By some means we obtained a little musty corn-meal which served to make our flour last longer. Our fuel was wood from the canyon, and, our team being poor and little food for it to eat, it was with difficulty we obtained even wood. As a light we were thankful to get tallow candles.

When Spring opened we found ourselves almost entirely without food and had to subsist chiefly on herbs and roots for a time. Here we were in the heart of a desert, a thousand miles away from civilization without food or nearly so, the soil barren and forbidding. . . .

I will here relate an incident of our seed time: My husband had taken a lot of land near what is now called the Sugar House Ward. He took his team and went to plow and prepare it for the seed. In due time he went to plant his corn and he found the ground as dry as ashes to a great depth. It seemed impossible to him for the seed ever to germinate in such a soil. He planted the seeds, however, knowing that if he did not plant he surely could not reap. He came home at night hungry, faint and weary. I was also very weary from the labors of the day. We had planted a garden near the house and I brought water from the City Creek in pails every day to water it (the creek then flowed down the east side of Main Street); and the water made the ground as hard as an adobe. We partook of our scanty meal and prepared to retire to rest. We then bowed ourselves before the Lord to implore His blessing to rest upon us. His Spirit did rest upon us powerfully in the gift of tongues and the interpretation of the same. My husband commenced praying in his own language and suddenly he broke out in an unknown tongue. I understood what he said. At first it was a reproof from the Lord for our unbelief. It was thus: "Have I not brought you all this way from the land of your enemies to this goodly land? and I will bless this land for my people's sake, if they will put their trust in me, and it shall bring forth in great abundance of grass, grain and vegetables of every kind, fruit also, of the choicest kind, and your tables shall be loaded with the best fruits of the earth. Only put your trust in me. Plant and you shall reap."

We arose and retired to rest, but not to sleep. Sleep had departed from our eyes. We were filled with wonder, love and admiration. We could not doubt more. We went to work with fresh courage. The earth yielded more and more each succeeding year, and in the year 1850, my husband reaped forty bushels of wheat per acre.

---

*Juvenile Instructor,* 19:35–36.

# "THE STORM WAS MUCH WORSE INDOORS"

## ELIZA R. SNOW

Our first winter in the mountains was delightful; the ground froze but little; our coldest weather was three or four days in November, after which the men plowed and sowed, built houses, etc. The weather seemed to have been particularly ordered to meet our very peculiar circumstances. Every labor, such as cultivating the ground, procuring fuel and timber from the canyons, etc., was a matter of experiment. Most of us were houseless; and what the result would have been, had that winter been like the succeeding ones, may well be conjectured.

President Young had kindly made arrangements for me to live with his wife, Clara Decker, who came with the pioneers, and was living in a log-house about eighteen feet square, which constituted a portion of the east side of our fort. This hut, like most of those built the first year, was roofed with willows and earth, the roof having but little pitch, the first-comers having adopted the idea that the valley was subject to little if any rain, and our roofs were nearly flat. We suffered no inconvenience from this fact until about the middle of March, when a long storm of snow, sleet and rain occurred, and for several days the sun did not make its appearance. The roof of our dwelling was covered deeper with earth than the adjoining ones, consequently it did not leak so soon, and some of my neighbors huddled in for shelter; but one evening, when several were socially sitting around, the water commenced dripping in one place, and then in another; they dodged it for awhile, but it increased so rapidly that they finally concluded they might as well go to their own wet houses. After they had gone I spread my umbrella over my head and shoulders as I ensconced myself in bed, the lower part of which, not shielded by the umbrella, was wet enough before morning. The earth overhead was thoroughly saturated, and after it commenced to drip the storm was much worse indoors than out.

Eliza R. Snow, in Edward W. Tullidge, *Women of Mormondom*, 350–51.

# "HE WAS HAILED BY US AS THE ARRIVAL OF AN ANGEL"

## ALICE BROOKS

*Alice Brooks (1835–1915), who traveled west with the Martin hand-cart company, recorded the following about her journey.*

Some days we traveled from ten to fifteen miles and one day we journeyed thirty miles. Two persons were assigned to each handcart and only seventeen pounds of baggage was allowed each passenger. Two ox teams accompanying the hand-cart company carried tents and rations. We usually pitched our tents at night near water and gathered buffalo chips for fuel. Having left most of our clothes behind, we were compelled to spread gunny-sacks on the snow for bedding. We often sat and held our feet in our hands at night to keep them from freezing. Our eatables consisted chiefly of flour, tea and sugar, and we had to depend upon the killing of buffaloes for meat.

We had to wade rivers, and finally in a very exhausted condition we were helped to the Valley by teams sent out to meet us, but we had spent three weeks in the snow before relief came. During that time, when our cattle gave out, we boiled their bones for soup, as there was no meat. We also roasted raw hides and ate them. At last we found ourselves encamped in a ravine near Devils Gate with just four ounces of flour to each person per day for four days. A great number of our people died, sometimes half a dozen a day, and on one occasion sixteen persons were buried in one grave. People would walk until exhausted and then drop down by the wayside dead, leaving their bodies to be eaten by wolves, as the survivors, on account of the frozen ground, were not able to dig graves deep enough to secure them from ravenous beasts.

In their starving condition both men and women seemed to become devoid of all human feeling and lost all affection for each other. The children's faces sometimes assumed the appearance of monkeys, and they would frequently grab pieces of food out of each others mouths and die crying for bread. We climbed mountains to get icicles off the sage brush and melted snow to obtain water wherewith to mix our flour.

At Devils Gate the people were called together for prayer and asked if they were willing to die if the Lord so willed it, or if they were sorry they had come. They all answered that they were willing to die if the Lord so willed it, but they were not sorry they had come.

Almost at the same moment was witnessed the approach of Joseph A. Young on a white horse. He was hailed by us as the arrival of an angel. Men and women surrounded him, weeping and holding onto him, pleading with him to save them from death. Elder Young went back and reported, and the next night we received a pound of flour each.

In traveling through Echo canyon, camp fires were built every quarter of a mile to thaw out those who lingered behind. At last we arrived in Salt Lake City, Nov. 30, 1856.

Alice Brooks, in Andrew Jenson, *LDS Biographical Encyclopedia,* 3:4–5.

# "SHE STRAPPED MY LITTLE
# BROTHER ON MY BACK"

MARGARET McNEIL BALLARD

The first ten years of my childhood was spent in Tranent, [Scotland,] but because of being a "Mormon" I was not permitted to attend the schools, and so I was entirely deprived of schooling while in the old country, and in pioneering there was little opportunity for education. During those ten years our family enjoyed the association of the Elders and Saints. My father was President of the Edinburgh Conference for a number of years. Therefore, the Elders visited our home often, and we were always glad to receive them, although many times I went to bed hungry in order to give my meal to the visiting Elders.

We had waited a long time to come to Zion, but my father was called by the Church to stay in Scotland and preside over the Saints in that Branch. When Father was finally given the chance to leave

Scotland he tried to persuade my mother to wait awhile—Mother
was about to give birth to her sixth child. Mother insisted upon
coming for she had faith that the Lord would take care of her.

Before we left, my mother took us to say good-bye to our
grandmother, my mother's mother, Margaret (Martin) Reid, but
she would not come to the door or let us in. My aunt came to the
door and said Grandmother didn't want to see us for we had
broken her heart because we had joined the Mormon Church.
Mother took us by the hand and we went home. Mother cried all
the way home.

On April 27, 1856 we left Liverpool for America. . . .

When we were all ready to start on our journey westward, my
father's team of five-year old unbroken oxen ran away, and we
were delayed. We had never seen oxen before, and the animals
allotted to us had to be roped and tied in order to yoke and fasten
them to the wagon. When they were released from the ropes they
became unmanageable and difficult to catch.

The company had gone on ahead, and as my mother was
anxious for me to go with them she strapped my little brother,
James, on my back with a shawl. He was only four years old [and I
was ten] and still quite sick with the measles, but I took him since
mother had all she could do to care for the other children. I
hurried and caught up with the company, traveling with them all
day. That night a kind lady helped me take my brother off my
back. I sat up and held him on my lap with the shawl wrapped
around him, alone, all night. He was a little better in the morning. The people in the camp were very good to us and gave us a
little fried bacon and some bread for breakfast.

We traveled this way for about a week, my brother and I not
seeing our mother during this time. Each morning one of the
men would write a note and put it in the slit of a willow stuck into

the ground to tell how we were getting along. In this way mother knew that we were all right. . . .

One night our cow ran away from camp and I was sent out to bring her back. I was barefooted and not watching where I was going. All of sudden I began to feel that I was walking on something soft and looked down to see what it could be. I found to my horror that I was standing in a bed of snakes, large ones and small ones. At the sight of them I became so weak that I could scarcely move. All I could think of was to pray. The Lord blessed and watched out for me so that I was protected from many similar experiences. . . .

Being alone much of the time I had to get across the rivers as best as I could. Our cow was a Jersey and had a long tail. When it became necessary to cross the rivers I would wind the end of her tail around my hand and swim across with her. . . .

Our food gave out and we had nothing but milk and wild rose berries to eat. However we did have a good team and could travel fast. We arrived in Ogden on the 4th day of October, 1859 after a journey of 1,035 miles from Woodriver. Although each day was filled with hardship and hunger, we thanked our Heavenly Father for His protecting care—care that made our trip easier to endure. I walked every step of the way across the plains, drove my cow and a large part of the way carried my little brother, James, on my back.

We camped on the outskirts of town. . . . Across the field from where we were was a little home and out in the yard was a big pile of squash. We were so famished that my mother sent me over to beg for squash, for we did not have a cent of money, and some of the children were very weak for want of food. I knocked at the door and an old lady came and said, "Come in, come in. I knew you were coming and have been told to give you food." She gave me a large loaf of fresh bread and said to tell my mother that she would come over soon. It was not long until she did come and brought us a nicely cooked dinner, something we had not had for a long time. This woman was surely inspired of the Lord to help us and we were grateful for her kindness. Bread never tasted so good before or since. . . .

At one time we ran right out of everything to eat and father had a few logs he could spare, so he went to a man and asked him if he would not give him some bran for them. This is all we had to eat for some time. This man found that we were in dire need of help and told the Presiding Elder that we needed assistance. A meeting was held and the people were told that they should pay fast offerings, which they did. The first fast offerings paid in Logan were then given to my father.

Father soon got work building a bridge, and after this we did not have it so hard. I carried water for the family all that winter from the north branch of Logan River which was about three blocks away. I had very little clothing on my body, and my feet were bare, often leaving blood stains on the snow. Sometimes I would wrap them in old rags but this was worse than ever because the rags froze to my feet.

---

Margaret McNeil Ballard, in Douglas O. Crookston, ed., *Henry Ballard*, 213–23.

BEST-LOVED STORIES OF THE LDS PEOPLE

# "PROMISE ME . . . THAT YOU WILL . . . GO TO UTAH"

## ADAH ROBERTS NAYLOR

*Brigham Henry Roberts faced difficult times as a child. When his mother, Ann Everington Roberts, emigrated from her native Great Britain to Utah in 1862, she lacked the funds to bring her entire family with her. She traveled with her younger children and left the two eldest behind—with plans for them to soon join her. She entrusted five-year-old Henry to the care of the Toveys, a couple who had recently joined the Church. Henry's subsequent challenges are told in this account:*

Ann was blessed with an abundance of vitality, and she worked early and late, often sewing far into the night, in her struggle to get warm clothing, bedding, and money enough to send for her children, but nearly three years had passed before she had accomplished her purpose. The clothing and bedding were sent to New York, the money to England, and Mary, now a girl of fifteen, was prepared for the journey, but no trace of the boy Henry could be found.

And so it was that a great search was set up in the branches of the Mormon Church throughout the British Isles.

The Toveys, tiring of the restrictions placed on them by the teachings of the Church, disappeared shortly after Ann left England, taking the boy Henry with them. Their sole earthly belongings were a violin, a Bible, and a bundle of clothing. It was summertime, and on foot they went through the green lanes of England. They worked a little at odd jobs and begged, and at

334

night they slept huddled together under the hedges. But when cold weather came they sought the cities, where shelter could be had at low cost and where Mr. Tovey, who was a stonecutter by trade, would sometimes find employment.

Both Mr. and Mrs. Tovey were given to drink, and many hours were whiled away at taverns where Mr. Tovey played his violin and Mrs. Tovey sang in a cracked voice, in return for which they were given free drinks and sometimes food. They taught Henry a number of old English ballads, and he would stand on a table and entertain the patrons by singing in a sweet childish treble, afterwards passing his hat for pennies. One day some soldiers, noticing the splendid rhythm of the lad, suggested that he would make a good drummer boy for the army.

When Henry was seven the Toveys, who had now changed their name to Gailey, quarreled seriously and decided to separate. Mrs. Gailey, Henry learned from their conversation, wanted to join a brother who had recently finished a term in prison, and Mr. Gailey, not wishing to be encumbered with a small boy and evidently remembering the comment of the soldier, took him to nearby barracks where he was accepted as a drummer boy in the British Army. Measurements were taken for his uniform, and Mr. Gailey was to return with him the following day, but that night, as Henry slept, his mother's face appeared before him. She was weeping, and the promise he had made at their parting flashed into his mind. "Promise me," she had said, "that if I am unable to send for you, that you will, when you grow to be a man, go to Utah." The dream awakened him and something within him said, "If you serve in the army you will never get to Utah." He got up quietly, and taking his clothes in his arms, crept down the stairs and out into the dark street. He stopped to dress and then started on his pilgrimage back to Thorplton where he thought he could find the elders who had known his mother.

For many weeks he wandered about, eating when he could find food and sleeping with other street urchins in empty boxes and doorways. He inquired everywhere for Mormon elders, but no one seemed to have heard of them, and so, overcome by loneliness and longing for the healing influence of the familiar, he retraced his steps back to where he had lived with the Gaileys. They welcomed him back, and life for him settled back into the old groove.

Ann had been in America four long years, and Henry had passed his ninth birthday when the elders found him. He was a sturdy lad, like his mother in appearance—the same clear blue eyes with the wide setting, the same fine head line, and the same air of serious earnestness. He could neither read nor write, nor did he know the letters of the alphabet, but necessity had made him a keen observer, and he was far older than his years. He joined his sister Mary at Liverpool, and late in April 1866, they set sail for America. . . .

[During the pioneer journey westward] he slept with the other men and boys under the wagons, shivering in the cold because the bedding sent by his mother had been lost, and the only covering he had was the flannel petticoat of his sister that was dropped down to him when she went to bed inside the wagon. He was up early and out to the campfire to warm himself; he liked to watch the sun pulling itself up over the edge of the earth, for its coming meant warmth and comfort.

During the day he made tours of inspection that often led him far afield. Once he was left behind and forced to swim the Missouri River before he could rejoin the wagon train. It was there that he lost his coat and shoes, a loss that filled him with a sad foreboding. He had lovely remembrances of his mother. Her clothes made by herself, often from cast-off garments of her rich customers, had a line and a style that gave her a fine appearance, and Henry thought her very beautiful. He remembered her exactitude about clean hands, well-brushed hair, and neat clothing, and the sight of his bare bruised feet made him miserable. . . . Along the trail they came upon a cluster of log cabins that had been burned and were still smoldering. Henry stayed behind to investigate. Sticking out between two burned logs were the . . . legs of a [dead] man, and on those legs were a practically new pair of shoes. He pulled and tugged until the shoes were free . . . then running swiftly he caught up with the train, and climbing quietly into the back of a provision wagon, he hid his precious find against the time when he should meet his mother—a great burden had been lifted from his heart.

In October they reached the Valley. As the long wagon train slowly wended its way through Emigration Canyon, Henry hurried ahead and, climbing to a high cliff, caught his first glimpse of Zion. . . .

The wagons rolled into the city streets, and at last the great moment had come. The lad rushed to the provision wagon where his treasure was hidden. They were a man's shoes, much too large for him—but they were shoes, and slipping his bruised and swollen feet into them, he marched at the head of the procession up Main Street to the Tithing Office, where his mother awaited him.

---

Adah Roberts Naylor, *Relief Society Magazine,* January 1934, 7–8.

# PRAYER

# "I Will Go and Find the Cow"

WILLIAM W. CLUFF

M y parents were living in Nauvoo, State of Illinois, when the incident I will here relate occurred. There were ten children in the family, only one being a girl. I was at the time ten years old. We were very poor, owning only one cow, on the milk of which we depended largely for food. In the spring of 1842 the cow strayed off. My father and three older brothers spent weeks during the summer in vain looking for her, and about concluded that she must be dead, and almost gave up in despair. I had repeatedly asked father to let me go and hunt for her, when he would reply, "What can you do when myself and the older boys have traveled the country over for miles around in a vain search?" But young as I was, my faith was that I could find the lost cow.

One evening in August father came home very weary and dis-couraged after traveling all day for her. I said, "Father, if you will let me take Charley" (an old horse), "I will go and find the cow." He said somewhat angrily, "Well, go my boy and learn that you are not so smart as you think yourself to be."

Early next morning I started off, taking the La Harpe Road, which passed near the "Big Mound," three or four miles east of the city, and in a prairie country. Here I had often herded cows with other boys from Nauvoo. Riding direct to the base of the big mound, I dismounted, and holding the horse by the bridle, knelt down and fervently prayed the Lord to direct me which way to go to find the cow. Then climbing up on the horse, I started due south; and notwithstanding there were numerous bunches of cattle in every direction, as far as the eye could reach, I did not turn to the right or to the left to examine any of them, although some were within a short distance of the direct course I seemed impelled to take.

After traveling a number of miles in the open prairie, and passing hundreds of cattle, I came to a fence, the end of which I could not see either to the east or west, and how far it might be across the field, or what was on the other side, I did not know; but the Spirit which had thus far impelled me I could not resist, so I dismounted and let down the stake and rider or worm fence, led my horse in, put up the fence, mounted and rode three miles due south across the field. When I came to the fence on the south side I again dismounted and let the fence down as before. Leading the horse through and putting the fence up, I found myself again in the open prairie, with numerous bunches of stock in every direction.

Mounting the horse, I continued on my due south course, paying no attention to the stock on either side of me. When I had gone about a quarter of a mile from where I passed out of the field, I rode right on to the cow, feeding alone some distance from any other animals. It was now late in the afternoon, and I was in a strange part of the country; but feeling elated and full of joy and thankful to my Father in Heaven, that he had heard and answered my prayers, I started to drive the cow in the direction of the city. In about two or three miles travel I came to the farm of old man Lot, on the Carthage road just east of Nauvoo, where I had once been to a general muster of the Nauvoo Legion, and then knew I was on the right way home, where I arrived late in the evening. My parents had been worried very much about me, but seeing the long-lost cow and my safe return all anxiety and fear turned into thanksgiving, and we were a happy family.

---

*Improvement Era*, 2:454–55.

# "TEARS FALLING FAST FROM HIS FACE"

⌒

## HENRY  G.  BOYLE

On the 7th of July, 1846, while I was waiting [at Council Point, near Nauvoo] for the [Mormon] Battalion to be organized and mustered into service, a stranger Colonel [Kane], arrived at the Point and obtained board and lodging at the same place. After gaining an introduction to me, he soon entered into an animated conversation relative to our people, their history, religion, etc. I found him to be a very pleasant and affable gentleman, and easy and fluent in conversation. . . . I soon found that his sympathies and good feelings were all in our favor. . . . He seemed to take in, and understand our situation, our motives and aspirations. He appreciated and praised our heroic resignation to the inevitable, and our determination to meet and overcome every obstacle and to bear uncomplainingly every trial. He noticed our simple trust in God, and our noble resolve to be happy amid the severest hardships and privations.

The Colonel often proposed a moonlight stroll through the woods. . . . During one of these rambles, we heard one of our men praying in secret in the skirt of the woods in the rear of our camps. Although we were not near enough to distinguish words or sentences, it seemed to affect the Colonel deeply, and as we walked away he observed that our people were a praying people, and that was evidence enough to him that we were sincere and honest in our faith.

Not long after this, when taking another walk, following a

narrow path through a thicket of undergrowth, we came suddenly within a few feet of a man who had just commenced to pray. As we wore on our feet Indian moccasins, we made no perceptible noise, and the man evidently thought himself alone and praying in secret. At the time, I was in the path just in the rear of the Colonel, who, on hearing the beginning of the man's supplication, halted, and, in doing so, turned half around, with his face in the bright light of the full moon, and in such a position that every feature was plain to my view.

I never listened to such a prayer, so contrite, so earnest and fervent, and so full of inspiration. We had involuntarily taken off our hats as though we were in a sacred presence. I never can forget my feelings on that occasion. Neither can I describe them, and yet the Colonel was more deeply affected than I was. As he stood there I could see the tears falling fast from his face, while his bosom swelled with the fullness of his emotions. And for some time after the man had arisen from his knees and walked away towards his encampment, the Colonel sobbed like a child and could not trust himself to utter a word. When, finally, he did get control of his feelings, his first words were, "I am satisfied; your people are solemnly and terribly in earnest."

---

*Juvenile Instructor,* 17:74.

PRAYER

# "You Will Find Your Oxen"

AUTHOR UNKNOWN

John Murray Murdoch, a convert from Scotland, crossed the plains in 1852 and settled in Salt Lake City. A few years later, in the fall,] he turned his oxen into a big field, thinking they could feed there until winter came. Then he could bring them home and feed them the hay [he had worked long and hard to store.] When winter came, he spent days looking for them, but no one . . . had seen them. . . .

After everything else failed, John sought the Lord in prayer. . . . As he prayed, a voice said, "You will find your oxen."

Still no word came. . . . Feed was scarce that year, and after John was offered a good price for [his hay], he decided to sell. He still had faith that he would find the oxen.

Next spring he was notified by Apostle Franklin D. Richards that a large herd of cattle was being brought to a certain corral in the city, and John thought he could buy a yoke of oxen from that herd.

When he went to look at the cattle, . . . he saw his own oxen [in the corral with the other animals.] He informed the men in charge that two of the oxen belonged to him, but they said that was impossible. He immediately went to Apostle Richards, and together they returned to the corral. The man in charge was not satisfied, as there were no marks or brands on the oxen. He asked if there were any others besides [John] who could identify them.

"Yes," he said, "every man, woman and child in the Third

345

Ward. We will not need them, however. If I call the oxen they will come to me, and if they will not own me, I will not own them."

"All right, try it," [the man] said.

John got off the fence and went to a place where the oxen could see and hear him and held out his hat and said, "Come, Bob." The ox came right up to him. He put his right arm over his neck and called, "Come under, Bright." The other ox came up and stood as if under the yoke. The two men clapped their hands and said, "These are his oxen, and no one can dispute that kind of evidence."

---

Unpublished manuscript, *The James and Mary Murray Murdoch Family Organization*, 213.

# "I CAN'T STAND THIS FOOD ANY LONGER"

I D A   M .   K I R K H A M

Joseph and Elizabeth Hunter Murdock were sent to the Muddy Mission [in Nevada] as colonizers in the early [1860s] and endured many hardships in caring for and supporting their family, and helping to establish a settlement. It was very hot in summer and their home was made mostly of woven willows. They raised hay and a great deal of grain, as many travelers passed their way and needed feed for their tired animals. Their food was poor and coarse—bran was used to make bread, and greens and roots were used for substance many a time.

Elizabeth was a good, faithful woman and willing to make her sacrifice in colonizing, but worried because her children were not thriving physically. One night as she was mixing the bran bread for the morrow, the tears fell heedlessly in the dough. She felt that she could not give her children this coarse bread again. After washing and drying her hands she walked out into the moonlight and, to use her own words, said: "Dear Lord, I can't stand this food any longer, please send us some white flour."

At three A.M., a team stopped outside their house and a man asked if he could buy feed for his horses. The sand was deep and his load was heavy and he needed feed badly. Joseph went out and gave him all the hay and oats he wanted and stood in the moonlight with his hands full of money as the man started to drive away. Just then he thought of his hungry family and called to the man and asked him what he had on his wagon. The man answered, "White flour, and anyone can have all he wants for what it cost me, as it is too heavy to pull all the way to California."

Elizabeth could hardly believe her eyes as she saw bag after bag of flour stacked in her bedroom. The next morning all the neighbors were made happy too. They had hot biscuits for breakfast.

---

Ida M. Kirkham, in Kate B. Carter, comp., *Heart Throbs of the West*, 10:123.

# "WE MADE LITTLE PROGRESS IN RAISING THE ANCHOR"

GEORGE Q. CANNON

W hile Brother Woodruff was speaking about what President Young had told him in Winter Quarters, respecting the Prophet Joseph's teachings, with regard to cultivating the spirit of the Lord, a thing came to my mind that I was taught in the same way in the beginning of my labors on my first mission. . . .

There were ten of us, of whom I was the youngest, wind-bound in the Bay of San Francisco, and we had been thus delayed for nearly a week near the Golden Gate in consequence of head winds. I dreamed one night that this party of brethren were heaving at the windlass, having a rope attached to it reaching forward to the anchor at the bow of the vessel. We were working with all our might endeavoring to raise the anchor, but seemingly we made but little progress. While thus engaged I thought the Prophet Joseph came from the after part of the vessel . . . , and tapping me on the shoulder told me to go with him. I went, and he climbed on to the forecastle which was higher than the main deck and on a level with the bulwarks, and there he knelt down, also telling me to kneel down with him. He prayed. . . . After prayer, he arose upon his feet. "Now," said he, "George, take hold of that rope"— the rope we had been pulling on with all our might. I took hold of it, and with the greatest ease and without the least effort, the anchor was raised. "Now," said he, "let this be a lesson to you;

remember that great things can be accomplished through the power of prayer and the exercise of faith in the right way."

*Journal of Discourses*, 22:290–91.

# A LOST LAMB

EPHRAIM LAMBERT

When my brother and I were about eight years of age, and were herding sheep, we lost a lamb on a certain occasion. We searched and hunted, but failed to find it, and we were afraid to go home without it, as our father was quite strict with his children. Having been taught the principle of prayer, we made up our mind to pray to the Lord, and ask Him to direct us, so that we could find the lost animal. Consequently, we knelt down and prayed, each in turn, and when we arose to our feet, we saw the lost lamb standing close by and in plain view. This may appear like a trifling affair to some, but it was the means of creating a faith in me through which the Lord has subsequently blessed me abundantly and preserved my life. Often, when I have been alone on the tops of high mountains, have I knelt down and lifted up my voice in thanksgiving to the Lord for the many manifestations of His goodness towards me.

Ephraim Lambert, in Andrew Jenson, *LDS Biographical Encyclopedia*, 1:477.

# "BE OF GOOD CHEER— YOU WILL BEAR A SON"

## MARGARET McNEIL BALLARD

On February 9, 1873, I gave birth to another son whom we named Melvin Joseph. Prior to his birth I had lost my twins in death, and my health was broken. I had the misfortune of having several miscarriages, and during the early stages of pregnancy, I was in danger of losing him also. My heart was broken. . . . Melvin was carried during a period of great trial in my life; a period of poverty, during a national depression, a season of crop failures, a very severe winter, and during the "underground." I had given birth to six children. Two had been taken in death in their infancy, just ten days apart. Sorrow and sickness had weakened my physical strength. My heart was sore, my arms were empty, for again the life of my unborn child was threatened.

For days and weeks I was bedfast, and I felt in my anguish that the "fruit of my womb was cursed." Like Rachel of old, my heart yearned for a child, and I cried unto the Lord, "Give me children or else I die." My husband had taken the children a block away to see a parade, and while he was gone I raised my trembling body from the bed and crawled and locked the door so that I might pour out my soul to God on my knees in prayer. I called to his remembrance my willingness to bear children. . . . I supplicated the Lord for his help. I felt that I had done all that was in my power, and I asked to know my standing in his sight.

God hearkened unto my prayer and a comfort was given to me. I saw no person but I heard a voice speak plainly to me saying,

"Be of good cheer—your life is acceptable, and you will bear a son who will become an apostle of the Lord Jesus Christ."

In due time my child was born; I did bear a son, my last son. We named him Melvin Joseph, and I know he is a chosen son of God.

His life was ever precious to us, and we both recognized in him a choice spirit. He was also honored by his brothers and sisters, although they did not know of the promise given him, nor did I ever tell him.

Margaret McNeil Ballard, in Douglas O. Crookston, ed., *Henry Ballard,* 230–31.

# "I Continued to Pray"

## JOSEPH F. MERRILL

I was reared in a family where prayer, night and morning, was always the order. I have seen my father sometimes too busy to stop to eat his breakfast, but never too busy to kneel with his family in prayer before he left, to thank the Lord for the prospects of the day, for the rest of the night, and to ask his direction and help in the labors of the day. I was taught to pray at my mother's knee, and when I could say my own little prayers, I was taught that it was my prayer; it should be said in secret, or at least to myself.

So I knelt on one side of the bed, brother on the other side, every night. He never knew what I prayed for; certainly I did not know what he prayed for. But when I was about ten years of age, I began to pray for a special blessing. But I did not get an answer. Why? Father had taught us that there are three factors that must characterize every prayer that the Lord will answer: We must pray for real needs—and even grown-ups, he said, sometimes ask the Lord for things they do not get, because they ask foolishly—we must pray worthily, and we must pray with faith.

In answer to my first prayer, no answer came. The faith was there, I felt, to the extent that I could exert it. The need was there, I felt certainly no doubt about that, but was the worthiness? I could always think of something, as I prayed night after night without an answer, that I had done that I should not have done, and so I continued to pray, feeling that when I could make myself worthy of an answer, I would get it.

It was after I had been praying nightly for five years that the whole family went, one Wednesday evening, in the month of February, into town and attended a Sunday School entertainment. My class rendered its number, followed by another that sang, and I remember some of the words of that song: "Keep on asking, God will answer by and by." To me that was a revelation. I kept on praying.

Some four years later, in the latter part of the month of August, 1887, in my nineteenth year, after I had been praying nightly for nine long years with all the earnestness of my soul for this special blessing, I was alone in the bedroom, and I said, half aloud, "O Father, wilt thou not hear me?" I was beginning to get discouraged.

Then, brethren, something happened. The most glorious experience that I have received, came. In answer to my question I heard as distinctly as anything I ever heard in my life the short, simple word: "Yes." Simultaneously my whole being, from the crown of my head to the soles of my feet, was filled with the most joyous feeling of elation, of peace and certainty that I could imagine a human being could experience. I sprang from my knees, and jumped as high as I could, and shouted: "O Father, I thank thee." At last an answer had come. I knew it.

Why did it not come before? I have thanked the Lord many times since that He withheld the answer. A few days after that, father said to me: "Would you like to go to Salt Lake City and attend the University of Deseret?"—a secret wish of which I had said nothing. I had finished, the spring before, what is equivalent in this day to a junior high school course, nothing more in the town. I wanted to go on and now I could. And as it turned out, after graduating at the University of Deseret, I went east and completed nine years of work in the field of science in four of America's leading universities.

Had I gone without an answer to my prayers at that critical moment in my life I might have forgotten to pray. But I think that I am here today—I think that I have been preserved in the Church, perhaps, because the answer to my prayer came at that critical moment, since which time never has a day passed that I have forgotten to pray. And as long as memory lasts I cannot forget the thrilling experience of that night.

---

Conference Report, April 1944, 151–52.

# "HIS FIVE DOLLARS SUPPLIED OUR NECESSITIES"

GEORGE Q. CANNON

One incident, I will relate, which occurred a few months after we went to Wailuku, to show how the Lord hears and answers prayer.

We were very much in need of some means to buy stuff for garments, etc. The natives were very poor, and we felt delicate about asking them for anything; but we knew that the Lord would hear and answer our prayers; so we prayed to Him. Brother Hammond had brought his wife and child over from Lahaina, and they were living, as I have told you, in the village close to Wailuku. He and I had to make a visit to a town about twelve or fifteen miles distant, and before starting, we had prayed to the Lord to open the way so that we might obtain what we wanted.

We had traveled from the house about three miles, when, in passing some houses which were on the beach, we met a man by the name of Freeman, an American, who accosted us and inquired if we had authority to marry. Upon our informing him that we had, he asked us if we could spare the time to stop at his house and marry him. We told him as it was on our way we would stop. I performed the ceremony, and at his request addressed the people who had assembled at the house. He gave us a five-dollar gold piece.

We had married many before that, but this was the first money which had ever been given to us. His five dollars supplied our necessities, for in those days we were content with very little.

354

I have always looked upon this as a direct answer to our prayers, for when we met the man he was evidently on his way to Wailuku, with his intended wife, to be married by the missionary there. The missionary missed the fee, but as he knew nothing respecting it, he was no poorer. I do not suppose he needed it as badly as we did.

George Q. Cannon, *My First Mission,* 180–81.

# "THE LORD KNEW WHERE THAT GOLD PIECE WAS"

## JOHN A. WIDTSOE

There were not many after-school jobs in Logan when I was a boy, but I found one that took only two or three hours a day. One day my employer told me I had done very well, and he gave me a five-dollar gold piece for my several weeks of work.

Five dollars! That was money! I was jubilant! I would give half of it to my mother, buy a new book, and save the remainder. Into the pocket of my trousers went the bright new gold piece, and off I ran to tell my mother of my good luck.

On the way home, I put my hand in the pocket to feel and caress the money. It was not there! Instead, I found a hole in the pocket through which the coin had slipped. It was terrible! I was so sorry that I sat down by the ditch bank and cried.

Then I slowly walked back the way I had come, looking every step for that gold piece. The sidewalk on Logan Main Street was made of planks. I looked in every crack for my lost fortune. Not a sign of it! Then I walked back over the same road, stopping, looking everywhere. No little shiny gold coin was there to lighten my heart! Again I walked slowly back and forth over the road I had been following when the precious coin was lost. But it was not to be found! It was lost for good.

Then I remembered that the Lord knew where that gold piece was, and that if he would help me, and wanted me to find it, it could not be lost for long.

So I got down on my knees behind a big tree and told the Lord all about my trouble, and asked him, if he thought it was the best thing for me, to help me find it. When I got up I felt so much better. I felt sure the Lord had heard my prayer.

Dusk was gathering. One could not see anything on the ground very clearly, especially a small piece of gold. But I walked right on, not so slowly this time, for I knew the Lord was helping. About halfway up the second block, there in the grass lay my lost five-dollar gold piece. It gleamed in the darkness, as if to say, "Come and take me; I want to make you happy." I almost shouted with joy. How glad my mother would be, and how I would enjoy that book I had planned to buy. I leaned up against the fence and said, "Thank you, O Lord, for finding my money for me."

Since that time I have known that the Lord hears prayers. And, since that day, I have been careful to have no holes in my pockets.

---

*Children's Friend*, September 1947, 46:369.

# "It Was Getting Darker All the Time"

## HENRY D. MOYLE

When I was a young boy, my father entrusted the family cow to my care, both at our home in [Salt Lake] City as well as at our [summer] home in the mountains [in Big Cottonwood Canyon]. My first trip from the city to the mountains with the cow was made on the back of my Indian pony. . . . It can be hard work leading a cow by a rope attached to her halter with the other end wrapped around the horn of the saddle. It took most of the day to get the cow just from Salt Lake City to the mouth of the canyon.

Around noon I stopped at a farm located on Highland Drive below Sugar House. I milked the cow to make traveling easier for her and fed the pony and the cow. The fresh warm milk tasted good with the sandwiches Mother had put in my saddlebag.

We began to climb the canyon road, and continued our journey uneventfully until early evening, when the cow suddenly balked. I lost hold of the rope and the cow took off up the hill in the thick scrub oak brush. I left my pony on the canyon road and went to find the cow. I climbed through the brush, but I could not find her, and it was getting darker all the time. When I felt I had done all I could to help myself, I knelt down to pray. I knew then that the Lord hears and answers our prayers when we do our part. I felt good when I stood up. I was not afraid any more. I walked a short distance up the hill and came upon an old irrigation ditch. A short distance up the ditch I saw my cow hidden by the bank.

After thanking the Lord for answering my prayer, I drove the cow ahead of me in the ditch until we came out into a clearing. I tied the cow to a bush, then went down the canyon road until I was once again seated comfortably on my pony. I retrieved the cow and soon arrived at our summer home.

If I were you I would pray and develop the ability of talking to the Lord and depending upon him to help when his help is necessary. You will find throughout life he will always be there to help you. Without his help, we do not accomplish much. With his help there is nothing we cannot accomplish if we will.

*Improvement Era,* 66:118–19.

# "I PRAYED TO THE LORD . . . TO GIVE ME WORK"

## ADAM S. BENNION

God does not always answer prayers miraculously. He often shapes events so naturally that we may scarcely recognize His hand in our welfare. But He is our Father—He will help us in the hour of need if we only will ask of Him as of a father—honestly and sincerely. Here is an extract from the journal of Brother Horace H. Cummings, Superintendent of Schools of The Church of Jesus Christ of Latter-day Saints, which shows with perfect clearness that God will bless His servants when they trust in Him and attempt to do His will:

"When I was old enough my father put me to work in the Deseret Mill near Salt Lake City in the finishing department. He told all of his sons that they might have one tenth of their wages and all their over time to spend as they pleased, while he took the rest to help maintain the family. My wages were nine dollars a week and fifty cents a night for working over time until nine o'clock.

"I saved most of my money and when about eighteen years of age I had enough to attend school at the Deseret University. Unfortunately, I was unable to register until the beginning of the second term and by the end of the third term circumstances forced me to quit. My father and oldest brother were both called on missions and that meant for me to leave school and keep the family.

"For any other reason, it would have been a matter of the greatest regret to have to leave school after going only two terms, or half a year, but it rather appealed to me as an honor that had come to us. So I quit school and began looking for work. Being the last of February or the first of March, there was little to be found to do. I visited the stores, the shops, the trunk factory, and made inquiries to find work on some of the nearby farms.

"Night after night I would come home with no prospect of work until I began to be discouraged. The baby was sick and mother was not very well, and the stock of family provisions was getting decidedly low. I began to feel that something must be done.

"Before being called on his mission, my father had torn down the rear part of our old home which was a small adobe hut, and had begun to build a commodious home for us to live in. He was only able to finish one room of the new house, however, so we were living in parts of both houses.

"The day that the situation reached the climax, I went back

into the closet of the new house and there knelt before the Lord in prayer. Now, of course, I had prayed to the Lord many times to give me work, but this time I had a peculiar, earnest determination to get what I wanted. I prayed with such earnestness that I cried. I fear my prayer was somewhat of a complaint, for I told the Lord He had called my father and brother to preach His Gospel and left me to support the family; that I had looked and looked for work and could not find any.

"To my great satisfaction, that very day saw an answer to my prayer. Two school trustees from the county were in need of a teacher in their district and had come to the city to get one. On making inquiry of Dr. John R. Park, the president of the university, where I had been attending, they had been referred to me as a suitable person to teach their school and after a short conversation they engaged me at $60 a month."

Adam S. Bennion, *What It Means to Be a Mormon*, 68–71.

# "FATHER, ARE YOU THERE?"

## HUGH B. BROWN

I shall never forget the words of my mother when I left to go on a mission sixty-odd years ago, when she said to me, "When you were a lad you often had bad dreams. You remember you would call out from your room and say, 'Mother, are you there?' And I would say, 'Yes, son, I am here. Everything's all right. Turn over and go to sleep.'" She said, "Now, my boy, you are going on a mission. You will be 5,000 miles away from me and I can't answer your call, but many times you will need to ask someone, 'Are you there?' Now," she said, "while you are gone, and the rest of your life, whatever happens, don't forget to call out and say, 'Father, are you there?' And I promise you, my boy, if you will do that, he will respond to you. You may not hear his voice; you will not see his form or figure, but you will know he is there, and he will support you."

I bear you my witness tonight that many times in intervening years I have called out to him for help, and I have needed it all the time.

---

Conference Report, April 1967, 101.

# "WILL YOU SPEAK FOR
# US TONIGHT?"

HOWARD W. HUNTER

Several years ago a young man came to my home to be interviewed for a temple recommend. He told me of the lovely
girl who had consented to be his bride. I knew his parents
were not members of the Church, and this fact led to our conversation. I asked him what had come about in his life to cause him to
be interested in the Church and to influence him to accept the
gospel and live its precepts. This is the story he told me.

Five years before this night we sat together, a little thing
happened in his life—a simple thing, yet so extraordinary that it
changed his course. He had been serving in the armed services
and had been sent to a university in the East for some specialized
training, along with two other young men.

The three of them traveled together on the flight which took
them to their destination, and on their arrival they went through
the procedure of registration and then were assigned to quarters.
They were to room together.

He said that during the time they had traveled neither of these
companions smoked, and he did not smoke because of his respect
for them.

After the three became acquainted with their new quarters
they drew straws for beds and then unpacked their cases.
Although they were not well acquainted, they spent the evening
chatting about their ambitions and their goals in life.

It was past the hour for a reasonable bedtime, and all evening he had been suppressing the desire for a cigarette. He finally suggested that they go to bed. The other two looked at each other, and then one of them said, "Shall we have prayer together before we go to bed?" Then to the other he added, "Will you speak for us tonight?" The two of them dropped to their knees, just as though they had done this all of their lives.

He said to me, "I was somewhat bewildered, but I followed their pattern and got on my knees." And as he did so, some strange fear came over him. He said to me, "I had never prayed in my life, but as this young man spoke to the Lord some warm feeling came over me—a feeling I had never experienced before."

They were soon on their feet, shook hands, and said good night to each other. In a few minutes they were in bed and the lights were out, but sleep did not come to this young man. Something had happened to him while he was on his knees, and he determined to find out what made these two young men different from other men he had known. . . .

These three servicemen went to school the next day and, because of their heavy assignments, spent the evening in quiet study, followed by the chitchat that preceded bedtime. Then it happened again—the same thing that had happened the night before. On this occasion the one who offered the words of thanksgiving and petitioned for the blessings of the Lord was the other of the two.

As the lights went out, one of them said to my friend, "It'll be your turn tomorrow night." For the second night sleep did not come quickly. The thoughts of the words which had been spoken puzzled him for some little time, and he wondered if he would ever be able to express himself on his knees as had been done by the other two.

The next day in the classroom the assignment of that evening kept coming back to his mind. He had the same feeling he had

had on many occasions in track meets when he was toeing the line in that tense moment just before the gun that challenged every ounce of strength.

He wondered about this fear that had come over him. In high school he had been a student body officer. For two years he had been a member of the debating team. Public speaking was not new to him, but this was different.

That evening, dinner was over and the three were studying, but it was difficult for him to keep his mind on the subject. He kept thinking of those few moments that would end the day. Then it came. All the courage he had mustered that day seemed to disappear from him and he said to the other two, "I guess I don't have much religion. One of you had better do this."

One of these young men, who had seen the same thing happen so many times during the two years prior to his military service, said to him, "Prayer is just a matter of thanking your Heavenly Father for the blessings you have received and asking him for the blessings you desire. It is just that simple."

With this encouragement he got on his knees and prayed—the first time in his whole life. For the next few weeks, every third night he took his turn and expressed appreciation for the things that the Lord had given to them and asked for that which they desired.

Then he went with the other two young men to the branch of the Church in the mission where they were attending school. Finally a period was set aside each night for a little discussion in which they taught him the gospel.

Then came the decision and the day he described as the greatest day of his life. One of these young men baptized him and the other confirmed him a member of the Church.

They were soon separated after this brief time in school. He finished his military training, filled a mission for two years, and then met this lovely girl who was now to become his companion for eternity.

It all started from a prayer that night. Prayer has changed many lives. It has had an effect on our lives, both yours and mine. Prayer is that which brings us in close communion with God.

---

*BYU Speeches of the Year,* 15 October 1963, 2–4.

# PROTECTION
## AND DELIVERANCE

# "I ENTIRELY LOST THE TRACK"

JEDEDIAH M. GRANT

In the year 1834, when Zion's camp was moving from Kirtland to Missouri, one day I left the camp and went out to hunt in the woods of Ohio, and strayed away from the camp some 10 or 11 miles. The camp kept moving on all the time, and I entirely lost the track, and having no compass, I knew not towards what point I should travel. I kept travelling on till the after part of the day; I then concluded I would pray, but I could not get any impression where the camp was. However, I soon after received an impression from the Spirit, the same Spirit we had in Kirtland, and the same Spirit we enjoy in this place; and immediately after receiving the impression, I looked before me, and there was the camp moving on in regular order. I could see it just as clear as I did in the morning; there were the people, the wagons and horses, all in their places as I left them in the fore part of the day, and I supposed they were not more than 80 rods off. But after turning away for a moment, I again looked in the same direction, but all was gone. Still the Spirit told me to travel on in the same direction I had seen the camp; I did so, and after travelling some 8 or 10 miles, came up with them, and when they first came in sight, they looked just as I saw them in the vision.

*Journal of Discourses*, 3:9–10.

# "RUN, YOU DEVILS, OR DIE!"

LORENZO DOW YOUNG

My mother was afflicted many years with consumption. I remember her as a fervent, praying woman. She used, frequently, to call me to her bedside and counsel me to be a good man, that the Lord might bless my future life. On one occasion, she told me that if I would not neglect to pray to my Heavenly Father, He would send a guardian angel to protect me in the dangers to which I might be exposed. . . .

[Years later, in Missouri,] Mr. Richard Welding, of whom I had bought my farm, came to me, accompanied by three or four others. He gave me warning to leave the country at once.

I asked him why I must leave, saying: "Have I not bought my land, and paid you for it? Have I not attended to my own business?"

He replied: "Mr. Young, we do not want you to leave. You are a good neighbor and citizen, and if you will only be man enough to renounce Joe Smith and your religion, we want you to remain with us, and I will protect you in your rights. The Mormons must all leave the country, and if you do not renounce them, you must go too."

I paid no attention to this warning.

Three or four days after this occurrence, four men rode up in front of my house, when I happened to be away, called Sister Young to the door, and again gave warning that we had better leave. . . .

About five days after this warning, early in the morning, I looked up the road towards Gallatin, and saw a man on horseback coming towards my house at full speed. As he rode up he inquired: "Is your name Young?"

I answered that it was.

He continued: "I have rode from Gallatin to inform you that, in two or three hours, there will be a company of forty men here, who assert that if they find you here, they will fasten you and your family in your house and burn it down. For God's sake, if you value your own life and the lives of your wife and children, do not be here an hour from now. I have come to give you this warning as a friend. Should it be found out that I have done so, I might lose my own life!"

I thanked him for his kindness, and he rode off rapidly towards Gallatin. I told Sister Young to prepare to leave at once, then attached my team to a light spring wagon, put a bed, a few cooking utensils, a trunk of clothing, and some food for the day into it. I got my wife, my four children, William, Harriet, Joseph and John into the wagon, fastened up the house and started for Far West.

I expected to return and get my goods. The next day I obtained some teams and started for my goods. I found the road strongly guarded, and the Missourians threatened to kill me if I went on. I never obtained goods, cows nor anything that I had left on my place.

This left my family very destitute, in common with others of the Saints who had been treated in like manner.

I had previously driven a fine yoke of oxen and a new milch cow to Far West, thinking I might possibly want to remove there; but Clark's army drove my oxen into camp and butchered them for beef. I was promised pay for them, but, of course, never received anything but the promise.

This was in October, 1838. I remained in Far West doing whatever was necessary for the protection of the Saints. I was on guard much of the time.

Major Seymour Brunson directed Brother A. P. Rockwood, and myself to take our horses and go out two miles north of Far West and patrol the country every night. If we saw a man, or company of men coming towards Far West, we were ordered to hail them and demand the countersign. If necessary, to make this demand the second time, when, if not given, we were to fire on them. When we arrived on the ground where we were to perform our duties, Brother Rockwood and I separated, taking different directions.

It was a moonlit night. I was on the edge of a prairie with my eye along the road, when I discovered a company of mounted men coming over a swell of the prairie. I retired into the timber and took a station behind the trunk of a large tree, under the shadow of its branches, and twenty or thirty yards from the road. As the company came opposite to me, I demanded the countersign twice, as I had been ordered to do. As they paid no attention to me, I made ready to fire, intending to shoot the leader, when a strong and sudden impression came over me to hail again. I did so, and ordered them to halt. This time the leader recognized my voice, and turning towards me, asked: "Is that you, Brother Lorenzo?" I also recognized the man as Brother Lyman Wight, and, as I answered in the affirmative, rode up to his side. We were glad to meet each other, and I was very thankful that I had not obeyed orders. He was on his way from Diamond to Far West, with a company of men to assist the Saints there.

Soon after this occurrence, I returned to Far West. I told Sister Young that I hoped to get one good night's sleep. For three weeks I had not had my clothes off to lay down, and I felt much worn.

Perhaps I had slept two hours, when I was awakened by the bass drum sounding an alarm on the public square. I was soon out to see what was the matter. There were five men on the square, of whom I inquired the cause of the alarm. They informed me that two of the brethren had been taken prisoners by the mob on Crooked River, tried by a court martial that day, and condemned to be shot the coming morning at eight o'clock. A company of men was wanted to go and rescue them.

Preparations were soon made, and in a short time, about forty mounted men, under the command of David W. Patten, were ready to start. We kept the road to a ford on Crooked River, twenty miles distant, where we expected to find the mob.

Just as the day was breaking we dismounted, about a mile from the ford, tied our horses, and left Brother Isaac Decker to watch them.

We marched down the road some distance, when we heard the crack of a rifle. Brother Obanion, who was one step in advance of me fell. I assisted brother John P. Green, who was the captain of the platoon I belonged to, to carry him to the side of the road. We asked the Lord to preserve his life, laid him down, ran on and took our places again.

The man who shot Brother Obanion was a picket guard of the mob, who was secreted in ambush by the roadside. Captain Patten was ahead of the company.

As we neared the river the firing was somewhat lively. Captain Patten turned to the left of the road, with a part of the command; Captain Green and others turned to the right.

We were ordered to charge, which we did, to the bank of the river, when the enemy broke and fled.

I snapped my gun twice at a man in a white blanket coat. While engaged in repriming my gun, he got out of range.

A tall, powerful, Missourian sprang from under the bank of the river, and, with a heavy sword in hand, rushed towards one of the brethren, crying out, "Run, you devils, or die!"

The man he was making for was also armed with a sword, but was small and poorly calculated to withstand the heavy blows of the Missourian. He, however, succeeded in defending himself until I ran to his aid, and leveled my gun within two feet of his enemy, but it missed fire.

The Missourian turned on me. With nothing but the muzzle end of my rifle to parry his rapid blows, my situation was perilous. The man whom I had relieved, for some reason, did not come to the rescue. I succeeded in parrying the blows of my enemy until he backed me to the bank of the river. I could back no farther without going off the perpendicular bank, eight or ten feet above the water. In a moment I realized that my chances were very desperate. At this juncture the Missourian raised his sword, apparently throwing all his strength and energy into the act, as if intending to crush me with one desperate blow.

As his arm extended I saw a hand pass down the back of his head and between his shoulders. There was no other person visible, and I have always believed that I saw the hand of the angel of the Lord interposed for my deliverance. The arm of my enemy was paralyzed, and I had time to extricate myself from the perilous situation I was in.

As soon as I had time to think, I felt that the inspiration of my mother's promise had been again verified. The appearance of the hand, to me, was real. I do not see how I could have been saved in the way I was, without a providential interference.

---

*Fragments of Experience,* 22–23, 48–52.

# "ONE MOVING MASS OF PEOPLE"

## AMASA LYMAN

When we were in Nauvoo, at the beginning of the last winter we spent in Illinois, about the time the clouds were gathering so thick, and the last storm began to break upon us, we heard the thunders and threatenings of our enemies wherein they stated that we were to be driven away.

At that time I was confined to my bed with sickness, but I heard the report of the proceedings day after day; but I could not come out to see the face of the heavens, to judge what the issues would be. To get away was impossible with me at that time, and we knew that the longer we stayed the more we should be oppressed by our enemies.

After I had commenced to recover my health, one morning, while lying in my bed in open day, as wakeful as I am at this moment, the surrounding objects which I could see when in my natural condition all in an instant disappeared, and, instead of appearing to keep my bed, I found myself standing in a place where those acquainted with Nauvoo and the location of the Printing Office, subsequent to the death of the Prophets, will remember. There was a vacant lot in front of the Printing Office; I stood there, and I heard a rumbling noise something like that which attends the moving of a mass of people. I turned round to look in the direction of Main street, and behold! the whole country was filled with one moving mass of people that seemed to be travelling directly to the point where I stood. As they approached somewhat nearer, they seemed not to be travelling on the ground, but somewhat near the altitude of the tops of the buildings.

At the head of the company were three personages clothed with robes of white, something like those which many of us are acquainted with. Around their waist was a girdle of gold, and from this was suspended the scabbard of a sword,—the sword being in the hand of the wearer.

They took their places with their faces directly west; and as they stopped, the individual in advance turned and looked over his shoulder to me with a smile of recognition. It was Joseph; and the others were his two brothers, Hyrum and Carlos.

I contemplated them for a few moments; but to tell my feelings would be impossible. I leave you to guess them; for it would be futile to attempt a description.

After contemplating the scene a few moments, I was again in my bed as before, and the vision had disappeared. This was my assurance, in the commencement of our troubles there, that I received of the guardianship that was around us and the protection that we were receiving from the hosts of heaven.

---

*Journal of Discourses,* 5:59–60.

# "THE LORD PERMITTED THE DEVIL TO TRY ME"

JACOB HAMBLIN

I labored with the company of pioneers to prepare the way for the Saints through Iowa, after which I had the privilege of returning to Nauvoo for my family, which consisted of my wife and three children. I moved them out into Iowa, 200 miles, where I left them, and returned 100 miles to settlements, in order to obtain food and other necessaries.

I was taken sick, and sent for my family to return to me. My wife and two children were taken sick the day after their arrival. We found shelter in a miserable hut, some distance from water.

One day I made an effort to get some water for my suffering family, but failed through weakness. Night came on and my family were burning with fever and calling for water.

These very trying circumstances called up some bitter feelings within me. It seemed as though in this, my terrible extremity, the Lord permitted the devil to try me, for just then a Methodist class leader came along, and remarked that I was in a very bad situation. He assured me that he had a comfortable house that I could move into, and that he had plenty of everything, and would assist me if I would renounce "Mormonism." I refused and he passed on.

I afterwards knelt down and asked the Lord to pity us in our miserable condition, and to soften the heart of some one to administer to us in our affliction.

About an hour after this, a man by the name of William Johnson came with a three gallon jug full of water, set it down and said: "I came home this evening, weary, having been working with a threshing machine during the day, but, when I lay down I could not sleep; something told me that you were suffering for water. I took this jug, went over to Custer's well and got this for you. I feel now as though I could go home and sleep. I have plenty of chickens and other things at my house, that are good for sick people. When you need anything I will let you have it." I knew this was from the Lord in answer to my prayer.

The following day the quails came out of the thickets, and were so easily caught that I picked up what I needed without difficulty. I afterwards learned that the camps of the Saints had been supplied with food in the same way.

---

Jacob Hamblin, in James A. Little, ed., *Jacob Hamblin*, 215–16.

# CATHERINE JENSEN'S PRAYER
# IS ANSWERED

### ALLA COVELAND

Catherine Christina Jensen . . . crossed the plains with a handcart company during the summer of 1857. During their travels they, by mistake, left the road and were lost for a day and a night. At this time they were without water. When evening came all were tired, worn out, and thirsty. As they retired

378

for night, prayers were offered, asking God to help them find their way and to find water before conditions became too serious.

. . . Being a very faithful woman, and in a delicate condition, [Catherine] was too thirsty to sleep. She began crying and prayed silently to her Heavenly Father, asking him to send water to them. While all the camp was quiet . . . she thought she heard water running. At first she thought it was her imagination, but soon she realized it was really water. She quietly crept from her bed and followed the sound. Sure enough, she found a small, clear, cold stream was running close to their camp. She drank all the water she could, then went back to camp and woke her husband. As she told him of the water, he said, "Catherine, you just dreamed it because you are suffering for water." But he finally consented to go with her to the place. He then rushed back to the camp and told the men. They watered their oxen, filled their vessels, and went back to bed. The next morning the stream had dried away.

Alla Coveland, in Kate B. Carter, comp., *Heart Throbs of the West*, 3:337.

# "MY RIFLE MISSED FIRE"

JACOB HAMBLIN

We surprised [a group of Indians] near a large mountain between Tooele and Skull Valleys. They scattered
in the foot hills, and the company divided to the right
and left to keep them from the mountains. I rode my horse as far
as he could go on account of the difficulties of the ground, then
left him, and secreted myself behind a rock in a narrow pass,
through which I presumed some of the Indians would attempt to
escape. I had not been there long before an Indian came within a
few paces of me.

I leveled my rifle on him, and it missed fire. He sent an arrow
at me, and it struck my gun as I was in the act of re-capping it; he
sent the second, and it passed through my hat; the third barely
missed my head; the fourth passed through my coat and vest. As I
could not discharge my gun, I defended myself as well as I could
with stones. The Indian soon left the ground to me.

I afterwards learned that as he went on, he met two others of
our company and passed them safely, as their guns also missed
fire. When the company gathered back to the place from which
they scattered, we learned that not one was able to discharge his
gun when within range of an Indian. One of the company
received a slight arrow wound, which was the only injury inflicted.

In my subsequent reflections, it appeared evident to me that
a special providence had been over us, in this and the two previous
expeditions, to prevent us from shedding the blood of the
Indians. The Holy Spirit forcibly impressed me that it was not my

calling to shed the blood of the scattered remnant of Israel, but to be a messenger of peace to them. It was also made manifest to me that if I would not thirst for their blood, I should never fall by their hands. . . . Most of the men who went on this last expedition also received an impression that it was wrong to kill these Indians.

Jacob Hamblin, in James A. Little, ed., *Jacob Hamblin*, 222–23.

# "OUR ENEMIES QUARRELED
# AND FOUGHT"

## JAMES S. BROWN

About the 5th of May, 1852, the whole people were called to assemble at the village of Tatake and prepare a feast, and at the same time to decide definitely what to do with the Mormon minister [James S. Brown] and his *pipis* (disciples). Everything was excitement. The young braves came armed with muskets, shouting and yelling, saying they were going to have a fat roast for tomorrow, while the old councillors, twenty-five or thirty in number, came with slow, quiet steps and grave countenances, and filed into the schoolhouse just at dark. Then the people gathered, loaded down with roast pig, and fruit, fish and poultry. They kindled fires and began shouting, singing, and dancing.

Soon the young braves were dancing around the house that

they were in; for by this time every member of the Church had come to one place. The mob seemed to be fully enthused with the spirit of murder, as they shouted, "Tomorrow we will have a fat young missionary for a roast!" Just then they fired a salute, seemingly under the foundation or sill of the house—a frame building. Then they commenced to tear down the post and pole fence that enclosed the premises. This fence, together with other wood, was piled up in a heap, as people in timbered countries stack timber to burn it off their land. Then the natives covered the wood with coral rock, as if they were going to burn a lime kiln. They kept up a continual howl all the night long, firing their guns, singing their war songs, and burning their campfires.

While this was going on, we held prayer and testimony meeting, never sleeping a moment the whole night. Many times we could hear the crowd outside boasting what a fine, fat missionary roast they were going to have *enanahe* (tomorrow).

Daylight came, and the village was all alive with people, as in America on the Fourth of July, at a barbecue. Soon the feasting began. The council had been all night in deciding what they would do with the Mormons and their minister. The provisions at the feast were apportioned to each village according to its numbers, and subdivided among the families, so that a full allowance was made for the Mormon *pupu* (party). They sent to me the portion of ten men, saying: "Here, this is for you, *Iatobo* (James); eat it and get fat for the roast," laughing contemptuously as they did so. By this time the whole people were in high glee, eating, drinking, talking, laughing and jeering, as if all hands were bent on pleasure only. When the feasting was over, all became silent, and it seemed as though everybody had gone to sleep.

By 1 o'clock p.m. all were astir again. Two great ruffians came into my apartment, armed with long clubs. They said they had been sent to order me before the council, and if I refused to come

they were to drag me there. . . . As quick as thought, the promises of President Brigham Young flashed through my mind; also the promise of Dr. Willard Richards, in which he told me, in the name of the Lord God of Israel, that though men should seek my life, yet I should return in safety to the bosom of the Saints, having done good and honor to myself and the church and kingdom of God. He also gave me instructions what to do; this was when starting on my mission. The next thought that came to my mind was: Have I forfeited those promises? The answer that came quickly from the Spirit was no; and this drove away all fear. Not a doubt was left in my mind.

Without hesitation I arose and walked out to the beach, where the people had assembled, the Saints following me. We passed by the log heap to the assemblage, at the head of which stood twelve or fifteen stout, athletic, young braves, with hair cut close. They were stripped naked to their breechclouts, and were oiled. They stood with folded arms, and certainly seemed formidable, although they were without weapons, for they had a fierce and savage look about them that must be seen to be realized in its effect.

As we came near, the man Tabate stepped out from the crowd and said, "All the Britons stand to the right hand with the sheep, and all the Mormons stand to the left hand where the goats are." Everyone responded to the order except two men from the Mormon party, who drew off to themselves and were neutral. At that, one faithful Mormon man named Rivae, and his wife, with an eight months old babe in her arms, stepped forward, well knowing what the sentence was to be. This brave brother said, "If you burn this man," pointing to the writer, "you burn me first." His heroic wife stepped forward, holding her babe at arm's length, and shouted, "I am a Mormon, and this baby is a Mormon. . . . You will have to burn all of us, or Mormonism will grow again." . . .

Pointing to the left and rear of the prisoner, to the log heap,

which was then at the zenith of its burning, with haughty demeanor and in an exulting voice, Tabate said, "Look there at that fire. It is made to consume the flesh off of your bones." In that moment the Spirit of the Lord rested mightily upon me, and I felt as though I could run through a troop and leap over a wall. "In the name of Israel's God," I said, "I defy ten of your best men, yea, the host of you, for I serve that God who delivered Daniel from the den of lions, and the three Hebrew children from the fiery furnace!"

. . . There was absolutely not one particle of fear or tremor in my whole being. But I did feel thankful for that great and marvelous deliverance, because in the very moment that I defied the host the spirit of division rested upon the judge who had passed the sentence, his counselors, and the executioners, insomuch that the counselors faced the executioners, and they grappled with each other in a sharp tussle. From that ensued a fight, until the whole people were mixed up in it. . . .

During all this time our enemies quarreled and fought with clubs and stones, pulled hair and screamed. They did not cease fighting till sundown. Then, with many sore heads, and more sore limbs, they dispersed, and I doubt very much if the majority of them knew what they had been fighting for. After they left, a feeling of quiet and safety pervaded the village, especially in and about our residence, such as we had not before known on the island, and for weeks everything was strangely peaceful. People who once seemed surly and defiant now had a tame and subdued expression in their countenances and appeared to prefer passing by unnoticed rather than otherwise.

Some two months later, I was traveling alone in the timber, and at a short turn in the road I chanced to meet one of the old councillors who decided that I should be burned. We were close together before we saw each other. At sight of me he turned and

ran as hard as he could, and I, without any particular object in view, gave chase and ran him down. I seized him by the neck and asked why he ran from me and why he was afraid of me. Said he: "Your God is a God of power, and I was afraid to meet his servant." I inquired how he knew that my God was a God of power, and why they had not burned me when they had decided to do so. He answered: "At the moment that you defied us there was a brilliant light, or pillar of fire, bore down close over your head. It was as bright as the sun. We remembered reading in the Bible about Elijah calling fire down from heaven so that it consumed the captains and their fifties, and we thought that you had prayed to your God of power, and that he had sent that fire to burn us and our people if we harmed you. The young men did not see the light. They were going to burn you, and we tried to stop them. So we got into a fight. Now we all know that you are a true servant of God."

*A String of Pearls,* 56–59.

# "HE WOULD NEVER RUN AWAY
# FROM PRAYERS AGAIN"

SOLOMON F. KIMBALL

It took a strong man two days to go to the canyon and get a load of wood. Then it took him two days more to chop it into firewood. This would last a small family probably three weeks or a month. It was nothing unusual to see a boy twelve or thirteen years of age driving a team to the canyon, in company with his father or brother, who also had teams to look after. Like conditions prevailed in the different avocations of life.

About the last of May 1865, our father, Heber C. Kimball, purchased quite a valuable work horse from the Knowlton family, paying them three hundred and fifty dollars, cash down. That evening he instructed David H. and myself to hitch up our teams the next morning and go to North Mill Creek Canyon, east of Bountiful, after wood. He entrusted the new horse to the care of David, who was but fifteen years of age at the time, I being three years older.

Every morning Father had family prayers, and he never allowed us boys to go to work until this was attended to. He would not only pray for us, but for the horses and wagons, and even the harness. The next morning David and I hitched up our teams bright and early and drove them out of the yard very quietly, so as not to wake our father. We well knew that we were disobeying orders, and that if he should happen to hear us driving out, he would call us back and have us put our horses back into the stable and remain until after prayers. . . .

Nothing unusual happened until after we had reached the head of the canyon, which is about seventeen miles from Salt Lake City. We loaded our wagons with wood, which had already been gotten out for us, and started for home, myself being in the lead. We had not gone far before the Knowlton horse began to jump about so frantically that my brother could not manage him. I stopped my team and ran back to where he was, and finally got the horse quieted down. I then told David that he had better drive my team, and that I would take charge of his.

We then drove on until we came to a very steep and narrow dugway, which was quite sidling in places. This was the most dangerous piece of road in the canyon. Not long before this, Father Kinney's son met with a terrible death in this same place. The wagon that he was driving tipped over into the creek, and fell on him. In those days we had no brakes on our wagons, and when we came to a hill that was too steep for the horses to hold the loaded wagon back, we locked one of the hind wheels and drove down in that way.

When David reached the top of this hill, he stopped his team as usual, locked the wheel, and then drove on down. I then drove my team to the brink of the hill, but before I could get it stopped, the Knowlton horse began to pitch and lunge ahead so frantically that it was impossible for me to stop him. I fully realized the awful position that I was in. Like a flash of lightning, the death of Father Kinney's son came before my mind.

David, by this time, was about fifty yards on ahead of me. I yelled to him, at the top of my voice, telling him to whip up, and get out of my way as quickly as possible. By this time my team was running. I had dropped one of my lines, and could do nothing but hold on to my load of wood as best I could. I was satisfied that if my team ran into his wagon, in such a narrow and sidling place, it would not only knock his outfit off into the raging torrent below, but that we would all go down together. The dugway next to the creek was probably twenty-five or thirty feet high, and almost perpendicular. The stream below was quite high and the bottom of it was strewn with huge boulders. The water rushing and beating against them on its downward course made it appear as white as snow. This also made such a roaring that we could hardly hear.

David looked back and saw my team coming at full speed. For the first time he sensed the danger that we were in, and immediately began to put the whip to his horses, letting them go as fast as he dared. By so doing he took his life in his own hands in order to try and save me, as well as himself. My binding chain began to loosen, and my wood commenced to bound about. Something had to be done immediately, as it was impossible for me to hold on much longer.

At the foot of this dugway was a narrow and dangerous pole-bridge that crossed this treacherous stream. On crossing this bridge with loaded wagons, under ordinary circumstances, we had our teams walk across it as slowly as possible. In a miraculous manner, David had managed to get his team across safely, had reached a little flat on the other side, and was out of danger a few seconds before I overtook him. But what was to become of me? I still held the right-hand line in my hands. As my team was headed, my left wheels would miss the bridge, on the upper side, at least three feet.

There was just one chance left for me. If I could steer my horses a little to the right and strike the bridge squarely, I believed that I would be able to cross it. If I should happen to miss it, even one-eighth of an inch, it meant certain destruction for myself and team. This was the danger spot of the whole canyon.

I made a superhuman effort. I pulled on the line as hard as I could under the circumstances, and managed to get my team turned a little to the right and came within two inches of running off the bridge, on the upper side, but went across alright. By this time I had completely lost my balance, and was just falling onto the heels of this crazy horse, when my team crashed into my brother David's wagon with such tremendous force that it drove a pole almost through the body of the Knowlton horse, killing him almost instantly.

So far we had not seen a human being in the canyon, and the lonely and dismal feeling that took possession of us nearly drove us wild. We began to realize the danger that we had just passed through, and our faces were as white as chalk, while our hearts were beating sledge-hammer blows. We were speechless, as well as powerless, and it took us some time before we could collect our thoughts.

The first words that were spoken were by David, who said that he would never run away from prayers again, as long as he lived. I felt a little more that way than he did, but said nothing. I offered up a silent prayer, thanking God, my Heavenly Father, for saving our lives in such a miraculous manner.

The next thing we did was to get the wagons and dead horse out of the road. We then tied [our] faithful . . . horse behind our wagon and drove homeward. We arrived at the Warm Springs about 7 p.m., being two hours late. . . .

When we met [Father] at the gate, his face was flushed, and he was unable to speak a word, while big tears were running down his cheeks. The next morning we were called into the prayer room with the rest of the family. . . . He hoped that it would be a lesson that we would always remember. Then we all kneeled down, and before he prayed many minutes, we could begin to feel the blood tingling in our veins; the Spirit of God rested down upon us in mighty power. Before he was through, there was not a person in the room who was not weeping. I had never heard such a prayer before, and what I heard on that occasion will remain with me as long as I live.

———————

*Improvement Era,* 9:554–57.

# "I FELT THAT SOMEONE WAS IN TROUBLE"

⌒⌐⌐⌐⌐⌐

NICHOLAS G. MORGAN SR.

On one occasion [in the late 1800s] when [Mission] President [John] Morgan was holding a council meeting with a group of traveling missionaries in the backwoods of Tennessee, a number of elders had reported very poor results in interesting people. In an endeavor to ascertain the reason for this lack of interest on the part of the people, President Morgan inquired of the elders reporting negligible results if they had sufficient money to purchase the food they had needed and lodging whenever it was necessary. The elders stated that they had; that they had never missed a meal and that they had been paying regularly for their lodging. So far as their travels were concerned, they were enjoying themselves greatly. The following morning, President Morgan directed Elder James Ford of Centerville, Utah, and his companion, two of the elders reporting unsatisfactory results, to start on their journey by foot to a hitherto unvisited section of the country and to travel without purse or scrip. . . .

It was early when they started. They had walked briskly until dark, without meeting anyone or seeing any habitation where food or lodging might be obtained. Nevertheless they continued on their journey. Shortly after dusk, very dark clouds developed in the sky and there was a great deal of thunder and lightning. The two missionaries quickened their pace but still the entire countryside seemed uninhabited. It started to rain, raining lightly at first, then very heavily.

Coming to a trail that led through some heavy timbers, they left the main road and hurried to the shelter of the trees. The rain rapidly developed into a torrent, and the elders were soon drenched to the skin. It grew desperately dark. The trail through the trees was a heavy one: sticky clay, making it most difficult to travel. Tired, hungry, and cold, they stopped to rest. The rain had ceased, but they did not know where they were or what to do. In that moment, Elder Ford's companion, trembling with cold and emotion, suggested that they kneel on the damp ground and pray; that President Morgan had promised them divine aid should circumstance require it.

Surely they had done their duty and were willing and desirous of carrying on. Surely God would hear and answer their prayer. Then on bended knees, far from home and loved ones, lost in what they thought was a wholly uninhabited country in the cold and dampness of the woods, the two young elders knelt in prayer. Elder Ford did the praying. He had prayed daily since he was a boy at his mother's knee, but never until now had he known the true meaning and power of prayer. He talked to the Lord as though he were very near, and pleaded for the help necessary to assist them out of their miserable dilemma; and as he prayed, they felt a divine influence about them and in that moment of supplication they received assurance that the Lord would help them to security and peace of mind. In closing his prayer, Elder Ford, in deep humility, thanked their Heavenly Father for his blessings and for his Spirit which had enlightened their minds and assured them the security for which they prayed.

They arose to their feet and scarcely had risen when they heard measured footbeats as though a horse was approaching; then through the darkness of the night, they saw the flickering light of a lantern through the trees, and they knew that someone was approaching. Not knowing what else to do, they stood still until the man with a lantern, astride his horse, rode up to them.

"What are you boys doing here?" the stranger asked.

"We are lost," the elders replied, "but we are very happy to see you."

The man dismounted. "Well," said he, "you boys are in pretty bad shape; you better climb onto this horse and I will lead you back to my house. I went to bed pretty tired tonight and I just couldn't go to sleep. I tossed and turned in bed with a constantly growing feeling that someone out here needed help. I don't know why I did it, but I got out of a nice warm bed and came out into the rain and cold and through these woods because I felt that someone was in trouble. I guess it was you boys who just wouldn't let me go to sleep." Astride the horse, the elders felt the warmth of the animal's body, and in their hearts was a deep gratitude for their miraculous escape.

Nothing further was said between them and the man until they arrived at his house and they had been given warm clothing and their hunger appeased. Then the man asked them what their business was and how they happened to be out in that part of the country. The elders explained to their benefactor the purpose of their mission and explained to him the first principles of the gospel. It was very late when they retired, but on arising on the following day they learned that the man of the house had left early to invite neighbors and farmers and friends in the valley to a meeting to be held in his home that evening in which the two elders would be the speakers.

The meeting was held; the house was crowded to its capacity. The two elders taught the first principles of the gospel of Jesus Christ, as revealed in this dispensation of the fullness of time. Filled with the spirit of their mission, they spoke with great power in the delivery of their message. The assembly was thrilled and other meetings were arranged. Soon one family and then another sought baptism until most of the people in the valley were baptized as members of the Church, and their benefactor . . . was made the presiding elder of the newly organized branch.

---

Nicholas G. Morgan Sr., in Bryant S. Hinckley, *Faith of Our Pioneer Fathers*, 252–55.

# "I Could Proceed No Farther"

## H . G . B .

I had stayed over Monday night at the house of a Mr. H——, who was preparing to move south with his family, and who prevailed on me to accompany him around by land. He offered to feed both myself and horse as far south as I desired to go, thus relieving me of any expense.

Mr. H—— had taken great pains to tell me of a Mr. O——,

who was very favorably inclined to our people and doctrines. He thought that I ought, by all means, to visit him, and that I could do so on the coming Friday evening, and join him (Mr. H——) on Saturday morning at Vallejo, on the proposed trip.

This all appeared right enough to me, as Mr. O—— lived nearly in a direct line from Petaluma (the place I would start from on Friday) and Vallejo.

Mr. O—— had often invited me to make him a visit, and I therefore promised Mr. H—— that I would accept of his kind offer, and meet him at Vallejo as proposed.

On the Friday following, I took dinner at A. J. Mayfield's, near Petaluma. Soon afterwards I caught and saddled my horse, when I began to feel opposed to going to Mr. O——'s.

I remarked to Mr. Mayfield that I was tempted to give up my visit, at which he and wife (who were both great friends of ours) began to insist that I must not fail to visit Mr. O—— and family, as they were very anxious for me to do so. His acquaintance and friendship, they said, would be a great advantage to me, as he was a man of wealth and great influence.

Having nothing to offer as an excuse for not going, I mounted my horse and rode away.

The distance was about four miles; and, as I proceeded, the same mysterious influence was brought to bear upon me that had saved my life on the [other] occasion. . . .

This aversion grew and increased upon me until I came in sight of Mr. O——'s house, which was located in a beautiful vale, some half a mile away. From this point I could proceed no farther, or, to say the least, it seemed madness to do so.

So powerfully was I impressed that some impending evil awaited me if I went farther, that I turned my horse about and started back on a gallop, which I did not break until I arrived at

Mr. Mayfield's again, feeling all the time as if I was fleeing from some great calamity.

The explanation I gave this family did not seem to satisfy them. I could see they thought me a little inclined to lunacy. However, next morning all was made plain enough.

Having given up my trip around the bay, I went, in company with Mr. Mayfield, to Petaluma, to take steamer and make my way by water.

We had been in town but a few minutes when we met with Mr. O——, who had come in to get out a warrant and an officer to arrest Mr. H——, whom I was to have met that same morning at Vallejo.

Mr. O—— had been robbed the night before of eight thousand dollars in gold, and he charged H—— with being the guilty party, which afterwards was proved to be true.

If I had not been prevented by a kind Providence, I would doubtless have been arrested at Benicia with him, as an accomplice.

The reader can easily perceive the dilemma this would have placed me in. And no doubt Mr. H—— and his family would have done all in their power to fasten the guilt upon me, in order to save themselves.

As soon as Mr. Mayfield and I were alone, he exclaimed, "O, I know now why you could not visit Mr. O—— last evening."

That family no longer regarded me as being superstitious.

. . . I considered this a wonderful escape from a terrible snare, and was full of gratitude, giving thanks to Almighty God for the same.

Since then I have given more heed to the still small voice of the Spirit, and, consequently, have escaped many snares and evils that I might otherwise have fallen into.

---

*Gems for the Young Folks,* 24–26.

# "I KNELT DOWN BY THE SIDE OF MY HORSES"

WILFORD WOODRUFF

One Monday morning, the Spirit watching over me said, "Take your team and go to Salt Lake City."

When I told it to my family who were at Randolph, they urged me strongly to stay longer. Through their persuasion I stayed until Saturday, with the Spirit continually prompting me to go home. I then began to feel ashamed to think that I had not obeyed the whisperings of the Spirit to me before.

On Saturday I took my team and started early. When I arrived at Woodruff, Bishop Lee urged me to stop until Monday and he would go with me. I told him, "No, I have waited too long already." I drove on, and when about twelve miles from Wasatch, a great snowstorm struck me. It was terribly blinding. In fifteen minutes I could not see any road whatever, and I knew not where to guide my horses. I left my lines loosely on my animals, went inside my wagon, tied down the cover, committed my life and guidance into the hands of the Lord, trusting to my horses to find the way, as they had twice passed over that road. I prayed to the Lord to forgive my sin in not obeying the voice of the Spirit to me, and implored Him to preserve my life.

At nine o'clock in the evening my horses brought me into the Wasatch station, with the hubs of my wagon dragging in the snow. I called upon Brother George Rowley, who was the only Latter-day Saint in that place. He received me kindly and assisted me to get my horses into the storehouse, but for which I think they would have perished.

I had traveled thirty-five miles that day, but I slept little through the night. I arose next morning and found the snow two feet deep and falling thick and fast. It looked very gloomy and I did not know what course to pursue. I could not travel the road, so I went to Mr. Haven, the Union Pacific agent, and asked him what chance there was to get a railroad car. He had no railroad car, he said, and if he had, he did not know how I could get my horses and wagon on board, as all the appliances for loading such articles were moved to Evanston, I could not buy any grain in the place, and the only hay there was, was in the hands of Mr. Hammond, an apostate Mormon, and a very bitter one. I brought from Randolph about one hundred pounds of hay, which was all the feed I had. The snow was rapidly covering up my wagon. I fed my horses a little hay, then went to the house and prayed to the Lord to deliver me.

In the morning it was still snowing furiously. I could see no deliverance for myself and team unless the Lord opened the way for us. I had to wallow to my arm pits in snow to get to my horses, or anywhere else. Mr. Haven sent to Evanston for a car for me, the night before, at my request, but how to get my wagon and team into it was the great question. My wagon was covered with snow and was some 300 feet from the station. There was no help except the Chinese section foreman. I spoke to him, but he said he had no right to take his men from the railroad to dig out a wagon and span of horses.

I then made my way through three feet of snow about 300 yards to the place where my horses were housed. I rubbed them down, caressed them, but only had a morsel to feed them. I then knelt down again and prayed earnestly to the Lord to deliver me and my team. It might be thought a little matter to allow the horses to remain and starve and take care of myself. But my team had wallowed through the snow some twelve miles to save my life, and I felt it my duty to do all in my power to save theirs. I prayed earnestly to the Lord to deliver me and save my animals from starvation. The Spirit of the Lord came upon me while praying, and I had a testimony that my prayers would be answered and that I should be delivered.

I arose from my knees and wallowed some sixty rods through three feet of snow to the telegraph office, and again talked with Mr. Haven, the agent. I told him he must help me. The Spirit of the Lord rested upon him and he said he would do all in his power for my deliverance. He went with me to see Mr. Carpenter, and the same spirit came upon him and he said he would do all he could. He then told the ten Chinamen to take their shovels and follow him. We all went to where the horses and wagon were, and it took us nearly five hours to dig them out and open the road to the station. Then we had to build a platform some ten feet high and cover it with coal cinders to get the horses up, but they would not walk the planks. I then went to Mr. Hammond, who had the only hay in the place, and asked him to sell me fifty cents worth. He got the same spirit as the others, put up the hay for me, and carried it to the depot. I laid it at the head of the platform, and both of the horses readily went to it. I then put them inside. We then took the wagon to pieces and lifted it up, one piece at a time, and placed it in the storehouse.

When the freight train came along, Mr. Haven stopped it and had the engineer bring up the car 100 yards, to the platform. In trying to get my wagon box in with the bows and cover on it, it became fastened, with one end on the platform and the other against the side of the car. The engineer would not wait any longer, but started off with his train and left me.

Mr. Haven then telegraphed to Evanston to send him an engine. While it was coming, we took off the cover and bows of the wagon box, and finally succeeded in loading my outfit. It was in order when the engine arrived. Mr. Haven ordered the engineer to hitch on to the car. He did so reluctantly as he had to travel something like 160 miles to get to Ogden and back, just to take me and my wagon and team.

I bade my friends good-bye, and as the cars started, I knelt down by the side of my horses and returned thanks to my Heavenly Father for the deliverance He had brought me. My clothing was wet, I having wallowed in the snow all day, so I put on dry ones.

We arrived in Ogden about ten o'clock, when I went to the home of Bishop Lester Herrick, and passed the night with him. Brother Herrick lent me money to pay my bill to the railroad, which, strange to say, was only $26.00. Had they charged me in full, their usual rates for car and engine and all that was done, it would have been $150.00.

On the 28th of November, I drove my team from Ogden to Salt Lake, where I arrived home with a grateful heart, to be delivered from my perils and find my family well.

---

Wilford Woodruff, in Preston Nibley, comp., *Faith-Promoting Stories*, 181–84.

# "SARAH FELT MOVED TO INVITE HIM IN"

## LEONARD J. ARRINGTON AND
## SUSAN ARRINGTON MADSEN

Sarah Farr Smith had just finished cleaning the kitchen after the family noontime meal when she heard a firm knock at the back door of her home at 23 North West Temple in Salt Lake City. Proceeding to the door, she was not particularly surprised to see a poor but tidy-looking gentleman standing on her porch. She didn't know the elderly man, but it was not uncommon for transients to come to her home from the nearby railroad station asking for a meal. As Sarah often tired of serving food at all hours of the day to whoever came by, her husband, John Henry, had purchased "meal tickets" to give to those in need, which enabled them to eat a satisfying meal at a nearby restaurant.

There was something different about this particular man, and Sarah felt moved to invite him in to her kitchen table. As he was eating, the man suddenly asked where Sarah's young son George Albert was. She indicated that he was outside playing in the yard. He then asked her to call the youth into the house so he could see him. Again she felt compelled to comply, although she was hesitant to leave a stranger alone in the house. She found George Albert, who was about eight years old, playing at a nearby two-story building north of their house, underneath a second-story balcony from which steps descended to the ground level. When she reentered her house with her young son at her side, the gentleman was gone. Sarah was searching through the house for him when she heard a

400

loud crashing sound outside. She rushed out to see what had happened and was astonished to discover that the balcony and staircase under which her son had just been playing had collapsed, sending large beams and pieces of lumber crashing down onto playthings he had left behind just moments before.

Leonard J. Arrington and Susan Arrington Madsen, *Mothers of the Prophets*, 123–24.

# THE WOLF AND THE SHARKS

$\frown$

E L A I N E    E A R L    R I C H A R D S O N

F ather (Orange Wight Earl) was born April 15, 1877 in Pine Valley, Utah.

When Father was very young he was hiking in the hills above Pine Valley when a huge white wolf appeared on the path before him. He was alone, with no stick, club, or gun to protect himself. But suddenly he knew through the Spirit what he should do. Father felt he should look the wolf squarely and steadily in the eyes while he slowly (so as not to startle the wolf) bent his knees until his hand touched the ground and found three small rocks. Then, he felt, he should slowly return to a standing position and toss a rock to the wolf. He did so. The wolf caught the rock in his mouth, then after a moment let it drop to the ground. Father tossed the second rock to the wolf. Again the wolf caught it in his mouth, then dropped it. He repeated the motion a third time, and again the wolf caught, then dropped, the rock. At that point, the wolf quietly turned and disappeared into the thick underbrush at the side of the trail. Shaken but grateful, the young Orange continued down the path to the village where his father was.

Years later, while serving a mission in Tahiti, Father was miraculously protected again. With some of the Tahitian natives, he swam a long distance out into the ocean and began to dive for pearls. The divers would swim down, locate the oysters, and put them in a pouch. When the pouch was half full or so, they would swim to a waiting boat, empty their treasures into it, and swim to a new location looking for more oysters.

The bay was dotted with bobbing, diving, swimming men. All at once the chilling shout of "Sharks!" pierced the air. The sharks quickly swam among the men, brutally attacking them, while the screaming natives thrashed wildly through the water, trying to get to their boats and to safety. But the Spirit whispered to Father to turn onto his back and float without moving a muscle.

When the school of sharks reached him, they abruptly parted, half of them going on one side of Elder Earl and half going on the other. After passing him they closed the opening and became one group again.

Father rejoiced in the power and inspiration of God that saved him from serious injury and possible death.

---

Elaine Earl Richardson, in Orange Wight Earl, unpublished history.

# "A BOLT OF LIGHTNING"

## HAROLD B. LEE

There was a severe thunderstorm raging near the mountains where our home was located. Our family, consisting of my grandmother, my mother, and two or three of the younger children, were seated in the kitchen before an open door, watching the great display of nature's fireworks. A flash of chain lightning followed by an immediate loud clap of thunder indicated that the lightning had struck very close.

I was playing back and forth in the doorway when suddenly and without warning, my mother gave me a vigorous push that sent me sprawling backwards out of the doorway. At that instant, a bolt of lightning came down the chimney of the kitchen stove, out through the kitchen's open doorway, and split a huge gash from top to bottom in a large tree immediately in front of the house. Had it not been for Mother's intuitive action, and if I had remained in the door opening, I wouldn't be writing this story today.

---

Harold B. Lee, in L. Brent Goates, *Harold B. Lee: Prophet and Seer,* 41.

# THE HOUSES WERE ALL IN FLAMES

## V. W. BENTLEY

I remember some twenty years ago when I was living down in Old Mexico. It was during the time of the Mexican Revolution when the famous bandit, Pancho Villa, was roaming the northern part of the nation, especially in the state of Chihuahua. The depredations and crimes that he had committed were too numerous to mention, as it seemed he was very fond of taking human life.

At this particular time, General Villa was in a very ugly mood because the United States had just recognized his opponent, President Carranza. This made General Villa a bandit and rebel, cutting off all possibilities of supplies from the United States. This naturally embittered him toward any American people, and he gave vent to his feelings in the form of hanging all Americans that he could find in the country that he rode over.

How well I remember we were living in the little town of Colonia Juarez and word came that General Villa and his whole army were passing to the west of us some thirty or thirty-five miles and were headed north. Of course, no one ever knew just what Villa's plans were or where he was going, as he was a man who did not divulge his plans to others but kept them to himself. It was particularly hazardous that he should be that close to us, as all means of escape had been cut off—the railroad had been destroyed, there were no automobiles, and all of our horses had been stolen so that we were virtually afoot. To have ventured out on any road leading toward the United States would have been suicide, as the entire country was thickly infested with roving bandits and rebels, so you can imagine us as the report came that General Villa and his whole army were camped just some thirty miles away. It was no wonder that consternation came over everyone.

However, General Villa did not come our way at that time, but marched straight for the American border. His men were starving and almost out of ammunition and war materials, and so he headed directly for Columbus, New Mexico, where he hoped to replenish the supplies his army so badly needed. However, when he reached Columbus, disappointment and tragedy met him. Instead of supplies and ammunition that he had worked for and hoped to obtain, he was driven back by the American soldiers and many of his men were killed and wounded, without their securing any of the provisions and ammunition they so badly needed.

As a result of their defeat, General Villa and his entire army turned south again and headed straight for the Mormon colonies. General Villa promised his men that when they got to the colonies they would be turned loose to loot and rob and steal or do anything else they wanted to without any restrictions. The only requirement was that they were to leave nothing alive in any of the colonies and were to burn everything that would burn when they went through.

How well I remember the anxiety we all sustained, as our scouts—sent out by my father, who was the president of the stake, to watch the movement of Villa and his army—came in and made their report. An experience that I shall remember all of my life happened one Sunday morning about 2 o'clock. There were four of us boys there at home, and we were suddenly awakened by two of these scouts who came to find Father and inform him that General Villa and his entire army had passed through the pass north of the colony and should be there by sunup or before. As I said, escape was impossible, and so we fully felt that it was to be our last day on this earth, as we knew that these rebels would leave no human being alive to tell the story.

The panic which followed in this little Mormon colony was very pathetic indeed. Mothers took their children down into the river bottoms and hid them in bushes, or covered them up with dead branches and then tried to cover themselves up with sand to escape attention. Others hid in trees or any place that offered any shelter at all where they might not be detected.

I remember well we could not find Father, and although it was 2 o'clock in the morning, he was out among the Saints, trying to lend encouragement and assistance wherever possible—we had no idea where he might be. Therefore, we four boys just waited there, deciding to face whatever befell us. It was some time before any of us could go back to sleep, but I remember finally we all did accomplish this, in spite of the tenseness of the situation.

To my dying day I shall never forget the beauty and serenity of that Sunday morning as the sun came up over the eastern hills. Birds were singing, and if there was ever peace on earth, it seemed to reign on that little colony that morning. We could not understand it as we had been sure we would all be dead before sun-up, but to our surprise, we could find no evidence whatever of General Villa or any of his army having entered town. We hurriedly dressed and began to investigate. Father soon came in and told us that he had been all over the colony, and it was plain to see that he hadn't slept a wink all night. He told us that to his knowledge, not a soldier had entered town. However, morning was still early, and we felt that perhaps they had been only temporarily delayed, so we waited, expecting them to come at any moment. But by noon not a soldier had entered the colony, and so we decided to send out scouts to investigate.

You can well imagine the prayer of thanksgiving and grateful joy to our Father in heaven when these scouts returned with the information that General Villa's entire army had come to the edge of the colony and for some inexplicable reason, instead of marching through the colony, as anticipated, had turned and gone way to the east and missed the town entirely. Our scouts followed them for some little distance to make sure that they had really passed us by before returning.

It was not until several years later that we learned the cause of this action on the part of General Villa. At that time, Father was serving as president of the Mexican Mission and was traveling with Elder Whetten throughout the mission and the state of Chihuahua. They had stopped for the evening by a spring. Hardly had they made camp when they were accosted by three soldiers. The men asked them who they were and when they were told who Father was, they told him that he was the man that General Villa would like to see, and they were sent back to take him to Villa's headquarters. General Villa was in the company of General Filipi Angeles, who was perhaps one of the greatest military geniuses and authorities on arms and ammunitions Mexico had ever produced. Father discovered later that it was General Angeles who had requested that he and his party be brought to General Villa's headquarters.

General Villa kept them there as his guests for nine days, during which time they were given the utmost in courteous treatment and the best of everything available in the camp. It was during this period that Father had an opportunity to ask General Villa why he had not come into the colonies and destroyed them as he had promised his men he would do when they were retreating from Columbus, New Mexico, after their defeat. General Villa turned to Father and in very positive language gave this explanation:

"Mr. Bentley," he said, "that is one thing I have never been able to understand myself. It might interest you to know that when we got to the edge of those colonies a great vision opened up before me, and instead of seeing those colonies as I remembered them, I could see the houses all right, but they were all in flames. I can see that picture now—those homes burning—and I felt that the heat would be so terrific that it would be unsafe for me and my army with our wounded men to even venture near. The surprising thing was that none of the men saw the same picture that I saw, and when I gave them the command to turn aside and march around the colonies, taking our wounded soldiers with us, many of them were very resentful and reminded me of my promise, but I turned to them and said, 'Can't you see the colonies are already on fire? It would be dangerous for us to go in!' But they couldn't see it. Because they couldn't, it angered me and I gave the command that any man who didn't obey orders should be shot.

"We marched around and it wasn't until we had gone miles that I came to realize that perhaps I had been mistaken and maybe those colonies weren't on fire. I turned around and looked toward them, but I could see nothing, yet I felt we were too far away to turn back, so we continued on. No, Mr. Bentley, I have never been able to understand it to this day, because I have learned since that those colonies were not on fire—that not a single home was burned, and yet I saw that picture as vividly as I see you standing in front of me."

Of course we realize why General Villa did not know or could not understand this vision which he saw. We know that it was the hand of the Lord, protecting His people when they were helpless to protect themselves.

---

V. W. Bentley, in Preston Nibley, comp., *Faith-Promoting Stories,* 54–58.

# "You Will All Come Back"

⌒‿

## ARCHIBALD F. BENNETT

War came to Canada when it came to England, on August 4, 1914. Canadian volunteers formed into contingents and soon took their place in the trenches beside troops from the Mother Country.

In Alberta was organized the 13th Canadian Mounted Rifles; and "C" Squadron of this regiment was made up largely of Mormon boys of American birth. They were sons mostly of parents who had settled in Canada in obedience to a call from the President of the Church. Living there, they felt an obligation to assist the country of their adoption in its day of need. They loved not war for its glamour and adventure, but they resented deeply the imputation sometimes heard that the Mormons were not loyal, and they stood forth in the ranks to disprove this assertion.

At a Sunday service held in the town of Taber, Alberta, on March 26, 1916, Major Hugh B. Brown, then commanding "C" Squadron of the 13th, made a ringing call for recruits. Nine boys responded, ranging in age from eighteen to twenty-one. We had grown up together in the Priesthood Quorums, the Sunday School and the Mutual; we had joined together in the fun of the dance and had competed in friendly contests of sport.

Just before we left home, Elder Samuel J. Layton was called to address the sacrament meeting. He had spoken but a few minutes when the Spirit of the Lord rested upon him. Under that prompting he promised this group of nine boys that if we did nothing while away of which our mothers would be ashamed we would all live to return after the war was over.

A few months later eight of us were in England; (one of the group had been detained in Canada;) and in the midst of the alluring temptations and lax moral standards of camp life we drew more closely together. In our tent at night we discussed the folks at home and the home teachings. We determined to try to observe those teachings more than we had before enlisting, and to prove worthy representatives of our loved ones. Regularly at night we knelt in a group in our tent and prayed God to assist us.

When granted leave, we sought out our Conference headquarters in London. There we were welcomed with true American hospitality by President James Gunn McKay and his missionaries. He even invited us to assist in street meetings and other Church gatherings.

I was appointed by him to attend a meeting of the South London Branch. I remember relating some of the testimonies gained in the army. When President McKay spoke, the Spirit of the Lord rested mightily upon him. He said how impressed he was with the story of our holding "family prayers." Then he told of the two thousand sons of the people of Ammon who had been taught by their mothers "that there was a just God; and whosoever did not doubt, that they should be preserved by his marvelous power." Turning to me, he said slowly and impressively:

"I promise you boys, in the name of the Lord, that if you will continue faithful to the commandments of the Lord, avoid the vices and sins of the world, and keep the Word of Wisdom, you will all come back and be preserved to fulfil a life's work."

I copy this promise from a letter now in my possession, which I wrote home to my mother immediately after the meeting.

We determined, in our little group of eight, that this was a reward worth the seeking. But as I look back I wonder at the temptations that came to us. Our best friends persistently offered us tobacco. "No use refusing," they told us, "when you're out in the trenches in France, standing all night up to your waist in icy mud, you'll be glad of a little smoke or a little rum to warm you up." "Oh, you won't drink tea! Wait till you've marched all day with nothing to eat, and when you go for your rations at night there's nothing but tea issued! Wait till you're out wounded in No Man's Land, perishing from thirst, and you see a shell hole, and you crawl over to drink some of the water that has seeped into it— and you find a corpse lying there! You'll be glad of a little boiled tea, won't you?" "What if you're about to go over the top, and you need something to brace you up—I guess you'll take your share of the rum all right." "There's no need to be squeamish about it; you'll have to give in sooner or later; it's absolutely impossible to get along out there without them; you might as well give in now and enjoy them."

We could not argue down our friendly tempters. They must know, for some of them had been in France for months. But the Lord had promised through his servants—had he asked something of us that was physically impossible?

I shall always think it a blessing that we came in our reading to the story of Lehi, who requested his sons to go to Jerusalem for the sacred plates. The older sons refused, saying the thing he asked of them was an utter impossibility. But Nephi said:

"I will go and do the things which the Lord hath commanded, for I know that the Lord giveth no commandments unto the children of men, save he shall prepare a way for them that they may accomplish the thing which he commandeth them."

One by one, or in groups of two or three, we went to France. We knew by then something of what we were entering. For, a few weeks previous, Binning, who slept beside us, announced one morning that he was on draft, and jubilantly he marched away. Up

411

the line he went. As he lay at night, sleeping with his comrades four abreast, a shell came hurtling over, struck their dug-out, strewed the bodies of Binning and a bed-mate all over the valley, and left the other two untouched! One morning Billy Sibley said smilingly, "Well, I am going to France, and I'll see some real action at last." It was reported that he had not been in the trench five minutes before he was killed. The papers were filled every morning with stories of the big British offensive on the Somme, and even the carefully censored communiqués gave the impression that hundreds of thousands of lives were sacrificed.

There came times in France when we did march many miles, and when, footsore and famished, we seized our mess tins and rushed to the camp-fire, only to find that nothing but tea was given that night. A few experiences like that and we learned to lay something by for lean days in the hour of "plenty." We took our turn in the trenches and crawled over No Man's Land; and we traded our rations of rum and tea and cigarettes for luxuries like jam and other foods that nourished. All of us had our individual experiences. Once, in hospital with the flu, and some complications, I was puzzled. "At this stage of your sickness," the attendants explained, "we serve you nothing but tea." "But I don't drink tea," I said. "Can't you get me some milk?" "It has never been done, but we'll try." So I was served milk instead of tea.

In November, 1917, came the charge of our squadron at Cambrai. Two of the group of eight took part. My horse went down as we crossed, swords drawn, over a frail bridge. Somehow I managed to fall free of my horse as he rolled over into the water, carrying the whole side of the bridge with him. I lost my sword in the water, but managed to strike the water a glancing blow, so that I did not sink, despite my heavy load, and managed to swim out. The troops passed before I could drag out my almost drowning horse, and all the while a German sniper made things intensely lively for me. A straggler came limping back. "Where's 'B' Squadron?" I asked. "Gone!" he said, "Surrounded and cut to pieces!" "Poor old 'B' Squadron!" I heard someone say.

Drenched and shivering, I waited through that long night. About 9 o'clock, some twenty comrades fought their way through and escaped to our lines. Near 2 a.m., ten more straggled through. That was all! Leslie Bigelow, one of the group to whom the promise was made, was among the lost! He had surely lived his religion and kept the Word of Wisdom. Had the Lord's promise failed?

In my Book of Remembrance I have a card, worn and faded, dated June 11, 1918, and postmarked Friedrichsfel bei Wesel. It came from a prisoner of war camp there. Along with it I preserve a picture of my friend Leslie in a prisoner's uniform, as I saw him in London the first Christmas after the armistice. He had seen many trying days and had suffered untold privations, but he came back alive and well. I saw him a few weeks ago in Canada, and he is still "carrying on."

I keep that little card and the photo, not alone because they remind me of the preservation of a friend, but because they are the symbols of a victory—an undying testimony to me that, if we do our part, the word of the Lord does not fail!

Others of the group are doubtless recording their own experiences. Lowell Duncombe was with the regiment ordered to charge, on their horses in full daylight, a wood bristling with machine guns. The Colonel objected to the order, saying it was madness to make that charge and meant certain death to the men. The Brigadier-General shouted peremptorily, "Charge that wood! I don't care whether a d—— one of them comes back!" They charged; and Sir Phillip Gibbs has written of what he termed the foolhardy venture, which in a few minutes left every horse dead upon the field. Fortunately, most of the men escaped, and Lowell was among those who, when his horse went down, crawled into a trench and escaped. Another soldier rode my horse into action that day—I was still in hospital—and the best horse I ever had there was killed.

In the spring of 1918 we charged afoot up a hillside. Before starting we threw off our overcoats in a pile. Just then a shell struck the pile and changed the coats into carpet rags. "Now boys," the Captain explained in even tones, "We are to go up the hill in waves. The first wave will probably get a good dressing down. You are to be the first wave. But, remember, there are many more to follow and support you."

The order was given and we stepped out into the open. A furious hail of bullets shrieked over and about us. We ran a few steps, dropped down for a minute, ran again, and so on until we reached the brow of the hill. Lee McOmber was shot through the ankle on the way up the slope. Charlie Tufts and I carried a box of machine gun ammunition between us. A shell struck a bank of earth on a level with our heads and a few yards in front of us. As it exploded, however, the particles were thrown upwards, and we escaped. Just beyond we came to a sunken road. Another shell struck right between our feet and exploded. We were knocked down and somewhat dazed; he had a few holes cut in his tunic; several on either side of us were stricken down or severely wounded; but neither of us was scratched!

I am told that as he ran forward to take the place of a machine gunner who had been killed another shell struck between his legs, but failed to explode. As I returned from carrying wounded to the dressing station, I fell in with some British troops coming to our support. The Major in command of the party was struck on the knee and it was shattered. With perfect self-control, in the midst of what must have been excruciating pain, he explained every detail of the plan we were to follow, before he would leave. We started through the wood single file. I was third in line. Shells were tearing through the trees and snapping them off like matchwood. Bullets were cracking on all sides of us, and an airplane added to the interest by firing upon us from overhead. A bullet struck and the first man crumpled; a second, and the next man groaned and fell stark. It was my turn next. I am thankful that it never came.

The boys of the troop who had remained back of the line with our horses prepared a sumptuous meal for us. "They will be good and hungry after this fight," they told themselves, "for they haven't had any rations for nearly two days. So we'll surprise them." Only six of us came back to eat it, and for once there was plenty.

Eight months more of active service followed. In a cavalry charge at Le Cateau, Charlie Tufts received a shrapnel wound on the hand and was in hospital for a month or so. The armistice found us in Belgium, in hot pursuit of the retreating enemy. Every one of the eight had had narrow escapes; two had been wounded, and one had been a prisoner of war for a year; but all of them came back home alive and well and all are alive today, spared for their life's mission. *The promise of the Lord was fulfilled.*

---

*Improvement Era,* 35:100–102.

# "YOUNG MAN, I BELIEVE
# EVERY WORD YOU SAID"

SHERI L. DEW

On Sunday evening the elders, dressed in black suits and bowlers, began their open-air assembly near the railway station in Sunderland [England]. As the meeting progressed, attendance increased steadily. Some persons became rowdy, and when the pubs closed, a large group of men, many inebriated, swelled the audience. In order to make themselves heard, the elders turned their backs to each other and shouted their message. Some persons on the periphery began to yell, "What's all the excitement?" Others shouted back, "It's those dreadful Mormons." With increasing pandemonium, the shout went out, "Let's get 'em and throw 'em in the river!"

The elders became separated, with the crowd pushing Ezra [Taft Benson] down one side of the railway station and his companion down the other. As he was pushed along in a man-made circle some ten feet in diameter, Ezra began to pray silently for help. "When it seemed that I could hold out no longer," he reported, "a big husky stranger pushed his way through to my side. He looked me straight in the eye and said in a strong, clear voice, 'Young man, I believe every word you said tonight.' As he spoke a little circle cleared around me. This to me was a direct answer to prayer. Then a British bobby appeared."

The policeman escorted Ezra home with strict instructions to stay put. But when his companion didn't return, Ezra disguised himself in an old English cap and jacket and set out to find him.

An onlooker who quickly saw through the disguise told Ezra that the elder's head had been "mashed in." Ezra started off in a sprint to find him and ran into the same policeman, who confirmed that the elder had had a nasty blow, but that he, the policeman, had helped him safely home.

"I went back to the lodge and found my companion disguising himself in order to go out and look for me," Ezra wrote. "We threw our arms around each other and knelt together in prayer."

---

Sheri L. Dew, *Ezra Taft Benson*, 62–63.

# "ALL THE MISSIONARIES MUST BE MOVED OUT"

JOHN ROBERT KEST

There was tension in the air that 26th day of August, 1939. For almost a year the people of Holland had clung desperately to the message of hope delivered by Neville Chamberlain, when, at the conclusion of the Munich conference of October, 1938, he had announced, his voice ringing with deep sincerity, "Peace has been preserved." . . .

On this blustery day, the mood of the Dutch matched the somewhat gloomy weather. The peace had not been preserved! A great many people sensed that at that very moment war was closer than it had yet been. . . .

Within the mission home there was also tension—and activity. Elder Joseph Fielding Smith, who was soon to direct the evacuation of the L.D.S. missionaries from Europe, was speaking with President Franklin J. Murdock of the Dutch mission. Intermittently throughout the day the telephone had relayed messages from various parts of the continent. From Switzerland, Denmark, and Germany the calls came. By early evening the telephone was ringing every hour or so. "Yes," Elder Smith was saying, "*all* the missionaries must be moved out of Germany, and that immediately." Grave message this, that we elders working in the office heard drifting from the president's office on the opposite side of the room.

Sometime after 10:30 p.m., President Murdock received a call from President Wood in Germany informing him that a number of missionaries were arriving in Holland by way of Oldenzaal, a tiny village on the eastern border of Holland, not more than seven kilometers from the German border city of Bentheim. A number of elders from Germany, he said, were to arrive sometime the following day. As a matter of fact, the six elders comprising the group at Bentheim crossed the border into Holland late on the night of the 26th but were hurried back to Germany after having emphatically been refused entry to Holland. This, President Murdock learned as a result of a phone call received much later that same evening.

Because of these phone calls and the help the elders at Bentheim obviously stood in need of, Elder Smith and President Murdock decided I was to go to Oldenzaal with sufficient funds to conduct the brethren from that point to the mission home. It was assumed, of course, that we would have no trouble transporting the elders across the border as we thought they had been refused entry because of lack of funds and not having had through tickets to England in their possession. I would be able to guarantee the government officials their passage to England, and would be carrying enough money to assure these same cautious officers the young men would in no way be a burden to the Dutch government while in Holland. . . .

It was necessary to arise about 5:30 a.m. in order to catch an early train to Oldenzaal. . . . There were innumerable delays. The train trip, which could usually be made in two hours, took well over four, and it was after 11 a.m. when the train finally arrived in Oldenzaal. The station master there, a portly fellow whose fantastic English phrases made me smile, proved very helpful. "Yes," he said, "a number of young American missionaries were sent back to Germany late last night and have not crossed back into Oldenzaal since." This was upsetting news, for we had fully expected the brethren to be waiting at Oldenzaal, needing only money and an assurance of transportation to England in order for the Dutch authorities to consent to their passage to The Hague. Even after the phone call President Murdock had received the previous evening, we thought the elders had been delayed by some triviality— probably minor border regulations. Already a good twelve hours had elapsed since they had been returned to Germany: something must be *very wrong* indeed.

Attempting to call Bentheim in order to learn the whereabouts of the elders proved of little value and after three hours I gave up the job as hopeless. Telephone connections with Germany had been cut off. (Afterwards it was found that the elders in Bentheim had been trying to call The Hague for hours, likewise without success.)

I phoned President Murdock in The Hague along about 2:30 p.m. and told him that it had not been possible to contact the elders, all attempts at phoning them had proved fruitless; it was impossible to contact Bentheim by phone. The station master told me the young men had been almost without funds and had nothing except cameras to declare at the Dutch border. It was obvious that they had no tickets in their possession and probably scarcely enough money adequately to take care of their needs. Therefore, the fact that they were obliged to return to Bentheim began to assume even more serious proportions. President Murdock had said the elders must be helped at any cost. "Do your best and use your judgment as to what should be done, Brother Kest." This advice that President Murdock had given me kept repeating itself in my mind. But what should be done at the moment?

The decision to go to the Dutch border had been made in such haste by Elder Smith and President Murdock that there had naturally not been time to obtain a visa, which would have legally enabled me to enter Germany. In fact, at the time no one thought such a move would be necessary. For an hour I phoned The Hague, the American Consulate, the Dutch Embassy asking if a visa might not somehow be arranged. They all said it was impossible. Hundreds of phone calls had been pouring in begging them to take care of stranded Americans and other Europeans who were desperately attempting to get out of Holland, and some of whom were begging help to extricate relatives and loved ones from Germany. It was impossible to handle the sudden abnormal volume. Their office forces had been working sixteen to eighteen hours straight; no help could possibly be given me.

After thoroughly discussing the matter with the station master and finding that under no circumstances would they allow the brethren to enter Holland, it became apparent that I must go into Germany, visa or no visa.

President Murdock had given me something over 300 guilders; it was thought this amount would take care of any eventuality which might arise. It took almost this entire amount to purchase tickets from Oldenzaal to Copenhagen, Denmark.

President Wood had said only the night before, that many missionaries had been pouring into Denmark, so it was reasonable to suppose the border there would still be open. It seems ten tickets were purchased, for it was a speculation how many brethren were stranded in Bentheim. The ten tickets used up nearly all the funds and I hoped there would be sufficient transportation to take care of the elders' needs.

The 2:30 train sped on toward Bentheim. Why the Dutch authorities allowed me to board that train, never asking for a visa, is a mystery; it was most irregular. Sitting tense and excited on the hard seats, the thought reoccurred again and again: "Is this the right thing to do?" Here I was speeding into Germany without a visa, under circumstances that were hardly promising, hoping somehow the brethren might still be there. The train stopped; we had arrived.

A moment later there was a sharp clicking of heels. German Blackshirts stepped quickly through the car, their eyes cold as steel, taking in at a glance the occupants of each car. Handing the leader my passport, the inevitable question was shot at me: "Why is no visa stamped on the proper page?" This thought suddenly flashed through my mind: "Brother Kest, you have always enjoyed acting. If you have ever acted a part well, do it now!" I explained in exasperatingly slow and deliberately incoherent English that at present I was living in Holland, had heard that some of my friends were in Bentheim and knowing that railroad and train transportation was being curtailed, wanted to visit them while possible. Suspicion shone from the cold eyes of the officers. I rambled on, deliberately, on utterly pointless tangents, hoping all the while they would have great difficulty understanding me, which they did.

Suddenly, curtly came the question: "Can you speak no Dutch? No German?"

"No," I replied, "I've been here a comparatively short while and have not learned the languages well. A few simple phrases I can understand—nothing more." It was fortunate that the German officer in charge spoke rather poor English. As I went on, talking disjointedly, tossing in a Dutch or German phrase here and there, the effect I wished to produce took hold of the men. They must have concluded that here was a simple, foolish American trying to see some friends for no good reason.

Inside the little cubicle in the station where they had taken me for questioning, they searched me thoroughly. What would they do to the precious tickets which I had in my suit coat pocket? This thought was paramount. In my possession was a folder in which were M.I.A. lessons written in English which we were translating into Dutch to be used the coming winter season. These they read over thoroughly, finally deciding they were harmless. They confiscated binder, papers, passport, *all* the money on my person and started going through each pocket in both coat and vest. I took the ten tickets out of my pocket and placed them on the table before me. *No one seemed to see the tickets.* The officer in charge gave me a receipt for the money, binder, papers and all my personal effects, and said, "You have forty minutes to catch the return train to Holland. After that time we cannot guarantee your safety."

Taking the tickets from the table I stuffed them in my pocket. *Not an eye flickered. I had the strong impression that the action had been entirely unobserved.* Hurriedly I left the station, my knees weak, my palms sweating. Few people on the street seemed to know where any American boys were staying, but finally someone directed me to the Hotel Kaiserhoff. There the elders were, trying to determine what course they should follow, as they were almost out of money and could no longer afford a hotel bill.

After quiet introductions and firm handshaking, my message was quickly delivered. Giving the tickets to Brother Ellis Rasmussen, who seemed to be in charge of the group, I told them quickly that these tickets from Holland might, with luck, insure their passage to Copenhagen. "You must leave immediately, brethren, and try to make connections into Denmark, as all railroad transportation is being cut off at an alarming rate!" The elders needed no urging, and in less than five minutes were ready, having very little luggage with them.

Quickly kneeling down, we . . . asked our Father that we might be safely conducted to our respective destinations. As the seven of us knelt in fervent prayer, we all felt a closeness and unity experienced very infrequently in life. We were truly united and prayed with power and faith, believing our request would be granted, for we realized the desperate nature of our situation.

After prayer we rushed to the station where Elder Rasmussen and his group finally managed to catch a train for Osnabrueck, finally getting to Hamburg and by wonderful circumstances catching an express train to Copenhagen—one of the last out of Germany carrying civilians.

After the brethren had left, and we waved each other good-bye, I hurried back to the office of the Blackshirts only a few yards away, where my passport and effects were being held. The station master gave me my money and papers immediately, but a Blackshirt guard stuck my passport in his wide cuff and marched insolently before me as the passengers boarded the train for Holland. The whistle of the train was blowing, and I noted the clock indicated only three minutes until departure time. What was going to happen? Finally the Blackshirt strutted over and with a sneer handed me my passport, muttering some deprecatory remark under his breath. He pushed me to the ticket window where I was obliged to buy a German ticket to Oldenzaal even though my Dutch ticket assured passage to Bentheim and return. It was necessary to run in order to catch the train—the wheels had just begun to turn. I sank into the seat, grateful for the brethren's escape and my own now certain and safe return.

Upon arrival in Oldenzaal, I informed President Murdock by telephone as to what had been done. He told me to stay in Oldenzaal that night, and if anything unusual occurred I would then be there to help. This I did. But the following day at noon, having received word from no one, I returned to The Hague.

The following Friday, September 1, war was declared. The night before, Elder Smith phoned from Copenhagen informing us that the elders had arrived in safety. Everyone had escaped from Germany. The Lord had indeed been kind. . . . It is my sincere testimony that the Lord does watch over his children today even as in days of old.

*Improvement Era*, 46:793–96.

# "WE TOLD HIM TO FOLLOW HIS IMPRESSIONS ENTIRELY"

M . DOUGLAS WOOD

On Friday, the 25th of August [1939], my wife and I were traveling in the company of Elder Joseph Fielding Smith and Sister Smith in northern Germany, after coming into the country from Denmark. Friday morning we received a telegram from the First Presidency, which was relayed from our office in Frankfurt to Hanover, telling us that we should immediately evacuate Germany. We were told to take our missionaries and go either to Holland or to Denmark. We were then six hours from our mission headquarters. [Brother Wood was then president of the West German Mission.] . . .

I went to the hotel clerk and told him to get me reservations on the plane to fly to Frankfurt. He looked at me and said: "Those reservations, I am sure, have been gone for some time. Frankfurt is on the main European line and all reservations on that line are reserved two weeks ahead. Now with this Polish trouble I am sure that you could not buy a ticket for any consideration."

I said: "Call them up anyway. Call the airport. We must have two reservations."

He scratched his head after he called and said, "There are two left."

I said: "That is all that we need, and thank you so much."

In an hour and twenty minutes we were in Frankfurt. . . . At home we immediately sent telegrams to all our elders telling them to pack their trunks and take them with them that night into Holland. We had called the Dutch consul for permission to enter Holland again and had received it. We decided on Holland as it was closer to most of our missionaries. We had 85 missionaries scattered from the Danish border on the north to Vienna on the south, which is quite a big territory. . . . It took a little time to get the telegrams off to our elders. We had also informed them to telegraph the office, or telephone, as they left, so that we could check on all of them.

Friday afternoon and evening we sat in the office receiving no telegrams or telephone calls at all. We wondered if the missionaries had received our messages. We tried to telephone to a few of them in order to check up on the telegrams, but were unable to get anyone on the telephone. Everyone else had the same idea, and the telephone wires were clogged. We tried to send more telegrams and were told that temporarily all the chances for sending telegrams anywhere were closed.

Early that morning, (Saturday), one of the elders called us by telephone from the Dutch border. He said: "President Wood, we have been here on the Dutch border for six hours and the Dutch will not let us in. We haven't a dime between us. What shall we do?" A person cannot leave Germany with any money because there is controlled currency there. The Dutch had given us permission to enter, but things had happened so fast that the consul in Frankfurt did not know of the new arrangements until we told him. The Dutch remembered the last war and the lack of food in their country, and they were determined to have no foreigners there at all.

I said, "Brother, if you will have faith, I will see that we get some money to you immediately."

We telegraphed money to those elders, and within five minutes after we had done so the operator called us and said: "We will not be able to take any more money by telegraph; however, I think I can get this last through."

About that time a radio announcement was made by the government, that after Sunday night at midnight, August 27th, the German government would not guarantee anyone his destination on the German railways. I shall never forget our feelings at that time. We had no telegraph nor telephone facilities, and railways were not available to us. We were not able to contact our missionaries, and we knew that most of them would be heading toward Holland. We knew they would arrive there without enough money to buy tickets to Denmark, and we knew that time was against us, with the railroads all being used for troop transportation. If ever we knew that we could do nothing of ourselves we were sure of it then. One of the girls took out our mission history and read how the missionaries during the last war [World War I] got out of the country. One of the elders was not able to get out during the war and a few of our missionaries had to crawl on their hands and knees and make their way out behind the Russian lines. We knew these things and we knew the intense feeling of the parents at home. We knew that each one of [them] was relying upon us to see that [their] son was safe. Conditions were so unsettled there. We had seen the treatment of the Jews and we felt that we must do all in our power to see that those missionaries were safe. We also knew that we would be helped. Every mother and father in America was praying for their missionary sons, and we knew that the Lord would help us if we did all we could.

About that time a big football player [Norman G. Seibold] came into our office, a fine Idaho boy, who weighed over 200 pounds. . . .

I said: "Elder, we have 31 missionaries lost somewhere between here and the Dutch border. It will be your mission to find them and see that they get out."

He set out for the Dutch border with 500 marks and tickets for Denmark and for London. We had heard that a few might be able to get into Holland if they had tickets for London. That was soon changed. After four hours on the train he arrived at Cologne, which is about half way to the Dutch border. We had told him to follow his impressions entirely, as we had no idea what towns these 31 elders would be in. Cologne was not his destination, but he felt impressed to get off the train there. It is a very large station, and was then filled with thousands of people. The call to arms had been given that day, and there were thousands of people going to the Polish border. There were many, many students returning to England, and many people returning from vacations before the train service stopped. There were so many people in the station that to find anyone there would have been next to impossible.

This elder stepped into this station and whistled our missionary whistle—"Do What is Right, Let the Consequence Follow."

Down in one corner of that station was an elder with an old couple who were also on a mission from America. They heard that call, and made their way safely to the train and were able to get into Holland with tickets for London. These three were stranded there. They couldn't call the office, as no more calls on telephones were accepted, and they had had nothing to eat all day.

At another border station going into Holland this elder arrived, after picking up missionaries along the way. As he rode along on the train he felt impressed at other stations to get out and whistle our call. At some stations he felt no impression at all, so he did not get out. At the border he found eight missionaries who had been locked in the station house all night. They were indeed glad to see the missionary from the office with tickets for Denmark, and money. A border officer stepped up and asked him how much money he had. He told him 500 marks.

He said to the elder: "Give me that money."

The missionary answered: "I will over my dead body. I was sent here to relieve these missionaries, and I will not give up the money." Just at that time a man in the other corner of the station was arrested for being a spy. Now a spy on a border is really something important at wartime, and he attracted everybody's attention. The moment the officer turned, the elders stooped down and made their way out of the station and out to the train. By this time the trains had stopped running regularly. These missionaries got on to unscheduled trains, traveled for fifteen or twenty minutes, and then they would get out at the next station. There they would stand until they felt impressed to get on another train. They had to transfer seventeen times on a route that regularly requires no more than two or three transfers before reaching Denmark.

At another station three of our elders were walking along the street. They were fortunate enough not to be locked up. A man came up to them and stated that he had seen them before, saying that he knew that they were Mormon missionaries. He said that he had been called to the Polish front and had 50 marks which he knew he would not need and asked if they could use this money. They were without a penny, so they took it. This amount paid their way back to the little town where they had come from the day before.

One of the elders had received his allowance from home the day before. All the other elders had used their surplus money to buy photographic equipment which could be taken out of the country. This young man went to town but felt so bad about everything he just couldn't spend that money, so he put it into a drawer and said for his landlady to give it to the poor Saints if he did not come back. He did come back, however. The train had a ten-minute wait, and he ran up to the dwelling, got that money, and it was just enough, within a few pennies for food, to pay their way to Copenhagen, Denmark.

We arrived in Denmark early Monday morning with 21 missionaries in our group. That morning we received a telegram from President Murdock saying 14 of our group had arrived in The Hague. We now had only 17 to worry about. About two o'clock that afternoon we received a telegram from the football player saying 17 of them were arriving that night at 7:30.

My dear brothers and sisters, these things I have told you today are true stories of our experiences in getting out of the country. They are testimonies that I am sure will remain with these missionaries all their lives. Almost every one of our elders could tell you a real faith-stirring story about his leaving Germany. We all arrived in Denmark with our hearts filled with gratitude and humility. One of our elders was asked if he was a bit anxious about going home on a freighter and being led out of Denmark by a German pilot through the mines.

He said: "That is child's play after the things we have been through in getting out of Germany. I don't think after all the trouble the Lord went to there that He is going to let us down in the middle of the ocean."

For further information on the withdrawal of European missionaries at the beginning of World War II, see J. Reuben Clark's report in Conference Report, April 1940, 19–20.

---

Conference Report, April 1940, 79–81.

# REPENTANCE

# "How Glad I Am to See You!"

## DANIEL TYLER

A man who had stood high in the Church while in Far West was taken down with chills or ague and fever. While his mind as well as body was weak, disaffected parties soured his mind and persuaded him to leave the Saints and go with them. He gave some testimony against the Prophet. While the Saints were settling in Commerce, having recovered from his illness, he removed from Missouri to Quincy, Illinois. There he went to work chopping cordwood to obtain means to take himself and family to Nauvoo, and provide a present to the injured man of God if, peradventure, he would forgive and permit him to return to the fold as a private member. He felt that there was salvation nowhere else for him, and if that was denied him, all was lost as far as he was concerned. He started with a sorrowful heart and downcast look.

While on the way, the Lord told Brother Joseph he was coming. The Prophet looked out of the window and saw him coming up the street. As soon as he turned to open the gate, the Prophet sprang up from his chair and ran and met him in the yard, exclaiming, "O Brother, how glad I am to see you!" He caught him around the neck, and both wept like children.

Suffice it to say that the proper restitution was made, and the fallen man again entered the Church by the door, received his priesthood again, went upon several important missions, gathered with the Saints in Zion, and died in full faith.

---

Daniel Tyler, in Hyrum L. Andrus and Helen Mae Andrus, comps., *They Knew the Prophet*, 53–54.

# "AN OVERRULING POWER BEGAN TO WORK WITH ME"

SOLOMON F. KIMBALL

Picket Post was an old government fort in Pinal country Arizona. . . . I opened a livery and feed stable at this place. Soon after, I formed a partnership with a man who had been well recommended to me. We did a good business, and made money.

President A. F. MacDonald, and my father-in-law, Francis M. Pomeroy, visited me about this time. Among the things they told me was this: that if I would do right, and pay my tithing, the Lord would bless me; but if not, things would not be well with me. Up to this time I had never given a cent of tithing in my life. I paid but little attention to what they said, and felt pretty well satisfied the way things were going. I did nothing towards living my religion. I was the only man in the place who claimed connection with the "Mormon" Church in any way. My partner kept the books and handled the cash, and I took charge of the other affairs.

One morning, he saddled a horse, and said he was going into the hills to collect a bill, and I have never seen him since. I learned afterwards that he had collected all bills, borrowed all the money that he could on our names, and drawn out what cash we had in the bank. He then crossed the line into Old Mexico, which was only seventy-five miles away.

After I learned that I was financially ruined, I began to think over what President MacDonald had told me, but it was too late then to "lock the stable door." I made up my mind to close this stable, and to lease a smaller one in another part of the town. That night I dreamed that I found two eggs, larger than turkey eggs. I broke one of them, and to my surprise found a large scorpion in it, which filled the whole shell. I felt tempted to open the other, but thinking that I might find something worse, changed my mind. When I awoke, the interpretation was made plain. I had already opened one feed stable, and knew the results. I did not dare to open the other.

My creditors were pounding me about, but I could do nothing for them. I became discouraged and almost heart-broken. My wife and child had gone to Mesa to visit her parents. The harder I worked to pay my debts, the blacker things looked ahead. I began to have horrible night visions. I dreamed that I was in hurricanes and earthquakes, even hearing the deafening sounds. I saw myself in company with some of my brothers on the brink of precipices, in the act of falling off. These things began to start my religious blood to circulating. It caused me to think seriously of the things my father had taught me, in years gone by. Satan was on the spot to magnify my troubles to the uttermost.

When I had reached the zenith of my trouble, as I supposed, I received, from my sister Helen M., a little book that had just been published, entitled *H. C. Kimball's Journal;* also a blessing given to me when I was but eight days old. I had never seen either of them before. This is the blessing, as recorded by President Willard Richards:

> A blessing upon the head of Solomon Farnham, . . . by President B. Young, with H. C. Kimball, N. K. Whitney and A. Cutler, at the house of H. C. Kimball.
>
> Solomon Farnham, . . . we lay our hands upon thy head, and bless thee. . . . Thou shalt not be a whit behind any of thy father's house in blessings, but shall receive them in due time, for thou shalt live to enjoy life, and the angels shall have charge over thee, and thou shalt have dominion over every

foul spirit, and over death itself, and possess great treasures of wisdom and knowledge; and we seal you unto your father and mother, and bless you with all the blessings of the new and everlasting covenant, in the name of the Lord Jesus Christ. Amen.

After reading the blessing over several times, carefully, I commenced to read the book. There was an overruling Power that began to work with me, but I did not know it. I little understood these things, then. I yet had to pass through severe mental suffering, in order to prepare me for what was coming. Satan had laid his plans to destroy me. If he could accomplish this, he would prove President Young to be a false prophet. By the next day I had read the book through. I went to bed that evening pondering over these things. I could not sleep. I felt evil influences gathering around me that I could not understand. It was so different from anything that I had ever experienced before. I had been taught to pray by my parents, but had neglected praying.

This oppressive spirit began to bear down upon me in great power. I felt that I could not endure it much longer. I soon found myself upon my knees, praying like a chaplain, but could get no relief. I was alone, and the town people had gone to bed. I walked the floor, and made a strong effort to cry, but this was denied me. I got down on my knees again, and told the Lord of all the mean things that I had ever done in my life, and it took a long time.

The harder I prayed the worse I felt, and the worse I felt the harder I prayed. I kept this up all night. It seemed like iron under my feet and brass over my head. I felt that I had been abandoned to the powers of darkness which were determined to destroy me. It was almost daylight, and I was about to give up, when relief came. The Lord had heard my prayers. Darkness had fled, and the heavenly influence that took possession of me almost lifted me from my feet.

For the first time in my life I received a spiritual communication from the heavens. My father, when I was a child, called me his spiritual-minded boy, and I enjoyed that gift to a great extent in my younger days. Here was so much greater that I could not help but clap my hands for joy, and weep like a child. This is the word that I received: "Return to the Mesa ward. Renew your covenants. Pay your tithing. Go to the temple, and have your wife and child sealed to you. Live the life of a Latter-day Saint, and then I will forgive you of your sins, and will bless you."

I felt as if my head were a fountain of tears. I continued to weep and to praise the Lord as long as I remained in that place. The people thought that I had gone crazy. By noon I had sold and given away almost everything I had. By three o'clock I said good-bye to Pinal, and have never seen it since.

That afternoon, in company with some of our Mesa boys, we drove out on the desert, about twenty miles, and camped for the night. The Spirit of the Lord had remained with me until this time. I could begin to feel it withdrawing from me. After supper I took my bed and went off about one hundred yards by myself. I felt as if I wanted to be alone. I made my bed, and after I had prayed, went to rest thoroughly worn out.

I slept pretty well until towards morning, when the Evil One made another assault upon me, only in a different way. As I lay on my back, I was unable to move a muscle, for at least an hour. I could not utter a word, not even whisper. Then the fallen spirits showed themselves to me, one at a time. All I could see of them was their heads and bodies down to their waists. They would pass in front of me, and then remain about a quarter of a minute and gnash their teeth, and make faces, and then pass on. Then another one would take his place. I never saw the same face twice, and they appeared to be all males. It would be impossible to describe the horrible countenances of these imps of hell. I knew that they could not kill me, from what the Lord had told me. Neither was I frightened of them, but it was a fearful position to be in. They kept this up until daylight, and then left me.

I got up and dressed myself, and prayed, but felt downcast all that day. We reached Mesa about noon. After dinner I sought President MacDonald, and related my experience to him. He advised me to say nothing about it to any one, but do as I was told. He said he would be a father to me, and assist me in any way that he could. I asked him what I should do first. He said, "Go to Brother C. I. Robson and ask him to rebaptize you." I told him that I was not on speaking terms with him. He said, "That makes no difference; go and ask his forgiveness."

I went down to Brother Robson's house. He was making cane molasses. I asked him if he would forgive me. He was so astonished that he came near falling over backwards. The tears began to stream down his cheeks, and he said, "Certainly I will, and I want you to forgive me," which, of course, I did. I then asked him if he would rebaptize me, and he said he would. He put his coat on, and we went up to the Mesa canal, and there he performed the ceremony.

I had a few horses and a couple of wagons left. The next day I met a brother who wanted to trade me a home for them. We closed the bargain. This gave me a cozy little home with about four acres of land already cultivated. I attended all the meetings, and was probably the most humble man in the place. I said nothing about my experience to any one, excepting my wife. Many of the Saints, as well as the sinners, could not understand the sudden change that had come over me. Some treated me well, while others looked upon me with suspicion. I attended to my family prayers twice a day and commenced studying the scriptures. I was trying to make up for lost time. I felt that I had come in at the eleventh hour.

That winter, Apostle Erastus Snow came down from Utah to organize us into a stake of Zion. There were probably five or six hundred saints in that part of Arizona, at the time. He had a hard time in selecting suitable timber [i.e., leaders] for this organization. It took him about three days to complete his work. I was acquainted with some of the men whom he had chosen to fill these offices. Some of the timber he used was somewhat warped and had some knots in it, but he did the best he could. Brother Snow had been a close friend to my father and mother, and visited them often when they were alive. Many times he had trotted me on his knee when I was small. During the conference, I kept listening, expecting to hear my name called, but was considerably disappointed.

After conference had adjourned, for the first time I began to feel my littleness. I wondered if it could be possible that I was a less worthy man than any of those he had chosen. Brother Snow could read my inmost thoughts. He understood me better than I understood myself. Before starting home, he took me by the hand, in a kind and fatherly manner, and said: "Brother Solomon, if you will continue to do right, I promise you, in the name of the Lord, that it will not be long before you will hold more offices than you will be able to take care of." He then prayed God to bless me.

This did me great good. I took hold of my religious duties with a vim, and never left a stone unturned. The worst thing I had to contend with was the self-righteous element. One prominent man, who was the best friend I had when I was doing wrong, was my worst enemy when I commenced to do right. His class could not bear to see me living my religion. They were continually throwing blocks in my way.

One day, at a general conference, one of them, in speaking of those who had been seeking after the things of the world, said it reminded him of Sol. Kimball. After meeting I called his attention

439

to it. I told him that I had been confessing my sins for the last three years. I thought that he ought to confess his own sins. He offered to apologize to me at the afternoon meeting, but I would not submit to it.

Some times I would feel quite discouraged. The way some of the brethren treated me, I began to feel like it was no use for me to try to do right. Some of them preached doctrine which, if true, would bar me out of the kingdom of heaven. And if I should happen to get there, I should be covered with scars. I imagined that they were talking to me all the time.

I heard so many of these things that I began to feel that I was throwing my time away in trying to work out my salvation. I became despondent, and thoroughly discouraged. I was between two very hot fires. I did not know what to do. I resorted to fasting and praying. I wanted to find out, if possible, whether my labors during the last three years had been acceptable to the Lord.

One morning, before breakfast, I went off into the desert, and prayed with great earnestness before the Lord in relation to this matter. After I had been on my knees for twenty-five or thirty minutes, I started back home thinking over these things. I had not gone far when the Spirit of the Lord, in a very satisfactory and comprehensive manner, informed me that my labors had been acceptable to him, and that my sins had been forgiven. It made such a deep and lasting impression upon my mind that I have never felt discouraged in relation to such matters since.

About this time there was a small company getting ready to go to the St. George Temple. I had a team and wagon. I sold my only cow to get an outfit to go along with them. The distance to St. George was five hundred miles, and two hundred of it over a very rough country. We made the trip in three weeks. After having my wife and children sealed to me, I felt that I had carried out

the instructions of the Lord to the letter. My heart was light, and
my sins were forgiven.

_____

*Improvement Era,* 9:685–91.

# A GOSPEL OF FORGIVENESS

## HEBER J. GRANT

A man was cut off from the Church for adultery and asked
to be restored. President John Taylor wrote a letter to the
brethren that had taken action against the man, in which
he said: "I want every man to vote his own convictions, and not to
vote to make it unanimous unless it is unanimous."

When the matter was presented and voted upon, the vote
stood half for and half against restoration.

Later he came up again, and a majority were in favor of his
being baptized.

Finally, all of the men that were at the trial, except one, voted
to let him be baptized. President John Taylor sent for me and told
me I was the only man that stood in the way of this man's being
baptized, and he said: "How will you feel when you meet the Lord,
if this man is permitted to come up and say he repented although
his sins were as scarlet, and you refused to let him be baptized?"

I said: "I will look the Lord squarely in the eye, and I will tell
Him that any man that can destroy the virtue of a girl and then lie
and claim that she was maligning him and blackmailing him, will

441

never get back into this Church with my vote. You said in your letter to vote our convictions, and I will vote them and stay with them unless you want me to change."

He said: "Stay with your convictions, my boy."

I walked to my home, only one block away. I picked up the Doctrine and Covenants. I was reading it prayerfully and humbly, and marking passages. Instead of its opening at the bookmark, it opened at the passage:

"Wherefore, I say unto you, that ye ought to forgive one another; for he that forgiveth not his brother his trespasses standeth condemned before the Lord; for there remaineth in him the greater sin.

"I, the Lord, will forgive whom I will forgive, but of you it is required to forgive all men." (D&C 64:9–10.)

I shut up the book and rushed back to the President, and I said, "I give my consent."

Brother Taylor had a habit, when something pleased him, of shaking himself and laughing, and he said: "My gracious, Heber, this is remarkable; what has happened?" And I told him. He said: "Heber, when you left here a few minutes ago did you not think: what if he had defiled my wife or daughter? And when you thought that, did you not feel as if you would like to just knock the life out of that man?"

I said, "I certainly did."

"How do you feel now?"

"Well, really and truly Brother Taylor, I hope the poor old sinner can be forgiven."

"You feel a whole lot better, don't you?"

I said, "I certainly do."

He added: "I put that clause in that letter for you and my son. You have learned a lesson as a young man. You have learned a good lesson, that this gospel is one of forgiveness of sin, of awful sin, if there is true repentance; and it brings peace into your heart when you forgive the sinner. It brings peace when you love the man that you hated, provided the man turns to doing right. You have learned a lesson in your youth. Never forget it." And I never have.

---

Conference Report, 5 October 1941, 148–49.

# RESTORATION

# THE DEATH OF ALVIN SMITH

<LUCY   MACK   SMITH>

O n the 15th of November, 1823, about 10 o'clock in the morning, Alvin [eldest brother of Joseph Smith] was taken very sick with the bilious colic. He came to the house in much distress, and requested his father to go immediately for a physician. He accordingly went, obtaining one by the name of Greenwood, who, on arriving, immediately administered to the patient a heavy dose of calomel. I will here notice, that this Dr. Greenwood was not the physician commonly employed by the family; he was brought in consequence of the family physician's absence. And on this account, as I suppose, Alvin at first refused to take the medicine, but by much persuasion, he was prevailed on to do so.

This dose of calomel lodged in his stomach, and all the medicine afterwards freely administered by four very skillful physicians could not remove it.

On the third day of his sickness, Dr. McIntyre, whose services were usually employed by the family, as he was considered very skillful, was brought, and with him four other eminent physicians. But it was all in vain, their exertions proved unavailing, just as Alvin said would be the case—he told them the calomel was still lodged in the same place, after some exertion had been made to carry it off, and that it must take his life.

On coming to this conclusion, [Alvin] called Hyrum to him, and said, "Hyrum, I must die. Now I want to say a few things, which I wish to have you remember. I have done all I could to

447

make our dear parents comfortable. I want you to go on and finish the house and take care of them in their old age, and do not any more let them work hard, as they are now in old age."

He then called Sophronia to him, and said to her, "Sophronia, you must be a good girl, and do all you can for father and mother—never forsake them; they have worked hard, and they are now getting old. Be kind to them, and remember what they have done for us."

In the latter part of the fourth night he called for all the children, and exhorted them separately in the same strain as above. But when he came to Joseph, he said, "I am now going to die, the distress which I suffer, and the feelings that I have, tell me my time is very short. I want you to be a good boy, and do everything that lies in your power to obtain the Record. Be faithful in receiving instruction, and in keeping every commandment that is given you. Your brother Alvin must leave you; but remember the example which he has set for you; and set the same example for the children that are younger than yourself, and always be kind to father and mother."

He then asked me to take my little daughter Lucy up, and bring her to him, for he wished to see her. He was always very fond of her. . . . I went to her, and said: "Lucy, Alvin wants to see you." At this, she started from her sleep, and screamed out, "Amby, Amby"; (she could not talk plain, being very young). We took her to him, and when she got within reach of him, she sprang from my arms and caught him around the neck, and cried out, "Oh, Amby," and kissed him again and again.

"Lucy," said he, "you must be the best girl in the world, and take care of mother; you can't have your Amby any more. Amby is going away; he must leave little Lucy." He then kissed her. . . .

As I turned with the child to leave him he said, "Father, mother, brothers, and sisters, farewell! I can now breathe out my life as calmly as a clock." Saying this, he immediately closed his eyes in death. . . .

Alvin was a youth of singular goodness of disposition—kind and amiable, so that lamentation and mourning filled the whole neighborhood in which he resided. . . .

Alvin manifested, if such could be the case, greater zeal and anxiety in regard to the Record that had been shown to Joseph, than any of the rest of the family. . . . Whenever Joseph spoke of the Record, it would immediately bring Alvin to our minds, with all his zeal, and with all his kindness; and, when we looked to his place, and realized that he was gone from it, to return no more in this life, we all with one accord wept over our irretrievable loss, and we could "not be comforted, because he was not."

Lucy Mack Smith, *History of the Prophet Joseph Smith*, 86–89.

# "A Personage Walked through the Room"

### ZEBEDEE COLTRIN

At one of these meetings after the organization of the school [of the prophets], on the 23rd January, 1833, when we were all together, Joseph having given instructions, and while engaged in silent prayer, kneeling, with our hands uplifted each one praying in silence, no one whispered above his breath, a personage walked through the room from East to west, and Joseph asked if we saw him. I saw him and suppose the others did, and Joseph answered that is Jesus, the Son of God, our elder brother.

Afterward Joseph told us to resume our former position in prayer, which we did. Another person came through; He was surrounded as with a flame of fire. [I] experienced a sensation that it might destroy the tabernacle as it was of consuming fire of great brightness. The Prophet Joseph said this was the Father of our Lord Jesus Christ. I saw Him. . . . This appearance was so grand and overwhelming that it seemed I should melt down in His presence, and the sensation was so powerful that it thrilled through my whole system and I felt it in the marrow of my bones.

The Prophet Joseph said: "Brethren, now you are prepared to be Apostles of Jesus Christ, for you have seen both the Father and the Son and know that they exist and that they are two separate personages."

---

Minutes of Salt Lake School of the Prophets, 3 October 1883, 58–60.

# "IT HAD BEEN PROPHESIED
# I WOULD BE THERE"

⌒

ORSON PRATT

I will pass over the first years of the organization of the Church and come down to the time when the Twelve were chosen. It was in the year 1835. In the preceding year a few of us, by commandment and revelation from God, went up to the State of Missouri in company with the Prophet Joseph Smith. By the direction of Joseph I was requested to stay in Clay County for a few months, to visit the Saints scattered through those regions, to preach to and comfort them, and to lay before them the manuscript revelations, for they were not then fully acquainted with all the revelations which had been given.

After having accomplished this work, and proclaimed the gospel to many branches of the Church in the western part of Missouri, I returned again a thousand miles to the State of Ohio, preaching by the way, suffering much from the chills, and the fever and ague, while passing through those low sickly countries, wading swamps and sloughs, lying down on the prairies in the hot sun, fifteen or twenty miles from any habitation, and having a hearty shake of the ague, then a violent fever, thus wandering along for months before getting back to Kirtland, Ohio, where the Prophet lived. In the meantime, however, I built up some few branches of the Church, and then started for the capital of the State of Ohio—the city of Columbus.

I entered the city, a stranger, on foot, and alone, not knowing that there was a Latter-day Saint within many miles, but, while

451

passing along the crowded streets, I caught a glimpse of the countenance of a man who passed, and whirling around instantly, I went after him, and inquired of him if he knew whether there were any people called "Mormons" in the city of Columbus. Said he: "I am one of that people, and the only one that resides in the city." I looked upon this as a great marvel. "How is it," said I, "that here in this great and populous city, where hundreds are passing to and fro, that I should be influenced to turn and accost the only Latter-day Saint residing here."

I look upon it as a revelation, as a manifestation of the power of God in my behalf. He took me to his house, and, when there, presented me with a paper published by our people in Kirtland. In that paper I saw an advertisement, in which br. Pratt was requested to be at Kirtland on such a day and at such an hour, to attend meeting in the Temple, that he might be ready to take his departure with the Twelve who had been chosen. The day and hour designated were right at hand; the Twelve were chosen, and were soon to start on their first mission as a Council. I had been travelling among strangers for months, and had not seen the paper.

I saw that I had not time to reach Kirtland on foot, as I had been accustomed to travel, and consequently could not thus comply with the request; but, with a little assistance, I got into the very first stage that went out, and started post-haste for Kirtland, and landed at Willoughby, or what was then called Chagim, three miles from Kirtland, to which I travelled on foot, reaching there on Sunday morning at the very hour appointed for the meeting, which I entered, valise in hand, not having had time to deposit it by the way. There I met with Joseph, Oliver Cowdery, David Whitmer, Martin Harris, and others of the witnesses to the Book of Mormon, besides several of the Twelve who had been chosen and ordained a short time previous. They were meeting on that day in order to be fully organized and qualified for their first mission as a council.

And, strange to relate, it had been prophesied in that meeting, and in prior meetings, I would be there on that day. They had predicted this, although they had not heard of me for some time, and did not know where I was. They knew I had been in Missouri, and that I had started from there, several months before, but the Lord poured out the spirit of prophecy upon them, and they predicted I would be there at that meeting. When they saw me walk into the meeting, many of the Saints could scarcely believe their own eyes, the prediction was fulfilled before them so perfectly. I look at these things as miraculous manifestations of the Spirit of God.

I was ordained, and went forth with the Council of Twelve. We performed an extended mission through the eastern States, built up churches, and returned again to Kirtland.

_____

*Journal of Discourses,* 12:87.

# THE TWELVE ON THE DAY
# OF THE MARTYRDOM

⌒

## B . H . ROBERTS

We here insert the location of the Twelve Apostles on this memorable day:—

President Brigham Young and Elder Wilford Woodruff spent a portion of the day together in the city of Boston, and were sitting together in the railway depot at the time of the massacre of the Prophets; they felt very sorrowful, and depressed in spirits, without knowing the cause.

Elders Heber C. Kimball and Lyman Wight traveled from Philadelphia to New York by railway and steamboat. Elder Kimball felt very mournful as though he had lost some friend, and knew not the cause.

Elder Orson Hyde was in the hall occupied by the saints in Boston, examining maps, and designating or pointing out each man's district or field of labor, in company with Elders Brigham Young, Wilford Woodruff and others, a part of the day. He felt very heavy and sorrowful in spirit, and knew not the cause, but felt no heart to look on the maps. He retired to the further end of the hall alone, and walked the floor; tears ran down his face. . . . He never felt so before, and knew no reason why he should feel so then.

Elder Parley P. Pratt was on the canal boat between Utica and Buffalo, N.Y., on his return to Nauvoo, and was much depressed in spirit; his brother William Pratt came on board of the same boat, and Parley asked him if he had any books or pamphlets containing the gospel of Christ, or the words of life; if so, to put them

454

under lock and key, for the people are not worthy of them for, said Parley, "I feel that the spirit of murder is in the hearts of the people through the land."

Elders Willard Richards and John Taylor were the only two of the Quorum of the Twelve who were not on missions, and the only two men who were with the martyrs when they fell and sealed their testimony with their blood.

Elder George A. Smith rode with Elder Crandall Dunn, from Napoleon, to Elder Noah Willis Bartholomew's, near Jacksonburg, Jackson county, Michigan, and felt unusually cast down and depressed in spirits. About five o'clock he repaired to an oak grove, and called upon the Lord, endeavoring to break the spell of horror which had dominion over his mind. He remained there a long time without finding any relief, and then went back to Brother Bartholomew's, and went to bed with Elder Crandall Dunn; he could not sleep, but spent the night in a series of miserable thoughts and reflections. Once it seemed to him that some fiend whispered in his ear, "Joseph and Hyrum are dead; ain't you glad of it?"

Elders William B. Smith, Orson Pratt, and John Edward Page are not mentioned.

———————

B. H. Roberts, in Joseph Smith, *History of the Church*, 7:132–33.

# REVELATION

# "You Shall Speak in Tongues"

SUSA YOUNG GATES

A meeting was again held, and after it was over the Prophet [Joseph Smith] baptized twelve persons, among whom [were] Lydia . . . , Mr. Nickerson, and all of his household. She who was always so sober and full of reflection had received the glad message with trembling joy. She was filled with a bright, peaceful influence and was full of gratitude that God had spared her to hear and accept his glorious gospel. . . .

So into the water goes Lydia with a light step and happy heart. She was so filled with the Holy Ghost while standing in the water after she was baptized that she was constrained to cry aloud, "Glory to God in the highest! Thanks be to his holy name that I have lived to see this day and be a partaker of this great blessing."

In the evening, the new members of the Church assembled in Mr. Nickerson's house for confirmation. God bestowed his Spirit very freely and the Prophet gave much valuable instruction.

Two more persons came to the Prophet and requested baptism at the meeting the next day. It was attended to and a branch of the Church was organized. Freeman Nickerson was ordained as the presiding elder.

The evening of this day . . . the family were all seated around the wide, old-fashioned fireplace in the parlor listening to the Prophet's words and full of rejoicing.

"I would be so glad if someone who has been baptized could receive the gift of tongues as the ancient Saints did and speak to us," said Moses Nickerson.

"If one of you will rise up and open your mouth it shall be filled, and you shall speak in tongues," replied the Prophet.

Everyone then turned as by a common instinct to Lydia and said with one voice, "Sister Lydia, rise up."

And then the great story of God was manifested to this weak but trusting girl. She was enveloped as with a flame, and unable longer to retain her seat, she rose and her mouth was filled with the praises of God and his glory. The spirit of tongues was upon her, and she was clothed in a shining light, so bright that all present saw it with great distinctness above the light of the fire and the candles.

Susa Young Gates, *Lydia Knight's History,* 20–22.

# "TWO FRENCHMEN WERE COMING UP THE TURNPIKE"

EDWARD STEVENSON

At one of our meetings, and it was a testimony meeting, Brother [Elijah] Fordham was speaking in tongues when two Frenchmen were coming up the turnpike road which passed close by the schoolhouse. By some means, perhaps by hearing their own language spoken, they were attracted to the window, where they asked a boy who was outside if he knew what that man said. Of course the boy did not know any more than did the speaker, for Brother Fordham did not understand any more about French that he did about Greek, for it was a spiritual gift he was then exercising. The Frenchmen testified that Brother Fordham was preaching the gospel to them.

---

*Juvenile Instructor* 29:524.

# "YOUR SON WILL ACT AS AN ANGEL TO YOU"

⌒‿

ORSON F. WHITNEY

Edward Hunter, the third Presiding Bishop of the Church, . . . was born June 22, 1793, in . . . Pennsylvania. [On] October 8, 1840, Edward Hunter was baptized by Elder Orson Hyde. . . .

At a subsequent visit of Brother Hyrum Smith, as they were walking along the banks of the Brandywine, the conversation turned upon the subject of the departed; and Brother Hunter was constrained to inquire about his children whom he has lost, particularly a little boy, George Washington by name, an excellent child to whom he was devotedly attached. "It is pretty strong doctrine," said Elder Smith, "but I believe I will tell it. Your son will act as an angel to you; not your guardian angel, but an auxiliary angel, to assist you in extreme trials." The truth of this was manifested to him about a year and a half later, when in an hour of deep depression, the little boy appeared to him in vision. Brother

Hunter says: "In appearance he was more perfect than in natural life—the same blue eyes, curly hair, fair complexion, and a most beautiful appearance. I felt disposed to keep him, and offered inducements for him to remain [but he could not]."

Orson F. Whitney, in Andrew Jenson, *LDS Biographical Encyclopedia,* 1:227, 229–30.

# "You Shall Have Plenty of Money"

## BRIGHAM YOUNG

On reaching Dublin, Indiana, I found my brother Lorenzo and Isaac Decker, and a number of other families who had stopped for the winter. Meanwhile the Prophet Joseph, Brothers Sidney Rigdon and George W. Robinson came along. They had fled from Kirtland because of the mobocratic spirit prevailing in the bosoms of the apostates.

Here the Prophet made inquiry concerning a job at cutting cordwood and sawing logs, after which he came to me and said, "Brother Brigham, I am destitute of means to pursue my journey and as you are one of the Twelve Apostles who hold the keys of the kingdom in all the world, I believe I shall throw myself upon you, and look to you for counsel in this case." At first I could hardly believe Joseph was in earnest, but on his assuring me he was, I said, "If you will take my counsel, it will be that you rest yourself and be assured, Brother Joseph, you shall have plenty of money to pursue your journey."

There was a brother named Tomlinson living in the place, who had previously asked my counsel about selling his tavern-stand. I told him if he would do right and obey counsel, he should have opportunity to sell soon, and the first offer he would get would be the best. A few days afterwards Brother Tomlinson informed me he had an offer for his place. I asked him what offer he had; he replied he was offered $500 in money, a team, and $250 in store goods. I told him that was the hand of the Lord to deliver President Joseph Smith from his present necessity.

My promise to Joseph was soon verified. Brother Tomlinson sold his property and gave the Prophet three hundred dollars, which enabled him comfortably to proceed on his journey.

---

Brigham Young, *Manuscript History of Brigham Young*, 24–25.

# "NOW, BRETHREN, WE WILL SEE SOME VISIONS"

AUTHOR UNKNOWN

Once after returning from a mission, [Zebedee Coltrin] met Brother Joseph in Kirtland, who asked him if he did not wish to go with him to a conference at New Portage. The party consisted of President Joseph Smith, Sidney Rigdon, Oliver Cowdery, and [Zebedee Coltrin]. Next morning at New Portage he [Coltrin] noticed that Joseph seemed to have a far off look in his eyes, or was looking at a distance, and presently he, Joseph, stepped between Brothers Cowdery and Coltrin and taking them by the arm, said, "Let's take a walk." They went to a place where there was some beautiful grass, and grapevines and swampbeech interlaced. President Joseph Smith then said, "Let us pray." They all three prayed in turn—Joseph, Oliver and Zebedee. Bro. Joseph then said, "Now, Brethren, we will see some visions."

[We] lay down on the ground on [our backs]. . . . The heavens gradually opened and they saw a golden throne, on a circular foundation, something like a lighthouse, and on the throne were two aged personages, having white hair and clothed in white garments. They were the two most beautiful and perfect specimens of mankind [Coltrin] ever saw. Joseph said, "They are our first parents, Adam and Eve." Adam was a large, broad-shouldered man, and Eve, as a woman, was as large in proportion.

---

Minutes of the Salt Lake School of the Prophets, 11 October 1883, 68–70.

# BRIGHAM YOUNG TALKS TO NORWEGIAN OXEN

B . H . ROBERTS

*This incident occurred on August 3, 1844, as Brigham Young was returning to Nauvoo with other Church leaders after the martyrdom of Joseph and Hyrum Smith.*

The Twelve continued their journey through the day and night by stage. While upon their journey they overtook a company of Norwegians who were traveling with ox teams, and heavily loaded wagons, one of which was stuck fast in the mud, blocking up the road, while several of them were whipping the oxen and bawling to them in the Norwegian language, which seemed to frighten the oxen, but they were unable to move the wagons on.

After sitting and looking at them a moment, President Young got out of the coach and stepped up, and took the whip out of the hands of one of the Norwegians, telling them all to stand out of the way.

He then talked to the oxen in a tongue which was not understood by Norwegians or English, and touching them lightly with the whip, they instantly pulled the wagon out of the mud and continued the journey, much to the astonishment of the Norwegians and the surprise and amusement of the passengers on the stage.

---

B. H. Roberts, in Joseph Smith, *History of the Church*, 7:224.

# "I WAS NEEDED BEHIND
# THE VEIL"

SUSA YOUNG GATES

That evening [January 11, 1847] Newel [Knight] was buried. No lumber could be had, so Lydia had one of her wagon-boxes made into a rude coffin. The day was excessively cold, and some of the brethren had their fingers and feet frozen while digging the grave and performing the last offices of love for their honored captain and brother.

As the woman looked out upon the wilderness of snow and saw the men bearing away all that was left of her husband, it seemed that the flavor of life had fled and left only dregs, bitter, unavailing sorrow. But as she grew calmer she whispered with poor, pale lips, "God rules!"

Time was empty of incident or interest to Lydia until the 4th of February, when Brother Miller, who had been to Winter Quarters for provisions, returned and brought tidings of a revelation showing the order of the organization of the camp of the Saints, and also the joyful news that Brothers E. T. Benson and Erastus Snow were coming soon to Ponca to organize the Saints according to the pattern given in the revelation.

On the day of the organization, Lydia returned from the meeting and sat down in her home full of sad thoughts. How could she, who had never taken any care except that which falls to every woman's share, prepare herself and family to return to Winter Quarters and from thence take a journey a thousand miles into

Malcolm McCool

the Rocky Mountains? The burden weighed her very spirit down until she cried out in her pain, "Oh Newel, why hast thou left me!"

As she spoke, he stood by her side, with a lovely smile on his face, and said: "Be calm, let no sorrow overcome you. It was necessary that I should go. I was needed behind the veil. . . . You cannot fully comprehend it now; but the time will come when you shall know why I left you and our little ones. Therefore, dry up your tears. Be patient, I will go before you and protect you in your journeyings. And you and your little ones shall never perish for lack of food." . . .

The little babe was a week old when a sudden severe rainstorm came up. Lydia told her daughter Sally to give her all the bedclothes they had, and these were put upon the bed and removed as they became soaked.

At last, finding the clothes were all wet completely through and that she was getting chilled sitting up in the wet, she said, "Sally, go to bed. It's no use doing any more unless some power beyond that which we possess is exercised; it is impossible for me to avoid catching cold. But we will trust in God; he has never failed to hear our prayers."

And so she drew her babe to her, and covered up as well as she could, and asked God to watch over them all through the night.

Her mind wandered back to the time when she had a noble companion, one who would never allow her to suffer any discomfort and who loved her as tenderly as man could woman. But now he was in the grave in a savage Indian country, and she was alone and in trouble.

As she thus mused, chilled with the cold rain and shivering, her agony at his loss became unbearable and she cried out, "Oh Newel, why could you not have stayed with and protected me through our journeyings?"

A voice plainly answered her from the darkness around her

and said, "Lydia, be patient and fear not. I will still watch over you, and protect you in your present situation. You shall receive no harm. It was needful that I should go, and you will understand why in due time."

As the voice ceased, a pleasant warmth crept over her and seemed like the mild sunshine in a lovely spring afternoon.

Curling down in this comfortable atmosphere, she went immediately to sleep, and awoke in the morning all right, but wet to the skin.

Instead of receiving harm from this circumstance, she got up the next morning, although the child was but a week old, and went about her usual labors.

Susa Young Gates, *Lydia Knight's History,* 71–73.

# "A Shining Substance"

## JACOB HAMBLIN

I dreamed, three nights in succession, of being out west, alone, with the Indians that we had been [fighting] about three years. . . . I saw myself walk with them in a friendly manner, and, while doing so, picked up a lump of shining substance, some of which stuck to my fingers, and the more I endeavored to brush it off the brighter it became. . . .

This dream made such an impression on my mind, that I took

my blankets, guns, ammunition, and went alone into their country. I remained with them several days, hunting deer and ducks, occasionally loaning them my rifle, and assisting to bring in their game. I also did all I could to induce them to be at peace with us.

One day, in my rambles, I came to a lodge where there was a squaw, and a boy about ten years old. As soon as I saw the boy, the Spirit said to me, "Take that lad home with you, that is part of your mission here, and here is the bright substance which you dreamed of picking up." I talked with him and asked if he would not go with me. He at once replied that he would.

The mother, naturally enough, in a deprecating tone, asked me if I wanted to take her boy away from her. But after some further conversation she consented to the arrangement. At this time I had not learned much of the language of these Indians, but I seemed to have the gift of making myself understood.

When I left, the boy took his bows and arrows and accompanied me. The woman appeared to feel so bad, and made so much ado, that I told him he had better go back to his mother, but he would not do so. We went to the side of a mountain where I agreed to meet the Indians. His mother, still anxious about her boy, came to our camp in the evening.

The following morning, she told me that she heard I had a good heart, for the Indians told her that I had been true to what I said, and the boy could go with me if I would always be his father and own him as a son.

This boy became very much attached to me, and was very particular to do what he was told. I asked him why he was so willing to come with me the first time we met. He replied that I was the first white man he ever saw; that he knew a man would come to his mother's lodge to see him, on the day of my arrival, for he was told so the night before, and that when the man came he must go with him, that he knew I was the man when he saw me a long way off, and built a smoke so that I could come there.

Jacob Hamblin, in Pearson H. Corbett, *Jacob Hamblin, Peacemaker,* 42–45.

# "THAT IS YOUR FUTURE HUSBAND"

## HANNAH CORNABY

Suitors came, my hand to claim," but as yet my heart gave no response to this symphony of love, although I appreciated the honor they sought to confer on me. My friends blamed me, and predicted for me the fate of an old maid. This, however, did not distress me, for my Bible said, "Be not unequally yoked with unbelievers," and, thinking myself a believer, I feared to be yoked with an unbeliever. None of those who had presented themselves had made any profession of religion.

But a day came when, as in all my life, I had been "led in a way I knew not"; so, with this important step it was the same.

One day I was in the town on business, walking along Market Street, intent only on the errand which called me there, when I passed a young man, an entire stranger to me. Now there was nothing remarkable in the appearance of this stranger, but something whispered, "That is your future husband." Surprised at this, I turned to take a look at him, and, to my annoyance, he had also turned to look at me. Ashamed of myself for this breach of street etiquette, I hastily resumed my way, and this stranger who had thus attracted my attention was lost to sight. Not so with the interest he had created in my heart. Business was for the time forgotten; I walked aimlessly on, thinking of this strange event, when I was met by my sister Amelia, who asked what had happened to make me look so pleased. I told her frankly of the singular circumstance just recorded. She smiled and said, "Oh, my romantic sister." I replied, "Do not make fun of me; I shall marry that man, or I shall never marry on this earth."

Months rolled on. I could not drive from my thoughts this singular incident, when, apparently by the merest accident, at the house of a friend, I met and was introduced to a Mr. Cornaby, who had come to Beccles to take charge of a public school. Here, dear reader, let me introduce to you my future husband; for in this gentleman I recognized the mysterious stranger who for months had filled my thoughts. Though perturbed and agitated, I concealed my emotion and left the house as quickly as possible; and in the quietude of my own room, I thought and prayed earnestly for the guidance of the Holy Spirit to direct me aright.

*Over time, a friendship developed between the author and Mr. Cornaby. The friendship led to deeper feelings. Finally, on January 30, 1851, the couple were married.*

Hannah Cornaby, *Autobiography and Poems*, 17–21.

# THE DISMISSAL OF DR. JUDD

⌒

BENJAMIN F. JOHNSON

With eight other Elders I was called by the General October Conference of 1852, on a mission to the Sandwich [Hawaiian] Islands. . . .

In passing through the southern settlements of Utah, . . . we were often invited to preach where we stopped for the night, or to spend the Sabbath. . . .

We all, alike, took part in the meetings, and shared the hospitality of the Saints. At Parowan we had an unusually good time, in a meeting of the Saints. The Spirit of the Lord rested greatly upon both hearers and speakers.

I was the last Elder called upon to speak, and only a few minutes were left for me to occupy. Being full of the good feeling and spirit of the meeting, I commenced, not only to bear my testimony to the truth, but to prophesy of the future of some of the sons of Zion who were then going forth as her ministers.

I predicted that, through faithfulness, the wisdom of heaven would increase with us; that while the wicked became weaker, the Elders of Israel would grow wiser; that the nations of the earth would begin to look towards Zion for counselors and statesmen, and that, if the Elders now going forth to the ends of the earth were true to their calling, they would not all fill their missions until some of them would be called upon to give counsel to some of the rulers of the lands to which they were sent.

After closing my prophecy and remarks, and I had time to

ponder on what I had said, I began to doubt the possibility of my predictions being fulfilled, and began to be troubled in mind.

For a time I could not divest myself of the feeling, that my prediction was ill-timed and not by the spirit of the gospel. I would sometimes query if the brethren did not regard me as a false prophet, or, at least, as an enthusiast.

When we arrived on the Sandwich Islands, we found the work of the Lord progressing. The Elders who had been laboring there were greatly rejoiced to see us.

After a general mission conference, most of the brethren left Honolulu for their fields of labor on the different islands. I was left at this capital city, in charge of the foreign interests of the mission, to preside over a small branch of Saints, which had been gathered from the foreign residents on the islands, and to preach to the people as I might find opportunity. I also assisted Elders Lewis and Cannon, in raising funds for publishing the Book of Mormon in the native language.

Owing to the conflicting interests of political and religious parties in the Hawaiian kingdom, it was in a weak condition. The various missionary interests had nearly changed into political ones. Dr. Judd, one of the missionaries sent out by the American Board of Foreign Missions, had long been the king's prime minister. Another missionary, by the name of Armstrong, was Minister of Public Instruction, and other Americans filled the offices of Minister of Foreign Relations, Chief Justice, Attorney General, etc.

This missionary-political power began to cause great jealousy, especially in the case of Dr. Judd. Through his political advantages he had acquired much wealth, and, apparently by its use, raised himself up to be a power behind the throne, greater than the throne itself.

King Kamehameha III, like George the III, of England, had not reached a high standard of virtue, or political economy. It was said that, for money borrowed of Dr. Judd, he had given a mortgage on the royal palace.

As he had no children of his own he had adopted as next in succession, two sons of his sister, who were princes of the realm. About this time two projects were deeply agitating the public mind. One was the annexation of the islands to the United States, the other, a British protectorate over them. Neither of these projects suited the interests of the young princes, or pleased the majority of the people.

There appeared to be but one thing upon which nearly all the natives could agree, that was opposition to Dr. Judd as the king's prime minister. He was, of course, sustained by some of his fellow missionaries, but appeared to be detested by the majority of those around him. Petition after petition was sent to the king, asking for, and even demanding, his removal. The court house and other large halls were crowded with indignation meetings, to protest against his being retained in office.

It seemed, at times, as though the people would break out in tumult and insurrection, yet the king made no move to give them satisfaction, and, for many days, no answer was given to their petitions.

All this time I had been a careful observer, and had attended their meetings. I had previously written a lengthy letter to the king, explaining the gospel as now revealed and the object of our mission to the islands.

This letter he had caused to be published in the government journal, both in the English and Hawaiian languages. Such was the impression the reading of it made on his mind, that he sent, through the Minister of Foreign Relations, to say that he would give us an audience at his earliest convenience. Up to the time of which I am writing, he had not found the convenient opportunity.

In the midst of this political commotion, I, one night, dreamed that I stood upon an eminence near a large mountain. I saw below me upon the bank of a small, but rapid stream, a large and rudely constructed frame building, apparently designed for machinery. It was not yet fully inclosed.

As I looked, I saw a dense smoke arise from the building, and heard the cry of fire from a large number of people.

It seemed that the wind blew strong from the mountain towards the building. The people came up on the opposite side of the building, to put out the fire, and they were blinded by the smoke which blew in their faces. I thought how foolish they were, to thus stay on the opposite side from the wind, to be blinded with the smoke.

Looking, I saw a bucket with a rope attached on a flume through which the water ran. I quickly took it up, drew it full of water, looked for the center of the fire, dashed it in, and, all at once, the flame was extinguished.

I thought a multitude of people came crowding into the building, wondering by whom the fire had been extinguished. Although I was with them, they appeared to comprehend nothing of my agency in the matter. I thought they were almost wild with joy, that the building, although somewhat charred and damaged, had been saved. They calculated that the damage the building had sustained was about fifty thousand dollars.

I awoke in the morning, strangely impressed with the dream. I related it to Brother Nathan Tanner, who was then with me. I told him I thought we should see its interpretation.

That morning, Brother Tanner called on one of the native Saints, who was living with Halalea, one of the highest native chiefs. He was a special friend of, and a counselor to, the king, and the man who carried him my letter.

He told Brother Tanner that the king had appointed him to come with Prince Rehoreho, to meet us that night at our rooms, lay before us the king's great political trouble, and get our counsel.

It came plainly to me, then, that therein would be the fulfillment of my dream. About ten o'clock the same evening, they called on us. They said the king was greatly exercised in his mind over the troubled condition of his government, and that he was not decided as to what was best to do.

He said that he could not trust to the counsel of his ministers, nor to the advice of the ministers of other nations then at his court, for all had some point to gain. Dr. Judd, in his past troubles, had been his adviser, and, in times of need, had supplied him with money.

It pained him, then, to turn out of office one who had so long been his friend, and, upon this subject, he wished us to give him our wisest counsel.

While Halalea and the prince were delivering their message, I was continually praying in my heart that the Lord would give us wisdom to say such things as would do honor to His cause, for I felt very small for such an important occasion.

After they delivered the king's message in full, I arose and told them that we were not sent to meddle with governments, nor to teach political science, but to preach the gospel of Christ as now revealed. But, inasmuch as the king was our friend, and desired counsel of us, we would give him such as the Lord would put in our hearts.

I told them the Bible said, that "when the wicked rule the people mourn;" that if Dr. Judd was really a good man and a true friend to the king, as the king had believed him to be, he would not now allow the king to be in such great trouble on his account, but, like a true friend, would resign his office for the sake of peace between the king and his subjects.

The fact that he was disposed to hold on to his office, at the expense of peace to the king's realm, showed, conclusively, that he was influenced by other motives than the peace and welfare of the kingdom. "We feel," said I, "that the present great political trouble and mourning is owing to Dr. Judd not being a good man, but wickedly holding a grasp upon the government office against the wishes of the people, for which there is no necessity, as the king has many true subjects of more than equal ability, any one of whom he could appoint as Dr. Judd's successor."

When I ceased speaking, the king's messengers clasped my hands and said: "The things you have told us we had not thought of, and they are true. The king will be glad when we tell him what you have said, for we can see it plainly, now. We will assure you that, at ten o'clock to-morrow, you will hear the king's herald proclaiming through the streets of the city that Dr. Judd is removed from office."

They left us with the warmest feelings of gratitude and friendship.

The next morning at ten o'clock, the heralds were heard proclaiming the dismissal of Dr. Judd. The news created wonder and astonishment among the people, and they hurried together with public demonstrations of joy. They greatly marveled and queried by what agency, or through whose influence this long delayed, though most desirable object had been attained.

As I had dreamed, so I saw the people greatly rejoicing, and, although I was daily among them, they had no thought that a Latter-day Saint could have had any agency in so important a matter.

At night the city was brilliantly illuminated. There were few windows in it that did not have, at least, one candle to each pane of glass.

In a settlement with Dr. Judd, as I had dreamed, the government found that it had lost fifty thousand dollars.

Thus my prophecy and my dream were fulfilled together, and peace returned to the people. Joy came to our hearts that the

Lord, through the inspiration of His Holy Spirit, had made us, His humble Elders, the means of giving saving counsel to princes.

*Fragments of Experience,* 75–81.

# "The Spot Where the Prophet Moroni Stood"

⌒⌒⌒

## AUTHOR UNKNOWN

In an early day when President Young and party were making the location of a settlement [in Manti, Utah], President Heber C. Kimball prophesied that the day would come when a temple would be built on this hill. Some disbelieved and doubted the possibility of even making a settlement here. Brother Kimball said, "Well, it will be so, and more than that, the rock will be quarried from that hill to build it with, and some of the stone from that quarry will be taken to help complete the Salt Lake Temple." On July 28, 1878, two large stones, weighing respectively 5,600 and 5,020 pounds, were taken from the Manti stone quarry, hauled by team to York, the U. C. R. R. terminus then, and shipped to Salt Lake City to be used for the tablets in the east and west ends of the Salt Lake City Temple.

At a conference held in Ephraim, Sanpete County, June 25th, 1875, nearly all the speakers expressed their feelings to have a temple built in Sanpete County, and gave their views as to what point and where to build it. . . . President Brigham Young said: "The Temple should be built on Manti stone quarry." Early on the morning of April 25th, 1877, President Brigham Young asked Brother Warren S. Snow to go with him to the Temple hill. Brother Snow says: "We two were alone: President Young took me to the spot where the Temple was to stand; we went to the southeast corner, and President Young said: 'Here is the spot where the prophet Moroni stood and dedicated this piece of land for a Temple site, and that is the reason why the location is made here, and we can't move it from this spot.'"

In Orson F. Whitney, *Life of Heber C. Kimball,* 435–36.

# "Don't Let That Woman Come into the Assembly"

## MATTHIAS F. COWLEY

On one of the three days during which the Dedicatory Services of the Logan Temple were held, President John Taylor and [Stake] President Charles O. Card stood at the top of the stairs leading to the assembly room and as the people were surging up the steps to get to the assembly room, President Taylor sighted a woman in the crowd whom he did not know but indicated her to President Card and said: "Don't let that woman come into the assembly; she is not worthy." Brother Card was greatly surprised and said: "Why not?" President Taylor said: "I know not but the Spirit of God said, 'She is not worthy.'" And so Brother Card went down the steps and met the woman and told her she would have to go back. Brother Card said to President Taylor: "She couldn't pass the door keeper without a recommend." President Taylor replied, "That matters not; she is not worthy." She did not raise much opposition when confronted by Brother Card when she showed her ticket of admission.

Brother Card turned her back and later on went to see her at her home and he asked her how she had gotten her recommend to go to the Temple, and she said there was a man in the ward who was not worthy of a recommend, but the Bishop gave him one, thinking it would make him feel glad to attend the dedicatory services, and also help him renew his religious duties. This woman happened to meet the man on the street and he asked her how she would like to go to the dedication of the Temple. She said she would like to but could not get a recommend. He said: "I have a recommend and will give it to you for one dollar." And so she got her recommend by paying this amount.

The thing in this matter was that the spirit of revelation was manifested in President Taylor who did not know personally the woman and had never seen her before nor ever afterwards. It was an instance in which was manifested the promise of Joseph Smith the Prophet to Elder Taylor in Nauvoo when the Prophet said to him: "Elder Taylor, you have received the Holy Spirit and if you are faithful in heeding its promptings the day will come when it will be within you a fountain of continuous revelation from God."

I was at the dedication of the Logan Temple but did not hear this but it was told to me afterwards. The following statement was uttered later by President Taylor to Brother Card and others: "Brethren, you may deceive the Bishop and you may deceive the Presidents of the Stake, and you may deceive the General authorities of the Church, but you cannot deceive the Lord Jesus Christ nor the Holy Ghost. You know yourselves better than anybody else and if there is anything wrong in you, now is the time to repent and make yourselves square with the Lord; and if you do not repent, the time will come when you will be humbled, and the higher up you get the greater will be your fall."

Matthias F. Cowley, in N. B. Lundwall, *Temples of the Most High*, 100–101.

# INSTRUCTIONS IN A DREAM

## FRANK ESSHOM

In a dream, or vision, there was revealed to [Jesse Knight] that Utah was for the Mormons; that the doctrine of the Church of Jesus Christ of Latter-day Saints was true; that Joseph Smith was a prophet of God; also, that if he went to a certain place (indelibly imprinted on his mind), that he would find a great vein of rich mineral, a mine. He followed the instructions given him in his dream, which took him to the now well-known Eureka mining district. There, away up on the mountain, he found the spot he had seen in his dream, and he uncovered the vein which led to a vast mineral body, which was opened up, only by much hard labor and many vicissitudes. Many times, for the lack of provisions, he would have to stop his work, but he never lost faith in his dream, and would return and continue his labor. At last the mine yielded the long sought precious mineral that made him a large fortune, which has multiplied and been added to.

Before his dream came true, and while he was laboring (as only one can who has faith) to take from "Mother Earth" her treasure, he met Wilford Woodruff, then president of the Church of Jesus Christ of Latter-day Saints, who prophesied that "he [Jesse Knight] would save the Church's credit." Not long afterward, the mine began to yield. The Church had outstanding notes upon which the interest was nearly due, the country was in a panic and money almost impossible to get. The first car of ore came from the mine and gave much greater value than was expected. When the miners and debts incidental to the production of ore had been paid, there was ten thousand dollars remaining, which amount Mr. Knight gave to President Woodruff, who paid the interest on the Church's notes, and its credit was saved.

From thence on, he knew the truth of dreams, visions and prophecies, that Joseph Smith was a prophet of God and that the Church of Jesus Christ of Latter-day Saints was the restoration of God's Church on the earth.

---

Frank Esshom, *Pioneers and Prominent Men of Utah,* 8.

# "THE EYES OF THE HEAVENLY HOSTS"

## WILFORD WOODRUFF

I believe the eyes of the heavenly hosts are over this people; I believe they are watching the elders of Israel, the prophets and apostles and men who are called to bear off this kingdom. I believe they watch over us all with great interest.

I will here make a remark concerning my own feelings. After the death of Joseph Smith I saw and conversed with him many times in my dreams in the night season. On one occasion he and his brother Hyrum met me when on the sea going on a mission to England. I had Dan Jones with me. He received his mission from Joseph Smith before his death; and the prophet talked freely to me about the mission I was then going to perform. And he also talked to me with regard to the mission of the Twelve Apostles in the flesh, and he laid before me the work they had to perform; and he also spoke of the reward they would receive after death. And there were many other things he laid before me in his interview on that occasion. And when I awoke many of the things he had told me were taken from me, I could not comprehend them.

I have had many interviews with Brother Joseph until the last 15 or 20 years of my life; I have not seen him for that length of time. But during my travels in the southern country last winter I had many interviews with President Young, and with Heber C. Kimball, and Geo. A. Smith, and Jedediah M. Grant, and many others who are dead. They attended our conference, they attended our meetings.

And on one occasion, I saw Brother Brigham and Brother Heber ride in a carriage ahead of the carriage in which I rode when I was on my way to attend conference; and they were dressed in the most priestly robes. When we arrived at our destination I asked Prest. Young if he would preach to us. He said, "No, I have finished my testimony in the flesh. I shall not talk to this people any more. But (said he) I have come to see you; I have come to watch over you, and to see what the people are doing. Then (said he) I want you to teach the people—and I want you to follow this counsel yourself—that they must labor and so live as to obtain the Holy Spirit, for without this you can not build up the kingdom; without the spirit of God you are in danger of walking in the dark, and in danger of failing to accomplish your calling as apostles and as elders in the church and kingdom of God. And, said he, Brother Joseph taught me this principle."

*Journal of Discourses,* 21:318–19.

# "GO TO LONDON TONIGHT"

## GEORGE H. BUDD

My father, George Budd, . . . came to America with the Maycock family, in 1859, being thirteen years of age. When a little over fourteen years of age he was given a job in a mail camp on the route to California. His special work was to care for mules used in hauling the mail, and one day while thus engaged a mail man drove into camp and said: "Boy, change the mules and drive to the next camp; I am too sick to go further, but the mail must go." My father replied, "I can't do that as I do not know the way and I do not know how to drive the mules." The mail man said: "Put these mules in the stable, put fresh mules on the wagon and get on the seat; I'll put the reins between your fingers and all you have to do is give the mules their head and they know where the next oat sack is. I'll stay here until you get back."

My father did as he was told to do by the mail man and was soon on the way, filled with excitement and wonder and not a little fear, due to the stories he had heard about highwaymen taking express and mail from the drivers, but he let the mules have their head and on he went out into the desert. Suddenly a man stepped onto the wagon, while it was moving, sat down beside my father, and said: "This is a beautiful day." My father replied, "Yes, it is a beautiful day," and wondered if this man would prove to be a highwayman. He looked at the man and said to himself, "No, he is too kind a man to be one of that sort." The man said, "Young man, you were born in a little village in the south end of Sussex County, England, and in that village there is a history of your family; some day you or some of your children after you will go there and get the history, and when you do, remember there is a work to do. Good day," and he was gone. He did not wait for the wagon to stop—just got off and disappeared.

As my father drove on he became curious and concerned. However, he did not feel alarmed, since the man proved to be quite different to what he had first suspected. He reached the other mail camp, but said nothing to the boy at that camp but changed mules, exchanged mail, and started back. As he proceeded he was thinking about what had taken place and much to his surprise the same man again stepped onto the wagon, sat down beside him and started to talk about that village in southern England and related the same story, telling him three times that he or some of his children would go there and get that genealogy. . . .

In September 1896, I was called on a mission from the Nineteenth Ward, Salt Lake Stake of Zion, and had to report to the old Historian's Office on a certain day to receive my appointment. Apostle George Teasdale and Pres. George Reynolds of the First Council of Seventy were present. Pres. Reynolds got up and turned to Robert Teasdale and said: "This young man is from the Nineteenth Ward and his bishop says you can send him to any mission you desire." Then Pres. Reynolds left. Apostle Teasdale, who had never met me before, looked at me so strangely that I became nervous and all I could think of was "islands" and in that day islands meant "cannibals" and that meant danger. He finally said: "What mission would you prefer?" I replied: "I have no choice," and he looked again and waited for my further reply, but I did not speak. Then he said, "Oh! every boy has some choice, what is yours?" I was still fearful of islands but said, "I feel that I would fill a better mission where you send me, than if I chose a place, for if things went wrong I might feel that I was in the wrong place." Brother Teasdale sat there for some time, and occasionally looked at me and smiled—then I would think "islands" again, with a lot of cannibals included in my thinking. He finally looked up from what seemed a deep study and said: "You go to England and get your father's genealogy. Does that suit you?" I thanked him and said, "Yes, very well," and he said, "Put him down for England."

Now let me say here that Apostle Teasdale did not know my father came from England, and had no way of knowing that my father's genealogy was over in England, so I always thought that he was most certainly inspired when he said, "Go to England and get your father's genealogy." . . .

I took my slip, which stated where I was to go, also giving some

instructions as to when to come back and what to do in the meantime. The call suited my mother and when my father came in from
some mining camp, where he was building a mill or had finished a
mill, he said the call was all right. He then . . . took this occasion to
tell me the above story and said it was the first time he had ever
mentioned it to a living soul. He said, "You'll get that genealogy
when you get over there." . . .

. . . One day [on my mission], after doing the housework,
while the other missionaries were out working, I had a strong
impression to go to London, and I could not drive away the words
that came into my mind—" Go to London tonight." When Pres.
Call arrived at the house I said, "I have an impression to go to
London tonight; may I go?" Pres. Call replied, "Why don't you wait
until there is an excursion, and save some money?" I said, "I don't
know, but that impression says 'Go to London tonight.'" "All
right," said Pres. Call, "go tonight." I went downtown to get some
things I thought I would need and one of the first things I saw was
"Cheap trip to London, tonight, six and sixpence." Just what I
needed, so I went to the station and bought my ticket and was
soon on the road to London.

I arrived early in the morning, at the St. Pancres Station,
London, and walked up to the old mission house, rapped at the
door, and who should open it—a friend of mine—William
Stoneman—from the Twenty-second Ward (later the Eighteenth
Ward). He was so surprised he could hardly speak but finally said:
"Boy, what are you doing over here?" I said, "I hardly know, do
you?" He said, "There is a cheap trip to Brighton today—two
shillings—come and go with me." I said, "Guess that's all right,
cheap trips seem to be what I'm looking for," and we went.

At the Brighton Station, Elder George Hilton, another man I
had known all my life, met us, and he said, "Boy alive, what are you
down here for?" I replied, "Don't know, cheap trip, maybe you

know why." He looked rather serious and said, "Yes, I think I do know why, and here it is. The other day I was tracting and found a cousin of yours and if you'll come along with me I'll introduce you to her." He knocked at the door and a lady came and he said, "This is your cousin, George, from America," and she invited us in, and requested me to stay with them while there, which I did.

One day my cousin said, "Let's go down the coast to Southwick and visit with my mother and then go over to Hyde and see the house where your father was born." . . . We went over to Hyde and walked along the path between the hedge, on either side, and came to the house that my father had described to me. We went in, looked around, and took a picture of the house, and took a piece of flintrock from the foundation. We were leaving the village when she remembered her cousin, William Budd, and said, "Let's go call on him." We knocked at his door and an old grey-haired man came. She said to him, "Cousin William, this is Cousin George's boy from America." I naturally expected him to say, "Come in, my boy, glad to see you," or to say, "Get out," as that was the way Englishmen treated me, either "come in" or "get out." But to my astonishment he did neither, and stood there looking and looking until I got nervous, and at last he said, "I have a history of our family for four hundred years." When I got my breath, I replied, "That is just what I am looking for." He said, "Come in; you can have it." . . .

Cousin William Budd was a warden of the Church of England and the minister of the church copied this information from the parish records and presented it to him. Cousin William said to the minister, "I don't know what I want of that information." The minister replied, "You may find a purpose or somebody else may have a reason to possess it." Cousin William gave me a nice room, fed me, and I stayed there and copied that record, covering four hundred years, and eleven generations. I had no understanding of genealogy at the time but I got what the man on the desert said was in that village. . . .

. . . I soon left that village and went back to my cousin in Brighton, where I wrote a letter to my father, telling him that I had the information just as he had told me I would get it.

As strange as it may seem, my father wrote me a letter, at the same time, telling me this story: He was up in City Creek Canyon, in company with Charles Evans, a son-in-law of Patriarch John Smith, prospecting, and at noon Evans was face down on the grass asleep, and my father was looking up into the sky through the trees and his uncle, William Budd, father of my cousin, William, appeared to him and said, "George, my son William is now giving to your son, George, the genealogy of our family, and when George gets home I want you to see that he does the work for me." Now my father was not visionary, he was not actively engaged in church work, but would fight for it anytime and anywhere, so nobody can say this was not real. Our letters crossed on the ocean; he received mine and I his, and this all goes to establish the fact that he did really see that man on the desert and that his uncle did really appear to him. . . .

. . . I have the record, just as I received it, and it is now transcribed on modern family sheets and on file in the Utah Genealogical Society Library. Every name that can be worked on, up to January 1st, 1946, has either been worked for or is now in the process of being worked for in the Salt Lake Temple.

---

George H. Budd, in N. B. Lundwall, comp., *Faith Like the Ancients,* 1:26–31.

# "I HAVE JUST BEEN TO AMERICA"

⌒⌣

ELAINE EARL RICHARDSON

In 1900, when my father (Orange Wight Earl) was twenty-three years old, he was called as a missionary to Tahiti. At the time he left his home in Bunkerville, Nevada, his father (Wilbur Bradley Earl) lay sick in bed with an asthmatic-type sickness. Orange feared that his father would die while he was away, but his uncle Joseph Ira Earl (who was also his bishop) gave him a blessing that he would see his father again before his father died.

One day in Tahiti Elder Earl felt deep sadness and concern about his father. His spirit was so heavy and sorrowful that he felt weary and unable to do any studying. In his depression, he lay down on his bed early in the evening. Later, when his missionary companion went in the bedroom to go to bed, he found Orange lying crosswise on the bed, so his companion could not lie down. The companion wanted to lift Orange's legs and pull him around in position lengthwise in the bed, but a force would not let him touch him. Shocked and amazed, the missionary went back to the kitchen, where he sat in a chair and pondered that peculiar and unexplainable happening.

After a time Elder Earl got up from the bed and walked into the kitchen. "I have just been to America," he said. "I visited my father in his bedroom in Bunkerville, Nevada, and talked to him there." Elder Earl explained that when his father saw him, he called to the rest of the family, "Here is Orange!" The family hurried into the room, but they couldn't see Orange. The father continued to speak happily to his son. His wife and children believed him to be having a hallucination due to his illness. After a time, Orange said, he saw his father die.

Surprised at Elder Earl's account, his companion told him, in turn, of how he had attempted to move him, but a force would not allow him to be touched.

Immediately Orange wrote a letter of sad consolation to his mother in America. Before the letter reached her, his mother wrote her own letter, telling Orange that his father had died and had talked about seeing Orange at his death. The letters passed each other in mid-ocean.

In a subsequent letter to his mother, Elder Earl wrote:

"Your letter bearing the death news of Father was no surprise to me, though it still continued and confirmed the heavy blow I received on the night of April 11th.

"Sister mentioned in her letter that father often called me and that one night I came and talked with him and that he called me and I answered him. He told you the truth when he said that I answered him, for I heard him call and I not only answered in word but I entered our big room, where I found father lying on the bed with his head to the west. . . .

"I do not remember saying but one word to Father and that word was 'Father.' I did not stay long with you, but before I left the room I watched father peacefully close his eyes in death. He looked as though he was closing his eyes in sweet slumber for the night.

"You see by this vision of the night that I knew and was caused to mourn father's death even before you. Yet you tell me that his final departure from this life did not take place until two nights later or on the 13th of April. But God in his mercy granted me the privilege in the vision of the night to answer the call of my father and to behold his face again in mortality and to see him pass the portals of death. . . .

"When the steamer arrived, my companion went for our mail. He did not get back until after dark. I met him some fifty yards from the house and my first words were, 'Have I got a letter edged in black?' to which he answered, 'No, all is well at home.'

We came into the house and with trembling hands I cut the seal while my eyes were so full of tears I could hardly see the letter. I drew forth the letter and these are the first words I read, 'Your dear Papa passed away on the 13th and was laid to rest on the 15th.'"

---

Elaine Earl Richardson, in Orange Wight Earl, unpublished history.

# "LYE WATER DASHED OVER MY FACE"

HAROLD B. LEE

Mother was making soap and had a large tub of lye preparation stored on a high shelf to keep it out of the reach of the younger children. She wanted to take it down, and since I was the only one home she enlisted my help. We climbed up on a chair and began to steady it down. When it was exactly above my head, our hold slipped and the tub and its burning lye water dashed over my face, head, and arms. As quickly as she could act, Mother seized me so I wouldn't run and kicked off the lid from a jar of beet pickles she had just made, and with the right hand cupped, dipped out the reddened, pickle vinegar from the beets over my burning face, neck, and arms to stop the eating of the lye and save me from being badly scarred. What could have been a tragedy was averted because of her inspired action. Often she was intuitively led by the Spirit.

Harold B. Lee, in L. Brent Goates, *Harold B. Lee: Prophet and Seer*, 39.

# "I Am Glad I Have Found You"

## MELVIN S. TAGG

In July of 1913, while on a tour of the northern wards, President Wood recorded an unusual experience. The group had held very fine meetings in four wards. At Frankburg the President received a message that there had been a death in his family. He was requested to return to Cardston. Instead of hurrying to catch the train home, he went into a room to pray. He said he felt impressed to go to the only telephone in Frankburg. He tried to phone Cardston but was not successful, for there was no Sunday rural telephone service.

Suddenly the phone rang, and answering it, President Wood heard a strange voice call out in the Samoan language, "How do you do, Brother Wood, I am glad I have found you." The speaker was a returned Samoan missionary whose father, a Mr. Swainston, had died. The family lived at Stettler, about 100 miles east of

Calgary, and they wanted President Wood to supervise the burial and funeral services. Then he realized the first message about a death in his family had been a mistaken effort to relay the message from Stettler. The unusual part of this experience is that the Stettler telephone operator had been trying for two days to locate President Wood. Suddenly she said she saw an unexplainable light descending from the ceiling to the hole on her switchboard for Frankburg. She plugged into it and made the contact with President Wood. Later the operator, who was not a member of the Church, said, "I'll never forget this occurrence, Mr. Wood!"

The President went to Stettler and made the necessary arrangements for the burial. The Methodist minister at Stettler had already heard of the unusual phone call and offered his chapel and choir for the funeral service. The service was well attended, and the family was especially grateful. Both President Wood's party and the family felt it was the "hand of the Lord" which helped to locate the northern wards' missionaries.

---

Melvin S. Tagg, *The Life of Edward James Wood, Church Patriot*, 83–84.

# "A PLACE OF REVELATION"

## JOHN A. WIDTSOE

Soon after my call to the apostleship, I was chosen a director of the Latter-day Saints Genealogical Society. . . .

My own genealogy required attention. After my mother and Aunt had filled their missions in Norway, they remained for the better part of a year to secure our genealogy. They brought home a list of about a hundred names of our dead relatives, and a book full of names of people who were probably related to us, but of their direct relationship we had no clue. This was disappointing. Temple work was done for the names of our family. Then the matter languished.

One Sunday morning when I awoke I had a distinct impulse to examine the book the sisters had brought with them, containing the list of blood relatives that they had collected. Obedient as I have always been to spiritual messages, I sought out the book, and studied it for five hours. I found that morning the key which has enabled me to secure thousands of desired names.

The temple is peculiarly a place of revelation. Many experiences have proved it. Perhaps the most impressive is this: For several years, under a Federal grant with my staff of workers we had gathered thousands of data in the field of soil moisture [Elder Widtsoe was a chemist by profession]; but I could not extract any general law running through them. I gave up at last. My wife and I went to the temple that day to forget the failure. In the third endowment room, out of the unseen, came the solution, which has long since gone into print.

It has been a joy to me to participate as often as possible in work for the dead. The sealing evenings when they, the long dead, have been sealed as husband and wife or children sealed to their parents have been unusually impressive.

John A. Widtsoe, *In a Sunlit Land,* 176–77.

# DISCOVERING PRICELESS FAMILY HISTORY RECORDS

## GEORGE ALBERT SMITH

Brother John A. Widtsoe had a remarkable experience . . . , when he was in Scandinavia and found a whole collection of genealogical records in a little store on a side street, which he felt prompted to visit without knowing why. The proprietors did not have any use for them, and he bought them very reasonably. They were Scandinavian genealogies that were priceless, but if he had not been praying about it, and if he had not been looking for them, and if he had not obeyed the promptings of the Spirit, he might not have found them. And these particular records could not have been duplicated nor otherwise obtained in any manner known to us.

The Lord has a way of accomplishing things that we are unable to do, and never asks us to do anything that he does not make the way possible. . . .

If you have something that the Lord asks or expects you to do and you don't know just how to proceed, do your best. Move in the direction that you ought to go; trust the Lord, give him a chance, and he will never fail you.

George Albert Smith, *Sharing the Gospel with Others,* 14–16.

# "ISN'T THIS BROTHER MCKAY?"

DAVID O. McKAY

On December 2, 1920, the late President Hugh J. Cannon and I were set apart for a special mission, to visit a number of the Latter-day Saint missions in distant parts of the world.

Among these was the Turkish Mission, of which Armenian Saints composed the principal part. It was then in a disorganized state, and the members of the Church who had not been killed during the Great World War or massacred by the Turks were so scattered that it was difficult even to know where they were situated.

December 4, we started on our mission.

In March, 1921, we learned that on a special fast day, contributions in the amount of several thousand dollars had been made for relief of the destitute in Europe and the suffering Armenians in Asia. We learned, too, that the First Presidency contemplated sending a special messenger to Syria to render personal aid to our Armenian Saints.

Our mission carried us to the Antipodes, and to a number of the South Sea Isles; so the year 1921 was nearing its close before we found ourselves sailing toward Port Said en route to Syria.

During the months intervening, we had received no word concerning conditions in Armenia. We did not know whether anyone had been sent with relief funds. We knew only that it was our duty to visit that mission and report to the First Presidency of the Church.

Inquiry by cable of the president of the European Mission brought us the information that Elder J. Wilford Booth [who spoke the Turkish language] was on his way to Aleppo. This was good news. The next thing was to locate him. We communicated with the United States Consul at Aleppo, and on November 3, 1921, at Jerusalem received the following telegram:

"Aleppo, November 2, 1921: Informed Booth en route Aleppo. Do not know whereabouts—Jackson."

My diary of that same date reads:

"We have no idea where he is, but shall leave Jerusalem for Haifa, en route to Aleppo, to-morrow morning. Have concluded to go by auto through Samaria, visiting Bible scenes."

At 3:30 p.m. of the same day, we ascended the Mount of Olives, and, choosing a secluded spot near where Jesus is supposed to have stood when he cried: "O Jerusalem, Jerusalem," . . . (Matt. 23:37), we knelt in humble supplication and thanksgiving to God. The substance of our prayer I need not give here, except that we prayed that we should be led by inspiration on our trip to the Armenian Mission.

Upon returning to the hotel, I felt strongly impressed that we should go by train and not by auto to Haifa. When I said as much to President Cannon, he replied, "If you feel that way, we had better take the train."

Our greatest desire as we neared this mission was to meet Elder Booth. Indeed, it seemed that our trip to Syria would be useless unless we should meet him. We were strangers. We knew no one. The branches of the Church in Syria were disorganized. True, we had some names and addresses; but we could not read them, since they were written in the Turkish language. Later, we learned that these addresses, even if we could have found them, were useless. The warning given us not to go to Aintab by a British government official as well as by the United States Consul at Cairo only tended to increase our realization of the need of meeting Brother Booth or some other person who could speak the Turkish language . . . and who knew where we might find our scattered people. We carried in our pockets a letter from President Heber J. Grant received at Jerusalem, in which he, too, expressed the hope that Brother Booth and we might meet.

Carrying out our impression not to go by auto through Samaria, we accordingly left Jerusalem by train at 6 a.m., November 4th. We knew that we should be compelled to remain one night at Haifa, before continuing our journey to Aleppo. Past experiences, one or two of which had been very annoying, had taught us the advisability of knowing the names of respectable hotels in each strange city we approached. This we usually obtained by inquiry at the town we were just leaving.

Shortly after leaving Jerusalem and before we approached a little town called Bitter, I said to President Cannon:

"Did you ask for the name of a hotel at Haifa?"

"No," he replied, "I didn't; did you?"

Now it was nothing unusual for me to forget a thing like that, but it was for Brother Cannon. Indeed, I do not recall another single important detail on the entire trip which he forgot or overlooked.

We both felt reassured and at our ease when he said:

"The Allenby Hotel runner is on this train: I will ask him when we get to Ludd." . . .

But, strange to say, at Ludd, we changed trains and were several miles away from there before we realized that neither of us had remembered to speak to the hotel man about a hotel at Haifa.

I have gone into detail about this seemingly insignificant matter because it has direct bearing upon what follows.

Arriving at Haifa, I said to Brother Cannon, "You take care of the luggage here, and I will try to make inquiry regarding a suitable place at which to stay."

I had some difficulty in doing so; but returned in five or ten minutes saying it seemed "Hobson's choice" between two hotels, so we decided to go to the one that had a "runner" waiting to take care of our luggage.

The delay caused by seeking information about hotels brought us to the station office door just at the same moment that another traveler reached it. He touched me on the shoulder saying, "Isn't this Brother McKay?"

Astonished beyond expression to be thus addressesd in so strange a town, I turned, and recognized Elder Wilford Booth, the one man above all others whom we were most desirous of meeting. We had met, too, at the most opportune time and place. Having known nothing of our whereabouts he had come from the western part of the world, hoping in his heart to meet us. Knowing from the cablegram only that he was en route to Syria, we had come from the eastern part of the world, traveling westward, praying that we might meet him; and there we had met at the very time and place best suited to our convenience and to the success of our mission to the Armenians. It could not have been better had we been planning it for weeks.

As we recounted to each other our experiences, we had

no doubt that our coming together was the result of divine interposition.

If Brother Cannon and I had taken an auto from Jerusalem to Haifa; or if we had remembered to secure the name of a hotel before we left the "Allenby"; or if we had thought to ask the hotel runner at Ludd; we should not have met Elder Booth at Haifa. It is true he would have been in town that same day, but he was intending to stop at the German "Hospice," where we should never have met him. He would have left by auto to Beirut; we, by train to Damascus.

Later developments showed that he would have been delayed at Beirut, while we should have been making fruitless search in Aleppo for the lost Saints.

Indeed, had it not been for our having met at Haifa, our trip to the Armenian Mission would have been, so far as human wisdom can tell, a total failure. As it was, among many duties and experiences, we organized the Armenian Mission, to take the place of the Turkish Mission.

This is only one incident of many which I might relate which have convinced me that if men will but seek the Lord in the right way, they will always find him. Truly, I can say with Benjamin Franklin, who evidently discovered the same truth:

"The longer I live the more convincing proof I see that God governs in the affairs of men."

---

David O. McKay, *Cherished Experiences*, 79–84.

BEST-LOVED STORIES OF THE LDS PEOPLE

# "HE HEARD THE VOICE OF HIS LOST SON"

Years ago an elder living in Canada was called on a mission to South America. When on the ocean the vessel was wrecked and the missionary was drowned, after being two days out of New York City. During this catastrophe, the elder and his companion became separated among the other passengers. The last seen of the elder was when his companion saw him clinging to some broken timbers. They waved at each other and said good-bye. The lifeboats searched in vain for the missing elder.

The parents of the elder who was drowned were officiators in the Cardston Temple. Only parents who have passed through similar experiences can know how these parents felt and especially when it is considered that but very few missionaries have lost their lives by being drowned as recorded in the history of the church. The wound was indeed deep in the hearts and affections of these fine parents and other members of the family. It was very difficult for them to be reconciled, but they carried on, however, as officiators in the temple, praying always that something would happen to alleviate their mental suffering.

One evening, several months after the accident, the father had finished his part in the temple and, very strange to say, he did not prepare to go home as had been his custom; but instead he went upstairs and sat down at a small stand in the celestial room, which is not far from one of the three sealing rooms. That evening I was officiating at the only one being used. The father wondered why he was sitting there alone, all members and officiators of the company having gone downstairs, and he started to leave the room, when to his great surprise he thought he heard the voice of his lost son, saying: "Father, you and mother have been greatly worried over my being shipwrecked but you wouldn't be grieved at all if you knew the missionary work I have been called to do in the spirit world where I am now laboring, which is more important than if I had gone to South America."

As the father seemed to awaken from the experience, he wondered if it was just his imagination about hearing from his son, and was about to leave the room when again the heavenly feeling came over him and again he thought he heard the voice of his son saying: "Father, you are in doubt as to my having actually delivered my message to you. To prove to you that you have heard from your missionary son, from the spirit world, Brother Wood will call you into the sealing room where he is officiating [and ask you] to bear your testimony, something he has never done before. He doesn't know you are here. This should be a testimony to you that you have heard from me, so that you and mother will no longer refuse to be reconciled at my passing."

The father wondered: "How will Brother Wood call me when he thinks I have long since left the temple?" He went downstairs and hesitated several times about going home, but after several attempts to leave the temple he went upstairs again, and on reaching the top of the stairs leading to the celestial room, was met by one of the brethren acting as a proxy, who said to him: "I am looking for you, Brother. Brother Wood wants you to come in the sealing room and speak to the few people there."

I shall always remember how I felt when the impression came to me to call for this certain brother. At first I thought to myself, "He has gone home. I have never asked anyone to speak in the sealing room, and no doubt this good man has gone home several hours ago." And yet the feeling was so strong, I asked the brother helping me to see if Brother——— was in the building; if so, please ask him to come here a few minutes and bear his testimony.

When the good brother appeared in the door of the sealing room, he seemed very pale but quite happy. He came inside and to our great astonishment told us with the finest spirit possible of his experience in receiving the message from his lost missionary son, and of how he wondered whether I would call him into the sealing room when I should know he had gone home. A very fine spirit was present, and how pleasing it was to all who knew him and his wife who were in the room when he said: "We will hereafter feel quite reconciled. It is a wonderful testimony to me and will be to his mother and all members of our family that the Lord certainly moves in a mysterious way to accomplish his purposes."

---

Edward James Wood, in N. B. Lundwall, comp., *Faith Like the Ancients,* 1:182–84.

# TRUTH

# WORDS OF THE LIVING PROPHETS

$\backsim$

## WILFORD WOODRUFF

I
... refer to a certain meeting I attended in the town of Kirtland in my early days. At that meeting ... a leading man in the Church got up and talked upon the subject, and said: "You have got the word of God before you here in the Bible, Book of Mormon, and Doctrine and Covenants; you have the written word of God, and you who give revelations should give revelations according to those books, as what is written in those books is the word of God. We should confine ourselves to them."

When he concluded, Brother Joseph turned to Brother Brigham Young and said, "Brother Brigham I want you to take the stand and tell us your views with regard to ... the written word of God."

Brother Brigham took the stand, and he took the Bible, and laid it down; he took the Book of Mormon, and laid it down; and he took the Book of Doctrine and Covenants, and laid it down before him, and he said: "There is the written word of God to us, concerning the work of God from the beginning of the world, almost, to our day. And now," said he, "when compared with the living oracles those books are nothing to me; those books do not convey the word of God direct to us now, as do the words of a Prophet or a man bearing the Holy Priesthood in our day and generation. I would rather have the living oracles than all the writing in the books."

That was the course he pursued. When he was through,

Brother Joseph said to the congregation: "Brother Brigham has
told you the word of the Lord, and he has told you the truth."

———

Conference Report, October 1897, 22–23.

# "IF HE SAYS IT IS TRUE, WILL
# YOU THEN BELIEVE HIM?"

⌒

## PHILO DIBBLE

One morning I was standing at my gate when two men
drove up in a two-horse wagon, and asked me to get in
and go home with them, about quarter of a mile distant.
On the way, one asked me if I had heard the news, and informed
me that four men had come to Kirtland with a golden Bible and
one of them had seen an angel. They laughed and ridiculed the
idea, but I did not feel inclined to make light of such a subject. I
made no reply, but thought that if angels had administered to the
children of men again I was glad of it; I was afraid, however, it was
not true. On my return home I told my wife what I had heard.

The next day I was intending to go fifty miles south to the
town of Suffield, Ohio, to pay some taxes, but my wife thinking
that one or two days would not make much difference about that,
proposed that we should hunt up those strange men in Kirtland.

The next morning I took my wife, another man and his wife,
and started for Kirtland. When we arrived there, the men we were

seeking had gone to the town of Mayfield, but were to return to Kirtland the next day. The following morning I hitched up my carriage and again drove to Kirtland, one of my neighbors accompanying us with his team and family. On arriving there, we were introduced to Oliver Cowdery, Ziba Peterson, Peter Whitmer, Jr., and Parley P. Pratt. I remained with them all day, and became convinced that they were sincere in their professions. I asked Oliver what repentance consisted of, and he replied, "Forsaking sin and yielding obedience to the gospel!"

That evening he preached at Brother Isaac Morley's, and bore his testimony to the administration of an angel at noonday. He then dwelt upon the subjects of repentance and baptism and the bestowal of the Holy Ghost, and promised that all who embraced these principles with honesty of heart should receive a testimony. He also requested all who wished to be baptized to make it manifest by arising. Five persons, among whom were William Cahoon and myself, arose. I then made preparations for baptism by borrowing a suit of clothes. My wife thought I was too hasty, and said if I would wait awhile perhaps she would go along with me. She was a Baptist by persuasion. I paid no heed to her, but went forthwith and was baptized by Parley P. Pratt. This was on the 16th of October, 1830. When I came out of the water, I knew that I had been born of water and of the spirit, for my mind was illuminated with the Holy Ghost.

I spent that evening at Dr. F. G. Williams'. While in bed that night I felt what appeared to be a hand upon my left shoulder and a sensation like fibers of fire immediately enveloped my body. It passed from my right shoulder across my breast to my left shoulder, it then struck me on my collar bone and went to the pit of my stomach, after which it left me. I was enveloped in a heavenly influence, and could not sleep for joy.

The next morning I started home a happy man. All my

neighbors were anxious to know the result of my visit to Kirtland, and I was visited by two Campbellite preachers, named respectively Scott and Williams, one of whom remarked, "Mr. Dibble, I understand you have joined the 'Mormons.' What reason have you to believe they have the truth?"

I told them, "The scriptures point to such a work, which should come forth."

He then asked me where I found it. I took the Bible and opened it where it speaks of truth springing out of the earth, and righteousness looking down from above. He read it and handed it to the other preacher. They made no comments.

I bore my testimony to them of what I had received, and Mr. Scott said, "I don't doubt, Mr. Dibble, that you have received all you say, because you are honest, but they are impostors."

I then asked Mr. Scott if he believed the Lord would bless the labors of a false prophet, to which they did not stop to reply but left, and told the people it was no use talking to me.

One of my neighbors came to me and said, "We have sent a man down to York State to find out the truth of this work, and he is a man who will not lie. If he returns and says it is false, will you believe him?"

I told him I would believe the truth, and asked him if that man (whose name was Edward Partridge) should come back and say it was false if he would believe him.

He replied, "Yes; for he is a man who would not lie for his right arm!"

I then added, "If he says it is true, will you then believe him?" to which he reluctantly replied that he would.

Shortly after this, however, when Brother Partridge wrote back and said that he had been baptized, and was then preaching the gospel, this man shunned me, and for a long time afterwards gave me no chance to talk with him. But when we met, I asked him what he thought of Brother Partridge, and he replied that he was honest, but had been deceived.

---

*Early Scenes in Church History,* 75–77.

# "I Consulted the Stars"

JAMES E. TALMAGE

Y ears ago, while a romping, careless school boy in far-off England, I was fortunate or unfortunate as you may choose to take it, to make acquaintance with an aged sage who placed implicit trust in the indications of the stars. . . . He supposed that he had found in me a promising student of astrological lore; so he devoted himself with great energy to instruct me. . . .

. . . Before I was ten years old, I had learned to cast the horoscope and to compute the benign and the malignant spirits of any person, the exact time of whose birth I could learn. My faith in these indications was so strong that I never could trust a school friend, boy or girl, who had been born under the ascendancy of Mercury or Saturn, and I think I would not have doubted a child of Mars, Jupiter, or the Sun though such a one had sought my life. . . . On rare occasions, when paternal permission was obtained to go a 'fishing, I was scrupulously careful to compute the position of the planets, and learn the hour at which the power of the Moon was weak; for the fishes being under the dominion of the queen of night would be protected during her reign.

But my faith in astrology was soon to undergo a change. Among my school-mates was a big blustering fellow, who ruled as the autocrat of the playground, maintaining his sway by force of animal might. We all acknowledged his supremacy and paid him tribute of our property, a five-fold tithe of our sweetmeats, marbles, and pins. And further, he compelled us to work his sums for him, to draw his maps, and write his essays, and if any such effort received less than high commendations at the class, the author of the work was sure to feel the might of offended majesty at the next recess. If any boy appeared to doubt his authority, or failed to pay him servile homage, the tyrant was apt to apply the effectual remedy of a severe drubbing which rarely failed to bring the rebel to a sense of his duty. . . .

But there came a day when I felt within me those swelling impulses that are known only to a would-be savior or deliverer of his kind. I consulted the stars; and determined to break the fetters that bound us and to set myself and my school-fellows free. My faith in the success of the undertaking was so unbounded that I had no thought of dividing the honors of conquest with anyone; I would fight the battle alone. Being on speaking terms with the autocrat's sister, I managed to find from her the date of Ben's birthday; but this was not enough, I must know also the *hour* at which this remarkable piece of humanity had made a first appearance on the earth. The girl, in entire ignorance of the purpose for which I intended to use the information, questioned her mother, and brought me word that it was within half an hour of midnight on a Friday. With this information I hurried home, and at once proceeded to compute his nativities, with as much care as if he had been a prince of the realm. Ah! I might have known it: the horoscope gave his character in detail: he was a son of Saturn, born when the planet was in ill-conjunction: what wonder then that he was untrustworthy, mean, and cruel? Then I cast the horoscope of the future, and found that at a convenient hour, five o'clock in the afternoon on Wednesday, the next day but one, his star would be declining, and mine would be in the ascendancy; this augured ill luck to him at that time and good fortune to me, in any undertaking. Surely the day of our deliverance was near at hand: the stars had promised to help me in my dangerous enterprise, and victory was assured. Brute force should be subdued by the power of superior knowledge.

So on the morning of the appointed day I confronted his saturnine majesty on the play ground, and challenged him to meet me that evening at five o'clock, boldly expressing my determination to show him who would be master from that time forth. His surprise made him dumb for an instant, then he indulged in a loud laugh and cuffed my ears; but this I bore with no attempt at retaliation, for the time of revenge had not yet come; besides, I consoled myself with the reflection that it is the lot of all heroes in the cause of liberty to suffer insult at the hands of tyranny. During the day I received many a hearty wish for success; but feeble faith in my cause was plainly portrayed in every face.

At five o'clock we were at the appointed place; a score of boys were there to see fair play done. My antagonist was nearly a foot taller, and fully a stone heavier than I, but these were trifles below notice; had I not the happy assurances of the stars that I should win? I made a speech to the burly fellow, setting forth a few of his many acts of oppression and cruelty, and closed with a studied flourish, declaring that henceforth we would be free. This was received with a laugh of derision by my opponent; and the hostilities began. They did not last long. The conflict though fierce was decidedly brief. I discovered myself by degrees, lying on the ground, cheek cut, eyes bruised, nose smashed, a couple of teeth loosened and a quantity of hair gone. The bully retired without a scratch.

As I slowly made my way homeward, I was in an unusually thoughtful state. I began for the first time in my life to have serious doubts as to the infallibility of astrological indications, after all. Amongst the family my appearance created considerable consternation; then my worthy sire reminded me of his oft repeated injunctions against fighting; and to impress the lesson firmly upon my mind he proceeded to illustrate his lecture by sundry strokes with the buckle end of a stout strap. This was convincing; my doubts vanished, and with them all my confidence in the horoscope. I knew that astrology was a fraud.

*Contributor,* November 1892, 33–35.

# "THEY PUT THEIR ARMS AROUND HIM AND WEPT"

WALLACE F. TORONTO

A short time after almost two million German troops had marched across the borders of Czecho-Slovakia [in 1939]—during that time of tension and terror, which inevitably resulted—a young German officer, a fine, straight, clean-looking fellow, walked through the door of our meeting hall in Prague [where a church meeting was being held]. We thought: Certainly, this is the end for us. The secret police have probably sent some one here to close the mission. Coming up he said: "My name is Brother R. (for obvious reasons it is felt unwise to give his name). I am an officer in the German Army. As soon as I had completed my official duties here in Prague, the first thing I set out to do was to find this branch of the Church in Czecho-Slovakia. With your permission, I would like to say just a word to this congregation." I replied: "Certainly, Brother R., we shall be happy to hear from you."

He stood up, and in a language which most of the people of Czecho-Slovakia detested, German, he had this to say to the members of the Church and to the friends who were present:

"Brothers and sisters, I come here not on an appointment of my own choosing. I come here as a servant of my government. I know we have brought you considerable distress and dismay. We have caused already much suffering. Nevertheless, you and I have something in common, something which oversteps the boundaries of race, language, and color. You and I have the gospel of Jesus Christ. Despite the fact that I speak German and you Czech, yet because of the gospel we still speak in common terms. The time is coming when we shall know this better than ever before."

I wish I had time to tell you all he said. Tears streamed down the faces of those Czecho-Slovakian people. As he walked down the aisle they stood up and put their arms around him and wept upon his shoulder. Every available Sunday—he believed in keeping the Sabbath—he was at the branch hall, doing his best to make the gospel of Jesus Christ a living thing among a subjugated people.

That is what the gospel of Jesus Christ does for a man. When it touches him it changes him, and he knows . . . that all mankind come of common blood, and that we are brothers and sisters in

the gospel of Jesus Christ, all having but one Father. These are . . .
truths which cannot be equaled any place in the world, outside
the plan of the gospel.

---

Conference Report, April 1940, 52.

# VALIANCE

# "I Told Them Joseph
## Was a Prophet"

BRIGHAM YOUNG

O n a certain occasion [in Kirtland, Ohio, in 1836] several
of the Twelve, the witnesses to the Book of Mormon,
and others of the Authorities of the Church, held a
council in the upper room of the [Kirtland] Temple. The question before them was to ascertain how the Prophet Joseph could
be deposed, and David Whitmer appointed President of the
Church. Father John Smith, Brother Heber C. Kimball and others
were present, who were opposed to such measures. I rose up, and
in a plain and forcible manner told them that Joseph was a
Prophet, and I knew it, and that they might rail and slander him as
much as they pleased, they could not destroy the appointment of
the Prophet of God, they could only destroy their own authority,
cut the thread that bound them to the Prophet and to God and
sink themselves to hell.

Many were highly enraged at my decided opposition to their
measures, and Jacob Bump (an old pugilist) was so exasperated
that he could not be still. Some of the brethren near him put their
hands on him, and requested him to be quiet; but he writhed and
twisted his arms and body saying, "How can I keep my hands off
that man?" I told him if he thought it would give him any relief he
might lay them on.

This meeting was broken up without the apostates being able
to unite on any decided measures of opposition. This was a crisis
when earth and hell seemed leagued to overthrow the Prophet

519

and Church of God. The knees of many of the strongest men in the Church faltered.

During this siege of darkness I stood close by Joseph, and, with all the wisdom and power God bestowed upon me, put forth my utmost energies to sustain the servant of God and unite the quorums of the Church.

---

Brigham Young, *Manuscript History of Brigham Young, 1801–1844*, 15–17.

# "I WANT YOU TO WORK FOR ME"

AUTHOR UNKNOWN

C harles Lambert had married during the first year of his residence in Nauvoo and undertaken the support of the brothers and a sister of his wife, who had recently been orphaned and were helpless. He felt keenly his responsibility, and wished for money as he never had done before.

While feeling thus he was passing along the street in Nauvoo one day when he met a well-dressed, genteel stranger who inquired if his name was Charles Lambert. On being told that it was, he said his name was Higgins, and that his home was in Missouri. With an ingratiating smile he said, "I have heard of your skill as a workman, and want you to go to Missouri and work for me. You are not appreciated or properly paid here. If you will quit the temple and go and work for me, you can name your own price and you will be sure of your pay. You see I have plenty of money with which to pay you." Suiting the action to the word, he thrust his hand into his pocket, and drew it out full of $10.00 and $20.00 gold pieces, which he displayed in a tempting manner, and urged him to accept his offer, and not to submit any longer to the unfair treatment accorded him at the temple.

With a gesture of impatience called forth by the intimation of unfairness, Father Lambert thanked the stranger for his offer, but said he couldn't think of accepting it. He said he had no complaint to make of his treatment at the temple, and the price others would pay for work they wished done would not influence him in the matter, as he intended to continue on at the temple from principle.

Bidding the stranger "Good-day," he turned to continue his walk along the street, but almost immediately the query arose in his mind as to how the stranger knew his name, and where he got his information from about his skill as a mechanic, and turned to take a final look at the stranger, when lo! he was nowhere to be seen. He had disappeared as completely as if the ground had opened and swallowed him, and yet he had not had time by any ordinary means of locomotion to get out of sight.

His opinion then was, and remained so up to the day of his death, that he had been talking with no other than Satan, the prince of tempters, and though he had not yielded to his tempting offer, he was vexed with himself for listening to him at all, and especially to his insinuations about the temple management.

---

George C. Lambert, comp., *Gems of Reminiscence,* 174–75.

# "I WAS NOT THE ONE TO GO"

SAMUEL W. RICHARDS

I n the winter of 1843–44, about six months prior to the death of the Prophet Joseph Smith, a messenger was sent to me from Nauvoo to ask me if I would be one of a company of pioneers to explore the Rocky Mountains and to find a place for the Church to go to. That request came from the Prophet Joseph Smith. At the time I thought it a little strange that I should be called upon for a mission of this kind, as I was but a young man, in my teens; but my acquaintance up to that time with the Prophet Joseph was such that I could not say no. I replied, Yes; I will do anything that the Prophet Joseph wants me to do, that is in my power to do. Consequently I gave my name in to be one of a company of twenty-four young men, who were selected to travel and explore the Rocky Mountains and find a place for the Church to go to, because the persecution was getting so strong then in Nauvoo that the Prophet Joseph foresaw that the Church would have to leave, retire from the civilized world, and go into the mountains. . . .

It was the purpose of the Prophet Joseph to come here [to the Salt Lake Valley] and locate with his people. He organized this company and held weekly meetings with them for several weeks in Nauvoo. . . . I attended four meetings of this company, and at one of them, which was in charge of Hyrum Smith, and three or four of the Twelve were also present, it was said that Joseph the Prophet had remarked that he wanted young men for that mission who could go up on the mountains and talk with God face to face, as Moses did upon Mount Sinai. When I heard that statement, I felt in my soul that I was not the one to go; and just before the meeting closed I got up out of my seat for the purpose of going to Brother Hyrum Smith and telling him I was not the one to go, for I did not feel that I could meet the conditions, but as I got up, there was a voice came to me, and I heard it distinctly as from one standing by my side, saying, "Stop; rest awhile."

I took my seat again, and instead of telling the Prophet Hyrum that I did not feel I could go, I went home, and before retiring I knelt by my bedside and prayed to my Heavenly Father. If I ever prayed in earnest, it was then, that I might know before morning whether I was a suitable one to go on that expedition, under the terms specified. The idea of going into the mountains and talking with God face to face, as Moses did upon Mount Sinai, was more than I, as a boy, could think of encountering.

No one perhaps need wonder that I should shrink from such a consideration. I retired to my bed and remained there about four hours, and during that four hours I got the answer to my prayer, and when I awoke I was prepared to go upon that journey and do just as the Prophet wanted me to do. During that four hours I saw all that I expect to see if I should live a thousand years. Someone came to me and told me where to go, and I performed that jour-ney that night while I lay upon my bed. I came to this valley first. I don't know how I got here, but I went down through these valleys and into southern California. It had been stated that possibly we might have to go that far. . . . I passed them all, and went on down into southern California. Then I was prompted to go farther, and I went into the northern part of Mexico. . . . Then I traversed this continent from end to end. I saw the Garden of Eden as it was in the beginning and as it will be restored again. It was a land filled with verdure and vegetation, and with all manner of fruits, on which man was living. I saw it filled with cities, towns and villages, and people happy, living under the administration of divine providence. It was a Garden of Eden in very deed.

Now, all this I saw while I was sleeping, and it was so impressed upon me that it can never be forgotten. I saw that this was the result of the Latter-day Saints coming to these valleys of the mountains and following the direction that the Prophet Joseph indicated.

Conference Report, October 1905, 87–89.

# "WITH GOD ALL THINGS ARE POSSIBLE"

HELEN M. WHITNEY

On the 3rd of February, 1846, I was married to H. K. Whitney, eldest son of N. K. Whitney, by Brigham Young. We were the last couple sealed in the temple at Nauvoo. We were among the exiles who crossed the river on the 16th of the same month, intending to go to the Rocky Mountains that year. But when the government demanded the strength of our companies to fight for them, we had to seek a place to quarter for the winter. I was sick most of the time while there. Some of the journey we had to walk, and our food being poor and scant, the infant and the aged, all classes, were swept off by death—the latter by scurvy and sheer exhaustion. The next year my husband was one of those chosen to go as a pioneer, and he had to go though the day of trial was upon me.

Our first born, a lovely baby girl, was buried there—we could not both live; but during those dark hours I had friends and the Lord was there. We had but few men, mostly aged and disabled, but to see the union of the sisters, the fasting and the prayers for the preservation of our battalion and the pioneers, and for the destroyer to be stayed, the great and marvelous manifestation, even to the power of the resurrection, experienced there, proved that they were encircled by a mighty power, and that "the prayers of the righteous availeth much." . . .

The next spring all were preparing to move, and as I was helping to put on my wagon cover I came near fainting and was prostrated on my bed from that time. I had a baby boy, born on the 17th of August, but he was buried on the 22nd—my twentieth birthday. This was the worst part of our journey, the roads being rough and rocky. I mourned incessantly, and that, with my intense bodily sufferings, soon brought me to death's door, but it was shorn of its sting. I was cold, but oh, how peaceful, as I lay there painless and my breath passing so gently away. I felt as though I was wafting on the air and happy in the thought of meeting so soon with my babes where no more pain or sorrow could come. I had talked with my husband and father (Heber C. Kimball), who were weeping as I took a parting kiss from all but my poor mother, who was the last one called, and who had sunk upon her knees before me. This distressed me, but I bade her not mourn for she would not be long behind me.

My words struck father like a sudden thunderbolt, and he spoke with a mighty voice and said: "Vilate, Helen is not dying," but my breath, which by this time had nearly gone, stopped that very instant, and I felt his faith and knew that he was holding me; and I begged him to let me go as I thought it very cruel to keep me, and believed it impossible for me to live and ever recover. . . . No one but God and the angels to whom I owe my life and all I have could know the tenth part of what I suffered. I never told anybody and never could. A keener taste of misery and woe, no mortal, I think, could endure.

For three months I lay, a portion of the time like one dead they told me; but that did not last long. I was alive to my spiritual condition and dead to the world. I tasted of the punishment which is prepared for those who reject any of the principles of the gospel. Then I learned . . . the difference between the power of God's priesthood, and that of Satan's, and the necessity of obedience to those who hold the priesthood, and the danger of rebelling against or speaking lightly of the Lord's anointed.

I had, in hours of temptation, when seeing the trials of my mother, felt to rebel. . . . I had loved my baby more than my God, and mourned for it unreasonably. All my sins and shortcomings were magnified before my eyes till I believed I had sinned beyond redemption. Some may call it the fruits of a diseased brain. There is nothing without a cause; be that as it may, it was a keen reality to me. During that season I lost my speech, forgot the names of everybody and everything, and was living in another sphere, learning lessons that would serve me in future times to keep me in the narrow way. I was left a poor wreck of what I had been, but the Devil, with all his cunning, little thought that he was fitting and preparing my heart to fulfill its destiny. My father said that Satan desired to clip my glory, and was quite willing I should die happy; but when he was thwarted he tried in every possible way to destroy my tabernacle.

. . . The Lord gave father faith enough to hold me until I was capable of exercising it for myself. I was so weak that I was often discouraged in trying to pray, as the evil spirits caused me to feel that it was no use; but the night after the first Christmas in this valley, I had my last struggle and resolved that they should buffet me no longer. [After much fasting and prayer], every day I gained till I had won the victory and I was just as sensible of the presence of holy spirits around my bedside as I had been of the evil ones.

It would take up too much room to relate my experience with the spirits, but New Year's eve, after spending one of the happiest days of my life, I was moved upon to talk to my mother. I knew her heart was weighed down in sorrow and I was full of the Holy Ghost. I talked as I never did before; I was too weak to talk with such a voice (of my own strength), besides I never before spoke with such eloquence, and she knew that it was not myself. She was so affected that she sobbed till I ceased. I assured her that father loved her, but he had a work to do; she must rise above her feelings and seek for the Holy Comforter. . . . Much more I said, and when I ceased, she wiped her eyes and told me to rest. I had not felt tired till she said this, but commenced then to feel myself sinking away. I silently prayed to be renewed, when my strength returned that instant.

New Year's day father had set apart to fast and pray, and they prepared a feast at evening. I had prayed that I might gain a sure testimony that day that I was acceptable to God, and my father, when he arose to speak, was so filled with His power that he looked almost transfigured! He turned to me and spoke of my sufferings and the blessings I should receive because of the same. He prophesied of the great work that I should do, that I should live long and raise honorable sons and daughters that would rise up and call me blessed, and should be a comfort to my mother in her declining years, and many more things which I have fulfilled. Many who knew me then have looked at me and seen me working with my children around me, with perfect amazement and as one who had been dead and resurrected.

I lost three babes before I kept any (two boys and a girl). My first to live was Vilate, who grew to womanhood and was then taken. Orson F. was my next, who has been appointed bishop of the Eighteenth Ward. [Subsequently, Orson F. Whitney was ordained an Apostle.] I had four more daughters, then a son, my last a little girl who died at five years of age; having had eleven children in all. My parents have left me and my heart has been wrung to the utmost, yet I have said: Thy will O God, be done.

Persons have sometimes wondered at my calmness and endurance, but I think they would not wonder if they had passed through the same experience. I have encouraged and sustained my husband. . . . At various times I have been healed. . . . I am still spared to testify to the truth and godliness of this work; and though my happiness once consisted in laboring for those I love, the Lord has seen fit to deprive me of bodily strength and taught me to "cast my bread upon the waters" and after many days my longing spirit was cheered with the knowledge that he had a work for me to do, and with him I know that all things are possible.

---

Helen M. Whitney, in Augusta Joyce Crocheron, *Representative Women of Deseret*, 110–14.

# "Holiness to the Lord"

## Theodore M. Burton

While [John R. Moyle] was working on the Salt Lake Temple, he lived in Alpine, Utah. . . . It was his custom to work on his farm Friday night and Saturday after he finished his work in Salt Lake. He would walk out to Alpine from Salt Lake after he had finished his shift of work as a mason on the temple and would take care of his farm chores and his irrigating, go to his meetings on Sunday, and then walk back to Salt Lake City to work on the temple Monday morning. . . .

. . . On one of these occasions when he had returned home for the weekend, he was taking care of milking his cow when . . . she kicked him and broke his leg. It was a nasty fracture of a compound nature and the bone stuck through the flesh. . . . They decided the only thing they could do under the circumstances was to cut off his leg.

. . . They gave him . . . a leaden bullet to bite his teeth on, tied him to a door [that had been pulled down off its hinges], and then with a bucksaw sawed off his leg, bound the flesh over the stump, and allowed it to heal. It is a wonder he didn't die of infection, but the Lord blessed him and the wound healed over. While it was healing, he got himself a piece of wood and carved out a peg leg. He fastened some leather to the top of the wood, padded it, and fitted it to his leg. As soon as the wound had healed sufficiently, he walked around the farm on that stump until he was able to stand the pain and had formed a callous over the stump.

When it had healed, he walked into Salt Lake as was his custom, to take up his work, for he had been called as a work missionary on the temple. And there, . . . he climbed up the scaffolding on the east side of the temple and carved "Holiness to the Lord."

Theodore M. Burton, in "Biographies and Reminiscences," unpublished manuscript, 201–3.

# "I KNEW MY FATHER WOULD GO"

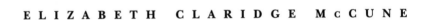

ELIZABETH CLARIDGE McCUNE

No place on earth seemed so precious to me at fifteen years of age as dear old Nephi. How eagerly we looked forward to the periodical visits of President Brigham Young and his company! Everything was done that could be thought of for their comfort and entertainment. And with all it was a labor of love. One of these visits I shall never forget.

We went out with our Sabbath Schools and all the other organizations, with bands of music and flags and banners and flowers, to meet and greet our beloved leader and his company. On this occasion the people were lined up on each side of the street waiting for the carriages to pass. Among them were twenty-five young ladies dressed in white, who had strewn evergreens and wild flowers along the path. Brother Brigham, Brothers [Heber C.] Kimball and [Daniel H.] Wells with the entire company, got out of their carriages and walked over the flowery road. When Brother Kimball passed me he said to the group of girls around me, "You five girls right here will live to be mothers in Israel."

530

The company having been taken to our home, the dinner was served. How we girls flew around to make everything nice. . . . As soon as they were seated at dinner, we slipped upstairs and tried on all the ladies' hats. That was a real treat. I venture to say that could the ladies have seen us next Sunday they would have been struck with the similarity of styles in Nephi and Salt Lake City millinery.

We all attended the afternoon meeting, [we] girls in white having reserved seats in front. The sermons were grand, and we were happy until President Young said that he had a few names to read of men who were to be called and voted as missionaries to go and settle up the "Muddy." This almost stilled the beating of the hearts of all present. Many of our friends had been called to go to settle the Dixie country, but the "Muddy," so many miles farther south and so much worse! Oh! Oh! I did not hear another name except Samuel Claridge. Then how I sobbed and cried, regardless of the fact that the tears were spoiling [my] new white dress. The father of the girl who sat next to me was also called. Said my companion, "Why, what are you crying about? It doesn't make me cry. I know my father won't go." "Well, there is the difference," said I; "I know that my father will go and that nothing could prevent him, and I should not own him as a father if he would not go when he is called." [Then] I broke down sobbing again.

Everything occurred to prevent my father from getting off. Just as he was nearly ready to start, one of his horses got poisoned. He had to buy another horse. A week later one of his big mules was found choked to death in his barn. Some of our friends said, "Brother Claridge, this shows you are not to go." My father answered, "It shows me that the adversary is trying to prevent me from going, but I shall go if I walk!"

---

Elizabeth Claridge McCune, in Susa Young Gates, *Memorial to Elizabeth Claridge McCune*, 17–18.

# "I WOULD BE A DEACON"

⌒

BRYANT S. HINCKLEY

In a conversation with Dr. [Creed] Haymond, James A. Farley, Postmaster General under President Franklin Delano Roosevelt, said: "I am a Democrat of some national prominence, and Reed Smoot is a Republican; but I consider him to be the greatest diplomat in the United States Government. He knows more of what is going on, attends more meetings, and is a better authority on all that goes on than anyone else I know. I wish we had more men exactly like him.

"I have been reliably informed that Reed Smoot was offered the nomination for the Presidency of the United States, on the Republican ticket, if he would deny his faith—his being a Mormon would make it impossible for him to receive any such a nomination."

Dr. Haymond continued: "Fifteen years later, Senator Smoot was in my office and during the conversation, I told him what James Farley had told me. He said: 'In two national Republican Conventions, I was offered the nomination for President of the United States, if I could turn against my Church.'

"I said to him: 'Wouldn't it be worth it?'

"He whirled on me, took me by the arm and said: 'Young man, maybe you do not know my stand in regard to my Church. If I had to take my choice of being a deacon in the Church of Jesus Christ of Latter-day Saints, or being the President of the United States, I would be a deacon.'"

---

Bryant S. Hinckley, *Faith of Our Pioneer Fathers*, 201–2.

# "I Thought You Were a Returned Missionary"

GEORGE ALBERT SMITH

The brethren have reminded me of one or two little incidents that I think I will relate. One has to do with a cigaret. One of our missionaries who filled a good mission came home and sought employment and was unable to find it here. He had been a smoker before he went on his mission but he had quit so when he came back and became a little bit discouraged, he took up his habit of smoking again.

About that time a non–Latter-day-Saint business man spoke to one of the prominent men of the Church also in business, and said:

"I need a man to come into my business, one that is capable and able to grow to take my place because I want to retire after a while. I can pay him a good salary and I have concluded that while I am not a member of your Church that I would like to have one of your returned missionaries. They have had such wonderful experiences, many of them. I have heard some of them talk. If one of them comes home and you know of him you don't need to tell him what it is all about but just send him to me with the understanding that there may be a position. I would like to interrogate him."

Not long after that the young man who had been seeking work visited the office of the brother who told me this story and he said to the young man, "I think I know where you can find employment." He sent the returned missionary to the individual who had told him without hesitation what he wanted.

This returned missionary was a fine intelligent young fellow, and he supposed it meant a job for him. Our Church businessman said, "I met the young applicant on the street two or three days after, and asked him, 'How did you come out?' He said, 'I didn't succeed. The man asked me a few questions and then remarked, "I think probably we had better not try it out together.""'

Some time later the two businessmen met and the member asked the non-member why the young man had not been employed. He said:

"When the missionary came into my office he told me you had sent him. He was a fine-looking young fellow and appeared satisfactory to me.

"As he entered the office, I was smoking my pipe and all at once he took a cigaret out of his pocket and lit it, and we started to talk and I said to him, 'I thought you were a member of the Church of Jesus Christ of Latter-day Saints.' He replied, 'I am,' and I said, 'I thought you were a returned missionary.' 'I am,' he answered.

"[I said,] 'I'm sorry, I wanted just such an individual as I think you might have been, but what are you smoking for?' and the young man said, 'You are smoking. Why shouldn't I smoke?'

"[I] said, 'The difference is this: You have been taught that it's not a proper thing to smoke; I was never taught that. You are violating the advice and desires of those that love you and I think there is no use discussing this matter any further. I will just say that I haven't any position ready for you and we'll part.'"

A fine position was lost to that young man because he had that filthy habit, and that's the only word that I can think of just now that exactly fills the bill.

Another instance that may be of interest. One of our missionaries returned from the eastern states where he had become

acquainted with a shop foreman in a large manufacturing establishment, and after returning home he tried for some time to
secure employment but was unable so to do. Finally he said to
himself. "Well, I believe if I go back East my friend there will give
me a job."

He was a very fine capable young fellow, but the friend that he
spoke of did not know that he was a member of the Church, so
when he went to him, and said, "I've come back. I wonder if you
will give me something to do," the foreman said, "Certainly I will,
come right in."

So the young man began work, in the very city where he had
been laboring as a missionary. He avoided the members of the
Church, he didn't even go to meeting, he kept away from them,
because he was afraid the men who employed him, who were not
members of the Church, would not give him the same kind of an
opportunity of advancement if they knew who he was. But he was
a good worker and kept at it for some time, and one day after he
had been there about three months, the shop foreman called him
and said, "You had better go upstairs. The president wants to see
you."

The president had told the shop foreman that he needed a
young man who had ability for another department. He wanted a
young man with a good education. He said, "Look around and if
you can find such a man as that, let me know." The foreman
replied, "We have just such a man working for us right now."

"Already in our employ?"

"Yes."

The president said, "That pleases me, send him up."

So the young man, not knowing what the circumstances were
reported to the president's office and said:

"I understand, Mr. Grant, that you want to speak to me."

He said, "Yes, have you been sent up by the shop foreman?"

"Yes, sir."

"Please sit down. I want to know something about you. I'd like to know where you are from."

"Well," the young man said, "I live away out in the Rocky Mountains." That was the first hedge.

"But what part of the Rocky Mountains?"

"I live not very far from Idaho."

"But what are you doing here?"

"Well, I'm here working as one of your employees."

"Were you ever here before?"

"Yes."

"Do you know anybody here in the city?"

"Not very many, just two or three."

"Well, I don't quite understand why you came back here for employment."

I want to say before going any further the president knew all about this boy. He had somebody check his record, and so when he kept hedging the president said:

"But who are your friends here?"

"Oh," the young man replied, "they're just people that work around town."

"But," the president continued, "do you belong to any church?"

"Well, not here."

"Did you ever belong to a church?"

"Yes, I did at one time," and the young man began to be afraid the president did know who he was and he didn't want him to find out now so he kept hedging, and said, "At one time I was a member of a church but I didn't take much interest in it and I'm not doing much at it now."

"What church was it?"

"Well, you'd call it the Mormon Church."

The president said, "Do you mean to tell me that you are a son of a Mormon family?" The boy knew the jig was up with him then, so he answered, "Yes, sir."

The president queried, "Do you mean to tell me that you would desert the faith of your parents when you had known that they were Mormons and desired you to be one?"

"Well, not exactly that."

"I'm afraid," the president said, "you're not much credit to them. If you haven't the courage to stand up for your faith, what good are you? Now I will be plain with you. I thought you were the man I was looking for for this position, but I want to say to you that if you would betray your parents and go back on the church you belong to I'd be afraid to give you any kind of a job where you have to handle money."

So the young man lost his opportunity because he did not have the courage to do his duty by his church and his family.

---

George Albert Smith, *Sharing the Gospel with Others*, 24.

# "PLEASE FIND THAT LITTLE GIRL"

## LLEWELYN R. McKAY

During the trip to Europe to dedicate the temple sites at Zollikofen, Switzerland, and at Chapel Hill, England, I noticed that no matter how fatiguing it was for father, he always shook hands with everyone present. . . . After the dedication at Chapel Hill I observed that father looked tired, and I decided to spare him the autograph signing if at all possible. . . . The first in line was a sweet little girl about nine years of age.

"May I have President McKay's autograph?" she inquired of me.

I began to find excuses, not knowing that father was just behind me overhearing the conversation. He put his hand on my shoulder and said, out of the children's hearing distance, "My boy, never hurt or disappoint a child. Children are most sensitive to praise, to criticism, and to recognition than we realize. I can take the time to sign these few autographs—it means a lot to these youngsters, and I wouldn't disappoint them for anything."

He turned to the little girl and jokingly asked, "Do you think I can write plainly enough so you can read it?"

The young girl wasn't sure whether or not father was in earnest and became flustered. At that moment, President Reiser interrupted to ask a pressing question, and a minute or two of conversation between the two men ensued. When father turned to the table to begin writing autographs, the girl had disappeared.

I have never seen father more upset. "Llewelyn," he called, "please find that little girl in the blue dress. I'm sure she has the impression that I didn't wish to sign her book. She misinterpreted my remarks. You must find her. She must not go home with this false impression!"

Before long branch presidents and mission presidents were looking for a little girl in blue, but all search was in vain.

During the drive back to London, father mentioned the incident again. One of the elders riding with us said, "We think we know who the little girl is, and the branch president in the village where she lives is going to inquire and will phone you tonight in London."

Sure enough, a telephone call came that night, and this is what father instructed:

"Tell that little girl I am sorry I missed her at New Chapel, and that I have asked the branch president to send her book to me by mail to Salt Lake City; I will sign my autograph and mail it directly back to her."

And he did!

---

Llewelyn R. McKay, *Home Memories*, 133–35.

# SOURCES

Andrus, Hyrum L., and Andrus, Helen Mae, comps. *They Knew the Prophet.* Salt Lake City: Bookcraft, 1974.

Arrington, Leonard J., and Madsen, Susan Arrington. *Mothers of the Prophets.* Salt Lake City: Deseret Book Co., 1987.

Ballard, Melvin R. *Melvin J. Ballard: Crusader for Righteousness.* Salt Lake City: Bookcraft, 1966.

Bennion, Adam S. *What It Means to Be a Mormon.* Salt Lake City: Deseret Sunday School Union, 1917.

Benson, Ezra Taft. *Crossfire: The Eight Years with Eisenhower.* Garden City, New York: Doubleday and Co., 1962.

———. *God, Family, Country: Our Three Great Loyalties.* Salt Lake City: Deseret Book Co., 1974.

Brown, Hugh B. *Continuing the Quest.* Salt Lake City: Deseret Book Co., 1961.

Burton, Theodore M. "Biographies and Reminiscences," from the James Henry Moyle Collection. Unpublished manuscript, 1974.

Cannon, George Q. *My First Mission.* First Book in the Faith Promoting Series. Salt Lake City: Juvenile Instructor Office, 1879.

Cannon, George Q., comp. *A String of Pearls.* Second Book in the Faith Promoting Series. Salt Lake City: Juvenile Instructor Office, 1882.

———. [George C. Lambert, pseud.] *Gems of Reminiscence.* Seventeenth Book in the Faith Promoting Series. Salt Lake City: Juvenile Instructor Office, 1915.

Carter, Kate B., comp. *Heart Throbs of the West,* 12 vols. Salt Lake City: Daughters of Utah Pioneers, 1939–1951.

————. *Our Pioneer Heritage.* 20 vols. Salt Lake City: Daughters of Utah Pioneers, 1958–77.

Corbett, Pearson H. *Jacob Hamblin, Peacemaker.* Salt Lake City: Deseret Book Co., 1968.

Cornaby, Hannah. *Autobiography and Poems.* Salt Lake City: J. C. Graham & Co., 1881.

Cowley, Matthew. *Matthew Cowley Speaks.* Salt Lake City: Deseret Book Co., 1954.

Crocheron, Augusta Joyce, comp. *Representative Women of Deseret.* Salt Lake City: J.C. Graham & Co., 1884.

Crookston, Douglas O., ed. *Henry Ballard: The Story of a Courageous Pioneer, 1832–1908.* Salt Lake City: n.p., 1994.

Dew, Sheri L. *Ezra Taft Benson: A Biography.* Salt Lake City: Deseret Book Co., 1987.

Earl, Orange Wight. Unpublished history. Typescript in possession of family.

*Early Scenes in Church History.* Eighth Book in the Faith Promoting Series. Salt Lake City: Juvenile Instructor Office, 1882.

Esshom, Frank. *Pioneers and Prominent Men of Utah.* Salt Lake City: Utah Pioneers Book Publishing Co., 1913.

*Fragments of Experience.* Sixth Book in the Faith Promoting Series. Salt Lake City: Juvenile Instructor Office, 1881.

Gates, Susa Young. *Lydia Knight's History.* Salt Lake City: Juvenile Instructor Office, 1883.

————. *Memorial to Elizabeth Claridge McCune, Missionary, Philanthropist, Architect.* Salt Lake City: n.p., 1924.

*Gems for the Young Folks.* Fourth Book in the Faith Promoting Series. Salt Lake City: Juvenile Instructor Office, 1881.

Goates, L. Brent. *Harold B. Lee: Prophet and Seer.* Salt Lake City: Bookcraft, 1985.

Grant, Heber J. *Gospel Standards: Selections from the Sermons and Writings of Heber J. Grant,* compiled by G. Homer Durham. Salt Lake City: Improvement Era, 1943.

Griggs, C. Wilfred, ed. *Apocryphal Writings and the Latter-day Saints.* Religious Studies Center Monograph Series, Volume 13. Provo: Religious Studies Center, Brigham Young University, 1986.

Hinckley, Bryant S. *The Faith of Our Pioneer Fathers.* Salt Lake City: Deseret Book, 1956.

Huntington, Oliver B. Journal, typescript, LDS Church Archives.

Jenson, Andrew. *LDS Biographical Encyclopedia.* 4 vols. Salt Lake City: Andrew Jenson History Co., 1901.

Johnson, Benjamin F. *My Life's Review.* Independence, Mo.: Zion's Printing & Publishing Co., 1947.

Jones, Daniel W. *Forty Years among the Indians.* Salt Lake City: Juvenile Instructor Office, 1890.

*Journal of Discourses.* 26 vols. London: Latter-day Saints' Book Depot, 1854–1886.

Kimball, Edward L., and Kimball, Andrew E., Jr. *Spencer W. Kimball.* Salt Lake City: Bookcraft, 1977.

Kirkham, Francis W. *A New Witness for Christ in America.* 2 vols. Independence, Mo.: Zion's Printing & Publishing Co., 1942.

*Labors in the Vineyard.* Twelfth Book in the Faith Promoting Series. Salt Lake City: Juvenile Instructor Office, 1884.

Larson, Andrew Karl. *Red Hills of November: A Pioneer Biography of Utah's Cotton Town.* Salt Lake City: Deseret News Press, 1957.

Lee, Harold B. *Stand Ye in Holy Places.* Salt Lake City: Deseret Book Co., 1974.

Little, James A., ed. *Jacob Hamblin.* Salt Lake City: The Church of Jesus Christ of Latter-day Saints, 1945.

Lundwall, N. B., comp. *Temples of the Most High.* Salt Lake City: Bookcraft, 1952.

———. *Faith Like the Ancients'.* Salt Lake City: Paragon Printing Co., 1950

Maeser, Reinhard. *Karl G. Maeser.* Provo: Brigham Young University, 1928.

McKay, David O. *Cherished Experiences from the Writings of David O. McKay.* Compiled by Clare Middlemiss. Salt Lake City: Deseret Book Co., 1955.

———. *Gospel Ideals: Selections from the Discourses of David O. McKay.* Salt Lake City: Improvement Era, 1953.

McKay, Llewelyn R., comp. *Home Memories of President David O. McKay.* Salt Lake City: Deseret Book, 1959.

Miner, Caroline Eyring, and Kimball, Edward L. *Camilla, a Biography of Camilla Eyring Kimball.* Salt Lake City: Deseret Book Co., 1980.

Minutes of the Salt Lake School of the Prophets. Papers of Zebedee Coltrin, LDS Church Archives.

Nelson, Russell M. *From Heart to Heart.* Salt Lake City: Russell M. Nelson, 1979.

Nibley, Preston, comp. *Faith-Promoting Stories.* Independence, Mo.: Zion's Printing and Publishing Co., 1943.

———. *Pioneer Stories.* Salt Lake City: Deseret Book Co., 1965.

Parry, Edwin F. *Sketches of Missionary Life.* Salt Lake City: G. Q. Cannon & Sons, 1899.

Pratt, Parley P. *Autobiography of Parley P. Pratt.* Edited by Parley P. Pratt, Jr. Salt Lake City: Deseret Book Co., 1985.

Roberts, B. H. *A Comprehensive History of The Church of Jesus Christ of Latter-day Saints,* 6 vols. Salt Lake City: The Church of Jesus Christ of Latter-day Saints, 1930.

———. *Life of John Taylor.* Salt Lake City: George Q. Cannon & Sons, 1892.

———. *New Witnesses for God,* 3 vols. Salt Lake City: Deseret News, 1909.

Smith, George Albert. *Sharing the Gospel with Others.* Compiled by Preston Nibley. Salt Lake City: Deseret News Press, 1948.

Smith, Joseph. *History of The Church of Jesus Christ of Latter-day Saints,* 7 vols., 2d ed. rev. Edited by B. H. Roberts. Salt Lake City: The Church of Jesus Christ of Latter-day Saints, 1932–51.

Smith, Joseph F. *Gospel Doctrine: Selections from the Sermons and Writings of Joseph F. Smith.* Compiled by John A. Widtsoe. Salt Lake City: Deseret Book Co., 1939.

Smith, Joseph Fielding. *Answers to Gospel Questions,* 5 vols. Salt Lake City: Deseret Book Co., 1957–1966.

Smith, Lucy Mack. *History of Joseph Smith.* Edited by Preston Nibley. Salt Lake City: Bookcraft, 1958.

Snow, Eliza R. *Biography and Family Record of Lorenzo Snow.* Salt Lake City: Deseret News, 1884.

*Speeches of the Year.* Provo: Brigham Young University, 1963, 1968. (This publication has been titled in several ways over the years; for example, *Brigham Young University 1990–91 Devotional and Fireside Speeches.*)

Stegner, Wallace. *Mormon Country.* New York: Duell, Sloan & Pearce, 1942.

*A Story to Tell.* Salt Lake City: The Church of Jesus Christ of Latter-day Saints, 1945.

*A String of Pearls.* Second Book in the Faith Promoting Series. Salt Lake City: Juvenile Instructor Office, 1882.

Swinton, Heidi S. *In the Company of Prophets.* Salt Lake City: Deseret Book Co., 1993.

Tagg, Melvin S. *The Life of Edward James Wood, Church Patriot.* Provo: Brigham Young University, 1959.

Talmage, John R. *The Talmage Story.* Salt Lake City: Bookcraft, 1972.

Tate, Lucile C. *LeGrand Richards: Beloved Apostle.* Salt Lake City: Bookcraft, 1982.

*The James and Mary Murray Murdoch Family History.* Provo: James and Mary Murray Murdoch Family Organization, 1982.

Tullidge, Edward W. *The Women of Mormondom.* New York: Tullidge and Crandall, 1877.

Whitney, Orson F. *Life of Heber C. Kimball.* Salt Lake City: Kimball Family, 1888.

———. *Through Memory's Halls*. Independence, Mo.: Press of Zion's Printing and Publishing Co., 1930.

Widtsoe, John A. *In a Sunlit Land*. Salt Lake City: Deseret News Press, 1952.

Woodruff, Wilford. *Leaves from My Journal*. Third Book in the Faith Promoting Series. Salt Lake City: Juvenile Instructor Office, 1881.

Young, Brigham. Manuscript History of Brigham Young, 1801–1844. Edited by Elden J. Watson. Salt Lake City: Smith Secretarial Service, 1968.

# INDEX